— HOW TO RESTORE —
BRITISH
SPORTS CARS

Jay Lamm

Motorbooks International
Publishers & Wholesalers ®

First published in 1992 by Motorbooks International Publishers & Wholesalers, PO Box 2, 729 Prospect Avenue, Osceola, WI 54020 USA

Library of Congress Cataloging-in-Publication Data
Lamm, Jay William.
    How to restore British sports cars / Jay Lamm.
        p.   cm.
    Includes index.
    ISBN 0-87938-567-7
    1. Sports cars—Conservation and restoration—Handbooks, manuals, etc.   2. Sports cars—Great Britain—Conservation and restoration—Handbooks, manuals, etc.   I. Title.
TL236.L35   1992
629.28′722—dc20   91-33927

On the front cover:*Two classic British sports cars. The white 1959 MGA Twin Cam is owned by Robert A. Koons, Jr., of Lansdale, Pennsylvania. The red 1963 Austin-Healey MkII 3000 is owned by Bob Weaver of Whitehall, Pennsylvania.* Mike Mueller

Printed and bound in the United States of America

Contents

Acknowledgments

The author would like to thank the following people and companies for their help in preparing this book: Tony Adams, Art's Auto Wrecking, Automotive Dismantlers and Recyclers Educational Foundation, Automotive Service Industry Association, Body English, Brooks Boliek, Dave Brownell, Jeff Burns, Channel Island Graphics, *Chatter* Magazine, Classic Motorbooks, Arleigh Closser, Corvette Fever, Robbie Darizell, Michael Dregni, The Eastwood Company, Tom Edgar, Embassy Photographic Supply, Jim Epstein, Mike Farber, Ellen Fern, Victor Frank, Elizabeth Gardiner, Tom Haddock, Bob Hall, Matthew Hall, Vernon Hall, Gail Heath, *Hemmings Motor News*, Mike Hohn, Ellen Houston, Joe Joffe, Matti S. Kim, Rick Kopec, Laguna Seca Raceway, Charlie Lamm, JoAnne Lamm, Mike Lamm, Robert Lamm, Darcy Leach, Beth Lunney, Dick Lunney, Alex Maduros, Matt Mazza, Moss Motors, Ltd., Motorhead Ltd., Nick Nicaise, Rob Nicholson, Brett O'Brien, Robin O'Brien, Tom O'Keefe, Lowell Paddock, Tim Parmley, Karen Penn, Jamie Pfeifer, Mick Pickett, Jim Poluch, Al Pruiett Restorations, Dave Pruiett, Putney & Perry Automotive, Erika Sandford, Dave Schillerstrom, SCRAMP, Tajel Shah, Tom Sisco, Tom Smitham, Smithsonian Institution Land Vehicles Collection, Society of Automotive Historians, Dave Solar, Special Interest Autos, Ross Stanfield, Mark Terrapelli, Billy Thompson, Sonny Tippe, Dale Wickenheiser, Roger White, White Post Restorations.

Introduction

My original idea for a book on classic English sports cars was something called *Keeping Your British Car Alive*. It was going to be a short, basic manual on the minor problems that cause ninety percent of the trouble with these wonderful but sometimes cantankerous cars.

The project grew quite a bit beyond that, but I think at its heart that basic idea remains: British sports cars are simple devices and, with a little understanding and knowledge, easy to work on. They are rarely cluttered with all the bells, whistles and smog equipment that covers the modern car. That's one element of their neverending charm.

This book covers simple fix-its to complete rejuvenations, but there's no way that any one book will tell you everything you need to know. Some of that knowledge will come from other books, some from friends and experts, and some from simply going out to your garage with wrench in hand and going to it.

The idea of this book is to bridge the gap between what you already know and what you'll need to know—how to follow the instructions, make the right choices and ask the right questions of your other information sources.

For some people, restoration is a chance to spend time by themselves; for me it's always been the opposite. To really have some fun, I need to have a friend or two around, to joke with, to pick their brains, to pool knowledge with and sometimes to commiserate with. Hopefully this book will do that for you. It will never take the place of Mike Hohn, Joe Joffe, my dad or any of the other people I like to work on cars with, but having one more friend and brain to pick never hurts.

There's not much more to do but jump right in. I suppose I could sing the praises of English cars for the next ten pages, but you, like anyone with good taste and common sense, obviously know them already.

Jay Lamm, 1991

1

Restoration Planning and Preparation

You bought this book for one of two reasons: either you've got a sports car in the garage that's starting to look a little weathered—okay, maybe it's completely beat—or you're thinking of buying one to restore. If you've already got a car lined up, hopefully this book will give you an idea of the amount of work ahead and how you'll go about doing it.

But if you're looking for a car to restore, choosing the right one will be the biggest aid to the whole project. The car you pick can make things hard or easy on yourself, your family, your accountant and every parts source between here and Australia.

There is no *right* choice to make when selecting a restoration subject, only the choice that's right for *you*. You have to think about how much time and money you want to put in, what you'll be able to do and what sort of results you want.

It might seem intuitive that you want an absolutely perfect car in the end, and the only choice is what *kind* of perfect car you'd like to wind up with. But in truth that's rarely the case. A perfect car that will drive the judges at Pebble Beach into a frenzy won't be much good for anything else. A top-flight show car can't be used for spirited Sunday outings, much less day-to-day driving, and it costs at least as much to make a great car into a Pebble Beach winner as it does to make a basket case into a great car.

TVR has been building light, sophisticated, limited-production sports cars for more than 30 years. Rare and fragile, it takes a dedicated person to restore and operate this sort of car; anyone can do it, but a more plebian MG or Triumph is, truthfully, a better subject for your first restoration. This TVR Mark 13 is on a scrutineer's ramp at Le Mans in 1962.

Despite its obscurity and rarity, a Morgan Super Sports Aero three-wheeler just might fit the bill for the beginning restorer. While most parts aren't readily available, the car was built so simply around its large JAP motorcycle engine that many parts can be fabricated without too much trouble.

Levels of Restoration

The Super Show Car

Starting with a serviceable Bentley, countless hours of your own time and over $100,000 you might get into the rarified top ranks of national competition. These days, there's just not much that can be done to keep the costs down on this kind of job. Every nut and bolt will be taken off the car and in all likelihood thrown away for a perfect replacement. The stitching of the door panels alone will take hours and hours of a professional's time. Every nut, bolt and screw in the engine compartment will line up perfectly with one another. And you probably won't be able to put any grease in the suspension joints—you wouldn't want it oozing back out again, would you?

The Darn Good Show Car

One notch down is a truly superb and correct car that'll maybe become a national marque winner, a rare Sunday driver and a source of constant pride the rest of the time. For something like this you could go the "easy" route—start with a sound E-Type, cough up about $50,000 to a professional restorer and show off the car. Or you could go the "difficult" route and invest a few thousand hours of your own time and cut that dollar figure in half or more.

The Club Show Car

Here's a nice and correct car that's useful for driving and occasionally showing off to the locals. Before a show, though, you'll have to strip apart the whole car, clean every nook and cranny, pick dead bugs out of the radiator, restitch any imperfect threads and just generally go to town on the thing.

Once you accept that you're not doing the restoration to compete in a major concours, though, you're freed up to do things in a much less-expensive fashion. The differences between a car prepared this way and a Pebble Beach winner are probably the kind most people would never notice,

This incomplete Jaguar E Type was offered for sale at a recent swap meet as a partly finished restoration project. So far, it looks as though the work has been done well, but who knows what kind of problems lurk inside. Basket cases or project cars such as this that are 90 percent complete often mean that the difficult-to-find parts or hard-to-complete projects are the ones that are missing or left to be done.

A second Jaguar E Type for sale, but this one is completely restored—and costs a lot more than the project E Type. In the long run, however, the restoration may run up larger bills than this finished car. The moral is that you may be better saving your pennies for the completed car.

Allard K and J Series cars came out of England in the late 1940s and early 1950s, featuring American V–8 power and what was considered sophisticated handling at the time. Tough to drive and hard to restore due to their limited production numbers, they're nevertheless collector's favorites. If nothing else, those Ford and Cadillac powertrains will keep chugging away forever.

but they cost a bundle. An old Healey could be brought to this condition (not including the price of the car, of course) for $15,000 or even quite a bit less—it all depends on what you can do yourself, how well you can do it, how much time you want to put in and how much money you can spend.

The Fun Car

You don't particularly want to show this car off anywhere, except maybe to green-with-envy neighbors and friends. If you're not interested in competition, the only person the car has to please is you. It might not do that unless it looks factory perfect, or it might do that as long as it gets you to the store and back without breaking down. A fun car can cost you just about nothing—a $900 MG and a hundred bucks' worth of junkyard parts might be all it takes. On the other hand, you could get caught up in the restoration and wind up sinking a fair amount of time and money into it just to please yourself.

This book is going to concentrate primarily on fun cars. It will give you a head start on building a Class A show winner, but at the same time not make you feel like a cheapskate if all you really want is a car you can drive, travel in and just enjoy.

Finding the Car

Where do you look for a car? Just about anywhere. A surprising number of great cars change hands simply because somebody left a note on the windshield saying, "Wanna sell this?" Sooner or later, the owner might just call you and offer a sale.

I try to stay off used car lots, since the dealer is no fool and he's got to make some money in the deal. If he can sell you the car for X dollars, then theoretically you could have bought it from the original owner for X-minus-Y dollars. Occasionally you'll find a good deal on lots, though; it's fun to look,

The Austin-Healey really filled the middle ground between entry-level Triumphs and the rich man's Jaguar. They still fit somewhere in between the two in price and performance, but for the most part the Healey's basic simplicity lends it to restoration while the Jaguar's complexity is harder to deal with. The only thing that can be tricky about the Healey is its rather strange internal structure. Erika Sandford

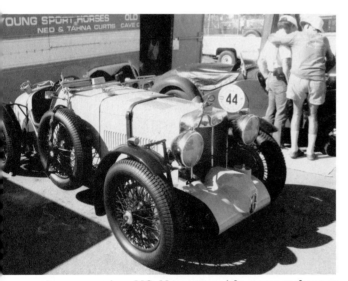

A rare racing MG Magnette with a supercharger mounted at the front of the car underneath the cowling below the radiator. This is a good example of a car that may be beyond the technical ability of many home restorers to work on as components like the supercharger require special attention. It may also be beyond the budget of many. Know your limitations before starting.

Cast-off cars seem to inevitably wind up under a tree. In truth, better they should be left completely exposed than offered this kind of protection: trees drip sap, big raindrops, nuts, bird droppings, leaves and even branches onto the vehicle, while offering it almost no protection from the elements. Expect a lot of superficial rust on this MGB and give the cowl vents a really good look—chances are they're clogged and corroded.

9

Only the Morgan Plus 8 carries on the tradition of the classic drophead British sports cars. Restoration of a Morgan can present more than its share of good, old-fashioned British sports car frustration, however. The chassis is wood, requiring some carpentry expertise, and the modern Rover V–8 engine can be difficult to find parts for in the United States.

A Morris or Austin Mini Cooper such as this pair battling it out on the racetracks in the 1960s may be an ideal first restoration project. Parts—except for some competition components—are relatively easy to come by and much of the car's construction is more straightforward than on, say, an early T Series MG.

regardless. If a used car dealer winds up getting something he considers an oddball in trade, he might be willing to part with it for not much money just to open up the space on his lot. It never hurts to ask—and lowball—the salesman.

The local newspaper want ads are probably the most likely place to find a good car, so get in the habit of going through them every day. Don't restrict yourself to the "Classics and Antiques" column; the cars in the "Imports and Sports" section are often just as good and a bit less expensive. Pay particular attention to an ad that's been running awhile—the owner might be getting disheartened and desperate to sell. (On the other hand, the car could be a real turkey.)

Local photo advertisers are also a good place to start, although the car can look much better in a grainy 2x3 in. black-and-white photo than it does in real life. Since these carry a number of cars in every issue, you should be able to get a good idea of what certain cars are going for in your area; there's a lot of regional fluctuation across the country. You'll also notice that the market has pronounced highs and lows: some cars will be advertised for ridiculously high prices, while others will be markedly lower than their brethren. Don't be afraid of the cheapies—a phone call about one of them might save you a lot of money in the long run.

Also keep an eye on club publications and specialty magazines; the chances of getting a really good buy through one of these isn't all that good, since other people with the same idea are probably looking through them, too. You're more likely to get a well-maintained car from a club or specialty magazine, though, because the owner at least knows enough about cars to know of the publication's existence.

One problem with shopping this way is that desirability of a car seems inversely proportional to its distance from your house. When I lived in California, all the great cars were in New York. Now that I'm on the East Coast, they've all moved to Los Angeles. Buying a car long distance is something I shy away from; the vehicle rarely lives up to your expectations when you see it in the flesh, and just transporting the thing across the country can cost $1,000 or more.

The self-named Bible of the old car hobby is *Hemmings Motor News*, a 700 page doorstop of a magazine that comes out of Bennington, Vermont. *Hemmings* is a great place to find cars—the largest single source around—but it's equally valuable just as a reference book. You can find advertisements for parts sources and clubs in it as easily as finding whole cars, and it gives you probably the best idea of what kind of money is being asked for certain cars around the country. (Bear in mind that prices from local sources tend to be a bit lower than those you see in national magazines.)

Hemmings also lists its cars in an organized fashion. Until recently, if you wanted to find an MGA Twincam you'd turn to the "M" section and scan through about a dozen pages of MGs, Maseratis, Monteverdis and Mercurys looking for the car you wanted. Recently they alphabetized each section, so it's easier to find just the car you're after—although you might miss the 1962 Maserati that way, of course.

A magazine like *Hemmings* can also hide your car in another place; always check the "Multi-make Cars" and "High-Performance" headings just to be sure you're not missing anything. Aside from *Hemmings*, smaller classified ad sections can be found in enthusiast magazines like *Road & Track* and *Automobile*, and in specialist magazines like *Vintage, Old Cars News & Marketplace* and *Cars & Parts*.

Getting Familiar with the Car

If you can get familiar with a car before you go out looking to buy your own, so much the better. It'll be easy if you absolutely, positively *must* have a very early E-Type. You can check books out of the library, phone the big wheels of the local Jaguar club for a chat and go for a ride in some prime examples of the car. The latter is the hardest, but probably most valuable, step. You might read that old E-Type gearboxes "whine pleasantly," but the only way to know if the car you're looking at is whining pleasantly or just making a racket is to hear a good one in action.

If you're just looking for a neat car at a good price and you don't particularly care which model it is, your research will be, by necessity, much broader. That still doesn't mean you can't trot down to the library to study up on the vehicle of the day.

Some people like to learn how to read the identification plate of the car; each one is located and structured differently. ID plates may (or may not) tell you when the car was made, what color the body and interior were and what options the car was sold with.

Trying to read the plate is always worthwhile once you've got the car in your garage. But while deciphering vehicle identification numbers (VIN) and the like can lead to some fascinating discoveries, I've learned to take the results with a grain of salt. There's simply too many variations and oddballs thrown into the equation; dealer-installed options won't be mentioned. Often valuable special equipment factory parts like axles, windscreens, intake systems and racing seats won't be mentioned either. And sometimes the ID plates are simply *wrong*. If you were to take a photo of the car coming out of the factory you might see that the information on the plate just didn't match the equipment on the car.

Club and parts supplier newsletters are also great sources. These will help you out once you've selected a car as well, by telling you about new parts on the market, special events and by giving you lots of technical tips. A club newsletter also gives you some names to start with if you ever get into trouble and need advice. Car clubs are more or less support networks—a group of people who are willing to help each other out in exchange for the same consideration later on.

The Hunting Expedition

Most of the car hunts you go on will begin with a phone call, and a well-thought-out call will save you a lot of unnecessary running around. The picture in your mind after reading an ad is almost always rosier than the car itself; the trick is to get the current owner to bring that picture further in line with reality.

I used to have a great set of questions in mind when phoning owners, but I'd always forget them once the guy started talking. Nowadays I have a list that I pull out before making the calls so I remember to ask everything I set out to. It's best to start out with general questions and then work up to the specifics.

This kind of serious grilling will save you an amazing number of unnecessary and time-consuming trips. Of course, it never hurts to go around and look at a few cars in the neighborhood just to get familiar with what's out there, even if you don't think you're going to buy this one. On rare occasions, you might even find that the car's in better shape than the owner portrayed. More often, of course, you'll wind up chasing down a "really good car with no rust, minor scratches and a sound engine" that's an obvious basket case on first sight.

Most people are honest—you just have to ask the right questions. Once you've decided that a car is

Phone Call Checklist

Some of these questions might seem frivolous at first, but the answers can be interesting. I try to mention before jumping into the list that I'm going to ask a lot of questions, and ask if the owner has the time to answer them or if I should call back later.

• Tell me the things wrong with the car. This usually gets an interesting response—either evasive or surprisingly straightforward. You learn more about the owner than about the car with this one.

• How many miles are on the odometer, and is that figure accurate?

• Do all the other gauges work?

• Does the car run? If so, does it smoke or leak? Almost every British car seems to leak some, and probably the majority smoke a bit, too.

• Has it been stored inside or outside?

• Is the car hard to start?

• Does it burn oil?

• Is there any rust, and if so, where is it? How bad is it?

• Any big dents? Any scratches, parking lot dings or things like that?

• In what condition are the bumpers and trim?

• What color is the car? You might not care if you plan to repaint it, but if you start with a color you like you might not have to repaint the inner doors, the trunk and under the hood.

• Is the color original, or has the owner found another color underneath? Is the paint shiny or dull, smooth or orange-peel-like?

• What options are on the car? Does it have overdrive?

• What's the condition of the interior? Do the seats have any tears? Is the dash cracked? Are the roof, headliner, and rear window in good

condition? If the car is a roadster, does it come with side curtains? Is there a tonneau cover or a top boot? How are the carpets and door panels? Does it still have all the door handles and other doohickeys?

• What kind of wheels does it have, disc or wire? How much tread is left on the tires? Tires might seem trivial, but don't kid yourself—four new tires can set you back as much as replacement seats and carpets.

• How good are the brakes? Do you have to pump them? What about the clutch?

• Does the car make any funny noises?

• Is there a radio? If so, is it stock or aftermarket? Does it work? How about the other electronics, like lights and turn signals; do they all work?

• Are there any spare parts that come with the car, or any manuals? Besides saving money, the car's owners manual will tell you what its problem areas are—those will be the greasiest pages.

• When can you see the car, and where? If it's far away, is the owner willing to drive it somewhere so you can meet halfway?

• What kind of maintenance does the car need, and how often? You and I both know that British cars require only slightly more care than newborn children; if this guy doesn't know the car needs a lube every X-thousand miles, watch out.

• One thing I *never* ask is the perennial favorite, "Why are you selling the car?" If the car has some ticking time bomb of a mechanical problem that the owner hasn't already mentioned, he won't do it now.

With English cars, of course, you have to give a lot of leeway for these answers. Almost all unrestored examples are going to smoke, leak, use some oil and make some noise, so don't be put off by a response like, "No more than usual." That's a fair and honest description in many cases.

worth going out and looking at, be prepared to do the job right. If the car's just around the block, you can give it a once-over and come back with the heavy artillery later; if it's a long way off, though, pack your gear.

Once you've shown up on the owner's doorstep the fun begins. Sometimes it's immediately apparent that you're not going to want to get involved with the car—say half the pieces are missing, chickens live in the trunk and the hardtop is in two pieces in two different trees. Even then, desperation will drive you on in some cases; perhaps the car is so rare that this is the only one you're likely to find. (Mind you, I don't recommend restoring a real oddball as a first effort.)

What You're Looking For

It's almost always cheaper to buy a car with good seats than to replace the seats yourself later. It's almost always cheaper to buy a car with good paint than to have it painted afterward. In the most general terms, except for cleaning and tuning, the closer a car is to the condition you want it to end up in, the better off you are financially. If you want to do a restoration for profit you're looking for a very rare car indeed; one that's priced like a beater but is, under ten layers of grime, in basically good

Simple and rugged, a lot of Triumph TR 4s are still on the road. Despite a recent rise in prices, old TRs are a good low-dollar entry into the hobby; they're simple, easy to restore and maintain, and lots of fun to drive.

shape. A car that just needs lots of cleaning and minor tuning *might* make money; most others will not. Exceptions might be cars in fine shape except for one big job—an engine rebuild, a new transmission, some paint and body work. These can often

---

Car-Hunting Tools

A complete car-search survival kit includes the following:

• Large screwdriver: Use this to poke around under the car for rusted-out panels. (Ask the owner for permission, of course, and don't go poking around a really clean car that's obviously sound.)

• Magnet: Bring this along, preferably the flexible, rubber-backed kind you'd use on the refrigerator. You'll go over the fenders and body creases looking for filler putty with this. The magnet will stick to real metal (unless the car's something like a fiberglass Lotus or an aluminum-bodied Aston, of course) and fall off of plastic filler. Most cars will have some plastic somewhere, so don't dismiss one because of a few repaired sections. Instead, pay attention to the size, number and *location* of the repairs. Cars with nonmetal sills, for example, should be avoided at all costs. The magnet will also show up any fiberglass replacement panels—beware of any car so equipped.

• Flashlight: Use this to look into nooks and crannies for rust, oil, loose parts, resident mice, black widows and so on.

• Hydraulic jack and jack stands: You'll have to get under the car to give it a good look-see, and using the owner's old Toyota bumper jack can take you out of the hobby for good.

• Dingy clothes and an old rag: Crawling in and out of an old car is a messy business, and you'll trash whatever you wear. The rag is to check oil and fluids, and to wipe off any crud from number plates and so forth.

• Compression tester and spark plug wrench: Never buy a car with a freed-up engine without first doing a compression test on all the cylinders. On an old MG this will take a few minutes; on an XJS you might want to bring along a sleeping bag in case you nod off somewhere between the number nine and number ten spark plugs. Compression tests are easy on inline cars and a little more hassle on V-8s and V-12s.

• Mechanic's stethoscope: Okay, this isn't really necessary, but I love these things—you might as well buy one now and use it. This is like your doctor's stethoscope except that it has an obscene-looking probe on the far end. Touch it to a mechanical component and you can hear the noise that particular part is contributing to the overall festival of knocks, whines and wheezes coming from the engine. This will tell you a lot about the water pump, the alternator, the valves, the fuel injectors and the all-important lower end. Listen for grinding, screeching and deep knocking from rotating parts; valves and injectors should all make the same noise in the same rhythm.

A real bonus—two matching wire wheels in the trunk of this MGB. Often a car won't have even a single matching spare.

bring down the price of a car almost as low as if several major jobs needed to be done.

If you want the fun and satisfaction of doing your own restoration, though, it's a wide-open field. After reading this book you should have a good idea of how various fixes are done and whether or not you want to get into them. The only thing left to do is to match the car to the jobs you'd like to tackle, whether painting, bodywork, interior rejuvenation, mechanical repair or a combination of all of them.

Okay. Armed with this knowledge, you arrive at the Dead TR Ranch. Walk around the car and take it all in; view the car under bright sunlight or, better still, fluorescent lights. Never buy a car you've only seen by dim illumination.

Does it match your expectations, or does just looking at it worry you? Your first feelings about a car are important—they rarely improve once it's in your garage. On the other hand, if you take a liking to it immediately it might be the beginning of a beautiful friendship. Just don't fall in love to the point that you're blind to any flaws you might find later in the checkout.

Open the doors and rock them back and forth on their hinges. The hinges—particularly on the driver's side—are a good indication of the car's true age. A 30,000 mile car shouldn't have doors that sag 3 in. when you open them; it's more likely to be a 130,000 mile car if they do. (Make sure it's the hinges—a cheap fix—that are bad instead of the whole door pillar, a heinously expensive fix.) Another good indicator is the driver's seat. It shouldn't be too torn up or too saggy if the car is supposed to be a low-mileage example.

Your full checkout will be done by combining all of the steps outlined as follows. Do them in any order you like, but I'd start with the rust checks first—finding a lot of rust will scotch the deal faster than anything else.

Rust and Structure—Your Main Concern

Your absolute A-Number-One time and money sink is going to be serious rust. Properly repairing

---

Cars to Watch Out For

When browsing car ads, there are a few kinds of cars that make me *really* nervous:

• "Just needs assembly": You have to ask yourself why the previous owner hasn't done it yet. Whatever made the reassembly impossible for him or her will probably do the same for you, and you don't even know for sure what that was.

Restoring a car is a big enough job when you're the one who took it apart and (hopefully) tagged and bagged all the parts. Restoring one from a mass of boxes is next to impossible—parts will be missing, others unlabeled and others just plain wrong. (Somebody with a lot of experience could make a fortune reassembling T Series MGs from crates—it seems like $1,500 disassembled Ts with disgusted owners are everywhere. Of course, it would probably take two sets of crates to make one complete car.)

• "Restoration almost complete": Here, you have the added worry of correcting all the mistakes the last guy made. The cheap and easy jobs will probably all be done—the tough and expensive ones are left to you. Be especially wary of cars in

primer. The body will look much better than it actually is, and primer allows rust to form on the metal while the car sits and waits.

• "Recently restored": In the best scenario, you've just aced yourself out of the fun of restoration. In the worst scenario, though, you'll be paying twice for a number of jobs—paying the owner for the paint job he did and then paying again to strip that paint off and do it yourself correctly. There's absolutely nothing wrong with buying a well-restored car; in fact, it might cost less in the long run than doing the work yourself. Buying one that's been poorly done, however, will cost a lot more than buying a solid but weathered example and restoring it yourself. If the "rebuilt" engine still knocks and wheezes or the "new interior" is of the wrong materials, you face the agonizing decision of living with them or starting all over.

• "Fascinating history": You have to take most of these stories with a grain of salt, although one will occasionally be true. As German car fans say, Hitler might have won the war if he hadn't been so busy registering all those Mercedes at the DMV.

Something as major as a collapsed rail can be hiding under an eaten-out inner fender. This discovery really needs to be made before you buy the car, not afterwards; the bill for this restoration might have just gone up another 25 percent. Robin O'Brien

This MGB's torn window looks pretty easy to fix, but the question is how much damage has leaking water done to the inside of the car?

rust even on a simple outer panel will involve you in all the most complicated steps of a restoration: cutting, welding, bodywork and painting. Rust on a structural member—a frame or a stressed point on

a unibody—is even more serious and time consuming to correct.

Rust is serious no matter where you find it, but on monocoque (also called frameless or unibody) cars it can be especially damaging. Unibody cars don't use a separate, heavy frame for most of their strength. On these machines a little surface rust on the outer panels is about the minimum you can accept without starting to give the car some serious thought. This usually appears as big, scabby areas or tiny bubbles under the paint, and is relatively rare.

Much more common is out-and-out rot, the sort that causes large paint blisters, peeling, and cracks and holes in the metal. In this respect Californians are lucky, because the chances of finding basically rustfree cars, even old ones, are pretty good. As you

What Do the Surroundings Tell You?

I used to believe I could tell a lot about the care a car received by looking at the owner, but that was just prejudice. It turns out that a lot of guys with perennial ketchup stains on their shirts and live turkeys in their living rooms have cars so clean you could do an appendectomy on top of them.

My father's pet theory says if the guy has other enthusiast cars around you should be worried. He feels the owner is likely to have done all the easy jobs and less likely to give you a low price. (Dad stays awake nights fantasizing about a retired accountant who owns a 1963 E-Type but really prefers his 1979 Ford Fairmont.) Personally, I *like* to know the guy's an enthusiast—it usually means the car has received the proper maintenance and care. This one's a mixed bag.

Pay attention to where the car is stored. Is it outdoors, and if so, does it look like it's been there for a couple of winters? Nothing causes hundreds of annoying little cosmetic and mechanical flaws faster than a few years in the elements. Is it under a sap-dripping tree? Does the family dog have a summer home in the passenger's footwell? Is it sinking into the ground through disuse? Has it been under a cover, and if so was it a good, breathable one or the plastic sort that traps condensation on top of the car and makes things worse instead of better?

The condition of this MGB's luggage rack should make you wonder about the holes drilled into the trunk. If they weren't painted before the rack was mounted there will be rust around them.

15

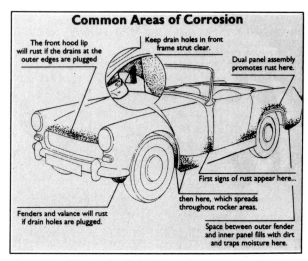

Common Areas of Corrosion

The front hood lip will rust if the drains at the outer edges are plugged

Keep drain holes in front frame strut clear.

Dual panel assembly promotes rust here.

First signs of rust appear here...

then here, which spreads throughout rocker areas.

Space between outer fender and inner panel fills with dirt and traps moisture here.

Fenders and valance will rust if drain holes are plugged.

A good guide to the initial rusting points of an MG Midget and Austin-Healey Sprite from the Moss Motors catalog. These areas are common to all British cars. Moss Motors, Ltd.

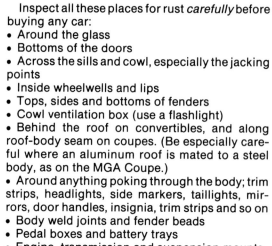

Rust Area Checklist

Inspect all these places for rust *carefully* before buying any car:
- Around the glass
- Bottoms of the doors
- Across the sills and cowl, especially the jacking points
- Inside wheelwells and lips
- Tops, sides and bottoms of fenders
- Cowl ventilation box (use a flashlight)
- Behind the roof on convertibles, and along roof-body seam on coupes. (Be especially careful where an aluminum roof is mated to a steel body, as on the MGA Coupe.)
- Around anything poking through the body; trim strips, headlights, side markers, taillights, mirrors, door handles, insignia, trim strips and so on
- Body weld joints and fender beads
- Pedal boxes and battery trays
- Engine, transmission and suspension mounts
- Frame welds

move into snowy areas or onto the coast near salt-water, though, some rust is almost guaranteed. Rust on nonstructural pieces—at the bottom of door panels, fenders and so on—is ugly and a pain to fix, but it's far from terminal. Structural rust—rot in frames, suspension mountings and stressed panels—*can* be repaired in most cases, but nine times out of ten it's cheaper and easier to skip the car and choose a better one.

When you're giving a car the rust once-over, pay particular attention to jacking points, the seat area, pedal-mounting boxes, and drivetrain and suspension mounting points. Also give a close eye to the wheelwells and the body around them.

Here's where your screwdriver is going to get its first workout, because you often discover lots of rust hiding behind innocent-looking accumulations of dirt and mud.

Any piece that makes a sharp return curve—the E-Type's nose, for example—can also hold water. Walk around the car and ask yourself where water could enter and then get trapped. A common place is in the frame or chassis channels. These are usually equipped with drain holes, but the holes get plugged quickly and water can sit inside and stew for years. It's a good idea to tap along the bottom of the car and look for places rusting from the inside

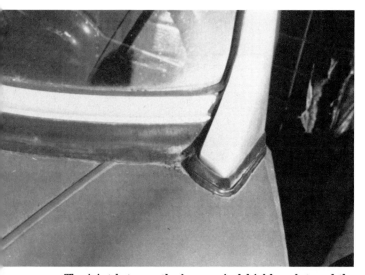

The joint between the lower windshield gasket and the pillar gasket traps water; this one's just starting to rust. It doesn't look terminal, fortunately.

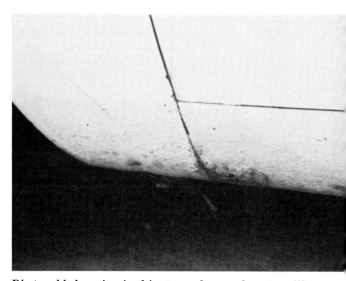

Big trouble brewing in this stressed area; the outer sill and lower fender will have to be cut out and replaced. Inner sill and fender are probably shot as well.

out. The joints between cross-members and the mainframe rails can be particularly nasty, and particularly dangerous if they go undiscovered.

Other vulnerable areas are the exhaust system—which is usually pretty rusty no matter how nice the rest of the car is—and around the battery, whether it's under the hood, in the trunk or behind the seats. The battery's going to have leaked acid on the surrounding metal and that area will often be particularly bad. Some cars have removable battery trays, but on others the damage is done to something much harder to replace, like an inner fender.

At this point of the search, you might notice some "English rustproofing": the only sound spots on the car might be the areas that have had leaking oil thrown on them for the last twenty years. Real rustproof undercoating, on the other hand, is a mixed blessing. As it ages it can lift off and allow water to work its way underneath. If any rubberized undercoating seems loose, pry a little up and have a look below. Sometimes there's a rust monster waiting there, sometimes not.

While you're under the car, look for whole panels that have been patched in after the car left the factory—a sure sign of major rust repair. Repair plates might mean the problem was corrected, but they could also mean that other areas are getting ready for replacement themselves.

Finally, lift up the carpets or mats in the interior, the trunk, the parcel shelf behind the seats and the well for the convertible top. All of these places tend to hold water, and if they're seriously rusted they'll have to go.

Interior Checkout

Every time you get into the car you're going to be staring at the interior; it's one of the most neglected yet most important parts of any restoration. A lousy cockpit will make you hate driving an otherwise perfect car, so try to start with as nice an interior as possible.

Back on the outside, go over the body piece by piece, looking out for any dings, dents and scratches you might have missed in your search for rust. Sight down the body panels in bright light to check for waves and small dents, especially at the beltline. If you have a pretty good idea of how you'd like the car to look when it's finished, you should be able to tell how much work it will take to get it there. On a daily knockabout driver, a few waves and chips might be acceptable.

On something that's going to be nicer, starting with a car needing "just a little" bodywork might be a waste of money. If you're going to fill the dings anyway, patching a few bigger dents won't be much more bother and a car so afflicted will cost a lot less to buy. Lots and lots of minor waves will be much more trouble to set right than some well-defined

Beautiful frame cross-members; no rust, no dents, not even any scratches. Few old unrestored cars (this MGB's got 100,000+ hard miles on it) will be this nice.

dents and dings, so watch out for those if the car is going to be patched up.

Flat, dull paint can often be brought back to life with lots of polishing compound and elbow grease. If the paint is a lacquer, orange peel can easily be sanded down with fine wet-dry paper, rubbed out, polished and made mirror-smooth. Orange peel and other surface flaws on enamel are more likely to be there for the life of the car, but you never know until you consult a professional.

The Mechanics: Steering and Suspension

If the car is roadworthy, the test drive (as described later) should give you a good idea of the condition of the suspension and steering. A car

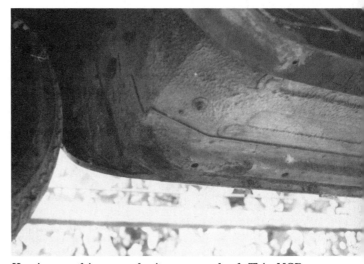

Here's something you don't see enough of. This MGB hasn't been particularly well cared for, yet the drain holes are all clear and there's no rust in the floor panels.

Interior Checklist

Things to look at inside the car:

• If the dashboard's cracked it will be a big job to replace unless you intend to tear the whole car down anyway.

• Look for signs of leaking around the windows, at the corners of the windshield and from the heater (up under the dashboard). Leaks around the window are generally easy to fix—leaks from the windshield and heater are bigger problems.

• Take stock of the seats: Do they move on their tracks, are they torn, do they sag? Separating seams on one or two panels, or a tear confined to one piece of a *sewn*—not molded—seat are no big deal. Many smaller tears or damage to embossed plastic seats and panels means a replacement, not a repair, will be needed.

• Check all the switches and slide controls to see if they're frozen in place. The choke cable is pretty easy to replace; ventilation slide cables are harder. Broken switches can often be fixed on older cars; on newer ones they'll have to be replaced.

• Look at the gauge faces and the condition of the chrome on the instrument panel. Refacing the gauges is a pain, but cleaning minor grime off the glass and bezels is pretty simple. An odometer that doesn't quite line up means the figure may be wrong.

• Look for chips and scratches on painted interior panels. If *any* panel needs repainting you'll probably have to do *all* of them to get a decent match.

• The carpets should be complete and reasonably clean. Wet carpets indicate a leak; the rugs themselves might be ruined and the floorboards below can be rusty. Threadbare carpeting can never be brought back, but this is one area where you might wind up ahead of the game—shabby rugs often lower the price of the car more than the cost of an easily installed carpet kit.

• Inspect all the weatherstripping, windshield rubber and window fuzzies carefully. Also look for traces of leaks around the glass, in the top well and at the tops and bottoms of the doors.

• Lift the handbrake to see if it works. If not, it probably just needs adjusting.

• Are little rubber and vinyl details like the shift boot and sun visors in good shape? Replacing lots of these can drain you of money in a big hurry—they'll be hard to find in a junkyard.

• Check out the door panels; simple sewn ones are pretty easy to recreate and replace. Complex panels with lots of stitching and pockets are harder to recreate, while embossed plastic panels are virtually impossible to fix—better ones will have to be found. While you're there, see if the windows roll up and down nicely, though it's usually not a big deal to fix them if they don't. Also check that all the armrests, handles and door trim pieces are in place. Again, this isn't a major expense if replacement parts are available.

• Look closely at the steering wheel. Cracked plastic wheels are possible but difficult to fix, and new ones can be relatively expensive. Vinyl or leather wheels can often be recovered by an upholstery shop for not too much money.

• Inspect any wooden panels for flaking varnish, stains, burns and delamination. Refacing flat wood paneling is a time-consuming but simple task—working on more complex shapes is much harder.

Reading Tread Wear

One of your best steering and suspension diagnostic tools will simply be inspecting the tread of the front tires. Tire wear patterns give you an idea of what flaws may exist in the front suspension; some of these symptoms and causes may appear at the rear, too.

Tread should be evenly worn across the face of the tire. If it's not, follow these guidelines:

• Even wear on one side only: Incorrect camber; also incorrect toe setting.

• Scalloped wear on one side only: Also called *cupping,* this usually indicates an unbalanced wheel. It can also be caused by loose tie-rod joints or bad brakes and shocks.

• Tread blocks worn at an angle across the tire: Also called *feathering,* this points to poor toe adjustment. It also might be caused by bad suspension bushings or damaged components.

• Tread worn in center or on both edges of tire: Caused by over- and under-inflation, respectively.

that steers well, doesn't pull to one side, is properly damped, has no wheel play and doesn't wander is probably healthy enough to let you skip these static tests. It is also, however, rare as hen's teeth.

A little slop in the steering (play) is almost inevitable, though by no means desirable. Even when the car's not moving, you can usually turn the wheel a few degrees to either side before it meets resistance; the thing is, just how much play is normal and acceptable varies widely from car to car and owner to owner. On cars with steering boxes, up to a few inches of play at center might be normal; on rack-and-pinion cars, the center play should be close to nonexistent. This is an area where prior experience with a good example of the car will pay off when it comes time to shop for your own.

If something seems wrong during the test drive or you can't take the car out on the road, you'll have to launch into the long and rather dull business of testing the springs and suspension by hand. To do this you'll need a helper, a good floor jack, a piece of timber to support the car, a crowbar and a set of strong jack stands.

With the car on the ground, open the hood and have your helper slowly turn the wheel back and forth across the play. If the steering column doesn't move, you might be looking simply at a steering wheel with stripped splines. If the steering column does move, look to see if there's any slop in the U-joints or rubber bushings along the column. Detecting some deterioration in the joints, however, doesn't necessarily mean you've found the root of the problem. Look farther down and see if the bottom of the column is turning at the same rate as the top. If it is, then the steering play is due to a deeper cause than worn joints.

Next, you'll notice an arm coming from the steering box called a *drop arm*. (On cars that use rack-and-pinion steering, instead of a single drop arm there will be a *track rod* coming from either side of the steering rack.) The drop arm or track rod moves back and forth to create the turning motion at the wheels. Grab hold of it and try to determine if the motion of the steering column is making it through the box. If not, the fault lies somewhere in the steering box (or rack) itself. This can be an expensive fix, but before you despair make sure that it isn't something simple like loose mounting bolts or an arm that's loose on its shaft. (Some boxes and racks are also adjustable, so it's possible that a simple adjustment is causing the problem—don't bet on it, though.) While you're playing with the steering box, look for cracks around the mounting holes or damage to the nearby frame members. Either one will mean big bucks.

While your helper keeps cranking, move on to the steering arms pivoting at the wheels, the track rods and idler (intermediate) arms. These should all move smoothly and smartly; no slop should be evident in any of the joints or threaded cups.

Next jack up the car at a strong point on the frame—not the suspension arm—and support the car on the jack with a stout piece of wood. (You don't want to bend the frame of an unfamiliar car or go through a rusted-out jacking point.) As the car is being raised, look closely at the front suspension as a whole; you're checking for any movement other than a normal pivoting action. Most suspension pieces will move freely in one arc or a predictable combination of arcs. Any straight movement, clunking or back-and-forth rocking is probably due to wear and should be investigated further.

Once the car is up in the air and supported soundly, rock the wheel with your hands in the twelve and six positions and then at three and nine. If there's any looseness or wobble, have your helper step hard on the brakes. If the wobble goes away, you're just looking at lousy wheel bearings, a minor problem. If the wobbling doesn't go away, trace it back to the source—it's probably at the main upper swivel, a costly repair. Destroyed rubber bushings, another likely culprit, are relatively cheap to buy but a pain to replace. Other points of wear or damage can be a big or a small problem depending on the car. Give the local alignment and brake shop a call to get an estimate on any flaws you find.

On cars with strut suspensions, the lower ball joints are also tested by aggressive fore-and-aft rocking of the wheel. Also inspect the fluid seal between the piston and the main chamber for

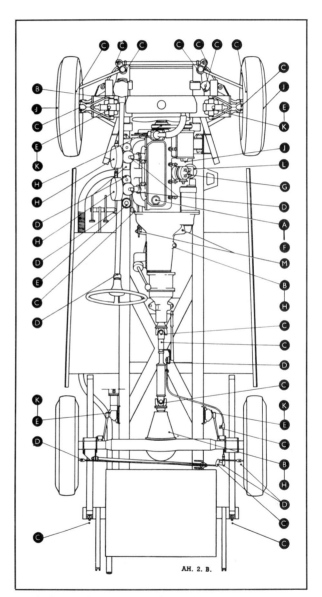

A 1956, Austin-Healey's lubrication—that's right, just lubrication—points show up the maintenance-intensive nature of British sports cars. Most of the blame laid at the feet of English engineers through the years really belongs with the owners. A well-maintained car, whether it's your own or one you're looking to buy, will be many times more reliable than one that's been neglected.

leaks, and the shock towers for rust and collapsed rubber mounts. Have your helper spin the steering wheel back and forth; any clicking sound at the top of the strut towers indicates wear of the top bearing.

Next look at the springs and shocks. Most English sports cars use lever shocks, which require more maintenance than tube shocks but last much longer if properly cared for. With the car back on the ground, the simplest check is to get it rocking up and down at one corner and then to let it go. The body should settle down after a single oscillation; if it keeps rocking, the shock is bad. Lever shocks *theoretically* can be rebuilt, but it's not a do-it-yourself job—you're looking at a replacement shock, which can cost a fair amount of money.

Springs are also easy to check out (unless you have a Mini-based car with Hydrolastic or Hydragas suspension—get a Mini book from a specialist or talk to a pro). Coil springs can sag and break; the latter will be immediately obvious and the former should show up as lowered ride height and fre-

Smog equipment like this MGB air-injection pipe has often been removed or bypassed by a previous owner; all the equipment may have to be replaced before you can register your newly restored car.

quent bottoming over the road. The coil spring pan (where the spring rests on the suspension) can also be damaged or loose, which often leads to a clicking sound as the car is bounced.

Leaf springs can also break or simply come loose from their mounts. Lever all around the front and rear of the leaf with a tire iron or crow bar to expose any weak joints. Both leaf springs and coil springs can be repaired or replaced with a few simple tools and a little know-how, but the parts can be costly and the work takes time.

Finally, check out the wheels themselves and see if all four and the spare match. Pressed-steel wheels are pretty tough; about the only thing to worry about is damage from an impact with a curb or another car. Look closely around the rim for dents, flattening and warping.

With wire wheels, a lot more can go wrong. Tap each spoke lightly with a pencil or small screwdriver; sound spokes make a nice metallic ring, while loose or broken ones make a hollow thud. Also make note of the condition of the knockoff cap inside and out, which can be expensive to replace on some cars. Stripped knockoff spindles can be another relatively costly replacement part.

The tires should have at least 1/8 in. of tread all around and no obvious splits, bald spots or ballooning. The size and type (radial, cross-ply and so on) of all four tires and the spare should match.

Under the Car

The first thing to do down below (once you've jacked and supported the car well) is to hunt down the source of any leaks you find. Often you'll see fuel or water dripping, but more viscous fluids like oil are harder to track down; they'll probably show up as a spot of moisture beneath a stalactite of sludge far away from the actual source. Leaks around the transmission, rear axle and engine gaskets are fairly common—almost universal, in fact—but they shouldn't be too active. See if any of these pieces have been banged up enough to explain the leak, or get ready to do some hunt-and-peck gasket replacement later. Clogged vent holes can also cause leaking from the transmission and rear end.

Leaks around the brake drums are also common, pointing to brake woes or axle-seal troubles. A weep down the brake backing plate usually indicates a bad wheel cylinder, which is a relatively minor repair. Sludge around the ends of live axles means bad seals, which are much harder to fix. Leaks from disc brake calipers often mean replacing the whole unit—a big expense.

If you intend to remove the engine and rebuild it along with the clutch, a leak from the rear of the block isn't any big deal. If not, a leak here is a major concern; it's probably a rear main seal, which will haunt you to the end of your days. If a leak is found and the clutch is juddery or vibrating intensely when you drive the car, a leaky rear main is definitely the culprit.

Under the car you're also in a good position to detect damage from accidents or a bent frame rail from serious bottoming out. Most English cars have about zip for ground clearance, so the frames do get pretty scuffed in normal use. Minor scrapes and dents are no big deal assuming they haven't bent the frame out of line. Bigger dents in the frame can give the car a weak spot that may fail later; if you have any doubts, take the car to a frame shop before you sign the check.

Check the fuel tank for dents (common) or leaks (also common) which might mean replacing the tank—a basically inexpensive but dangerous job.

Under the Hood

Look into the brake and clutch master cylinders to see if they're full. The fluid should be reasonably clean, although anything short of the LaBrea tar pits can be considered normal.

Pull the dipstick out and look for signs of water—actual bubbles or a milky look to the oil. Water in the oil often means a crack in the block or head (a serious matter), a bad head gasket (less of a problem but still a pain) or a faulty crankcase ventilation system (no big deal to fix, and this can also explain leaks from the oil pan gasket). Even if just a bad crankcase breather caused it, though, water in the oil can quickly cause serious lower-end damage.

Open the radiator and look for scale and rust; lots of it means a radiator boilout (not much money) and possibly clogged water passages in the engine (big bucks later on). Oil floating on the water indicates the two more serious scenarios of water in the oil—engine cracks or a bad head gasket.

Look for major leaks from between the head and block, which might point to a warped head or at least a bad head gasket. Check oil pressure lines and fittings for leaks, and look for crud around the crankcase breather—a sign of bad rings, bad bearings or clogged water galleries. Take a look at the air filters. Brand-new ones don't tell you much, except that the owner's no fool. Really grungy ones should tip you off that the car hasn't received the world's best maintenance. And inspect the wiring under the hood closely—is it a rat's nest of splices

<table>
<tr><td>

Static Brake Checks

Minor brake work isn't hard or expensive, but it's a nuisance you can live without. Major work can cost major bucks, mostly in the form of parts.

A seriously rusty rotor will need replacement, as do most leaky calipers. Leaky master and wheel cylinders are cheap if they can be rebuilt, costly if they must be replaced—you won't know until you get there, so assume the worst. Cracked rubber hoses will have to be replaced.

Get in the car and push on the brake pedal; it should be hard and firm, not mushy. Sponginess means there's air in the lines, from simple neglect or a more serious matter. If the brakes pump up—go firm after a few hard stabs—a simple bleeding might cure the problem. If the system refuses to pump up or immediately goes soft again, there's probably a more serious flaw somewhere down the line.

</td></tr>
</table>

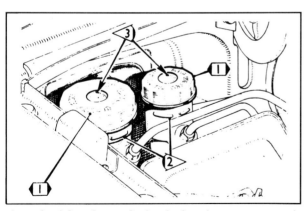

A good trick to learn the level of maintenance a car's received is to study the brake and clutch reservoirs (2). The caps will fuse to the reservoirs through electrolytic corrosion if they're not removed from time to time, so a well-maintained car shouldn't be affected. Also check the vent holes (3) in the caps. If these are closed off it's a good indication that the owner didn't know much about what made his or her car tick.

This car will have you chasing electrical gremlins for a while, so take that into account when you make your bid.

and worn insulation or is it basically sound and neat? Lots of guerilla wiring means lots of electrical trouble down the road—a big inconvenience.

Look closely at the carburetors and fuel filters, which should be clean and not leaking. (The main source of fuel leaks from the float bowls are bad needles and seats, a small repair. These will also keep the car from running well.) Also make sure that the carbs and intake manifold are tight on the engine and that there are no obvious vacuum leaks anywhere, like a broken vacuum hose or a missing plug. (If the car idles fast but the adjustment screws are backed off all the way, a vacuum leak is likely. Usually the fix isn't major.)

If the car is equipped with smog equipment, it had better all be there and working unless you live in a state that doesn't make a smog check a mandatory part of the registration process. (Laws vary from state to state, but it's becoming more common for smog equipment to be the financial responsibility of the seller, not the buyer. Check with your local Department of Motor Vehicles to get the full scoop before proceeding.)

Reading Tailpipe Smoke

Smoke from the tailpipe can tell you a lot about the engine. Some cars will smoke all the time, but others need a little hand—while the car's still cold, have a friend or the owner stomp on the gas while you stand in back. Look for:

• White smoke: This is usually water; if it goes away quickly it's probably just natural condensation and nothing to worry about. If it stays with the car for a long time or seems particularly heavy, cooling water is getting into the cylinders—a bad head gasket or cracked head are the most likely culprits.

• Blue smoke: This is oil. Oil usually enters the combustion chambers through bad valve guides and seals; that will mean a costly head rebuild at least. It can also indicate worn piston rings or cylinder bores (expensive) or a faulty crankcase breathing system (not so costly). Worn rings and bores should show up on a compression test; most valve problems will not. (To check the bores and rings correctly, squirt a little oil into a suspect cylinder and test its compression again—it will rise significantly if that's the problem.) A little oil smoke at the first startup that quickly goes away usually means a not-too-serious upper-end problem; the work will still have to be done, but not in a tremendous hurry.

• Black smoke: This is almost always unburned fuel. Black smoke usually means the car is tuned poorly or there's something not quite right in the carbs or choke. It's possible that the owner has done this intentionally, however; an overly rich mixture will help keep temperatures down in a car that has cooling problems.

The Test Drive

Assuming the car runs, take it out for a serious test drive. Before you leave the driveway, though, put up the top and roll up all the windows. Not only will that make noises more apparent, it keeps you from falling in love with the car on the spot. The first thing to check is simply how well the engine starts; it should fire off reasonably quickly and settle into a nice, even idle. If the owner wants to be the one to start the car, he's probably already learned the proper tricks and procedures. Don't let that put you off; a lot of English cars seem to need a familiar hand at the key to light off easily. Just make sure you learn the "half-choke, half-pedal, crank the key once, bow toward Mecca and two Hail Marys" routine before you drive the thing away.

With the engine running, listen for any knocks, particularly deep ones from the lower end. (Once the car is hot, check for knocks again. Deep knocks that stay or appear once the oil is thin and hot are bad news. Ones that have gone away are a sign of the same problems, just further down the road.) Light, consistent tapping is more likely to be a valve out of adjustment, which is less of a problem.

Treat the car gently at first, keeping one eye on the road and one on the gauges. The water and oil temperature should come up to operating range within five minutes or so of normal driving, and the ammeter or voltmeter should stay in the charge range all the time. (It might dip into the discharge range at idle if the car is a little off song, but it should leap back up as soon as you're off the line.) The oil pressure, meanwhile, will fall as the car warms up. Every engine operates in a different pressure range (the gauges are usually off a bit as well) but the pattern should be the same: high pressure when cold, nearly as high pressure when

---

Reading Spark Plugs

The spark plugs will also tell you a lot about the state of tune, if not so much about the overall condition, of the engine. Watch for:

• Light gray, brown or tan deposits: These are normal.

• Dry, fluffy black deposits: Such deposits are carbon fouled, due to overly rich mixture, excessive choke or clogged air cleaners.

• Wet, black deposits: These are oil fouled, due to bad rings or guides. They also can indicate bad ignition to that plug (wire, rotor, cap or plug may be defective) or too cold a plug type.

• Burned, cracked insulator or very worn electrode: These result from pre-ignition (pinging) due to wrong fuel or spark timing. They are also caused by a poor cooling system or overly lean fuel mixture.

revved up warm and lower pressure at idle. Check with a club or a manual to learn the proper pressure range for the car you're driving.

With the engine idling, engage the handbrake and slowly let out the clutch. If the car stalls, great. If it drops a few hundred rpm but keeps running, the clutch is slipping—a big expense. And if it pulls away, the handbrake is broken or misadjusted—not such a big deal. The brakes should be firm; sponginess indicates that bleeding is needed (very minor expense), or there is more serious trouble (could be costly). Bear in mind any brake problems *before* you get out in traffic.

Okay, you're ready to hit the road. As soon as you put in the clutch you're back on the job—listen for a quiet grinding noise with the clutch pedal in, indicating a worn clutch throwout bearing (an inexpensive part but a royal pain to get to).

On older cars, first gear may grind a bit going in. Some early cars didn't have any synchromesh on first gear; others lose their synchros quickly. If it's common to the car—here again, your local club will help you out—and you can live with it, fine. Otherwise, a big-ticket transmission fix will be called for.

Notice if the clutch engages smoothly; sharp jerking and grabbing indicate glazing, wear or oil on the clutch face (at least an expensive clutch job and possibly replacing a rear main engine seal as well). More gentle jerking can mean loose U-joints or even something as esoteric as cracked motor mounts or a balance weight that's fallen off the driveshaft. (A missing weight is usually obvious as a clean rectangular patch on the shaft.)

Listen for any untoward noises from the suspension, the body or the running gear as the car starts down the road. A deep knocking (that might disappear at speed) indicates lower-end troubles and big bucks. Whining gears may or may not be "normal" for the car, but a chattering gearshift lever or one that pops out of gear is definitely not. Figure worn selector mechanisms and a fairly large repair bill, though you might get lucky and only have a misadjusted linkage.

Light, metallic squeaks from the brakes are probably not too serious; lower grinding noises most likely are. Sharp clunking over potholes and tar strips could point to bad springs, worn suspension bushings, dead shocks or missing bump stops. (On the other hand, it could be nothing more serious than a jack bouncing in the trunk.) Try to recreate the noise when you get back to the owner's house by bouncing the car on its springs, and hunt down the source of the thump.

If possible, have a friend follow the car as you make the test drive. He should be looking for smoke from the tailpipe, any shimmying as it moves down the road and a crab-like stance to the car. If the car does turn out to be crabbing—the rear doesn't quite follow in line with the front—think about

giving up right then. That usually means the frame is out of alignment and the car isn't worth bothering with.

So Now That You've Got a Car . . .

You've driven (or pushed) your new car into the garage. Your husband or wife can't see it yet, but underneath all that grime and neglect rests a jewel of English craftsmanship.

The loving spouse walks around the car, giving it a look generally reserved for household pets who've made an indiscretion on the mail carrier's shoes. You're beginning to sense that a cut-to-the-bone phrase is about to be uttered.

"Okay," says the spouse. "*Now* what?"

Ah! An excellent question.

Tools You'll Need

You don't need a full set of brand-new Snap-On tools for good results from your restoration, not that you wouldn't love to have them. On the other hand, filling your toolbox with rusted-out, Made-in-India bargain tools is a sure way to at least get frustrated, if not maimed, somewhere along the road. Trying to wrestle with a cheap tool will take

---

Test Drive Checks

While out on the road, try these tests:

• Step on the brakes gently from about 50 mph. If the car pulls to one side or another it probably means some brake (or even suspension) work is in your future. Don't try the next test if this is the case.

• On a clear stretch of road, try a panic stop from 30 mph. Again, the car shouldn't grab or pull to one side.

• Shift into top gear going up a hill at about 25 mph and punch the gas. If the clutch slips—the engine speeds up without pulling the car along with it—expect to be changing it soon. (Even if it's just a matter of adjustment right now, the clutch face has probably taken a beating in the meantime.)

• Gently loosen your hands on the wheel; the car should track straight and true. If it wanders around the road, suspect the steering box, wheel bearings or ball joints. Shimmying or vibration points to bent or loose suspension parts, or dragging or warped brakes. Pulling to one side could be bad axle or suspension alignment, an under-inflated tire or improper castor at one wheel. All of these symptoms can also be nothing more serious than unbalanced wheels, poor alignment or improper toe and castor settings, though, so if you really want the car, consider paying for a professional alignment and wheel balance before signing the check. You'll need to do it anyway if you buy the car.

all the fun out of a repair and do a lousy job in the process.

Your tools must simply be good enough to do the job quickly, correctly and *safely*—loose-fitting wrenches will slip off a nut, rounding out the fastener and busting your knuckles in the process. Bad pliers are great at pinching (it hurts to even think about it) that tender piece of skin between your thumb and forefinger. And a badly fitting lug wrench is much better at barking shins than removing wheels.

If you already have a tool kit lined up, you should know from experience which tools work and which don't. Obviously, no one expects you to go out and replace every screwdriver that's a little scuffed up, but if you've found yourself regularly referring to one particular tool as "That damn box-end wrench," I'd replace it now. Retire the old one to the second string. (Or, if you *really* hate the tool and never want to see it again, loan it to a friend.)

Before getting rid of a tool completely, remember that they metamorphose as they age; a small Phillips screwdriver enters the lowest toolbox drawer in the fall and emerges the following spring as an awl. A bent old ratchet handle goes to sleep one night and awakens as a cheater bar the next morning. (I still haven't figured out what changes into those $1.99 socket sets that keep turning up, though.) I believe very strongly in the saying, "The right tool for the right job." It's just that the right tool for some jobs is an old worn-out version of another tool. Don't throw away a worn-out screwdriver or file until you know there's no other use for it.

When you do go out to buy new tools, you can often tell just by looking whether something is high quality or not. Thin chrome plating and cheap plastic handles are generally a tip-off that the job being done will look no better than the tool itself. Occasionally you can find good tools on sale or good used ones at garage sales and swap meets, but by and large you're best to stick with brand-name tools from a reliable store—preferably with a lifetime guarantee. You can bring these back fifteen years later and get a replacement on the spot, even if the breakage was your own fault.

The Tool Kit

Whether your car uses metric, SAE, UNF or Whitworth fasteners, you're going to want a com-

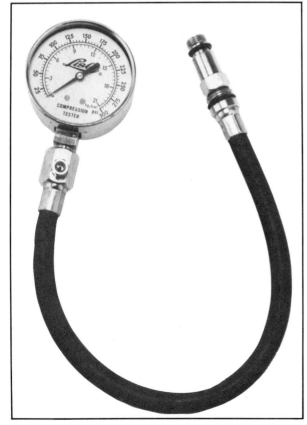

A compression gauge is your first and best tool for testing an engine. The Eastwood Company

A low-cost micrometer can tell you what kind of fasteners your car uses; the tool sizes should be common knowledge on more common cars, though.

plete set of the appropriate tools on hand to do even a relatively minor job. No list of tools needed will ever be complete, but here's a list of some basic items you'll need as you work through your car. The sockets and wrenches are listed in metric sizes; similar SAE (Society of Automotive Engineers) or Whitworth sizes should be substituted as necessary.
• Medium-size ½ in. drive socket wrench, sockets from 7 to 21 mm, and a large, medium and small extension. You'll probably need to fill in a few socket sizes on either end later
• Large ¾ in. drive socket wrench, sockets from 13 to 23 mm and a spark plug socket, medium extension and U-joint coupling. Also, a ¾ to ½ in. step-down adapter of the highest quality
• Standard screwdrivers, from tiny jeweler's to colossal self-defense size. Six should do it
• Phillips screwdrivers in the same sizes
• Short-shaft Phillips and standard screwdriver, medium-size head
• Complete set of Allen wrenches
• Full set of open-end wrenches, 6 to 19 mm. You'll have to acquire more as needed
• Full set of box-end wrenches in the same sizes
• Hacksaw with various blades
• Set of large, medium and small self-locking pliers
• Medium-size standard pliers
• Medium-size slip-jaw pliers
• Small needlenose pliers
• Medium-size awl
• Medium-size wire cutter or stripper. (Get a good one, the cheapies are lousy.)
• Standard household hammer (about 1 lb. head)
• Small, medium and large size chisel. Get nice ones at first—you can pick up ratty ones later for dirty work

• Ten inch crescent wrench. Hopefully you'll never need to use it—crescent wrenches should be a last resort—but you'd better have one handy
• Ignition or spark plug feeler gauge, 0.0005 to 0.0050 in. widths

A rolling two-ton hydraulic jack is about the least you can get away with for serious work.

Using a mechanic's stethoscope to check individual fuel injectors on a Rover V–8.

Jackstands are essential to doing most restoration work and sound jackstands protect your life when you are underneath the car. Make certain you have good, sturdy stands before you hoist the car on top.

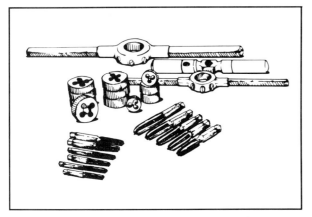

A tap and die kit will be invaluable during the restoration of almost any British sports car to clean up threads on original bolts and cut new threads into bolt holes. You may end up needing more than one set depending on the car you are restoring: some cars will require standard inch tools while others will need a Whitworth kit. Moss Motors, Ltd.

- Hanging shop light
- Utility or matte knife with extra blades
- Medium-size scissors
- Torque wrench with ¾ in. drive. (I prefer the clicking type, but gauge-type wrenches will work fine.)
- Large metal trash can with cover
- Large, well-charged A-B-C fire extinguisher

Those are the absolute must-haves for day-to-day work, but they're just the beginning. As you go on and do more and more things, you'll find the following tools become necessary:
- Full set of body files
- Large, medium and small sanding block
- Plastic spreader or putty knife
- Voltage or ohm multi-tester
- Soldering gun and electrical solder
- Plastic shrink tubing, all sizes
- Good hydraulic jack, at least two-ton capacity
- Highest quality jack stands (at least two)
- Set of brake (flare) wrenches (they look like a cross between open- and box-end wrenches)
- Medium nut breaker
- Electric two-speed drill with full set of metal bits
- Wire sanding wheel for electric drill
- Angle grinder
- Eight-foot tape measure
- Flat-faced body hammer
- All-purpose body dolly
- Solid steel pipe (to use as a cheater bar)
- Compression tester
- Set of medium or large size C-clamps
- Welding goodies, as needed
- Upholstery tools, as needed
- Sandblasting kit
- Circlip pliers
- Inductive timing light
- Mechanic's stethoscope
- Gear puller
- Buffing wheels, buffing machine and compounds
- Spray painting equipment, as needed
- Strong air compressor

More esoteric tools—there's no end to them—will be picked up constantly as you go. By the time you're done, you'll have at least twice as many tools as the ones listed here.

Space, Helpers and Attitude

A large, covered garage is far and away the best place to do your restoration. The more room you have, the better—cramped quarters mean lost parts, frustration and not much fun. Working in a space that's too small also increases the likelihood of accidentally knocking over or otherwise damaging things.

No matter how much space you're working with, keeping it neat and organized will speed things up and make the work enjoyable. There are few things in life more frustrating than spending thirty minutes looking for the right tool to perform a thirty-second job.

One of the best ways to get more space in your garage is to designate another area for "cold storage." This can be inside the house, in the rafters of the garage, on strong shelves you put up yourself; it doesn't matter where, as long as the parts will remain clean and dry and can't be easily gotten to by thieves and vandals. And though it's not often convenient, you can even rent a space in a public

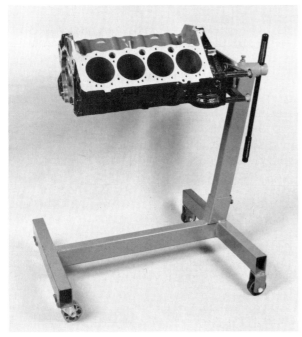

A strong engine hoist is well worth the investment if a rebuild is on your docket.

storage building to stash your parts until they're needed. (A friend of mine actually rebuilt an entire Mustang in a public storage room—the manager never did figure out why he would spend fourteen hours every Saturday in his shed.) Good covered work and storage space is valuable, so use it wisely.

No matter where they go, it's imperative that parts are stored someplace they can't fall over, be bumped into by kids and assistants and won't get things dropped on them. Scratching a newly finished part before it even gets put on the car is a supremely irritating experience. Glass and light assemblies are particularly vulnerable—wrap them in cloth and store them in strong boxes until you're ready to use them.

You might not think garage space is important if you plan to do most of your work outside. Granted, the sunshine and breeze make for a pleasant workday, but it's no substitute for a good garage. You want a work space that's well lit and comfortable when the weather or the light outdoors is bad. Comfort is a huge factor in enjoying the work—warmth, light and the ease of hooking up electrical tools can make all the difference. Hook up an old radio if you like to listen to music, but only one you won't mind ruining; it's likely to get a few good oil and paint baths before you're done.

You'll often find yourself doing jobs that require more than one set of hands. Finding helpers is usually pretty easy, since many people enjoy playing do-it-yourself restorer when they know the bills aren't theirs and they can quit anytime they feel like it.

Kids are especially fun to have around as "helpers," though I use the term advisedly. Children are great at doing things the dangerous way, so you'll have to keep a close eye on them. In the long run, pint-size assistants will probably also cost you more time than they'll save you. They have fun and you have fun, though, so it shouldn't matter.

Just remember that it's easy to get frustrated sometimes in the process of the restoration—don't take it out on people who are just trying to help. Quite frankly, restoration can be a good test of parenthood and, for that matter, marriage. If you've got to curse someone, it should be the engineer who ran the main dog bolt all the way through to the trunk.

The international monetary unit of payment for auto restoration helpers seems to be beer. I'm not going to say "never allow alcoholic beverages in the garage," because it's silly to assume anyone who likes a beer while he or she works is going to heed my advice anyway. Quite obviously, though, the wisdom of allowing yourself or your friends to get liquored up around power tools, hacksaws, chisels and welding equipment is rather questionable. The work will be slower and less accurate, if not downright dangerous.

One of the most important elements of a restoration, however, is one that can't be expressed in a book; it's your frame of mind. If you want to actually *enjoy* restoring a car, you have to have the right attitude. You have to be willing to persevere to finish the job, but at the same time you have to step back when you get frustrated or angry and let things alone. This not only allows you to cool off and remember you're supposed to be enjoying yourself, it usually winds up being faster in the end—the madder you get, the lousier your work gets and the longer it takes. Go inside and watch TV for a spell; cars aren't animals, they won't die overnight. But don't let things sit disassembled for too long. You'll forget how they go back together, and they can rust while you wait.

Don't be ashamed to call in the cavalry if you find yourself over your head. It's imperative that you establish a support network of people familiar with the car and its problems. No matter how smart you are and how good your manuals may be, there are simply going to be things that aren't covered. And if you have to take something to a professional for repair, don't despair. The day you spend at the office earning the money to pay him might be more fun than the day you'd spend at home trying to fight with the component.

Learning to Do the Work

Some people are born with the ability to recognize how mechanical assemblies go together and operate; others aren't. You'll sharpen this skill quickly as you work, but there's some inherent talent to it you can't do much about. I think everybody, though, has more of this talent than they realize.

Whether you're a natural mechanic or not, there are some resources you'll need to do the job. The most important is finding a good shop manual for your particular car. This shouldn't be one of those $15 Parts-R-Us specials that covers every Triumph from 1952 to 1970. It should be a legitimate service guide for the make, model and as few years as possible.

You'll usually find that there's more than one manual out there—a factory service manual, an aftermarket service manual, a restoration guide to your particular car, an engine rebuild guide, a complete body and paint book you can understand and so on. Buy each and every one you can lay your hands on. It might cost you $150, but it will be the best investment you make in the entire restoration. Each book will answer some questions that the others don't, the kind you might never answer on your own. Read these books like the Bible; get familiar with them backward and forward, make notes in the margin, clip drawings and diagrams in the appropriate pages. And remember that the car is more important than the book—keep it at your side and don't be afraid to look something up just

The sound metal on this MGB GT might make it a better restoration subject than the car that would receive its parts.

because you'll get the pages dirty. If you think of it beforehand, you can make enlarged photocopies of certain sections.

Where do you find manuals? Swap meets are a good place to start, as are parts suppliers. Automotive mail-order book suppliers are probably the best source, and I quite frankly have to mention Classic Motorbooks, the distributor of this book. Robert Bentley, Inc., also does the fantastic service of reprinting factory manuals, and Haynes and Chilton offer less precise but more generalized manuals on many English cars. Classic Motorbooks carries them all, though, so you get a good idea of what's available through their catalog. Other literature sources are listed in the appendix.

English manual writers have the blood of Shakespeare in them, and their sentences tend to be a little obscure, like "Prise the swarf ring home a little proud and rap smartly on the shank with a clevis sammy." (The proper response, of course, is "Huh?") Sometimes it's hard to tell if they're giving directions to repair a part or get to the local pub.

A little imaginative translation usually gets you through, but sometimes it's actually necessary to write out their directions in English; I'm not sure what language the original is in. There's a translation glossary included in this book that will help, but sometimes you just have to go over the sentence four or five times before divining its meaning.

A good restoration guide to your particular car is almost vital; try to look over a few and find a writer or a series you can relate to. I've become very fond of Lindsay Porter's guides—they're well thought out and he approaches restoration from the do-it-yourself point of view.

Following guides and manuals is 100 times easier if you actually understand how the parts in question are supposed to work, and what function they serve to the car as a whole. If you've never worked on a car before, you can attend a basic automotive repair class at a local community college. It's probably easier and just as effective, though, to find a good book explaining basic automotive theory and read through it yourself. One of my favorite things about older British cars is that there's rarely anything on them that's more complicated than a basic book can explain. All the systems work in basic textbook fashion—there are few tricky or non-intuitive elements.

Probably the best way to learn the work—the way most people get into this hobby—is by working together with someone who already has a fair idea of what they're doing. If a friend or relative does a lot of restoration work, apprentice yourself to him and learn as you go. If not, try to get involved with a local sports car or one-marque club; some of the people you'll meet are almost certainly in the process of a restoration right now. Since it's doubtful you'll be able to find anyone to go through your entire restoration with you, go through theirs with them.

Finding Parts

If something's broken you have three basic alternatives; fix and refinish it yourself, find a used part or buy a replacement.

Fixing and refinishing parts is something that will be covered as we go along, though by and large the method is perfectly clear. Finding replacements is not so intuitive.

Used parts, obviously, will be less expensive than new ones. They're usually kind of tatty and often have the same problem as the part you're replacing, but going with all new parts can bankrupt you. I generally stick with used parts when I can, digging them up in junkyards, swap meets and through ads in the enthusiast magazines. I've gotten into the routine of combing the better local junkyards every now and then just to see what they have—often I'll wind up buying something just in case I need it later. It's wise to keep on top of the best yards, as their turnover can be quite high; good used parts may show up one day and be gone the next.

The pick-it-yourself type of junkyard is usually the cheapest source of parts around. You pay a buck or two to get into the yard, bring your own tools and yank the part you want off a derelict by yourself. These yards also make for great instruction sessions—you get to learn how the piece fits on the car without scratching up your own vehicle in the process. Bring your old part with you if possible to make sure you get the right one off the scrap car. (Have the yard stamp or mark it as you go in so you won't have to pay for it when you leave.)

These yards often give guarantees for a few bucks above the price of the part; get them every time. They may also ding you for a core charge—to

Taking Stock of Missing Parts

Once you've made your rust checks and gone over the inside, it's time to take serious account of what's missing and what will need to be replaced.

Obviously, the more common a car is, the cheaper and easier it will be to replace missing parts. On old and rare cars, finding something as simple as a name badge can be virtually impossible, so take missing pieces especially seriously with oddballs and orphans. The exception may be those parts of a limited-production car that are shared with a more common brand. Many of the taillight assemblies, for instance, used on special-bodied cars are pirated straight off a plebeian production model.

Don't assume that finding parts will be easy just because a car is relatively new, however. You'll have much better luck getting a new trunk hinge for a 1956 Triumph TR-3 than for a 1976 Triumph Stag.

Before offering to buy a car it's always a good idea to find out what it will cost to replace all the missing items *new*. (Assume, for now, that nothing will be available in junkyards or swap meets.) Take that amount off of your purchase price.

get that money back, you have to bring your old part and the receipt back to the junkyard. If you're replacing a ratty but functioning component, it's usually best to eat the core charge and save the old part as a back-up. (This, of course, also applies to items you're tempted to throw away. Save everything that has a glimmer of value left in it, even just as trading stock.)

Used parts you don't pull off yourself are more expensive, but usually still much cheaper than new ones. Here you'll phone the yard or drop by, ask the man at the counter if he's got a trafficator wand for

Parts Cars

Parts cars can be a great way to get a lot of needed parts cheap. They can also cause some hassles, so let's go over both sides of the issue.

On the plus side, a parts car can quickly provide you with enough spares to far outstrip its purchase price. It's also a good guide to assembly and disassembly if you get confused. (The opposite side of your own car often serves the same purpose.) If the part you need is actually on the parts car, it's fast and easy to just go out and yank the thing—no waiting in line or for the UPS courier. There's also the possibility of trading parts from the car that you don't need for ones you do.

Sometimes one good assembly will make a whole parts car worth the money: a transmission, an engine, even a set of carburetors can be worth more than the purchase price. Finally, when you're done, parts cars have scrap metal value—usually about $50 or $75 worth.

On the minus side, parts cars take up a lot of space you could use for other things. They invite thieves and vandals into your yard, and frequently the same parts are worn on the parts car as your own—obviously, if the seats and top are as bad as the ones you've got now they won't do you any good. Parts cars may not, on closer inspection, provide you with much of anything you can use: no sound body panels, no interior parts, no working accessories or mechanical components. You've got to choose your parts car wisely, and ask yourself if the parts they do offer are good enough to go on your car.

Parts cars also frequently have the wrong equipment on them. A 1967 MGB parts car will be of remarkably little value if you're restoring a 1979 car. The carburetors, interior, springs, electrical components and much of the engine won't interchange.

Parts cars are usually junkers that have expired of natural causes, but those aren't often the best deals. A better bet is a good car that was totaled in a wreck. The body or frame might be shot but the important things—gauges, seats, engine components, shocks and so on—are often quite nice. If the car died a natural death, usually all the parts have deteriorated at the same rate—beyond usefulness. Similarly, a sound car with a blown engine or transmission might be picked up cheaply indeed. It can be used for parts, or as a basis for rebuilding a second car with a simple component swap.

Where do you find parts cars? Usually the same places you'll find regular cars, through the want ads or bulletin boards around your area. But often you can pick up parts cars just by noticing one that's rusting away in somebody's yard and asking the owner if he wants to sell it. You might also ask your friendly neighborhood salvage man to keep his eyes open at auctions for a likely candidate.

Another great source is abandoned restorations: a disassembled or half-finished car is almost impossible to bring back to life, but it can be a great scrounger. This, of course, cuts both ways. It means your own restoration, if you get it apart and can't finish it, isn't much good to anyone else except *as* a parts car.

a 1934 MG NA Magnette and, when he's done laughing and can get up off the floor, he'll send somebody out to the yard to look and pull the part for you. (This kind of place gets really huffy if you call it a junkyard. It's an auto recycler or automotive dismantling center, or pretty soon, I suspect, a pre-owned component boutique.) Again, try to get a guarantee on used parts from a dismantler.

New parts are great when you can afford them, and often you'll have no choice. You just won't be able to find the part anywhere else, or a used one simply isn't good enough. Not only will the part be clean and ready to go, it ought to darn well *work*— something you can rarely be sure of with used parts.

In the long run, new parts are the easiest way to go. If you're lucky enough to have a good parts source nearby you can just get in a car, drive there with the old part in hand and pick up a new one— fast and expensive. Getting to know the people at your local parts house is also a good way to get advice, recommendations and to find out about new repair and refinishing methods. If you spend a lot of time bugging your local parts place for advice, go ahead and give them some business from time to time. If it costs a couple of dollars extra to buy a

part from them, let them have your money and keep the relationship worthwhile for both parties.

A slower but less expensive method is to call a good mail-order parts supplier, though if speed is important, you can often get a part shipped overnight or second-day air for not much money. You'll get very familiar with at least one of these mail-order companies, and they can be an even more valuable source of information, aid and comfort than a local supplier. To survive, a mail-order company must have enough experience with the particular parts they stock to really know their stuff.

A good parts house will make you part of the family—include you in their technical mailings, give you a chance to write letters to their experts or their newsletter, and let you know of fun or interesting events happening in your area. A good parts house will just plain know a lot about the car you're working on, and they'll be happy to share their knowledge with you. After all, it's in everybody's best interest that you get your car up and running. In the end, a good supplier genuinely enjoys working on and preserving nice cars.

Cleaning the Car

It's vital to start with as clean a car as possible. Chapter 9 of this book contains a short section on general cleaning once the car is back together. That will go a long way toward knowing how to do the initial cleanup job as well.

I can't stress enough how starting with a clean car makes your work easier—it makes all the difference in the world. You can actually see how things go together and come apart. You don't constantly get grease all over yourself and your tools. You can tag wires and fittings without the labels getting smeared or falling off.

Steam or chemical engine cleaning is the first step (as outlined in the engine chapter). But full degreasing and cleaning of the entire car—body, chassis, suspension, interior—is critical if you want to get through this restoration. Try to scrape up and bag as much caked grease as possible first; you can add it to your toxic-crud box for later disposal. Start with the grimiest pieces and work your way out, remembering to support the car on jack stands and remove the wheels to get at the wheelwells and suspension. After a thorough cleaning, you're often amazed at just how good the condition of the car really is. Sometimes, of course, you uncover more problems lurking under the dirt and grease—well, better now than later.

Find and remove all the papers and extra parts from the car, and file and store all of them safely— don't throw anything away yet, particularly papers. You'll probably find receipts, registration papers, even paint codes and instructions lurking about inside the car. It may take a couple of days to do it all, but they're days well spent.

Degreasing an engine compartment is an art in itself. The engine of this Austin-Healey was covered with the usual grime, grease and dirt of years of driving and storage. It's wise to degrease the engine before taking it apart so you don't get dirt inside and to make the job that much more easy and pleasant. Chemical sprays can help but they are also often toxic; lye also works, but is difficult to safely dispose of. The best route is often to go to the local self-service car wash and use its system, complete with its proper drainage. Robin O'Brien

As you work on the car, it's also important to immediately clean parts as you remove them; that's always your first order of business. Commercial degreasers, kerosene, aerosols and soapy water are your best weapons for most jobs, as are soft plastic brushes and clean rags. Cleaning the parts lets you see what you're doing and prevents crud from gumming up the works once you've fixed the darned thing. It keeps grit and grime from falling in your eyes while you work. It keeps you from losing things constantly, and keeps your work space neat and comfortable. Parts are easier to identify when they're clean, and easier to disassemble—small fasteners often hide beneath layers of grease and grime.

Get in the habit of constantly cleaning your hands as well. The best gift to the do-it-yourself restorer might be waterless hand cleaner. Smear the stuff on your hands, work it in and wipe yourself down the moment you get greasy. Keep rotating your rags as they get greasy, and wash them often with lots of detergent.

Planning, Tagging and Bagging

The easiest (and probably most fun) part of a restoration is taking things apart. Given a pot of coffee and twenty-four hours you could disassemble a Jaguar down to its last nut and bolt with no trouble at all. The difficult part is getting it back together.

You have to know how things came apart if you want any prayer of getting them back together again. You might think that the exploded diagrams in your manuals will make this perfectly clear later—they won't. Keep track of the disassembly, mark every part so you know what it is and where it goes, and keep different parts together in a logical place and fashion. Don't trust yourself to remember anything!

Always keep paper and pencil handy, and make drawings and notes of the entire disassembly: how parts fit together, where they go, how wires are clipped to one another, what rod goes in what hole and so on. Also make a note of everything you break, lose or need. Put tags on all wire connections, keep all the bolts and doodads together with their proper assemblies in strong plastic bags or other storage containers, and put one label on the outside of the container and another on the inside, just in case.

Get into the habit of always threading as many fasteners as possible back into their holes as soon as you can—that's the best way to avoid losing them or forgetting where they go. (While I'm thinking of fasteners, two tips: never reuse a cotter pin, and never thread a bolt into a blind hole with water or oil in the bottom. The fluid will keep it from seating and possibly damage the surrounding metal.)

While you're doing the actual work, keep nuts and bolts and clips in a clean jar or plastic container as you remove them, never on the lip of the engine bay or the ground. And don't bite off more than you can chew at any one time. By working in subassemblies and organizing everything as you go, you'll save countless hours of frustrating searching and fiddling when the time comes to get things back together.

The Parts Organizer's Hall of Fame

To keep parts well organized and readily available for reassembly, use the following items:
• Margarine tubs with clear lids: These are fantastic for keeping small parts together and clean.
• Heavy zip-lock plastic bags in all sizes: Get the good, heavy, name-brand variety, perhaps fifty each in sandwich, regular and jumbo size. (You'll need many more, but this will keep you going for the time being.) The newer bags with write-on strips are a real blessing, but always toss another label inside with the parts. Plastic bags will tear, though, and most are dissolved by gasoline and solvents. They have their limitations.

As soon as you figure out how to remove a trim piece—here it's a pot-metal trunk hinge from an early Healey, which is simple enough unless the studs strip themselves out of the hinge—drop the part in a labelled bag or container. Don't wait even to remove the next one; you'll get confused and pay for it later. Robin O'Brien

• Twist ties: These are great for keeping long, thin assemblies together, for holding wires up out of the way and for affixing labels to unruly large parts.

• Paper labels and tape: A necessary evil, masking tape is hard to write on and the cheap stuff never sticks. Mailing labels and other self-sticking papers usually leave lots of glue behind and are hard to remove. Never use sticky labels or tape on a refinished part. Colored labels can be handy for keeping different types of parts straight. To preserve the writing on the label, consider covering it up with clear plastic tape.

• 35 mm film canisters: These are good for very small parts. Most canisters are opaque, but Fuji makes them in transparent plastic. Ask your photographer friends to start saving them for you.

• Duct tape: There's no end to duct tape's uses, but one of the best is keeping large, unfinished assemblies like bumpers and brackets together. Duct tape leaves lots of glue behind, so only use it on a part you can clean with mineral spirits later. Duct tape is also good for sealing up boxes and bags, wrapping around tool handles to keep them from scratching, and holding together large components like transmissions that have had their fasteners removed.

Disassembling a British sports car is quick, easy and fun. The trouble is, if you don't take your car apart with method to the madness, you'll have a difficult time ever putting it back together. There are steps to take when disassembling a car that will help you in the end. First, take photographs of the area you are breaking down so you'll have a reference as to how it was assembled in the beginning. Second, as you take apart complicated assemblies, draw diagrams in a notebook showing the position of the components, nuts and bolts and where the washers all came from. Finally, sort your parts into ziplock plastic bags with identifying notes in each one. Then store all of the plastic bags for one assembly in its own box with a notation as to what it is. Organization is half of the battle in a good restoration job. Robin O'Brien

• Twist-on paper tags: Twist-on tags are much better than stick-ons when you can use them. The part, of course, will need to have a hole you can stick the wires through.

• Insulated single-strand copper wire: Copper wire is much better for holding large assemblies together than baling wire; the insulation keeps it from scratching. The wire should be thick enough to hold its shape after being bent, but not too thick to be easy to use.

• Large garbage bags: A mixed blessing at best, these are rarely strong enough to support a part that's large enough to need them, and since they're opaque you'll have a hard time knowing what's inside. They are good, however, for sealing up and protecting a large part while it's being safely stored.

• Paper bags: Paper is weak to begin with and useless once it gets soaked with oil and solvent. These usually make more of a mess than they're worth, except when used as a diaper to soak up excess grease and oil while the part is being protected by something else.

• Large cardboard boxes: Cardboard boxes aren't all that strong, and smaller parts are easy to lose in all the flaps and pockets. They're good for holding parts that are already protected in bags or tubs, though, and there's not much of an alternative in most cases. Heavy plastic crates are the best thing to use, but these are expensive and hard to come by.

• Cameras: After thoroughly cleaning the car and before you start taking things apart, take a ton of photos. Try to cover absolutely everything in detail—the linkages, the wiring, the suspension joints, the brake assemblies, the interior layout, the seat patterns, the trim fasteners. It might take 100 or more photos, and most you'll never need. The ones you do need will be a godsend, though. A Polaroid or other instant camera is best, although the film is expensive and can add up in a hurry.

As you work through the car, it's a good idea to take more photos as more layers are revealed. If you take off a brake drum, shoot a picture of the guts before disassembling them. If you pull off the carbs, shoot the throttle cable and linkage arrangement first. I've heard of people using home video cameras for this application, and I think it's a great idea. Obviously you're not going to want your camcorder laying around the garage and getting degreaser all over it, but it's not a bad idea to shoot the whole car before taking it apart—that just might save your bacon.

How Far Should You Go?

This is a complicated question that you have to answer for yourself. There are basically three ways to go about a restoration: by attacking parts and problems at random as the mood strikes you (repair, not restoration), by making a concerted game plan and correcting all the faults one at a time while the car's still together (staged restoration), and by taking everything apart right from the start and working it all over one step at a time (frame-up restoration).

The first option, repair-as-you-go, is certainly the easiest. You're probably not going to end up with a really nice car as a result, but if all you want is a serviceable driver there's nothing wrong with that. Some hard-core enthusiasts may look down their noses at you, but don't let them bug you—it's your car, after all.

The staged repair, where you make a list of all the flaws and work through them one by one, reassembling the car as you go, can definitely result in a real show-stopper. There are some advantages to doing it this way: the costs of the restoration are spread out over a longer period; it takes less space to do a staged restoration than a frame-up job; and you can move the car, drive it to the shop and sell it again before the restoration is completely finished. Perhaps most importantly, a staged restoration lets you drive and enjoy the car in the meantime; it won't be off the road for the entire time.

Most serious restorers swear by the frame-up restoration, though. If nothing else, this actually saves money—you do everything once and do it right. It also saves time in the long run, since you're not constantly disassembling something to get at something else. You'll do less damage to good parts while working on bad ones, and it's easier to plan the most efficient attack if everything is exposed at once. There's a very satisfying sense of a beginning and an end with a frame-up job, and the finished results are usually better. It's easier to paint, clean and refinish parts that are completely off the car and away from everything else. You're less tempted to leave alone something that's not quite perfect, because it's less of a hassle to deal with it if it's sitting out in the open instead of hidden by other pieces. It lets you do metalwork without worrying about damaging rubber and wiring and wood elsewhere in the car.

Seen as an entire project, a frame-up restoration is simply more complete, easier and cheaper than a staged one. That doesn't mean a frame-up restoration is necessarily the best answer, though—it has some serious problems. The biggest two are the fact that the car is off the road for a long period of time, and that the expenses all come at once. You can stretch out a staged restoration for years but a frame-up job ought to be done as quickly as possible, because until the car's all back together it's basically junk. It's much easier to get confused during a staged restoration, it takes more space to do the job and if you can't finish the restoration for one reason or another you'll lose just about every dollar you've invested. It's also much harder to move the project around your garage, and harder

to get the car and its parts to any professional who's going to be working on it.

And quite frankly, many cars simply don't need a frame-up restoration. Unless every area of the car needs attention, simple repair or a staged restoration might give you satisfactory results with a lot less time and expense than a frame-up job.

I've tried not to gear this book toward any one of these alternatives more than the others. The tips and procedures mentioned by and large will be useful for whatever kind of approach you choose. I have, though, written this book mostly for the person who's restoring a car for fun, not profit. As you go through it, bear in mind that consistently sticking to the cheaper, more labor-intensive alternatives can add up to a considerable savings no matter how you approach the job.

Time and Money

Which brings us nicely into the subjects of time and money. Here are two more areas that are hard to get a grip on without knowing about the car's original condition and how it's supposed to end up. There are simply no hard-and-fast rules for figuring out these details, only some general guidelines.

A frame-up restoration can easily take a couple of years of evenings, weekends and vacations, if not more. A serious, concerted, every-free-moment job can conceivably be done in a couple of months, but that's virtually unheard of for do-it-yourself restorers. A staged restoration can take even longer, though you won't notice it as much since you'll be driving the car in the meantime. And in all fairness,

Factor transportation into all your dead-car purchases. Renting a trailer for a cross-town jaunt won't cost more than $100, but transporting a relic from New York to California can be a $1,500+ proposition. If the car is close enough to fetch on your own, you'll probably be able to cadge a trailer—and maybe even some help—from your new friends in the local marque club. Don't forget to chain the car down tightly. Robin O'Brien

time is largely a factor of how good a mechanic you are. Somebody with a lot of experience and a gift for auto repair will be able to blow through a restoration in a quarter of the time it would take a novice.

Your own ability—whether you can tear something down and rebuild it off the top of your head, or if you have trouble screwing in a light bulb—needn't affect the finished product. Perseverance and hard work will ultimately make up for any skill and talent you lack. Realistically, though, ability has a bearing on the amount of time it will take to finish the job; the more talent you have mechanically, the faster it will go.

Money is equally hard to get a handle on. The costs of a professional restoration were touched on earlier in this chapter, and you must realize that not just a Jaguar can run up a $50,000 restoration bill. A 1976 Midget could do it just as easily, though only a loon would think it was worth it. Professionally reconditioned MGBs and TR-4s appear on the market from time to time for $10,000–$18,000; privately reconditioned examples might cost half that, so there you have an idea of just how much of the cost is labor (which the pro includes), how much is the car (the value of your own example) and how much is parts (which both pro and amateur must factor in).

You can get a worst-case scenario easily enough by simply pricing out all the parts you'll need new and adding them together, plus about 30 percent for tools, rentals, errors, paint and body filler, solvents, sandpaper and so on. Tack on dollars for any jobs you aren't planning to do yourself—paint, engine work, welding and so forth—and there's a fair estimate of what the restoration *could* cost. Not what it *will* cost, however, since you'll keep prices down by rejuvenating a lot of parts and doing work yourself. (Take a look at the number of "$20,000 invested, sell for $8,000 or best offer" ads in the paper and you can see how important it is to avoid doing things the expensive way wherever possible.)

For the average restore-it-for-fun type who plans to farm out a few of the big jobs (engine rebuild, paint and the like) it's often fair to take the original value of the car, compare it to a very good example and figure that the difference is about what the restoration will cost.

It's important, of course, to budget more than you think you'll need; if you run out of money halfway through the job you risk losing everything, to say nothing of being pretty darned mad about the whole experience. Budget realistically for each phase of the restoration, add about a third again for a cushion and see if the numbers work out for you. For someone serious about saving (and ultimately making) money on the restoration, lots of labor and attacking every job yourself is where the profit comes from. An experienced restorer with all the right tools at his or her disposal might be able to do a very nice restoration for the price of salvage parts and materials alone—maybe as little as $1,500. A beginner, however, will be looking at a much larger investment to do the same job.

2

Bodywork Restoration

Bodywork is definitely the big leagues. It can be as minor as popping out a dent with the heel of your hand or as major as splicing a new front clip onto the car. But whatever job you do, the results will be staring you in the face from that day on.

This section covers a lot of ground: beating, filling, shaping, cutting, welding and so on. The first thing to do, though, is to take stock of what your car is going to need. You ought to do this as soon as it's sitting in your garage—familiarity will blind you to flaws that other people might notice right away.

Take some black-and-white pictures of the whole car—both sides, top, front, back and any interesting details—before you get too far along with the project. Make two copies of each.

With a grease pencil or permanent marker, go over one set of photos and mark *every flaw* you can find on the body. Small dents and scratches might be hiding next to bigger ones, so get up close and go over every inch of the car. Use your fingers as well as your eyes; they're more sensitive than you think.

There's just no sense in trying to resurrect parts like the trunk and bumper of this Austin-Healey 100 when replacements are easily and inexpensively available. The rust on the trunk's too deep and the missing plating on the left of the bumper makes it a goner. Robin O'Brien

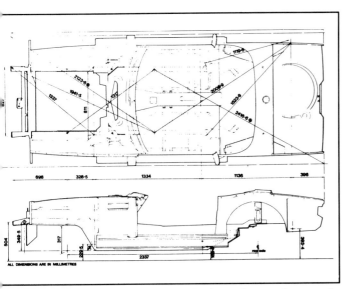

If a car is stripped down to the frame it never hurts to do an alignment check; a chart like the one for Jensen-Healeys shown here should be in your manual or available through a specialist. Rarely will you find a problem on a car that looks okay, but since a true frame is critical for safe handling this is a chore you should do whenever you have the chance.

(Light cotton gloves can sometimes increase the ability of your fingers to detect flaws.)

Mark down each flaw on the photos with a code you can remember, like S for scratches, H for high spots, D for dents—you get the idea. That way you won't forget to take care of something until after a new coat of paint makes it glaringly obvious.

For the second set of pictures, go over every inch of the car with a magnet and mark down the areas of plastic filler. Body damage that crosses into an area of filler will have to be treated specially—either the filler will have to come out, or you'll have to avoid beating those panels to bring them up or down.

A magnet will also tell you if the trunk, hood, doors or hardtop are aluminum.

You learn to do metal, you learn to do fiberglass, and then look what happens . . . how are you at cabinetmaking? This early Morgan shares a characteristic with plenty of prewar sports cars and postwar estate bodies, that of a stressed wooden structure that rots away fast. Motorhead Ltd. of Virginia had to cut a whole new set of pieces from original templates to get this car back in the shape you see here. Motorhead LTD.

The main front panel of an Austin-Healey bolts and screws on in a few key locations. You'd think removing these bolts should make it easy to remove the panel, but you'd be wrong; hidden around the cowl are eight rivets that have to be drilled out after removing all the nearby goodies like the demister vents. It's a classic example of the importance of marque-specific manuals; if you don't know about the rivets in advance, you'll inevitably try to pry the cowl up first and destroy it in the process. Robin O'Brien

Quite a startling change from start to finish on this Austin-Healey 100; all the forward panels were rotten, so the stripping had to go beyond the axle line. When it's all put back together, though, the trouble seems worth it and then some. Robin O'Brien

Panel Beating

Before you can fix up most dents and damage with filler you have to get the metal close to the correct shape. It takes years of practice to get really good at panel beating, but doing a job that's just a base for plastic filler is much easier.

There are, of course, things you can do to damaged panels that are faster and easier than beating. One is simply getting behind the dent with a pry bar or your fist and pushing it out—not usually possible, but great when it works. Occasionally, you can push a dent out so well you'll never know there was any damage; that's pretty rare, though.

Another method is to use a *slide hammer*, a long rod that passes through a heavy weight. You drill a hole (more often a number of holes) in the dent and attach the hammer with a self-tapping screw. Then whack the weight up to the top of the rod and the force pulls up the metal. This usually leaves some high spots, though, and obviously some holes. Slide hammers are only good for rough work—try

to get a dent too close to perfect with one and you'll do more harm than good. There are literally hundreds of gadgets—drill-mounted pullers, suction cups, spring picks and so on—that are supposed to replace panel beating. None of them does much good on high spots, however, and high spots are actually a bigger worry than dents. Dents you can fill; high spots must be brought down to or below their original contours. (To check the area for high spots, make a few crisscrossing passes with a long, rough body file. Any high spots should show up as extra-shiny metal.)

The odds are that at some point you'll have to resort to panel beating. The idea behind panel beat-

A professional can make up metal panels on a wheeling machine if you get stuck for a replacement. Be prepared to pay for the extensive labor, however. The Eastwood Company

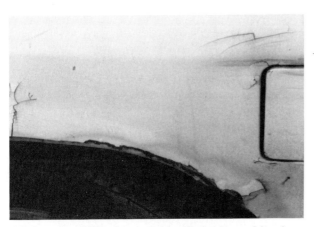

All the evils of filler in one fender: Paint is cracking from filler laid on too deeply, covered rust is peeking out from under the ruined fenderwell and ripples near the fuel door must have looked bad from day one.

The infamous MGB door crack. A new door or skin is the only answer.

Large suction cups can sometimes yank a gentle dent right out of the metal, leaving no trace of damage behind. It's often worth a try. The Eastwood Company

Flat faces of the body hammer must be kept clean and undented or the flaw will transfer to the work with every blow.

ing is to determine the forces that caused the damage and repeat them in the reverse order and direction. That means usually attacking the indirect damage first—the waves, ripples and buckling—before moving on to the impact site itself.

Your most often used tools will be a flat-body hammer and an all-purpose dolly. To lower a high spot, first remove all the undercoating and gunk from behind the metal. Gently heating the outside of the panel will usually soften up undercoating so it can be removed with a scraper. Finish it off with solvent and a wire brush.

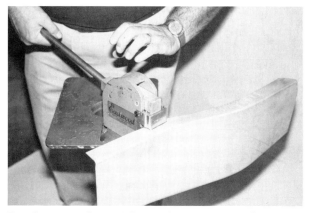

Bench-mounted panel former lets restorer make simple panels from steel stock. Pre-formed panels are easier if you can get them, of course. The Eastwood Company

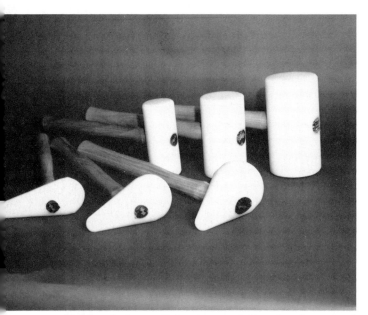

Rubber body mallets are great for aluminum and stainless-steel work. Large panel forming can also be done with rubber instead of metal hammers.

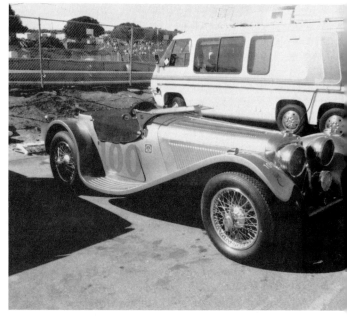

Clamshell fenders might vibrate enough to crack plastic filler right out; top-quality panel beating and maybe a little body solder are the order of the day. Besides, only a Visigoth would use plastic on something like this Jaguar SS–100.

Once the panel is clean on both sides (dirt or flaws will damage the faces of the hammers and dollies and transfer those flaws to the working surface), start by tapping on the ridge with the hammer while holding the dolly underneath, bridging the gap. Soft, glancing blows should be used, increasing in pressure as the metal comes closer to its original form. (To check that your blows are falling square, start by first pounding on a soft piece of wood. When you've mastered that, move on to a piece of scrap metal and get comfortable with the tools before turning to your car.) Rock the hammer between your fingers and palm rather than holding it firmly and using your elbow or wrist. To find the dolly under the metal, first strike gently around the area with the hammer; where it springs back the most is where the dolly is located.

This is called, fittingly enough, *on-the-dolly* beating. Working down a ridge with on-the-dolly beating is easiest if you use light blows and lower it a little at a time, instead of flattening one spot completely before moving on to the next.

You'll almost always want to work alternately on the highs and lows, though, so you'll also need to master *off-the-dolly* beating. Here, you strike the nearby high areas while pressing up with the dolly on the low spots. Alternating between the two methods every few swipes—the imaginatively named *on-and-off-the-dolly* beating—will do the

best job. You'll lower the highs and raise the lows simultaneously.

The real danger in panel beating is that all your pounding might stretch the metal. If this happens you'll wind up with more trouble than you started with, unless the stretching is very minor and can be hidden below some filler.

Stretching means you've thinned out one area of the metal; what was pushed away bunches up and causes ripples and waves. Stretching can also be caused by excessive heat or the accident itself. You'll recognize it by feeling the waves, by seeing a bowed surface in the metal or by finding a dent that pops in and out without resting in its original location.

If the metal does stretch you'll have to shrink it back down. This can be done on small areas with a *shrink beater*, a hammer with a cross-hatched face that forces the metal into a compact pattern. (You can also use *shrinking dollies* from behind to get the same results, and cut way down on the surface refinishing needed in the end.) Aluminum can be shrunk back when cold, but on steel you might have better luck if you warm the surface gently with a butane torch.

More serious stretching requires heat shrinking.

Heat Shrinking

Heat-shrunk metal will never be exactly right, and you'll need to use filler to finish the job. That's no big deal, since anyone who's not a seventy-eight-year-old panel-beater from Modena, Italy, will need filler to finish most *any* job. But heat-

---

Panel-Beating Tools

Listed here are a few other tools you'll find useful for panel beating:

• Bumping blade: Slap this blade back and forth over small ridges and high spots. You can use a dolly behind large areas, but smaller jobs don't require one. Bumping blades are only good for relatively minor damage.

• Spring beater: This consists of a spoon of spring steel that can spread out the force of your hammer blows. (Put the spring between your hammer and the metal.) It can preserve the paint job on a minor lowering repair if used properly.

• Pick beater: Hammered up from behind small dents, the pick beater can raise them if used *gently*. Work too hard with a pick and you'll get a pimply, brittle surface.

• Curved dolly: This is a shaped dolly that copies the curve of the metal you're trying to repair. The metal should flatten out onto it like a mold.

• Heavy spoon: Part pry bar, part dolly, this can be used for both purposes. A pointed spoon is about the best thing for getting into headlight lips, roof creases and similar places. Use it to first lever the metal close to the proper contour, then flip it around to be a dolly for the final pounding. A heavy spoon is also good as a chisel for separating inner and outer panels so you can get in for the actual repair.

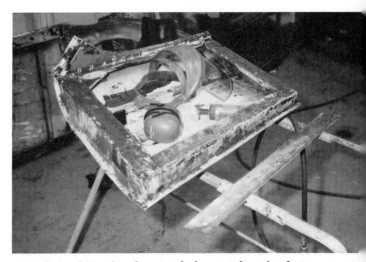

A good panel stand makes stand-alone work easier, but it's not absolutely necessary. Two sawhorses will do the job—they'll just seem a little rickety. This stripped-out Austin-Healey 100 door is ready to be worked on. Mounted on a solid stand, the angle grinder, face shield and ear protection are ready to go. Obviously, the door frame itself is going to need some work, too. Robin O'Brien

Despite its rather dirty appearance, this used Jaguar E Type sheet metal can be dipped or blasted and will finish up beautifully.

shrunk metal rusts very easily, too; it should be scoured to brightmetal and painted immediately after finishing.

Heat the center of the stretched area cherry red with a soft oxyacetylene nozzle, taking care not to burn right through. Then remove the flame and quickly put a dolly under the hot spot and beat around it with a hammer; the final few blows should be on the dolly itself. (Beware of too much beating, which will just stretch it more.) When the metal cools down to black again, quench it with heavy rags soaked in lots of water. (Don't quench it while it's still red-hot or the metal will become brittle.)

The rags themselves can retain a lot of heat—don't touch them without heavy gloves or you'll get burned.

In general, it's better to under-beat a panel and finish it off with plastic filler. The true perfectionist might try to beat out a panel entirely, but it will take infinitely longer and the results might be worse to look at. You're certainly welcome to spend the rest of your life replacing a Nautilus machine with a body hammer; a filler-free body is a legitimate source of pride. But people who are intent on a "no Bondo" finish shouldn't denigrate those of us who'd rather spend the next five years driving our cars instead of whacking on them. It's the final look that counts, not the bragging rights.

Work Hardening and Annealing

A lot of pounding and hammering can work-harden the metal, making it brittle and easy to crack; this takes awhile with steel, but aluminum hardens quickly. The answer is to anneal it before you apply any filler and move on. Annealing steel is done by simply heating the whole area to a cherry red and then slowly removing the heat and letting the metal cool off again. Aluminum shouldn't be heated beyond a dull glow, and should be immediately quenched with plenty of warm water.

Body Filler

Plastic body filler—in America it's often called Bondo, the brand name of one of the more popular varieties—has a terrible reputation. It doesn't deserve one. Plastic filler is *great* stuff, one of the best inventions since the knockoff wheel. The only trouble is that it's so darned easy to work with that people abuse it. Their shoddy work makes the whole product line look bad.

This swatch of poorly applied filler will have to be chipped out before things can proceed here, but the fragile nature of the panel means you'll have to go carefully. In bodywork it's easy to make things worse instead of better. Robin O'Brien

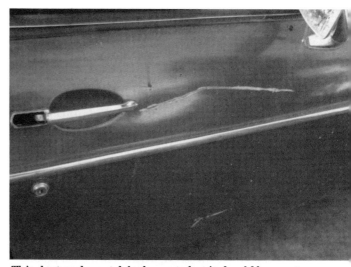

This dent and scratch looks nasty but it should be easy to fix. You should pound out the dent first, but plastic filler would probably do the job by itself.

Plastic filler should only be used as a finishing tool. You'll still have to pound any big dent almost all the way out, and lower any high spots before the filler can be used to good effect. But rough pulling and lowering is fairly easy, it's the much more time-consuming business of making a "pretty close" repair into a "just right" repair that Bondo and its brethren replace. The objective these days isn't to get a dented panel perfect again—it's to get it close enough to let a well-applied, light coat of filler perfect it for you.

In light of the ease with which filler can be applied correctly, it's amazing how many people have found ways to do it wrong. Probably the most common mistake people make with fillers is not using a large enough block or body file when sanding down the repair. Unless the sanding board rests on sound metal on either side of the dent, the filler will be brought down too low and there will be a wavy, uneven hole where the dent used to be.

Another big no-no with filler is an improperly feathered edge, which shows up under paint as an odd circle in the middle of an otherwise good panel. (For an explanation of feathering, see the painting chapter.) And using filler on door edges or other places where it's likely to get nicked off is asking for trouble. Here it's best to pound out the edge really well, keep the plastic to a minimum and go with a filler that includes chopped bits of fiberglass. (This is tougher and more resilient than plain filler, but a little harder to work with. The sanding is more dangerous, too—you have to wear a good mask to avoid sucking in fiberglass particles.)

The biggest mistake of all is assuming that filler is a structural replacement; it's strictly for looks, and never for use on a stressed part or panel in danger of failing. A rusted-out sill will collapse just as fast whether it's got filler in the holes or not, and the resulting accident will be just as deadly. Structural pieces of the car like cowl braces and suspension

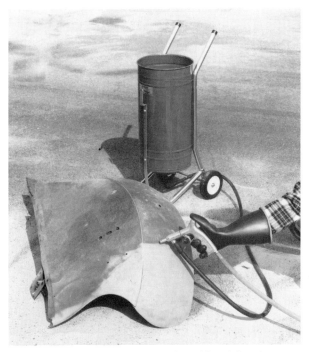

A small home sandblasting tank and head that connects to your own compressor will get you started in blasting. A small home system is pretty slow but it does the job on rust and paint. The Eastwood Company

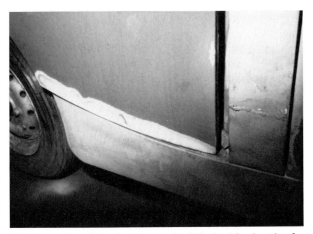

The lower lip of the fender can be filled with plastic; the sill must be replaced with steel.

The easiest way to remove surface rust is with a spot sandblaster; a wire wheel and sandpaper will also do the job, though. The bare metal under the rust will have to be treated with rust remover and high-zinc primer to keep the rust at bay. The Eastwood Company

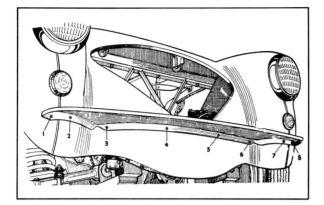

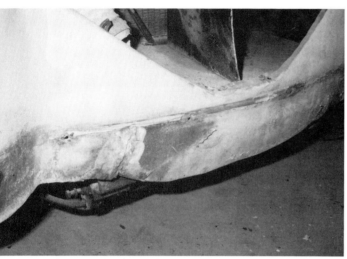

When you see something like this in your manual, start thinking about what it tells you; the fact that this Healey bumper sill traps dirt and stones under the bumper line means you can expect to find problems in the hidden area below. Pull the panel on a real car and, sure enough, you've got rust and impact cracks to contend with. Robin O'Brien

mounting points should *never* be fixed with plastic filler. You can fill a small dent in a sound sill with plastic, but anything that's big enough to compromise a structural panel's strength has got to be repaired with steel. A coverup repair in this area is a short step away from time-delayed manslaughter.

You can slap today's fillers on to a surprising depth without them cracking, shrinking back or falling out in chunks; that wasn't true with the fillers of the recent past. If you have to fill a hole more than maybe 1/3 in. deep, though, it's best to do it in layers. Leave the repair "a little proud," as the English would say, so you can sand it down flat without worrying about holes and chips that need touching up later.

Mind you, to make a repair in plastic you have to have something for the filler to stick to. In cases where the metal is simply gone—usually where a

rusty spot has been cut away—you're going to have to give the filler some kind of backing. That backing should be a new piece of steel that's been welded or brazed into place. On a car that's soon going to the graveyard, though, you can slap in most anything to give the filler a base: a pop-riveted aluminum panel, a swatch of fiberglass or even a piece of aluminum screen bonded into place with filler around the edges. These are on-the-cheap repairs, of course, and they're neither long-lasting nor "correct."

Applying Plastic Filler

The steps to filling a dent with plastic should be a breeze if you've done the rough work correctly in steel. Once the dent has been pounded close to, but a little lower than, it's proper contours you're ready to start with the plastic.

Clean out the area with solvent to remove any grime and crud. Sand down the entire area to clean metal, using a grinding wheel or rough sanding disc. Make a final pass with a stiff wire brush or wheel to get the last bits of paint out. Then rough up the surface with a scribe or coarse sandpaper, and wipe out all the grit.

Mix up a little plastic. It comes in two parts, filler and hardener, and once you've mixed them the clock is running. Only blend as much as you can use between the time you start working and the time it begins to set up. Depending on the ratio and the weather, filler will set up anywhere from five minutes to an hour or more after mixing. The exact ratio of filler to hardener isn't critical if it's close to the manufacturer's specifications. Just remember that more hardener or hot weather makes the filler set faster; use less hardener in the summer, more in the winter.

Spread the filler into the repair area. A flexible plastic spreader usually comes with the kit, or you can buy one at body and paint supply stores. These flexible spreaders are about the only tool that works. Some people use metal putty knives, but these make it hard to get a well-contoured finish.

Fill the repair (using more than one coat if needed) until it's just a bit higher than the surrounding area. (If you're a bit off, though, it's no big deal. You can just sand down the excess or add another coat later.) Once the filler has set up thoroughly, go after it with a long sanding board and 60 grit open-face dry paper or a dulled single-cut body file. By resting the edges of the tool on the undamaged metal to either side of the repair you'll avoid ripples and low spots.

Spray a quick coat of primer over the repair to show up major sanding scratches, chips and holes. You might also want to run a straightedge over the surface just to make sure you haven't created a low spot somewhere in the filler.

Patch up sanding marks and other errors with stopper (also called spot putty). Stopper is somewhat thinner than filler and takes a little longer to dry, but it spreads very nicely into little flaws. (You can also apply a thin film of regular filler in a pinch.) Finish off the stopper with medium sandpaper, then go over it once more with fine paper to remove the scratches. Once the edges are properly feathered you should be ready to go.

If the repair was a big one, I'd recommend guide coating the panel before proceeding with a final primer coat. You'll often find that there's still a long way to go.

There are a couple of tricks that are good to know when using plastic body filler. Most of them have to do with the tools you use: the plastic spreaders, for instance, must be absolutely clean and can't have any nicks on the spreading edge. (To clean a spreader, by the way, it's actually easier to let a whole wad of filler dry onto it rather than trying to scrape most of it off wet. Once the filler sets up you can just bend the spreader and the whole chunk will fall off.)

Mix the filler and hardener only on a clean, dry surface that you can throw away, like a good stiff piece of cardboard. Any grit or dirt that gets into the filler will play havoc with the repair, either by showing up as streaks or by creating a little air pocket that collapses later.

Use only the same brand of filler and hardener, and stir the filler well if it looks separated when you first open the can. Also, never let any filler that's been mixed with hardener come into contact with the rest of the can—not even a crumb. The whole can will harden and be ruined.

Some skilled bodymen can take a grater-type file to not-quite-set filler and quickly plane it down as easily as cutting through old cheddar cheese. I've never had any luck with this, though—I always try to grate the filler off too dry, which just makes scratches, or too wet, which just makes a complete mess. Incidentally, filler will often skin over and look dry on the surface before it really *is* dry underneath, so give it a little extra time before going after it with a file or sandpaper.

Body Solder

Everyone should try body soldering (also called leading, lead loading or a number of unprintable expletives) at least once, if for no other reason than to understand why plastic filler is such a blessing. Back when Triumphs ran at Le Mans and the terms Nissan and SCCA were never used in the same breath, lead loading was the accepted way to make body repairs. These days, plastic filler has made using the stuff virtually a forgotten art.

In all fairness, though, lead has one definite advantage over plastic filler: it actually adds some strength to the repair, while plastic just sits there like a lump and keeps the paint from falling off. Lead isn't nearly strong enough to use as a struc-

Paint should be sanded back a couple of inches from any joint about to be soldered.

tural repair medium, but on something that's going to be subjected to a lot of flapping and banging—a clamshell fender, for example—it might still be a better choice than plastic. Then again it might not: body solder is expensive, tricky to use and amazingly toxic.

Describing lead loading is sort of like telling someone to fly by flapping his arms—it sounds a whole lot easier than it really is. It's certainly not impossible for an amateur to do a good job, though, and with a little practice most people get the hang of it. The real trouble with lead is not so much that it's impossible to work with, it's that working with plastic filler is so much *easier*.

Anyway, to start with you'll need a mild flame source like a butane torch or a very soft gas welding flame. You'll need the correct kind of solder—basically an alloy of thirty percent tin and seventy percent lead—and the correct, matching flux or solder paint. Pick these up from an automotive supply source; the stuff you get down at Pablo's Plumbing Pavilion won't do. You'll also need some oiled wood or stainless-steel spreaders and a piece of scrap metal.

In addition you'll need a spotless work surface, so thorough preparation and cleaning is called for. A localized shot of sandblasting works wonders and also removes an inch or two of paint from around the area, which you'd need to do with sandpaper otherwise.

Traditionally you'd coat the repair area in flux and a light solder covering, which was something of a job in itself. These days you can do just as well with solder paint, a solution that includes flux and powdered solder in suspension. Once you paint it on, play the flame over the surface until the solder paint "flashes over"—turns shiny instead of dull gray. Then you stop, let it cool down and clean off all the black crud that was thrown around in the flashing process. A moist rag should do the trick.

The next step is to heat a couple of inches of the panel while simultaneously *warming*—not melting—the solder rod itself on the edge of the flame. When the metal is hot enough and the solder is properly warmed, touch the rod to the metal, give a twist, and a glob of the solder will stick to the car. To prevent the heat from distorting the panel (and interfering with the surrounding solder globs), keep quenching the surrounding areas with wet rags.

Once you've managed to deposit a glob or so every inch or two and cleaned everything up again, go back and heat each glob until it starts to melt. At first it will be crumbly and brittle, but soon it softens like butter and you can smooth it right into the repair with a wooden or stainless paddle. (Wooden paddles have the unfortunate habit of burning, of course, so I'd stick with stainless for now.) If you can get a nice, even, slightly raised bead over your repair you deserve to be pleased with youself. At this point lead loading can be very rewarding and more than a little fun.

It ceases to be fun quickly, however, if you overheat the solder; it will go too soft and run right down the side of the repair. If you had the foresight to place some scrap metal under the repair area, the solder will fall onto it and not be lost forever. (You can melt all the runoff into a new bar later and save a few bucks.) If not, the solder seems to make beeline right for your socks—this is definitely not a job for low-top tennies.

If all goes well, finish off the job with a dull single-cut file on the bodywork and a good air filtration

system over your mouth and nose. (Lead dust isn't the best thing in the world for your lungs.) Go after the solder with light, smooth strokes at no particular angle—just keep changing direction. You don't want to use any power tools, which will chew up the solder and put lots of lead in the air. For the finish work, a few swipes with some fairly coarse sandpaper ought to do it.

If the repair isn't quite perfect, you can either take the brave route—attempt to add more solder without letting what's already there melt and run off—or chicken out and finish off with a little plastic filler. The former lets you proudly thump your car's fender and declare "No Bondo!" to the envy (and great annoyance) of your friends. The latter is more likely to keep you out of a mental hospital.)

Guide Coating

Once you've filled in a low spot, patched up all the scratches with stopper, sanded it down a million times and primed it, you're still not quite ready to paint. If the repair was extensive, now comes the guide coat. On very small patches guide coating might not be worth the bother—of course it can't hurt, either.

Guide coating is a trick that lets you see how well your repair really worked. In primer you still won't be able to see some of the high and low spots, chips in the filler, scratches and so on that you've left behind. Primer's flat finish keeps you from using reflections on the surface as a guide to minor flaws. You'll pick up lots of invisible flaws with your fingertips, but even they're not the perfect test.

There are two things you can do. Some people simply run some water over the repair and sight across the area. The water gives enough gloss to pick up waves and valleys, but it hides chips and scratches. High-build primer may or may not fill those in later.

The better method is to spray some contrasting paint over the repair in a light, misting coat. Avoid reds, yellows and oranges, which can show through later coats. Once the paint dries, go over the area with medium open-grit dry paper on a professional longboard (or a long, straight chunk of wood). As you sand (in straight lines, changing direction 45 deg. every half-dozen strokes) the paint will come off the high spots first. Mark these and prepare to deal with them. The low spots, scratches, chips and other imperfections will show up as areas where the paint doesn't come off. When all's right with the world, the paint will come off the entire area at about the same rate—but don't expect this to happen the first time. A repair maybe a foot or two long is almost *guaranteed* to need touching up.

In the low spots, scratches and chips you can just sand out the paint again and slap in filler or stopper as needed. The high spots could possibly put you right back to square one. Those will have to

A stripping disc makes short work of the last remnants of paint and crud before filling or priming. The Eastwood Company

be pounded down as before—don't even *think* of building up the surrounding area with filler.

If your pounding lifts any of the filler off the metal, you're going to have to go in, chisel all the old filler out and start all over. That's why it's so important to use caution when pounding metal.

After repeating the whole process of pounding, filling, stopping, roughing and guide coating what might seem like eighty or ninety times, you should be done. (If it really *does* take you several tries, don't worry—filling and smoothing are skills that come quickly. For now, at least, be happy that you're taking the time to do it right.)

Welding

Unless you're doing a minor restoration, welding is going to come into the picture at some point. You won't necessarily have to do the welding yourself, you can farm it out, assuming you can get the pieces that need welding out of your garage and down to a shop.

Hiring someone else to do your welding can be impractical for a really big job, but it can also save

time and money in the long run—it all depends on how much (and what) you're going to need to do. If you only need to get a few seams welded at the tops of your doors it doesn't make much sense to buy a

A good, welded joint on the outside of this panel—the inner fenderwell still needs joining.

Full body protection should be worn during all welding, but especially when arc and MIG welding. An extra eye shield is needed for electric welding.

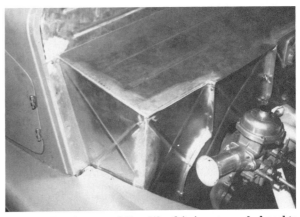

Lovely aluminum welding like this is extremely hard to do. Here a Morgan firewall and inner cowl have been fabricated from scratch. It's work for a pro.

welding kit and learn to use the thing. On the other hand, you can rent the equipment; that leaves learning to use it, which will take some time. If you've got to cut patches into three different fenders, though, it might pay to learn welding from scratch, buy the equipment yourself and practice until you're ready to move on to the car. The amount of practice you'll need depends on the equipment you use and your own skill.

In this section I'll describe some different kinds of equipment, tell you what they can and can't do, tell you what your alternatives are and talk about some of the things you might come up against when doing the work. I'm not going to pretend to tell you *how* to weld, though. That's a subject worthy of much more discussion than I can present here, and as they say in the welding business, "What you don't know can hurt you a whole lot."

Most community colleges have welding classes you might want to attend. Though there are some very good books on the subject, there's nothing like actually seeing it done right.

Welding is simply the fusing together of two metal pieces with heat; the pieces melt, their molecules flow together, some more metal is often added for additional strength, and when they cool and harden again they make one continuous part— at least that's how it's *supposed* to work. In practice, there's a lot that can go wrong. The metals have to be compatible with each other, although that's not such a big problem with cars, since most everything on them is steel. Still, you'll occasionally find yourself trying to join mild steel to high-strength steel, which you won't be able to do.

The welding gear must be adjusted correctly and held at the proper distance from the work, or else too little or too much heat is applied; the joint either doesn't hold or you burn right through. And if you're using a welding rod, that has to be the correct type as well; if not, it rolls off the weld and onto your shoe.

With all kinds of welding, both pieces of metal must be very clean indeed—any impurities will weaken the weld or keep it from taking at all. And with all kinds of welding there's a good amount of danger involved for both you and your belongings. That shouldn't be surprising; after all, welding is nothing more or less than directing enough concentrated energy to melt steel.

Oxyacetylene Open-Flame Welding

There are two practical ways to get the heat needed to fuse metal: electricity and an open flame. Oxyacetylene (open flame) welding is what we usually think of when we talk about welding. Here, oxygen and acetylene are stored in tanks, then mixed in the proper proportions to give a hot and controlled flame. The flame is played over the metal being welded until it's hot enough to melt,

and a treated steel rod is fed into the flame to add some more metal into the joint and build it up.

Oxyacetylene welding has some drawbacks. Most notably, it takes a long time for the metal being welded to get up to the proper temperature, and that gives the surrounding metal a chance to heat up in the meantime. That can result in distortion— rippling and buckling caused when some sections of the metal heat and expand at a different rate from others. You can get around distortion in large part by tack-welding a panel into place in different areas and doing your full weld in small sections that are allowed to cool before moving on. Distortion can also be removed after the fact with some time-consuming metal skrinking, pounding and filling. If you can avoid it in the first place, however, you're definitely best off to do so.

Since oxyacetylene welding puts more into the whole panel than other types of welding it also raises the danger of an accidental fire away from the joint. (With any welding job fire is a major concern; you need to have a good extinguisher nearby.) Any bushings, wood, wiring or cloth in the immediate vicinity can easily go up in flames.

Open-flame welding also takes a fair amount of skill. You have to move the welding flame at the right speed and keep it the right distance from the panel; you have to play the rod into the flame at the right speed; and you have to watch out for burning right through thin sheets of metal.

From a safety standpoint, open-flame welding is a mixed bag. Aside from the inherent danger of having all that energy in your hands, the tanks themselves are dangerous to have around: A solid rap on the acetylene tank can make it explode, and just getting grease in the oxygen line can cause a spontaneous fire. Acetylene is also expensive, although in truth most do-it-yourself sets don't even use it; they use MAPP gas, a safer and easier to handle alternative.

You can expect sparks and molten metal to fall down around your feet, and the light from the welding kit is so intense that special goggles are needed. In this regard, though, open-flame welding actually has an advantage over electric welding; the light put out by some electric systems is so intense you need to bundle up like Nanook of the North to avoid getting a sunburn.

Dangers aside, an open-flame kit is a handy thing to have around. You can use the flame not only to weld but also to free frozen nuts and bolts, to braze, to solder and (with a special attachment) to cut metal. As handy as open-flame welding is, however, electric systems like MIG and arc welding are very practical alternatives.

One of the big pluses of open-flame welding is that since you can control the temperature of the flame, you can also use the kit to solder and braze. Soldering is covered elsewhere in the bodywork section, but brazing is another metal-joining technique that merits discussion.

Brazing

Brazing, which is done at a lower temperature than welding, doesn't fuse metal to metal. Instead, it glues the two pieces together with molten copper. The pieces don't combine with each other, but the copper does combine on a molecular level with whatever's being brazed, so the joint is remarkably strong—not strong enough to repair structural pieces, but certainly good enough to hold a fender patch in place.

A brazed structural repair is grounds for failing a safety test in many of the states that require them, and it should be.

The real advantage to brazing is that it's not likely to cause distortion, and the heat needed is low enough that any welding set with a neutral flame will provide it. You can even, just *barely*, get enough heat out of a butane kit to braze, although the joint usually isn't very strong. Brazing is also faster than welding and not as critical—if you make a mistake, you can soften the braze with heat and reposition the panel.

No matter what the heat source, the procedure is the same: Start with two extremely clean surfaces (that meet in a lap joint—butt joints won't provide enough area for a good brazing job) and heat them to a dull red. The brazing rod will melt when it contacts the hot surface and flow into the joint. You don't want to use too much braze, just enough to make the repair.

Arc Welding

An arc welding system is inexpensive to set up and run, but it has some serious limitations. The way the system works is simple: You attach the pieces being welded to a ground, while the welding arm of the arc kit is positively charged. The arm ends in a sacrificial rod of welding material, and when you get it close enough to the negatively charged workpiece a spark jumps from rod to panel, creating the heat for welding. The rod melts and drips into the joint, and there's your weld.

That's how it's supposed to work, and in an expert's hands it usually does. However, you have to be precise with an arc kit. The tip of the rod needs to be kept at the correct distance from the work at all times, and since the rod is melting, its tip is constantly moving back up toward the welding arm. You have to move the rod constantly closer to the work while at the same time moving the welding arm along the seam so that it welds rather than cuts right through.

Arc kits are no good for thin sheet steel (like the kind used for most British body panels) because the intense heat put out usually burns through the metal before you can move the welder. And while the more expensive arc kits run on DC (direct current) and don't burn through as quickly, welding sheet steel by arc even then is a tricky business.

With various attachments, many of the difficulties of arc kits can be avoided. There are spot welding heads, stitch welding heads and all kinds of other goodies you can buy to "hop up" the hardware. By and large, though, these ask you to make some compromises in exchange for the added ease of use.

One attachment that extends the usefulness of an arc kit is a carbon-arc brazing arm. Here the

The ground terminal must be fit to clean, sound metal for electric welding. The Eastwood Company

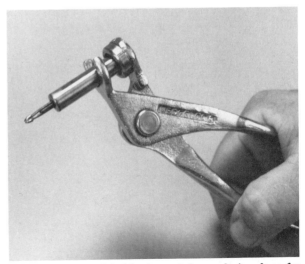

This clipping tool holds the metal panels in place for welding or brazing. The clip fits through a drilled hole and can be reused. The Eastwood Company

spark jumps between two sacrificial carbon rods to provide the heat to melt a brazing rod. While carbon-arc brazing is not likely to cause distortion, it's no easier to do than regular arc welding; you have to concentrate on a lot of things at once. And like traditional brazing, carbon-arc brazing isn't strong enough for structural repairs, only cosmetic ones.

Arc welding makes its own impurities as it goes through the air, so the welding rod has to be coated in flux to exclude air from the weld while everything's taking hold. The slag from the flux has to be removed later when the weld has cooled down again, but that's no big deal—it shouldn't take more than a few quick raps with a chisel. And arc welding doesn't heat up the surrounding metal as much as open-flame welding, so distortion is kept to a minimum.

Arc welding works best for big, heavy work: bumper brackets, major frame components, making your own tools and the occasional non-car household job like welding up a fence. For all intents and purposes, body splicing can't be done.

Since the most common uses for a welding kit on a car are attaching body sections and freeing frozen nuts, the arc system is probably not the best alternative for do-it-yourself auto restoration. And arc welding, like MIG, TIG, spot and any other electric welding, will destroy an alternator or generator that's still hooked up to the car. (You have to disconnect these before starting the work.)

Arc welding also has one particularly dangerous side effect: the arc itself is an intense source of both visible light and ultraviolet radiation. Standard oxyacetylene welding goggles aren't enough to protect your eyes; you need special UV protective lenses. And you have to cover your entire body to avoid getting sunburned from all those UV rays—not that doing *any* kind of welding with bare arms is smart. One of the biggest dangers of arc welding is that someone else—a kid, a neighbor or a pet—

might walk in and look at the pretty fire without the proper protection. That can lead to arc-eye; about half a day later they'll feel like someone's stuffed sand under their eyelids. People with arc-eye need to get to a hospital as soon as possible to prevent further damage to their vision.

MIG Welding

MIG welding is like arc welding in principle, but with a couple of helpful twists. First, MIG kits eliminate the necessity to feed a rod into the joint; a wire automatically feeds down into the work at a preset speed. As long as you keep moving the welding arm across the joint at the right rate you'll get a nice, even weld with just one hand. The other neat trick with MIG kits is that an inert gas—argon, an argon and carbon dioxide (CO_2) mix, or even just plain CO_2—is automatically pumped over the welding area to exclude the air. There's no slag created that needs to be chipped off later, and no cruddy oxides on the weld itself.

The gas also cools off the surrounding area rather nicely. That keeps distortion way down, making MIG a good option for letting in body panels and patches. MIG welding can also be set up for use on aluminum, although the more exotic TIG welding system does a better job. And it's just the thing to use on areas of high-grade steel, which react badly to the high heat input of an open-flame welding system. (High-grade steel appears mostly, if at all, around the seatbelt mounts of old sports cars. Newer cars like the current Corvette use it all over the place, but you're not likely to find much on an old MG.)

The drawbacks of MIG welding are the same as with arc welding—the light's intense and dangerous—along with a few of its own. Any surface to be MIG welded must be exceptionally clean, the wire and inert gas that you use cost money to replace, and the kit won't do anything but weld; no freeing nuts, no brazing, no cutting. It welds so well, though, that many people start out with a MIG kit and then use other tools—a small butane or MAPP setup and some body saws—to make up for the things a MIG machine can't do.

Spot Welding

Perhaps the simplest and cheapest option for the do-it-yourselfer faced with some minor welding is a simple spot welder. This is a miniature version of the robot-controlled machines that do much of the welding on a real assembly line: two welding arms are normally placed on either side of some overlapping metal pieces and a current is passed between them. The heat fuses the metal in that one spot, making a characteristic dimple and a very strong (albeit small) weld. Spot welders are a no-fuss, no-muss tool, and offer a much simpler alternative to the other sorts of welding gear out there.

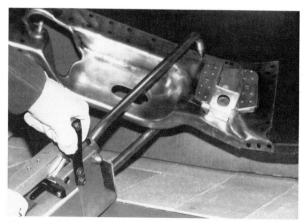

A spot welder makes fast, easy joints. Definitely a basic do-it-yourself tool. The Eastwood Company

The problem is, spot welding is all they do. About the only thing you're going to find a spot welder useful for is welding in small panel patches, tacking on door skins, fixing new fenders in place and things like that. Those, of course, are the jobs you usually need a welding kit for in the first place! You might be able to get by with a spot welder and nothing else if you're doing minor repairs.

Spot welders can be had with such a variety of different shaped arms that you can get them into the most unlikely places, so you shouldn't worry about not being able to get the welder where you want it. You can also find stitch welding attachments for electric kits that essentially make the same joint from one side only.

If you decide to take care of your own welding, you'll probably find that no one setup is going to do everything you want. An open-flame kit will come the closest; it does everything, just not everything *well*. For someone with one project and not much desire to get into welding in a big way, a low-cost MAPP kit makes good sense. MAPP kits are cheaper to buy into than acetylene setups and safer to have around. (The lower the cost of the kit, generally, the harder they are to use, however.)

If you're going to be doing lots of different household welding jobs over a long period of time, an arc kit with a carbon-arc brazing attachment might be a better investment. Arc welding is inexpensive, and good for the kind of heavy-duty work that most nonautomotive applications call for. If you just need to attach one fender or let in a couple of seams, however, a simple spot welder might be sufficient.

For serious, long-term automotive work, think about a decent MIG setup, cost notwithstanding. You can always worry about filling in the jobs MIG won't do later, by renting an open-flame kit when you need one, investing in a low-cost MAPP setup or even using a butane torch to free stuck nuts and heat up body solder.

Once you've settled on a welding kit to buy, though, you should sit down and ask yourself one thing: is it a sound investment in time and money? You can have a pro do a lot of welding for you before your own equipment will pay for itself, and you won't have to spend two nights a week at welding class. It all depends on the car, the job and your own desire to get behind the torch.

Patching Panels

Now, I said I wasn't going to discuss *how* to weld, and I meant it. I will, however, talk a bit about how to apply welding to the project you're working on.

A restorer usually wants to weld so he can let in new pieces of metal to replace those that have

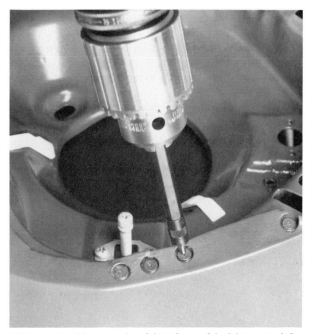

This spot weld removing bit takes a big bite out of the outer panel but leaves the inner one complete. Grind down the spots and the inner panel will be like new. The Eastwood Company

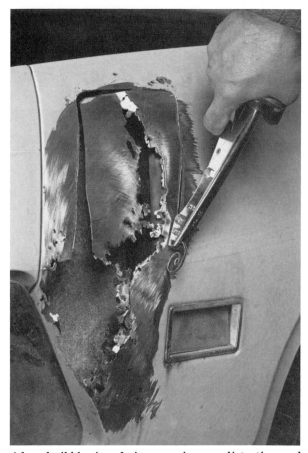

A hand nibbler is safe, inexpensive, nondistorting and easy to use. The Eastwood Company

rusted away. For surface rust, you can generally get away with sanding the spot down to clean metal, applying lots of rust remover, spot puttying the area if needed, shooting on a high-zinc primer and painting up the repair as you would any other. And many areas where rust has perforated the metal can be cut out and replaced *without* welding; a screen can be bonded into place to hold body filler

(a cheesy repair at best) or a patch panel can be attached to the car with braze. Even large sections like fender bottoms can often be brazed, rather than welded, into place. Structural parts like frames, sills and cowls, though, or big panels that are unsupported except by the joint you make, need to be welded in. Structural repairs simply

This dimpling tool recesses holes so rivets can be hidden below filler. The Eastwood Company

Air-powered nibbler makes fast, smooth cuts. The Eastwood Company

Lower fender panel gets cut clear through with an angle grinder; the edge will be cleaned up and straightened, then the replacement panel will be measured and cut to size. The Eastwood Company

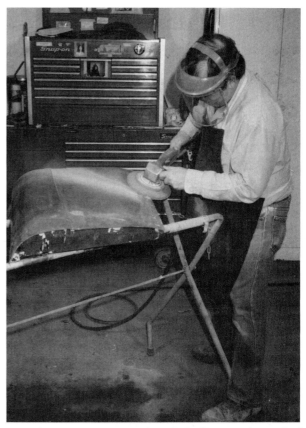

With the paint already stripped, the first step is to grind the heavy scale and crud off the entire area to be worked. Gloves would be a good idea here. Robin O'Brien

50

won't be covered here, but welding or brazing surface panels into place will.

Before you can splice in a replacement panel, of course, you have to get the old one off. You can cut it off with a welding cutter, which is fast but leads to distortion. You can slice it out with a rotary cutter or body saw, which will make a lot of sparks and chips but leave you with a pretty sound panel. Or you can go after it with a *nibbler*, either hand, air or electrically powered. Nibblers are slow, and a hand nibbler will leave you with aching palms long before you're finished, but they're safe, clean and inexpensive. Nibblers also leave the metal with the cleanest, smoothest edges.

Opening up a hole in a rusted panel will give you access to the panels beneath it, and you'll probably

To repair a panel where rust has eaten through a hole, first grind away the metal all around the hole.

With the finish ground down smooth, the area to be replaced is obvious. A nice straight cut along the rotted section of the door cuts away the whole panel. Robin O'Brien

The bad section of metal around the hole is then cut away with a nibbler.

Access is gained to the rotted frame underneath. All this work will eventually result in a perfect door, but a sound replacement would have been easier in the long run—if one could be located. Robin O'Brien

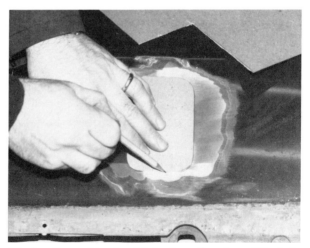

Mark a line out to about 1 in. from the edges of the hole and draw a template for your patch on a piece of cardboard.

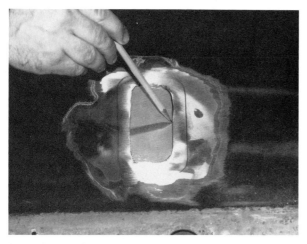

Place the cardboard template underneath the panel and mark the outline of the actual hole.

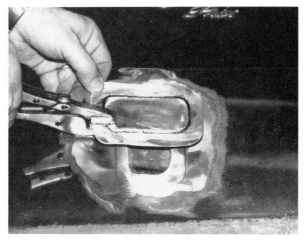

You can then cut a sheet steel patch to the shape of the template, and flange it to the dimension of the hole with a flanging pliers.

Then place the patch behind the panel and drill holes through both the panel and patch for rivets.

find that they're rusted out as well. There's no point in trying to cover up a rusty inner fender with a new outer skin; on top of making the car unsafe to drive, the rust will eat back through the new panel in no time flat. A car is built sort of like an onion. As you peel each layer back, you have to inspect the lower one for rot, and keep peeling if you find it.

If you're welding on a replacement panel you don't technically need to create a flange, you could butt weld the piece. For most welding and all brazing, though, a flange makes things easier. The new panel or the old one can receive the flange—it doesn't matter which—and the resulting lap joint

You can then rivet the patch in place with the flanged section pointing upward.

Body filler—in this case aluminum-fiberglass reinforced plastic—can now be spread over the area.

will be easier to work with and connect together. Flanging tools are inexpensive and easy to use.

You will, however, need to remove all grease, dirt and especially rubberized undercoating from the area being welded. Anything else that's flammable, such as wood, suspension bushings and obviously any fuel lines, pumps or tanks, will have to go as well. The danger of a fire while welding is incredibly great—you must have at least one good A-B-C extinguisher handy at all times. An old bottle of dishwashing soap filled with water will handily put out small wood and rubber fires without making you stop what you're doing, but it's no substitute for the real thing.

The repair patch will have to be held in place while you're welding or brazing it in. There are a number of commercial clamps and button clips that will do the job, and a combination of these, pop rivets, sheet-metal screws and C-clamps should get

When the filler has set up, smooth it over with a body file and then sand with fine-grit wet-and-dry sandpaper to prepare for priming and painting. The Eastwood Company

The usual trunk floor rust in an Austin-Healey. Robin O'Brien actually bought this car just because it had problems like this—it's a subject vehicle in the Rebirth of a Classic *cable/video show he hosts—but if the beginner can stay away from big holes like this one, he or she ought to.* Robin O'Brien

Replacement Panels

With the growing popularity of auto restoration in general and British cars in particular, there's been a great upswing in the number of replacement panels available to the do-it-yourself restorer.

It used to be that if you wanted to replace a section you had three alternatives: go to a junkyard and cut that piece off another car, buy the whole panel from a dealer or fabricate your own panel in a workshop. Today there's a fourth and very practical alternative—buying ready-made patches from a parts supplier.

• Junkyard panels: These are the cheapest but not always the best alternative. All the panels in the junkyard might be as bad as your own. Many junkyards don't allow you to cut up a complete panel and pay for just part of it—if they let you do metal cutting at all. You might distort or otherwise damage the panel while you're trying to take it off. (Body nibblers are a big help here, though.) Or you might cut away too little of the panel. Always take much more than you think you'll need.

• Factory panels: When they're available factory panels cost a lot of money; you'll also have to buy the whole thing, not just a section of it.

Factory panels come primed, but the primer is only for shipping. They have to be stripped, checked for flaws, filled and guide coated like anything else.

• Homemade patches: Simpler patches can be made from scratch, particularly if you're good with a rolling machine or body hammers. For the most part, though, anything but square and flat sections should be purchased ready-made.

• Aftermarket patches: Many parts sources will sell you either an entire panel or just the part of it that usually rusts out. These are often reasonably priced and of fairly good quality.

Just remember a few things no matter where the panel came from. First and foremost, sheet metal is *sharp*, particularly if it's been cut at home. The edges will cut you unless you wear the proper thickness gloves to protect yourself.

You'll also probably find that your replacement panel doesn't fit as well as it should. Bolt holes might be in the wrong places, body creases might not line up or the dimensions of the part could simply be off. You'll be ahead of the game if you make sure the panel fits exactly or go back and modify it before you try to fasten it to the car.

Bolt-on fenders (Austin-Healey shown here) are obviously easy to tackle. A new or used one may still need a few bolt holes redrilled and a complete strip, fill and guide coat. Robin O'Brien

you through. Make sure that the panels match up perfectly before you fix them in place. You'll never get another chance if you're welding them, and it's a waste of time to braze something twice.

To get the panel cut and fit correctly will take a lot of measuring and effort. If you're using a premade patch panel, lay it over the area to be cut out and mark its outline in permanent pen; measure the flange you're going to make in the new or old panel and draw in a new line that much lower minus about ⅛ in. That should be the cut line, but measure both panels and the overall size of the finished panel a few times again just to make sure.

If you're brazing a patch into place, go ahead and lay a few dabs of braze on the corners and step back from the work. If it's not perfect, you can still soften the braze with heat, reposition the panel and try

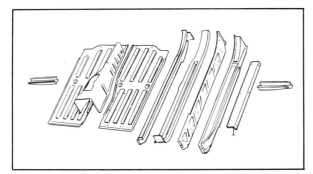

If you've got the guts and the talent to tackle them, new structural panels for most cars are readily available. The car must be kept perfectly true while the old panels are cut out and the new ones are patched in. It's basically a job for a professional or an experienced do-it-yourselfer. Moss Motors, Ltd.

again. Once everything lines up perfectly, finish the connection; the remaining seams can be filled, filed and painted later. If you're welding it in, tack weld a couple of corners in place first. You'll still have to grind or drill the welds out if something's wrong, but that's better than grinding off the whole panel. Once the panel is correct, tack weld it every half foot and do short seam welds in different areas to finish the job, instead of starting from one side and working all the way around.

Replacing an entire fender can actually be trickier than just letting in a patch, depending on how the fender mounts to the car. Some fenders simply come off with a few bolts—if yours does, you're lucky. You can replace the outer skin, at least, without any cutting or welding.

Others will be spot or seam welded into place, probably at the top and bottom. (Bottom welds fix the outer fender to the inner wheelwell. Inner fenders are sometimes hard to come by as replacements and might have to be made up from curved steel stock.)

Full welds must be ground down with an angle grinder. Spot welds are easy enough to remove if you can get to them. You can drill them out conventionally or with a spot-weld-removing bit, which will open a bigger hole in the outer surface but leave the inner surface intact. If an entire fender is being replaced, it often helps to cut the old one away right below the beading. This will help you get a clear shot at the spot welds underneath. New fenders should be attached the same way the old one was, with spot or seam welds in all the appropriate areas.

Doors

One of the most abused pieces of the car body is also one of the easiest to repair: the doors. They regularly take hits in parking lots, rust out from the bottom and get punched in during accidents. On at least one car, the MGB, the outer door is almost a routine replacement item; a crack forms in the metal right below the vent wing after few miles indeed.

Fortunately, since doors aren't held on too tightly in the first place, repairing and swapping them is a pretty simple task. I say *pretty* simple because you're still involved with bodywork and you're still likely to run into some pitfalls. The first hassle can be removing them: older doors usually are screwed on at the hinges, but newer doors hang on hinges that are welded into place. With older doors it's usually easiest if you unscrew the door from the hinge rather than pulling the hinge off the car. With the weld jobs, you often need a tricky tool from your auto parts store to drive the hinge pins out.

If the hinges do screw on, replacing them with new ones is relatively easy and you ought to do it. The first thing you notice about a lot of old cars is that the doors sag when they're open, and bounce off the sill plates when they're closed. New hinges make a better first impression for the car—it seems much more solid. Of course, replacing the hinges makes re-hanging the doors a bit more challenging, so you have to add that into your equation.

Whenever you remove a door, pay close attention to any shims or spacers that come off with it. These will have to go back on in the right place and the right order. (The same applies to the door striker and latch plate.)

Re-Skinning Doors

Often doors simply need to be re-skinned. Now when the average British restoration nut gets to the subject of re-skinning doors he or she just about jumps out of his or her chair with delight. It seems so easy! It is, in fact, probably the simplest metal repair you can do short of a simple hood or trunk swap. But even at that, re-skinning a door means removing it, grinding out some welds, gutting the door itself, and lots of whacking and thumping with a hammer and wooden blocks. Personally, I'd rather sit in a comfy chair with a list of

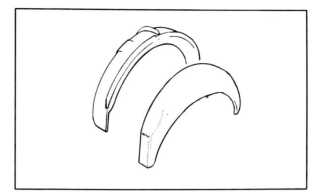

New fenderwells are critical if the old ones are rotten. Just fixing the outer surface will give you a repair that's temporary at best and dangerous at worst. Moss Motors, Ltd.

junkyards and try to find a replacement door over the phone. In the long run, that's often cheaper as well as being faster and easier. Finding a good replacement at a decent price isn't always possible, though, so read on.

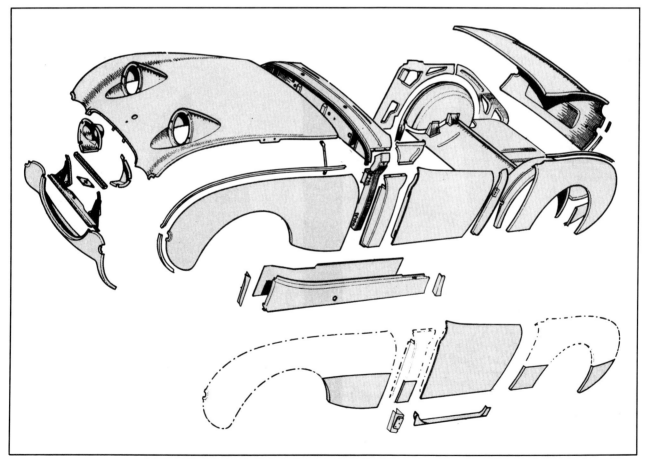

Replacement panels for an entire Sprite—or for that matter just about any popular car—are now available for the do-it-yourself market. Some will bolt right in, but most require welding. Moss Motors, Ltd.

This early Austin-Healey had identical rust perforations behind both doors. Robin O'Brien

To re-skin a door means just that. The door is made up of a frame around which has been folded a metal outer skin. Remove the old metal skin, fold on a new one, weld it in place at a few key spots and you're ready to go. (Actually, there may be some rust damage to the frame, too, which will have to be patched the same as anything else. You also need to remove the old door handle, any clips for tonneaus or side curtains, the weatherstripping along the window channel and so on.)

To get started, remove the interior door panel as outlined in chapter 4, preserving as much of the panel and your own knuckle skin as possible. Save the clear plastic or paper vapor barrier that sits behind panel—it keeps moisture from chewing up the door panel and needs to go back in.

Strip out the guts of the door, unless you've got something like a TR3 or a Morgan that doesn't have any guts (door guts, that is) in the first place. Next, remove the door from the car. This is often a two-person job; otherwise the door might fall to the

When the skins were peeled away, the results were predictable—the inner pillar has been chewed away right where you would expect it to be. Robin O'Brien

Another route you may choose to go is to start from new with your MGB body. Enter the Heritage bodyshell manufactured in England from the original dies. The Heritage MGB bodyshell is available in the United States from Victoria British in Lenexa, Kansas.

ground. With later cars, government-mandated crash bars make the doors heavy enough to warrant a jack for support.

Getting the skin off is usually quite simple. (By the way, do door work with the door resting on a sheet of plywood rather than a hard cement floor.) Most skins are held on by a crimped edge around the frame and spot or tack welded into place at a few key points. Grind off the crimped edges and welds and the skin should fold off easily. The edges of the old skin will be razor sharp, so wear the requisite rhino-hide gloves.

Try to remove the skin as intact as possible, and save it for later. You might need to use it as a template for cutting a new hole for the door handle or simply shaping the new skin to size. You might also find that there's some insulating or sound-deadening material glued to the inside of the door skin. That'll have to be replaced once the new skin's on and the inner door is painted. Make a note of the size and location of any pads for now.

If the frame also needs repairing, cut and patch the damaged area as you'd patch a fender or body panel. Many parts vendors offer new door frame sections already made up—you just cut off the old rusted section and weld in the new one. (Take precise measurements to make sure the cut and re-fit section are perfectly in place.) The replacement panel should match the original *exactly*, of course, or the door will never close right no matter how much twisting and torquing you do later. Take care of the framework before putting the new skin on, and prime and paint it with high-zinc, rust-resistant coatings. Any rust left inside the door frame will eventually work its way back out through the skin.

After the frame checks out, hold up the new skin to the frame and check for a *precise* fit; if it's out of line, you'll never get the door hung correctly again. Hold it there with high-quality locking pliers, a few self-tapping screws, or pop rivets where the welds would normally be. You're ready to start folding over the edges.

This is another two-person job. You or your assistant holds the door while the other person starts gently folding the lip all the way around. There are special crimping tools you can buy to make it easier, but you can also do the initial folds with a hammer and dolly, going little by little all the way around the door until the skin grips the frame on all sides. Then hold the door against a block of wood while the inner edge is hammered down flat and neat. (You might have to cut out some small wedges from the inner lip to get a good flat surface on the corners. It sometimes helps to hold another block of wood between the hammer and the edge being pounded down, too.)

Fitting Doors

At this point, it's a good idea to fit the door back to the car and make sure all that whacking and pounding didn't warp the frame. A warped door is different from one that's just not hung right. Doors can be adjusted up and down, in and out and back and forth by playing with the hinges and latches. If one corner or two diagonal corners don't line up with the neighboring fender, though, the door is warped. That's not something you can adjust in the traditional way.

You can still set things right as long as the skin and frame haven't been welded together yet. The most efficient way for us do-it-yourself types is a crude, effective and eminently satisfying little trick. Just leave the door bolted to the pillar, place a longish piece of 2x4 between the door and jamb on the nearest *unraised* corner and give the door a good shove against the wood. Elegant it's not—Phil Hill would probably die of apoplexy if he saw you—but it works. (The slam-the-wood-in-the-door trick will also cure minor warps on a door that's never been taken apart or one that's already been welded back together.)

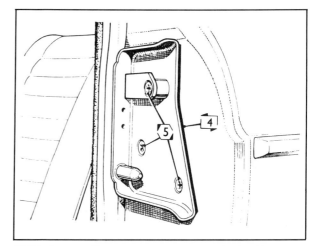

MGB door strikers use two pretty typical adjustment methods. Shims are added or removed at location 4 to raise or lower the striker relative to the door pillar, while the screws at 5 allow some fore and aft movement.

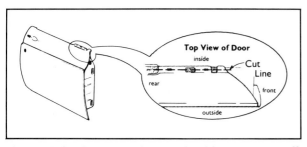

The welds holding door skin on should be pretty small and easy to handle. Cut as close as you can and grind away the rest. Moss Motors, Ltd.

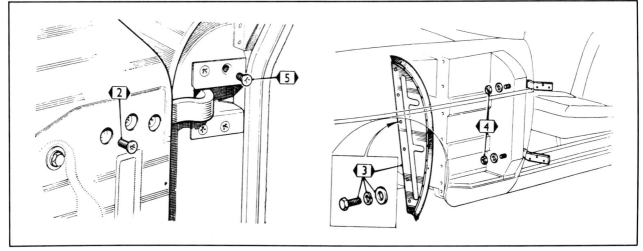

There are times when you could just throttle English engineers. MGB/MGC door hinges definitely apply; to get the hinges off the car you have to go in the other way

and remove the fender baffle for access to the nuts in back (3 and 4). If you can get away with it, just pulling the doors off the hinges (2) will be easier.

Once the door checks out when bolted to the car, put a couple of spot or tack welds where the pliers, screws or rivets were and remove the door once again. Finish off the welding and you're ready to put body sealant in all the inside edges, make sure the drain holes are clear and prime and paint the inside of the door skin. (Pay special attention to any holes or scratches on the inside of the door—that's where rust will form.)

Whether or not you put the door's guts back in before you put it on the car again depends on whether the added ease of access justifies the added weight. Before you do your final door adjustments, though, the guts have to be in place—their weight will make a difference in how the door hangs. Give the moving parts of the door an even,

light coat of white lithium grease before closing everything up.

Fiberglass

Fiberglass—also called plastic, glass, glass-fibre, Fiberglas (the trade name of Owens-Corning's product) and GRP (for Glass-Reinforced Plastic)—is truly amazing stuff. It's light, strong, versatile and currently the only practical alternative to metal for auto bodies. Unlike steel, fiberglass also never rusts. It sometimes develops other problems, though, as you'll see later.

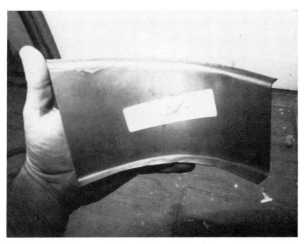

Replacement panels for this vulnerable spot are made for just about every type of popular British sports car. This one for an MGB will slot right into the area—certainly the easiest solution to the problem.

Even on this beautifully prepared Lotus Elan you can see the small waves that scare many companies away from fiberglass. It's a gorgeous car, regardless. Mike Lamm

Glass-reinforced plastic is an ideal medium for low-volume car makers; the cost of building small numbers of fiberglass bodies is negligible compared to hand-formed metal ones or tooling up to mass-produce them in steel. Fiberglass bodies have been the salvation of Lotus, TVR, Reliant and tiny companies like Fairthorpe, Berkeley and Marcos; they allow these cottage-industry builders to compete, price-wise, with the bigger manufacturers. The low cost of startup also lets car makers redesign their fiberglass bodies fairly often; they don't have to justify their tooling costs with 50,000 copies of the original design. Even traditionalists like Morgan, AC and Daimler have played around with plastic bodies, attracted by the low initial and per-unit cost. Higher production makers have shied away from GRP because of the lower per-unit cost of steel in large numbers and, more importantly, the better finish a metal body can give.

Fiberglass does have some definite drawbacks compared to steel and aluminum. In theory, GRP is stronger than steel ounce for ounce; in practice, few fiberglass bodies are that much lighter than their steel counterparts, and they're inevitably thicker. Fiberglass also tends to break up over time; the vibration it's subjected to eventually causes it to split and crack at stress points. These cracks—called, fittingly enough, stress cracks—point out what is probably the biggest weakness of GRP: it doesn't handle localized stress very well. A good fiberglass body is reinforced with metal plates at key spots to help spread out the load, and some manufacturers are better at doing this than others. You should look for cracks around the fenders, the hood hinges, near any trim strips or mirrors and especially in the door posts before buying any fiberglass car.

Fiberglass works because it combines the unique characteristics of two materials—spun glass strands and hardened plastic resin—into a composite that's stronger than the sum of its parts. The real workhorse of fiberglass is the resin, which is a chemically hardened compound sort of like the clear plastic used for paperweights.

The resin is made up of long chains of molecules which are free to slip and slide past each other as they see fit. Add a chemical hardener (technically a catalyst, usually methyl-ethyl-ketone peroxide, or MEK), though, and the chains begin to stick together in a complex, rigid mesh.

The reaction also takes an accelerator (technically an oxidizer and usually cobalt napthenate), but this is usually included in the resin when you buy it. If it's not you'll have to add it later. *Never* mix raw hardener and accelerator, unless you want a homemade explosion on your hands.

There are actually two distinct types of resin, polyester resin and epoxy resin, but in car repair you'll be dealing solely with polyester resin. Epoxy

Engaged in the traditional Chapman salute, this all-glass Lotus Elite probably presented its restorer with some problems. Since the Elite uses stressed fiberglass of varying widths as its load-bearing structure, any repair work has to be absolutely precise.

resin is stronger and it bonds better to nonfiberglass surfaces like metal and wood, but it's more expensive than polyester resin, harder to work with and exceedingly toxic while wet. (You wouldn't

The All-Glass Lotus Elite

The vast majority of fiberglass bodies are completely unstressed—they just sit atop the frame and add virtually nothing to the overall strength of the car. But in 1957, Colin Chapman, the head of Lotus, introduced a show car built around a complete fiberglass monocoque. It had no frame as such; its strength came from the shape and construction of its fiberglass bodyshell. That car would become the road-going Lotus Elite.

Chapman thought he really had something there, and he almost did. The problem was, and is, that GRP simply wasn't strong enough to be used by itself as a primary structure. The Elite just couldn't take the pounding of the open road, and that's why so few of them are still around today—and why trying to resurrect a beat-up Elite in your basement is almost impossible. The car's strength depends so much on precise thicknesses and shapes of fiberglass that it's almost beyond the ability of the do-it-yourselfer to make major repairs on one. On just about any other fiberglass car, though, body repairs are quite simple.

Chapman's idea came back to life when new composites like Kevlar and carbon-fiber were developed that were stronger than GRP. Today most top-notch racing cars are made of advanced composite monocoques; that construction is due to appear in road-ready supercars any day.

want to drink two fingers of polyester resin either, but it's not as deadly.)

Resins come in different varieties depending on whether they're to be used for the final outside coat of a composite or one of the inside layers. (Most fiberglass repairs are done with more than one sheet of glass.) Resin for the inner layers—lay-up resin—never quite hardens all the way on the surface, while finishing resins acquire a hard, shiny coat when dry. Here, too, you needn't worry about the distinction; in auto repair you can usually use a general-purpose resin, which combines some of the qualities of both types.

Now resin by itself isn't good for much of anything—it's extremely hard but also very brittle. The actual strands of fiberglass are called the reinforcing material. Fiberglass is made by taking a special molten glass and mechanically stringing it into long, thin fibers. The fibers are woven into cloth or chopped up and re-formed with binding agents into a mat. You'll use fiberglass mat for almost all of your auto body repairs, but fiberglass cloth is a little stronger—and therefore a better choice for making guerilla floorboards, covering gaping holes in fenders and things like that.

In truth, the strongest fiberglass repairs are made of a composite of mat and cloth; here too, you'll be dealing almost exclusively in mat so you don't need to worry about selecting and arranging composites. Mat goes around corners quite nicely once it's wetted down, something that most cloths won't do, and it's strong enough for body repairs.

Fiberglass is sold by its weight for a given size; the heavier the glass, the thicker it actually is. Some genius, however, decided to use two different scales: Mat comes measured by weight per square foot, while cloth is measured by weight per square yard.

While it's important to know what materials are available and how they all work together, you don't need to be an expert on the subject to do the work itself. If all you aim to do is patch up the nose of your TVR Tasmin, the procedure is quite simple.

All you need to know is what weight of fiberglass mat you'd like to use, how many layers you want to apply, how to mix the hardener into the resin and how you're going to go about applying it to the car. As long as you start with quality materials, fiberglass repairs are a breeze. Start with the cheap stuff and you'll be sorry.

Now bear in mind that while resin is hardened by chemical reaction, heat is still at the root of the process. The chemical reaction merely supplies that heat from inside the resin itself.

So what, you ask? So, the temperature of your working area will directly affect the amount of hardener you want to add to the mix: the hotter the day, the less hardener you use. Most resins are only designed to be used between about 70 and 85

deg. Fahrenheit, with hardening or flow trouble starting to appear on either end of the scale. If you have to work in particularly cold or hot weather, you'll need to get a special resin formulated for the conditions.

In general, the amount of hardener mixed in is minuscule—maybe a few drops per quart. Each container of resin and hardener will give you the appropriate ratios on the label, and it's best to stick with resin and hardener that have been made for one another by the same company.

The more resin you use on a given repair, oddly enough, the faster it will set up. Polyester resin can set up hard enough to be sanded in anything from a half an hour to an entire day or more, depending on the amount of hardener, the depth of resin and the ambient temperature. The average mixed resin will start to gel in the pot after about sixty minutes. The curing process can actually go on for as long as two weeks, but the repair should be workable not long after the resin first appears hard, say a couple of hours at the most.

Raw resin, by the way, will eventually harden in the can even without help from an added chemical. You should buy your resin from a store that moves a lot of material, and keep it in a cool place. Buy only enough resin to last for the next couple of months; the economy-size tub will set up long before you get a chance to use it.

Mix resin and hardener in a clean metal, plastic or unwaxed paper container. Clean coffee cans are ideal. (The wax from a Dixie cup will mix with the resin and give you spotty results, and styrofoam cups don't work because the resin eats right through them.) Mix up only as much resin and hardener as you can use before it sets up—shoot for about fifteen minutes' worth at first and you'll be fine.

Be prepared to toss out the mixing pot, as the acetone (the normal thinner) to clean it would probably cost more than the pot itself. Also make sure you don't stir pure resin with a stick that's already touched the mixed stuff. It will set up in a couple of days and be ruined.

For the most part you'll be applying resin to mat with a paintbrush, so this should also be a cheapie. You can clean the brush with acetone before the resin sets up, but once it's hard the brush is useless, and usually you'll be so busy fiddling with the wet repair that cleaning the brush is a low priority. (Avoid brushes with painted handles—the resin can dissolve the paint and carry it into your work.)

A good pair of scissors is a must for cutting the reinforcing material, and a sharp matte knife is no substitute—knives tend to tear mat, not cut it. You'll also want some plastic spreaders or stiff rubber squeegees. These are used to smooth everything down, remove the excess resin and get any little bubbles out of the way. (Excess resin makes the repair brittle and likely to crack, so you want to make sure that you only wind up with enough to wet down and saturate the mat.) Finally, you may or may not want to invest in a rolling tool made especially for driving the resin into the mat. This is a handy but not necessary addition.

The weight and number of mats used, as well as the application methods themselves, depend on the repair. But before getting into that, the requisite safety warnings are in order.

At this early stage of the game, the best rule to remember is not to bite off more than you can chew; wet fiberglass is messy stuff, and getting a big piece of it to do what you want can be a disheartening experience.

The normal procedure involves laying up many sheets of glass in place of the damaged material, almost always from behind. To lay up a section, you generally coat the area with a fair amount of resin, press new mat over it and gradually dab on more and more resin until the whole mat is moistened. (As soon as it's saturated it gives up its original whiteness for a translucent appearance.) Wipe away excess resin with a spreader or squeegee and clean up any drips and runs.

The really neat—and potentially dangerous—characteristic of fresh resin is that it melts into the old fiberglass a little and makes a good, strong joint. The danger, of course, is that the new resin can actually damage panels that were okay when you started working.

The most common flaw in fiberglass bodies, however, doesn't even need to be laid up with new mat. The minor stress cracks that seem to appear on most cars after they've been on the road awhile can simply be sanded away, touched up with fresh resin and finished with plastic filler.

Of course, nothing is ever quite as simple as dabbing some resin in a crack and being done with it. Repaint that repair and chances are the surrounding paint will quickly soften and lift up. It's advisable to strip the entire panel of paint before even starting any sort of fiberglass repair, and just any old stripper won't do. Most paint strippers will also eat fiberglass; you need one specially formulated for GRP. These aren't quite as fast as regular paint strippers, but they do the job.

You also have the unorthodox alternative of taking the paint off with a razor scraper. I'm not sure how I feel about this, but I've seen it done and it does work—at least on Corvettes, which might have stronger panels than some English cars. With this method the paint is simply scraped off dry—you get the blade under the finish and go nuts. You'll inevitably cause some scratches and nicks in the fiberglass, but nothing that 80 grit paper and some resin gel (a special fiberglass touchup solution) can't take care of.

As the damage gets more serious, the procedure for repairing it gets more and more complicated. Cracks running deeper into the body but not all the way through need to be sanded out and the panel roughed up about 4 or 5 in. beyond the crack itself. Then two layers of 1 oz. mat should be laid up in the resulting hole to build up strength. Any remaining depression can then be filled, and the whole mess will sand down nicely with 100 grit and then medium-grit dry paper on a longboard.

You start getting into serious work with bigger flaws. Unlike metal, fiberglass doesn't dent; it

---

Fiberglass Safety Guidelines

Some fiberglass safety tips from GRP to remember:

• Resin and hardener in wet form are very toxic. Avoid getting them in your eyes especially, and avoid breathing the fumes. If you get lightheaded while working with fiberglass, get out of the garage and treat yourself to some nice clean air.

• Read the manufacturer's label. This will tell you what to do in case of accidental ingestion or irritation.

• Work only in a well-ventilated area or outdoors. If you're outdoors, think about working upwind from the fiberglass itself.

• Always wear good rubber gloves when working with wet or raw fiberglass. Little pieces of raw mat will break off in your skin and the liquid components are highly toxic.

• Wash up well when you've finished. If you do get strands in your skin, cold water and moisturizing lotion should relieve some itching.

• Fiberglass strands thrown up in the cutting and sanding process can cause serious lung irritation. Always wear a good filtration mask or respirator when cutting or finishing off fiberglass. It's also a good idea to clean up all the sanding dust at the end of the day—it'll get airborne later and cause trouble.

• Both the resin and mat are highly flammable. You can put a mild heat source up to your repair to speed the drying, but it *cannot* be one with an open flame. You also have to store unused mat and chemicals away from water heaters, bare bulbs, welding kits and other sources of ignition.

• The smoke from burning fiberglass is a veritable witch's brew of nasty and carcinogenic chemicals. If the glass goes up and can't be immediately controlled, get yourself out of the area pronto. And if you decide to burn some hardened fiberglass off of a valuable tool—I don't recommend it, but some people do this anyway—do it outside and keep the fire well away from your face.

cracks, splits and occasionally falls out in chunks. Anything that's gone all the way through the body has to be attacked from the rear, and sometimes getting to the rear of a panel is the toughest part of the job. It might break your heart, but you often have to cut out a section of an inner panel just so you can fix some damage to an outer one.

Fixing Holes in Fiberglass

Repairing tears and letting in major patches are slightly more complicated jobs than patching a simple hole, but you'll use the same skills on all three. Holes are commonly punched into fiberglass bodywork by an impact with a sharp object like a fencepost or even a vandal's foot.

Once you can get to the back of the panel, rough up about half a foot around the hole with 100 grit sandpaper or an angle grinder. To keep excess resin from squirting out the front and oozing over otherwise good bodywork, cover the front of the hole with masking tape. This keeps the amount of extra work down and saves resin.

Four or five layers of 1.5 oz. mat are then laid up from the rear and allowed to dry. When dry, the masking tape is removed and the hole is patched with filler and dry sanded, first with 100 grit open paper and then medium grit. The procedure here is the same as for a metal panel: don't sand too deeply into the filler or you'll wind up with a noticeable depression in the repair area. Prime the area, guide coat it if you wish and fill in any sanding marks or pinholes with spot putty. Sand again with medium and then fine paper and prime once more—that's all there is to it.

To fix tears and splits and even to splice in new pieces, you only have to add one more weapon to your arsenal: clips. You can get all kinds of ready-made clips from a fiberglass supply store, but there's no reason not to make your own. Drill a hole every couple of inches in an inch-wide strip of aluminum; then cut the strip to give you several pieces with a hole at either end.

These clips screw into the outside of the body to hold the two repair edges together while the fiberglass is laid up and cured in back. You'll need to drill small pilot holes for the clips (a drill bit made for metal is ideal) and use sheet-metal screws or pop rivets to keep things in place. Use something to support the fiberglass from behind when drilling through—a piece of wood is fine.

Fixing Splits and Tears in Fiberglass

When repairing splits and tears, simply clip the broken edges back together, rough up the rear of the area for 6 in. on either side of the flaw and lay up four or five strips of 1 oz. mat. When the repair hardens, remove the clips, cover up the tear with plastic filler and sand as usual. (You might find that dabbing some fresh resin over the old torn fibers will hold them in place better for sanding.)

An alternative to sticking plastic filler in the remaining outside crack is to bevel the edges and lay a few thin strips of 1 oz. mat in the resulting vee. Finish that off with spot putty and the joint will be stronger than the surrounding panel.

If a torn section has begun to delaminate, cover that area with glass from behind and be ready to sand right through the old layers of bodywork. Again, you can lay up a mat or two on the outside to bring the repair to the point where a minimum of filler is needed.

Letting in whole patches is much easier to do in GRP than a similar repair in steel would be. If you happen to be there when the accident occurs, try to pick up as many of the pieces as possible—a slightly embarrassing but wholly worthwhile business. It's sometimes possible to just patch the old pieces back in and go on from there.

The other alternative is to find a replacement panel, either a new one from a supplier or one cut out from a scrapped car. (Books on fiberglassing will even tell you how to mold your own new panels if a replacement can't be found.) Since fiberglass cars are usually made up of a number of small panels that come off separately, make sure you can't just replace the whole fender or door instead of patching and filling the old one.

Whether you can replace the whole piece or not, taking panels from scrapped cars is usually cheaper than buying them new. It sometimes gives you a better fit as well; many aftermarket fiberglass panels are only a close—but not perfect—match for the original. And if patching is called for, be sure your replacement panel either fits *exactly* or is way too big. Cutting a bare inch or so from a piece of fiberglass can be tricky. If you find yourself in the junkyard with a hacksaw, it's better to cut too much panel rather than too little.

Patching Fiberglass

Once you have access to the back of the panel, letting in a large patch of fiberglass is easy.

Pencil closely around the area using a straight-edge to make your cut lines. Cut the damaged area, leaving as much of the original glass intact as possible. (Cured fiberglass cuts easily with a hacksaw, sabre saw or jigsaw equipped with a blade designed for metal. You can also get special angle-grinder blades made for cutting through GRP.)

Measure the hole and transfer those measurements to your replacement panel, or better still lay the new panel over the old one and trace out the cut lines from behind. If you cut away too much from the patch panel you can still proceed with the repair—you'll just have to patch the remaining hole as you would any other.

Drill a few pilot holes in the repair panel and start some clips, then check for fit. At this point a friend can hold it in place or you can just use tape. Secure the pilot clips in the adjoining panels of the car. Be gentle with the panel while it's only held in a few places—it'll tear easily.

Drill and place clips every six or so inches on flat surfaces, on either side of any corners, and on either side of any characteristic ridges or bumps. Run masking tape along the outside of the seam and lay up new fiberglass from the back as normal—six sheets of 1 oz. or four of 1.5 oz. mat should do it.

Whether you're using a new panel or one from a junked car, before cutting it's a good idea to make sure it's the right one. If something major like a character line doesn't match, you're in trouble. Since fiberglass panels are relatively inexpensive to play with at the factory, minor (and sometimes pointless) variations are often made from one year to the next. You can always drill and patch any holes that don't correspond, but if, say, a bulge for the side lamps is missing you're going to have to either get the right panel or splice in another section later.

Whenever you replace a whole fiberglass panel, make sure that you've remembered to include any metal stress plates in the repair. And if you're already patching up a tear or a hole, you might consider throwing a few extra layers of mat around the general vicinity just to strengthen the area. You don't want to add 80 lb. of glass to a sports car, but if a sill has already torn once you should think about preventing a second occurrence.

Chrome Brightwork

No amount of mirror-smooth paint will hide sorry brightwork, and unfortunately, most trim pieces are just that. We think of chrome plating as a tough, rust-resisting surface protector, but in reality it's not all that strong.

Plated parts are in fact relatively weak and porous; without a protective layer of wax, water will soak right into the steel below the chrome and eventually show up as pockets of rust. The plating process also weakens parts, so I have to raise my eyebrows when people chrome suspension arms and the like.

Aluminum and stainless-steel trim can be brought back to life in a few basic and rewarding steps—their shine depends only on the surface of the metal itself. Chrome parts are a lot harder to deal with, so let's go over them first.

Most of the time scabbed chrome can be brought back more or less to life without resorting to replating. Don't kid yourself, though; a cleaned chrome piece will rarely look as good as a new reproduction or NOS (new-old-stock) part, and a new part might not look as good as a high-quality plating job. Most factory and repro parts simply aren't given the lustrous, deep plating that a whole lot of money can buy from a professional shop.

If the chrome plating is worn off there's nothing to do but replace or replate the part. If it's still intact, though, try cleaning it up by starting with a nonabrasive chrome cleaner and lots of elbow grease. If that doesn't salvage the chrome, move on to a nonabrasive body polish. From there try good old Brasso, which has enough mild abrasives in it to quickly cut through not only grime and oxidation but also the chrome plating itself—be careful with the stuff. The last resort is to call in the heavy artillery: an electric buffing wheel using at first mild and then more and more abrasive rouge compounds. (Rouge is a fine polishing compound sold in sticks.)

An electric wheel and rouge will quickly zap right through any crazing and discoloration, but it's hard not to go through the chrome too. Use the wheel at low speed and be as gentle as you can on the metal—even if you shine the chrome up nicely, cutting through it at any point will lead to rust later. After any sort of cleaning, seal the chrome with a good, hard coat of carnauba wax as soon as possible. The more abrasive the cleaning method,

It's always a littly funny the things that a restoration hands you on a plate. This pretty sick-looking Healey has an almost perfect grille; one thing like that pays for a lot of cheaper repairs somewhere else. Robin O'Brien

63

This beautiful Jaguar SS–100 looks like its owner has a friend in the chroming business. Damage to the headlight buckets would be very hard to fix, but where could you get replacements? Take the job to a pro—thin buckets are easy to damage and almost irreplaceable. Erika Sandford

the more important it is to seal the chrome afterward.

By this point you'll have one of three things: a nice clean piece of chrome, a decent piece of chrome with hairline crazes, tiny rust pricks or a yellowish haze marring the overall finish, or a piece of shiny metal with the chrome plating worn straight through. The former means you've done what you wanted to and the latter means that fixing the part is now out of your hands. That leaves just the middle scenario to worry about.

Chrome pits because water finds its way to the steel beneath the chrome. A good cleaning will usually remove the rusty brown spots but leave the shiny pits behind, and these can never be removed by hand. Assuming you can live with the pits, it's important to treat them with a rust remover to prevent them from turning brown again and continuing the deterioration. Do this *immediately*, not tomorrow or the next day.

When choosing a rust remover, make certain that it dries to a light enough shade to blend in with the chrome. Silver, light gray or even glossy white will do—avoid rust removers that dry black or red. Wipe this onto the part and let it dry for the recommended time, then go back and remove it with a rag moistened in mineral spirits. The remover should remain in the pits while coming off the chrome plating itself. Just to be safe, try coating a small hidden area of the chrome first before slapping rust remover all the way across.

A yellowish haze means that the lower layers of nickel and copper are starting to show through the chrome and become oxidized. Many people think of this yellowish tint as a dignified patina of age and

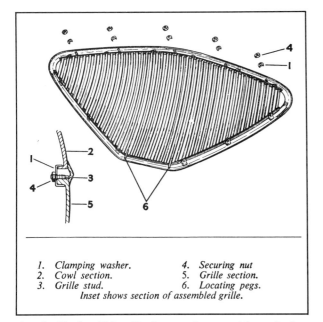

1. Clamping washer.
2. Cowl section.
3. Grille stud.
4. Securing nut
5. Grille section.
6. Locating pegs.
Inset shows section of assembled grille.

Austin-Healey 100 grille fixes to the car with studs that run right through the front panel. Getting access to these often means pulling a fender, but from there things should be pretty easy. Think ahead, though, to what can go wrong; at least one of these studs will probably let go, and dissimilar-metal corrosion might make everything brittle.

Lovely chrome fuel filler costs less new than stripping and replating the old one would have.

leave it be. If you can't get used to it, though, the part will have to be replaced or replated.

Replace or Replate?

Chrome plating—or at least any chrome plating worthy of the name—is actually a three-layer affair. Over a perfectly smooth metal base, the plater electrically deposits a layer of copper and then one of nickel before the final chromium coating is applied. These lower layers add the depth and bluish luster associated with high-quality plating, and the heavier the base coatings are, the richer the shine. The entire process is a time-consuming one, and very expensive machinery and chemicals are involved. The resulting bill reflects all this, and in many if not most cases, replacement of a part will be cheaper than replating.

It can be very frustrating trying to find large chrome pieces in a junkyard. If the junker died of neglect its chrome is usually shot as well, and if it's a sound car involved in an accident the bumpers and grilles are the first to get mangled. Smaller parts like instrument bezels and rearview mirrors can be easier to find in a junkyard, and a good thing—they can be almost as expensive to replate as much larger pieces. Junkyard pieces probably won't be perfect, but they might be good enough to respond to a cleaning that wouldn't faze your own parts. One brand-new piece of chrome can make the rest of your cleaned-up parts look bad, so a junkyard part might be a better match in these cases. Thin, brittle, plated pieces like headlight buckets are especially hard to repair if they get damaged—leave that job to a pro or replace them with new ones.

If you follow a particular piece of trim through the whole plating process it's easy to see where the costs and problems can accrue. I don't want you to get the idea that any plating job will be the kind of horror story that follows; if you have good communication with a good plater you can be completely satisfied with the results and the price. If you just drop off your parts at the first plater in the Yellow Pages, though, your experience is more likely to be like this one:

Let's say the grille on your Austin-Healey 100-6 is looking a little shabby. You drop it off at Chet's Cheap Chrome and say you'll be back in two weeks. Now, Chet Senior was probably in the back room watching TV reruns, so he didn't get a chance to warn you off—he makes his real money plating chrome toaster ovens and he'd rather not be bothered with fiddly old car work.

Since you're gone, though, he puts Chet Junior on the job. The first thing Chet Junior must do is disassemble the grille—pull off all the fasteners, remove the 100-6 badge and separate any removable bars from the backing frame. He then has to rough-clean all the parts before ushering them through a cleaning bath, and before you know it

Exhaust fumes and neglect have caused craters and pits in the bottom of this MGB overrider; it could be replated, but a junkyard spare would only cost about $10. Dave Solar

Chet's invested two hours and a dip in the grille and you're looking at $130. It takes him another hour to straighten two bent bars: there's $40 more. All the buffing and cleaning he's done has worn the crisp edges off the grille bars by now, but the parts had to be cleaned somehow.

Then he gets to the diecast 100-6 badge and the fun really begins. The badge is made of plated pot metal. (Pot metal is a porous diecast material often called Mazak in England, an acronym for magnesium-aluminum-zinc-and-Krome.) He buffs and sands the badge completely to get out as many of the little pits as possible, since pot metal is very porous and pits badly. Then he takes a tiny craft drill with a small burr tip, usually the ubiquitous Dremel-Moto, and roughs out each individual pit that remains. Finally he has to anneal a bar of copper—heat it to a glowing red and immediately quench it in cool water—before he can rub it over the pockmarks to fill them up again. The badge, which by now is missing most of its sharp contours, is finally ready to start the stripping and chroming process along with the other pieces.

After lunch, Chet Junior gathers the badge up with his cheeseburger wrappers and throws it in the trash, and you just got lucky. You could have bought three new repro badges for the price he would have charged for all that work.

The main parts of the grille, meanwhile, are ready to proceed. First they're dipped in a chemical stripping bath to remove all the old grease and crud. The plated layers are then stripped by reverse electrolysis, and the bare metal gets a pleasant acid bath to eat away any remaining rust while the dollar signs keep rolling. Chet Junior inspects the parts again, finds some more pitting and does another buffing job; he also finds a crack in one of the bars and has to braze it back together. The parts have to be cleaned and bathed one more time, and finally they go on to the copper plating bath. Two hours later they come out of the copper bath, are buffed once again and have to be treated to *another* copper layer. Finally, the parts proceed—after more cleaning—to the nickel bath and then on to the faster chrome-plating tank. The yellowish haze that remains is cleaned off in the final rinsing job.

You go to pick up your grille. Chet Senior feels bad about losing the 100-6 badge, so he knocks $20 off the final price, and you have to admit, the chrome looks fabulous. Some of the details are gone from the grille, though, and then you get the bill. The next thing you remember is waking up two days later in the cardiac ward.

The biggest mistake you made should be obvious—you have to get very familiar with the plating shop and the person doing the work if you want good results at a good price. If you'd stuck around and spoken to Chet Senior, he probably would have talked you out of the whole procedure. Many platers would simply rather not bother with walk-in auto plating—the customers demand too much and aren't knowledgeable about the procedure itself.

But let's say you asked a guy with beautifully replated parts on his own Healey where he'd had the work done, and he recommended Bill's Bumpers of Beauty. Bill could have told you right out whether or not the job was worth doing, he would have told you to replace the badge rather than trying to replate it and he might have told you that disassembling, straightening, brazing and cleaning the parts yourself would bring the price of the whole job way down.

He might also have told you that if you liked the job they did on the grille you'd want to make your next order include more parts—the per-unit price often goes down as the size of the order goes up. He would have explained the difference between show chrome—the costly, thick and beautiful plating used on top-flight show cars—and the thinner, cheaper varieties, and given you some idea of when it would be cheaper to just scrap a piece and start with a new one. Finally, he would let you know if his shop was capable of repairing any damaged parts or if they were even salvageable by someone else. Severely rusted parts—those with holes peppered right through the metal—or those with serious crash damage are usually goners.

Preparing Your Chrome for the Plater

You can do a lot of things to make plating work cheaper and more successful. Some platers won't take pieces that have been prepared beyond disassembly, since they don't want to be blamed for any work you've done incorrectly; others are willing to give you more leeway.

Any chrome piece should be disassembled and cleaned before taking it to the plater. Bumper brackets and overriders should be removed and the rough dirt and grease should be taken off with kerosene. Riveted assemblies are usually best left in one piece throughout the whole process, but discuss each piece individually with the plater. Special markings and angles should be pointed out to the plater so he can avoid buffing them into oblivion.

If a pot-metal part absolutely can't be replaced, you can buff it down, ream out the pits with a craft drill and fine bit and fill them with annealed copper yourself before plating. No plater in his right mind will guarantee a successful job on a part like this— it's simply too iffy a proposition. But many will give it a shot if you let them know you understand that the plating just might not take. (Pot metal is so porous that the acids used in cleaning often spoil the plating job itself.)

Also, let the plater know about any repairs you've already made in braze or solder so that he can be especially gentle with that piece.

And finally, choose your plater carefully. It's better to send out your plating to a respected specialist located far away than try a local one at random and hope for the best. If you do send out your plating, of course, you should spend some time on the phone with the plater discussing what sort of work needs to be done.

Repairing Broken Chrome Trim

One other thing worth mentioning before moving on to aluminum and stainless steel is the repair of broken chrome pieces. If something is broken in an exposed area and a replacement isn't available, it's possible to have the part stripped by a plating shop, welded or brazed, smoothed and then rechromed. If the break is in a hidden area or existing joint, however, the repair can often be done at home without the need for replating.

Broken pop rivets, of course, can simply be replaced, but often parts are spot welded or soldered together at the factory. The repair is usually a simple soldering job. To join light chrome pieces back together, the best method is to coat both pieces with a thin coat of resin-core solder and then clamp them together while playing a mild butane flame over the area. The solder will soften and reset almost immediately, making a joint that will stand up to light-duty use. For larger pieces you'll have to add a little solid flux to the joint before joining the pieces. Often this type of work will discolor the surrounding chrome, but Blue-Away will bring it back to life quickly—just don't break the joint while you're cleaning it up. (Blue-Away is easiest to find in motorcycle shops, where it's sold for chrome exhaust pipes.)

Brazing and spot welding will add too much heat to the part to save the plating, so you're right back where you started from. Occasionally, though, you can get away with making large repairs on a hidden area with fiberglass. Rough up the back of the pieces well with coarse sandpaper before trying this fix, and use epoxy resin for extra strength.

Stainless Steel and Aluminum Brightwork

Though it will never have the depth of chrome, aluminum and stainless trim is a real blessing. You don't have to worry about cutting through a thin top layer, just getting a smooth surface to the part. Since they don't rust in the traditional sense, these pieces usually don't deteriorate as badly as neglected chrome, either.

For both types of material you'll need buffing compounds or rouge of various grits, a few buffing wheels and a good set of protective eyeglasses. You can buy a professional buffing machine from a tool supply store, but most people seem to prefer salvaging an old washing machine motor and fixing it to their workbench by guerilla engineering. (In theory, an old appliance motor is risky since you don't know the rpm range you'll be dealing with, but I've had no problems with them.) The only thing you have to buy beside the motor, wiring and switch is a threaded end shaft from a hardware store so you have something to bolt the buffing wheels onto.

Buffing wheels come in different roughnesses, and you'll need at least one each in an abrasive grade, a mild grade and a fine grade. Buffing wheels remove oxidation and crud from your parts while smoothing out small scratches and nicks, but they get contaminated in the process. It's important to start with as clean a part as you can—go over the work piece with #00 steel wool and degreaser before starting the buffing process—and to clean the wheels as you go. To clean off a buffing wheel, hold a clean piece of scrap metal up to the spinning wheel every minute or two to scuff off the accumulated crud, or use a legitimate buffing rake.

The procedure for buffing both kinds of metal is basically the same. After cleaning them, apply a little coarse buffing compound to the coarsest wheel (by pressing the compound against it while

Buffing motor, wheels, rouge, wheel rake, breathing filter and eye protection—a full kit for reviving stainless steel and aluminum. The Eastwood Company

it's spinning) and gently apply it to the part. Hold the part so that it will fly away from you if it catches on the wheel.

A chart (available where you buy your buffing compounds) will tell you which compounds and wheels of a particular brand to use on which types of metal. Generally you do three steps: rough compound on the rough wheel, mild on the mild and fine on the fine, but this can change depending on the brand of buffing compound and the part in question. Clean the parts with alcohol between each step and dry well. The final buff will bring the surface to a remarkable, mirror-smooth finish, though you might have to remove some buffing crud with Glasswax. Finally, leave a good coat of carnauba wax on the part to prevent oxidation.

While stainless and aluminum trim is easy to bend and dent, it's also easy to set right again. Just remember how soft the metal you're working with is; use only rubber-faced hammers and rubber, wooden or sandbag dollies. Gross scratches and dents should be pounded smooth, roughed quickly with 150 grit sandpaper, glossed over with 400 grit to remove the sanding marks and then buffed out as usual.

Thin aluminum-alloy and stainless-steel trim gets beaten up easily. Gentle beating with a rubber body mallet and a sandbag or wooden dolly ought to bring it back to life.

Happich Simichrome is the traditional favorite for cleaning dirty but sound aluminum and stainless steel. The Eastwood Company

3

Priming and Painting

More than any other single factor, the quality of the paint job will determine how your car looks and, consequently, what it's worth. A knowledgeable person can see through a bad paint job to the vehicle underneath, but no one will pay much for the car one way or the other.

Do-it-yourself restorers have very different attitudes about painting cars. Some people would never dream of applying their own paint; others would never dream of paying some guy in overalls and an air mask to do it for them. For those in the latter group, the ones who put a lot of time and effort in their work usually wind up with excellent results; the ones who want to get in and out as quickly as possible wind up with a mess.

If you decide to do your own painting you'll find it one of the most rewarding jobs of the restoration, but I'd strongly recommend doing some serious research on the subject before tackling the job.

Power sanders and buffers have revolutionized auto restoration; it's almost impossible to imagine doing the whole job today with elbow power. Because they're so quick, though, a power unit can quickly wear through edges and corners; you've got to be careful. The Eastwood Company

There aren't enough pages in this book to thoroughly cover painting, but there are some excellent books on the market dedicated to the subject.

Looking for a Professional

Applying paint isn't all that hard—it's just a matter of patience, preparation, trial and error, and common sense. Painting is *exacting* work, however; if you're the sort of person who hates attending to lots of details, it might be better to let a professional shoot the car. Let's look quickly at that alternative first.

A good professional paint job won't be cheap. You can spend anywhere from $99 to $4,000 and beyond for a pro to coat the car, but (up to a point) you get what you pay for. If you go with an Honest Earl's paint job you'll be wasting your money. You might as well spend the cash on spray cans and do it yourself in the backyard. With some looking around and research, though, you might be able to find an excellent drop-off-the-car-and-wait paint job for less than a thousand bucks. As the price goes down much more than that, the quality of the paint job itself and, more importantly, the pre-shoot prep work seems to fall off dramatically.

For a pro, shooting paint onto the car is relatively fast and easy. The expensive and annoying task for him is removing all the trim, masking anything that's left and prepping the panels by stripping, sanding, filling small dents and priming. (Filling anything larger than parking-lot dings is going to up the cost of a pro job considerably.) Most professional shops are willing to take on an owner-prepped car for a lot less money than one straight off the road. Doing all the prep and body work yourself will make the cost of the actual spraying job quite competitive with buying your own spray equipment. The savings are determined by how much of, and how well, the prepping was done beforehand. It's a matter for negotiation with the manager or owner. He or she will talk not only about money but also about what they expect you to do and how.

You should pick a paint shop as carefully as you'd pick a surgeon. Look at the facilities—do they seem clean and well organized? Talk to previous customers—are they pleased with the shop's work? And take a look at some recent jobs—are they up to the standards you demand for your own car?

Selecting a paint shop is also a matter of personal rapport. You're going to be asking a lot of questions and your car is going to demand a lot of time from the painter; he or she should be willing and able to talk to you. It helps if the painter is a car enthusiast. For many paint shops, classic cars and their owners are simply a pain in the neck—they'd rather make money by doing volume work for people who aren't particularly critical. This attitude isn't confined to shops specializing in new cars, either; some "restoration" painters have the same idea. To them, your classic car is just one more classic car, not something special. Avoid these guys like the plague.

Once you've settled on a shop, get everything in writing: what kind of paint will be used, how much of the prep work you'll do yourself, how long the spray job should take and what the total cost will be. When it's all over, you'll see your "new" car for the first time.

Sanding

Before you can even think about painting, you have to master the simple but tedious job of sanding. I've always hated sanding, or at least ever since I flattened out a whole Chrysler Imperial by hand and lost my fingerprints for two weeks. But getting out the old paper and bucket is a necessary evil, and if it's done right it's not nearly as unpleasant as if it's done wrong. I won't tell you it becomes fun, however.

Needless to say, the correct grade of paper speeds things up and does the best job. In principle,

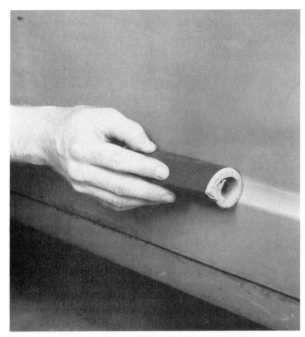
Foam professional sanding blocks can be bent to any shape to smooth out difficult contours. The Eastwood Company

you do the real work with a rough grade of paper, then go over the surface again with finer and finer grades to take out the scratches from the paper you used the last time around. Of course what you're sanding determines what kind of paper you start with, work down through and finish with, and it seems like each job has its own requirements. You smooth out old paint for a respray starting with a medium-grit paper, and then you go straight to fine; for color sanding between coats you just flash over the whole thing with fine-grit from the start; for bringing body filler to order you use 60 grit—there's just no end. (Incidentally, if you want to avoid some infuriating accidents, try to keep your

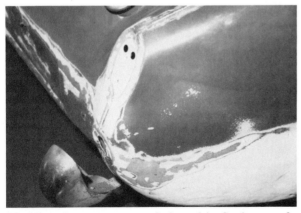
There's a long way to go before this Sprite can be painted—the chips must be sanded out, all the edges feathered and the lower panel needs to be smoothed, filled once more and guide coated before proceeding.

Traditional sanding blocks save your fingertips and prevent ripples and waves. The Eastwood Company

different grades of paper in separate places on the shelf.)

Usually you have a choice between dry sandpaper and wet-dry. I'd almost recommend the wet-dry variety and leave it at that, but there are a few advantages to the dry stuff. Wet-dry sanding puts water in contact with bare metal, so if it's not dried off completely it can speed up the rusting process. Okay, so you dry everything off—big deal.

Another problem with wet-dry sanding is that the water runs off and hides in cracks and crevices, under pieces of trim, inside mechanical parts and so on. Again there's a rust worry, but a more immediate problem is that the water can shoot back out when it's hit by the blast from your spray gun. That means stopping what you're doing and possibly re-prepping the whole panel. The best solution is to simply blow out all the nooks and crannies with compressed air.

Wet-dry sanding also creates a considerable amount of paint residue, which has to be washed off before you can go on. Dry paper leaves grit and sometimes powdered lubrication behind, so you have to wipe down any panels that have been dry sanded, too. You don't generally have to sponge them off, though; with wet-dry you do.

Using wet-dry paper is much easier than dry sanding, though. It's faster because the water lubricates everything and carries away a lot of the paint, it's less expensive since you can use the same paper over and over again, and it gives better results since the paper doesn't constantly go from Super-Rough Chew-it-up to Superfine No-Grit without you noticing. (Use any paper once the grit has worn off and you'll soon have Popeye's fore-

arms; it takes a lot longer for a piece of wet-dry to go bad.)

One of the first assumptions most people make about sanding is that it's a great way to remove crud from metal surfaces—that seems, after all, the whole point. Well, it is and it isn't. Sanding definitely chews right through the top layers of whatever is ailing your metal. But at the same time, it shoves tiny particles of whatever that stuff is down deeper into the metal itself.

If it's rust you're trying to cure, just sanding it off won't do the job. The only real cure—cutting out the metal and starting all over again—is often worse than the disease. (You can prolong the patient's life considerably without amputation; guerilla rust repair was talked about earlier.) By trying to sand off rust, you're actually reseeding the metal with smaller, better distributed particles of rust. Whisk away as much rust as possible with a wire brush and wipe with solvent before sanding.

Similarly, merely sanding over grease and dirt isn't going to give you a clean, paintable surface. You have to clean off all the junk *before* you start sanding, or the impurities will interfere with whatever you put on top of them—paint, filler and so on. This is especially true on thin or exposed pieces like body panels. Tougher and less obvious pieces are more forgiving, like frame tubes, bumper brackets and suspension arms. You can often simply blast, sand or wire brush these and get away with a good solvent wipe and a coat of rust remover before you begin painting. If you tried to get all the crud off of something like a rear leaf spring before you started sanding, you'd be wiping it down for the rest of your life.

How to Sand

Now that you know all the rules and regulations about sandpaper, you're probably thinking you might have to go out to the garage and use some. Fear not—here are some more things to know that will put off that fateful moment a few more pages.

First, use a sanding block of some sort whenever possible. This can be a professional tool you buy in paint or auto supply stores, or just a scrap of hard rubber or wood with some paper wrapped around it. A block gives you something to grab, covers a lot more area with every stroke than your fingers will and doesn't cause waves and ripples the way simple hand sanding can. It also saves your fingerprints.

Second, get creative with your blocks. Use the rounded back of a regular block, paper wrapped around a dowel, or wood with a unique curve to fit into odd-shaped areas. Be careful to use this type of block only on the fender lip or body ridge it was intended for.

Third, if you can't get a block into the area you're sanding, sand with the flats of your fingers (not the tips) and go at right angles to the fingers them-

---

Wet-Dry Sanding Tips

A couple of hints for sanding with wet/dry paper:

• Get the good stuff. The added life span will more than pay for the higher cost.

• Use a bucket to supply the water, not a hose, and add a drop of dishwashing soap. Soap lubes everything and keeps the water from rolling right off the paint.

• Change the water frequently and every time you go to a finer grit.

• Make *sure* that all the water's off the car when you're done and blow out all the cracks.

• Sponge off all the colored glop the sanding leaves behind.

• Clean the paper if you drop it. Any dirt or grease on it contaminates the metal.

• Wet-dry *does* wear down the same as dry paper, it just takes longer. Keep an eye on the condition of the paper, and chuck it when the grit wears down.

selves. Otherwise, each finger makes its own groove.

Tip number four, straight scratches don't show through paint nearly as much as circular ones, so sand in straight lines. Usually that means you go a half-dozen strokes in one direction, then another half dozen at 45 deg. to the first direction, over and over.

Tip number five, when using electric (or air-powered) sanding machines, the weight of the machine is usually enough to do the job. Leaning on the thing just bogs it down, cuts the paper or causes it to eat into the metal too quickly. Be especially careful around edges—power sanders will burn through paint like nobody's business. (Power polishers will do it too.)

Tip number six, always sand "over the hill" when smoothing a surface for painting. On a curved piece like the top of a fender, sand up and down, not side to side. This cuts way down on ridging and waves. (If you're trying to sand down plastic filler, you're going to have to get creative.)

Finally, feather the edges to blend a repair in with the old sheet metal.

Feathering is critical, and it's more of a habit than a skill. The idea is to make a smooth transition from the repair to the solid paint or metal. To do that, you'll have to sand a slope about 3 in. out from the edge of the repair for every coat of paint you're trying to feather back. Use fine paper and remember that you're trying to make a very smooth slope—lighten off the pressure as you get to the outer edge of the feather.

Removing Trim and Bumpers

Most professional shops would rather mask a part than remove it. Masking is faster, and to most customers the results look about the same. But to someone who's developed an eye for cars, a little overspray here and there is the hallmark of an incomplete job. The only way to guarantee that a part won't be subjected to overspray (or damaged by the masking process) is to remove it from the car. Only when that's not practical or feasible should you mask something.

Chrome bumpers should be the first thing to go. These can be a pain to remove—the nuts and bolts have often been frozen solid since the time of the dinosaurs. Generally, bumpers are held on to heavy brackets with heavy nuts and bolts, and it takes a seriously heavy wrench to remove them. Of course you can't always *get* a heavy wrench back there, so a few days of soaking with WD-40 or a similar loosening agent will make things a whole lot easier. (When putting the bumpers back on, it's a real treat to fit stainless-steel fasteners—they'll still be free when it comes time to paint the car again ten years down the road.) It's sometimes also easier to remove the mounting brackets from the car instead of the bumper from the mounting brackets.

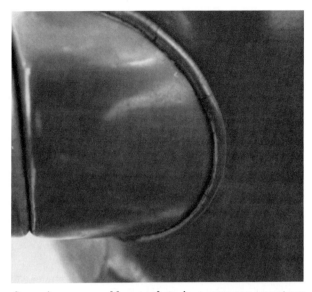

Spraying over rubber gaskets is a common amateur mistake. You don't think it will be obvious, but it looks terrible.

Most of the time it's easy to see how the bumpers come off; on newer cars, though, you might find a few twists. Energy-absorbing bumpers (used from the early 1970s on) usually mount onto two hydraulic pistons and the bolts are stuck somewhere down in the bowels of the front and rear ends. Other bumpers mount directly onto the body itself, and to remove them you have to go behind the sheet metal and undo a nut on the inside. (Just

Body decals can be a real pain. To get them off, try warming the decal with a heat gun and covering them with grease overnight; if that doesn't do it, go in with contact cement thinner. Anything stronger might lift the paint, so check solvents on a hidden section of the paint first.

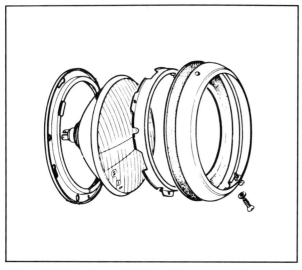

If headlight bezels are held in with setscrews the removal method is obvious; if not, the bezel may be snapped into place or secured by the headlight ring itself. Moss Motors, Ltd.

what good these bumpers are supposed to do I'll never know.) On still another car, you might have to lift up a rubber rub strip on the face of the bumper to find the bolt heads holding the unit on. Also don't forget to undo any wiring for turn signals, license plate lights or what have you before pulling off the part. Finally, it's best to have a helper nearby to support the bumper before you undo that last bolt. Otherwise, you can get 50 lb. of chromed steel square on your toes.

Figuring out how to remove other bits of trim can be more difficult. To pull the headlights, the first step is usually removing the outer chrome bezel. This can be secured by a few screws around the edge, or more often a single setscrew at the bottom. Sometimes, however, there are no apparent securing fasteners at all—these bezels are usually spring-loaded or snapped onto the body. Try fudging these off gently by twisting them a quarter turn. If that's no go, then it's possible that the headlight itself should come out first to reveal the bezel mountings. In these cases, you usually loosen the two headlight adjusting screws at the front of the

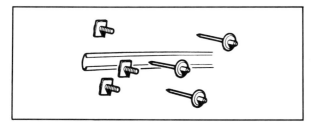

Rivets and clips are both used to mount trim. When drilling new holes for the clips, don't forget to prime and paint the bare metal edges to beat rust. Moss Motors, Ltd.

unit and rotate the retaining ring just enough to free it from the screws—you'll see what I mean when you're there. (Hold on to the headlight unit so it doesn't fall forward and break itself or its wires.) Once the retaining ring is off, you can ease the headlight forward, remove the wires (marking them as needed) and have a look inside the headlight bucket. The mounting method should be fairly obvious from this vantage point.

Taillights present a similar problem—usually a screw or two holds the plastic lens in, and by removing that you'll see a few more screws holding on the rest of the assembly. These screws (or small bolts) usually fit into captive nuts, but these may be missing or broken. Other taillights simply press through the body and nuts hold them from behind—even speed nuts occasionally. The only difficulty here can be getting access to the back of the assembly through the trunk. Sometimes you'll have to remove a finishing panel or two to get there.

Trim strips, emblems and chrome spears can be a bear to remove without breaking them in the process. Strips and spears generally snap onto clips, springs or rivet heads in the body. The difficult part is unsnapping them without bending the willowy strips themselves. Sometimes they pop straight off, but usually they slide off in one direction only and you have to gently tap them along with a rubber hammer. Whichever mounting method is used, try the wrong removal technique and you're likely to trash the strip. Make sure you know how the part went on before you try to take it off. Your service manual will help.

A few strips and emblems actually bolt on from behind or are held by speed nuts. These are usually a breeze to remove, but occasionally there's trouble; sometimes it seems the manufacturer mounted the thing and then welded a reinforcing panel behind it. (They didn't, although I do suspect that Standard-Triumph used a trained octopus to fit the lettering and emblems to the TR-3.) The only thing you can do is to wriggle your fingers or a small screwdriver into any access holes and try to gently lever the speed nuts off. There's a risk of breaking off the mounting tabs, so be careful.

If the piece still won't come off and other restorers don't have a solution, you have basically two options: masking and prying. Masking is probably the better option; even though it undoubtedly will collect some overspray, at least the piece will remain intact. It's better in these cases to lightly mask an emblem—you can remove overspray with a wooden toothpick, thinner-soaked cotton swabs and wax. Touching up surrounding areas that *should* have been painted is much harder.

If you can fit a hard piece of plastic between the offending part and the bodywork, you can try to pry it off and hope that something gives underneath. Usually this does nothing more than break the emblem, bend the metal and leave bits of fastener stuck inside the bodywork. Unless the part is already loose, this isn't the way to go.

It's possible, of course, that the piece you're trying to remove is glued onto the car. A lot of smaller emblems, especially plastic ones, are held on with strong contact cement. To remove one of these, *don't* try to lever it up with a screwdriver. Instead, run a thin-bladed putty knife up into the joint and slide it along to break through the cement. Levering will only break the emblem and bend the metal below it. (Before removing a glued-on emblem, take precise measurements of its location so you can get it back on correctly later.) Once the emblem is removed, gently scrape away the heavy glue left behind and clean up the rest with a mild solvent like contact cement thinner.

An outside mirror can be held in place by a set of screws on its base or by difficult-to-reach nuts inside the sheet metal. Radio antennas usually screw into a base on the car, the base itself fixed from behind by a single big nut. Trunk handles and door locks usually mount the same way—a large single nut fits around the barrel of the lock from behind. These are by no means the only mounting methods for these kinds of pieces, however. The best rule is to explore the backside of the part before proceeding; the method should be apparent once you've gotten access.

Door handles are rarely a big deal to remove, but getting to them can be a hassle. Usually the handle is simply held in place with nuts or bolts from behind, but getting to those mountings can mean pulling the door panel and sometimes the window glass and regulator as well.

The grille of the car should be pulled off before painting too, and often this seems like a bigger job than it really is. Postwar grilles are rarely more than decorative pieces, so usually they're just held in with screws around their periphery. To pull a stamped aluminum grille you might have to do nothing more than take out a dozen sheet-metal screws and unclip any wires that get in your way. On other cars it might not be so easy—you may have to take out the radiator just to get to the bolts holding the grille in from behind.

One mistake made by many restorers is leaving rubber pads and gaskets in place during painting. It costs little time and money to remove *all* the pads from underneath locks, handles and mirrors and replace them with new ones later, but the difference is tremendous to the finished product. Removing rubber from around the windows and windshield is a little harder but no less important. (Actually, removing the gasket under a roadster's windshield can be a pain—sometimes you're better off to mask it as mentioned later.)

Once all the trim and associated parts have been removed from the car, you need to attend to mask-

This isn't going to make a good base for new paint; dirt is actually trapped in the old paint job and the missing chip would have to be smoothed out and feathered, starting with a good sandblasting. All glass and chrome must be removed before blasting.

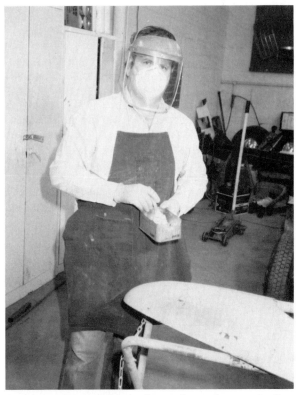

Serious stripping chemicals require serious protection, and it's always best to avoid them if you can. This guy's doing everything right, though; he's got face protection and a heavy apron, his nose and mouth are covered by a fiber filter, he's keeping the chemicals in a solid metal container, and there's a drop-cloth on the floor to catch whatever poisonous blobs fall to the ground. Robin O'Brien

There's one really easy way to strip a frame down in an instant. A bare Austin-Healey frame is connected to a forklift . . .

all the edges, go over it with wax and silicone remover again and then shoot a primer coat. If you're using enamel or two-pack (isocyanate) paints, you can often get away with shooting nonsanding primer over the filler and bare spots and using the old paint as your undercoat everywhere else. For lacquer, it's best to prime the whole car.

Depending on the type of paint being sprayed, you may also need to use an *isolator* to prevent chemical reactions between layers. If you do spray an isolator, make sure you put the first new coat of paint on within the time limits given.

Why would there be a reaction? Lacquer can't be sprayed over enamel or the solvents will blister the lower layer and ruin the paint job. Enamels can usually be sprayed over lacquer, but just to be sure it's best to stick with the same kind of paint for the respray. To see if the original paint is a lacquer, try rubbing a little lacquer thinner on a hidden spot. If the paint starts to come off, it's lacquer. If it curdles and wrinkles, it's probably enamel. If nothing happens at all, it's either a two-pack isocyanate like Imron or a really tough enamel.

If the current paint is too thick (more than a couple of thin resprays over the original), the wrong type or just too poor to use as a base you'll have to strip it off. (Look for orange peel, blistering, tiny cracks or bubbles, pinholes, large cracks from too many resprays or fisheye-like circles under the paint.) Generally the easiest way is with a chemical stripper, although it's also possible to power sand through the old paint or have it removed by a commercial stripping shop in a chemical bath. Chemical stripper is seriously caustic stuff, and it will irritate your skin unless you wear the proper heavy rubber gloves. It will also play havoc with any

ing off the remaining holes. Holes should be taped up from behind to keep paint from shooting through and fouling up the doors, engine, wheels or whatever's back there. Wires for lights and the antenna need to be marked, pushed back through the body and then protected behind the tape.

Stripping Old Paint

You don't necessarily need to strip off all old paint. Tired old paint *can* make a fine base for a new finish. You will have to wipe all the old paint down with wax and silicone remover, though—that's one cleaner to remove wax and silicone, not two different steps—smooth it out with medium and then fine paper, do any bodywork and feather

When the Austin-Healey chassis is pulled out of the witches' brew, it looks like it just rolled down the assembly line—notice the slurry of crud coming off the rising frame. Chemical dipping really does the trick, but it's costly and toxin-generating. Rebirth of a Classic

. . . and submerged in a pleasant chemical bath. Gallons of caustic chemicals are then poured in and the whole assembly is left to stew.

rubber, cloth, vinyl or plastic parts it meets on the car. Finally, it goes without saying that *all* the stripper has to be removed before any further work can be done.

Spread the stripper on and the first coat of paint will wrinkle and come up quickly. The lower, older coats will take longer, but eventually they, too, will come off. You'll have to get the stripper into nooks and crannies with wire and plastic brushes. It's important to make sure that all the stripper and old paint is gathered up and thrown away before moving on to the next steps. Sweep and sponge it up and dispose of it in a covered metal garbage can.

After stripping, you'll probably have to sand the whole body down with medium paper or a stripping wheel to get the last remnants of paint and crud off; you'll also probably find a lot of rust that needs dealing with. After *thoroughly* removing all traces of stripper, you might want to consider a full phosphoric acid wash as well to make sure the surface is clean and well etched. Follow the directions on the container carefully to make sure all the acid is neutralized and removed before proceeding.

Once the car is stripped, the metal is immediately under attack from oxidation. Try to get it primed and painted as quickly as possible once you've set the ball in motion.

Masking

Unless you've removed every last nut and bolt from the body of the car, you're still likely to have to do *some* masking; a good job here can make or break the finished product. Too little or just plain bad masking will lead to overspray on parts that shouldn't be painted. This can usually be cleaned up with thinner later, but there's a great risk of damaging the new paint in the process. Too much masking, on the other hand, will create a noticeable ridge between the masked part and the new paint layer, which can't be easily corrected. So, it's better to mask too little instead of too much.

The first thing to do is to start with high-quality masking tape. Go to a paint store—not the local supermarket's hardware aisle—and buy the good, brand-name stuff in 1 in. and 3 in. widths. The cheap stuff stinks—it either doesn't tear when it should or does tear when it shouldn't, and the edges are never strong enough to keep paint from seeping up underneath.

Once you've got good tape, keep the edges clean and fuzz-free by storing the unused rolls inside a plastic bag. If the edges do get fuzzy, you can try to clean them with a clean rag moistened with a little rubbing alcohol. However, too much alcohol and the glue will come off; too much fuzz left behind on the tape and it won't make a neat seal. Toss the roll either way, it's relatively cheap. Also avoid hitting the edges of the tape—every time you get around to that dent again the tape will tear or it just won't lay flat.

The best method I've found for masking off large sections like windshields is to first lay down a single piece of tape very carefully along the edge being protected. Then come back with another strip taped on top of that one a little behind the edge to hold down the protective sheets of paper. The second strip, of course, doesn't need to be laid as precisely, which is a good thing as the protective sheeting will be hard to work with. (Most pros use heavy sheets of butcher-type paper to mask large

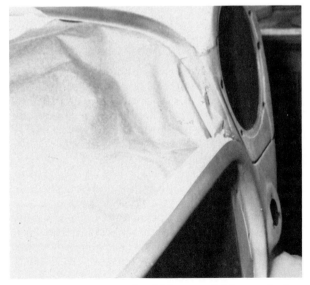

Engine compartment should be completely masked no matter what; even if the bay is getting painted too, do the jobs in two different sessions.

Items like turn signal lamps should always be removed, not masked, when painting. The new rubber gasket will look great on the finished car.

areas, but for do-it-yourself use I've had no problems with a few layers of newspaper. Some people say that the newsprint can bleed onto the masked surface, but it's never happened to me.)

Masking should be completely free of folds—they can trap dust and then let it be blown back on the paint. If you wind up with any folds, smooth them over and tape them down. Naturally, tape up any seams in the protective paper as well.

Applying the edge of the masking can be a time-consuming job. Try to slip the edge of the tape under any lips of trim and fold it back around, rather than just running it down to the painted surface and trimming it with an X-acto knife. If you do accidentally get tape onto a surface that's going to be painted, make sure all the glue is removed with alcohol before you go on.

If you're spraying the same color over an existing coat, you can leave weatherstripping in the doors, hood and trunk to help seal off those sections.

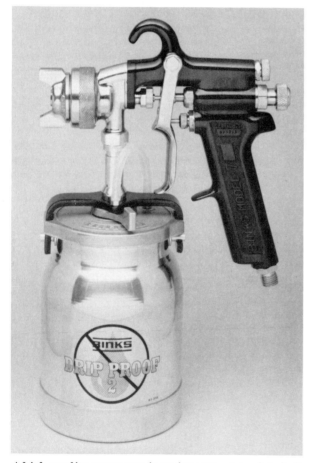

A high-quality spray gun is an investment; maintain it correctly and you should never have to buy another one. Think about getting a gun you can grow into. A slow and cheap unit may be fine for your first restoration, but if you'll want to upgrade for the next car it makes sense to start with the right piece in the first place. The Eastwood Company

You'll have to replace the weatherstripping later, of course, and this won't do the whole job. Thoroughly mask off the engine compartment, trunk and interior to avoid accidents. (Weatherstripping that doesn't merely clip into place can be removed with naphtha, which will soften the glue. A heat gun on the back of the panel will also soften it up enough to let you take the stripping up.) I usually try to fold back sill trim and carpets so I can get the masking material down below them to really be safe.

If you're changing colors you have to paint everything—inside the trunk, the doorjambs, under the hood, the engine compartment and so on. Changing colors on a car that's not completely disassembled is a major task. Unless you're planning to remove the engine and most of the interior, I wouldn't recommend it.

When the time comes to take the masking off there are a couple of different methods you can use. Some people like to leave the tape on until the car is completely dry. That way they avoid the risk of messing up the paint in the removal process. The trouble is that the tape can pull a chip of paint off of the body as it's removed. It's sometimes possible to free the chip with an X-acto knife and lay it back onto the car with a dab of thinner afterward, but sometimes the entire panel needs to be resprayed. For my money, it's safer in the long run to *very carefully* remove the tape while the last coat of paint is still a little wet—too wet to crack or make little strings when the tape is removed. By rolling the masking back on itself while you remove it, you can keep it from dragging on the freshly painted surface. Fortunately, sports cars are small enough that you should be able to avoid touching the car with your own body while you're pulling up the masking. Your only concern beyond that is to make sure dirt and hair don't fall onto the paint.

Spray Guns

The type of compressor you have in your garage will dictate the sort of spray gun you should use. If you already have a compressor kicking around from some earlier work, then you're going to have to tailor your gun to match it. If not, you can go about things the other way around—choose the gun and then buy a setup lock, stock and barrel to match it.

I'd avoid running right out and buying the best, most expensive spray gear you can lay your hands on, though. Yes, the expensive gear covers more area with each pass; yes, it makes a better spray pattern; and yes, it will probably last longer than a cheaper kit. But as a home restorer, you have to consider how important those three things really are.

The pros justify expensive equipment largely because it lets them spray a broader swath with each pass. That means they work faster and get paid more in a day. For those of us who aren't on a time clock, however, speed isn't important—in fact, it's not even desirable. We want to take our time and work methodically. It's easy to get so carried away with a powerful spray gun that paint winds up all over the garage, the washing machine, the lawn mower and even the dog.

And while a top-of-the-line spray rig will put out a better spray pattern, is it cost effective to buy a professional setup costing ten times as much as an entry-level kit when it's certainly not going to give you ten times the results? It might give you slightly better results, or then again it might not be any improvement at all. If you don't do a lot of spraying, chances are you'll make the same mistakes with a pro setup that you would have made with an entry-level one; that small difference in spray quality will be erased in your first session of roughing down the paint.

Since we restoration-for-fun types have all this extra time on our hands, the actual finish straight from the gun isn't nearly as important to us as it is to the pros. Professionals need to get perfect results as soon as possible. Sure, we'd love to have them too, but we don't really *need* them—we can always go back later and do damage control. We can respray whole panels, pick dead bugs out of the paint with tweezers and color sand a rough lacquer job until it shines like glass, all without worrying about work backing up in the shop. Why spend money on twenty-year-old scotch when you're going to cut it with soda and lime?

All we really need is a setup that's predictable—one that's not going to shoot big blobs out one minute and clog to a pinhole the next—and not so slow and weak that it's truly annoying to use.

How durable does this equipment need to be? It needs to be reliable and consistent for as long as we intend to use it. While a pro might shoot a dozen cars a month, folks like you and me will be lucky to do a dozen cars in the next five years. Any decent gun should last that long with proper care.

If all this sounds like you simply have to cut corners and accept a substandard paint job, fear not: there's no reason why we average guys can't get top-notch results. Since it's *our* car, by taking extra time and care we can make up for a large amount of missing practice and amateur equipment. (And by reading up on the very latest tricks and technology, we might even have an advantage over a pro. Chances are he's painting cars the same way today that he did when he learned how to do it years ago. The only thing we can't do that he can is to make it look easy.)

Your compressor will determine your gun type. That's because two factors—the amount of air the compressor pumps and whether or not it has a receiving tank—need to be considered. (Any spray

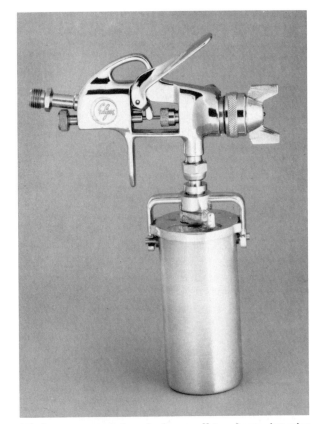

Mini spray gun is handy for small touchups, interior work and spraying small parts.

system designed for automotive use should include a moisture filter and water trap to prevent oil and water from entering the spray gun and fouling the paint.)

There are two main types of spray guns, pressure feed and suction feed. Pressure-feed systems pump air into the paint pot, which pushes the paint into the spraying stream. Suction-feed guns operate kind of like a carburetor's venturi chamber; the paint pot is vented to the atmosphere, and atmospheric pressure pushes the paint up into the airstream because a low-pressure area is created by the gun. (You can read up on venturis and pressure zones in chapter 6, or just take my word for it.)

Suction-feed guns need a whole lot of air, so to use one you'll need a fairly large compressor—larger than most amateur setups. And a suction-feed gun will run through a fairly large receiver tank in no time flat, so don't expect a big tank to make up for a small compressor. Suction-feed setups are the kind you see around professional shops most of the time, but one of the main reasons is that suction-feed guns usually cover more area with each pass. Unless you wind up with a gun that gives ridiculously small coverage, that's not too high on our list of priorities. (The higher you go in quality, the more guns seem to be of the suction-feed variety. Again, though, how much money do you intend to spend for all this equipment?) A pressure-feed system makes more sense for most people.

An added benefit of this kind of gun is its ability to get thick glop like spray putty up out of the paint pot. If you plan on coating your car with about 10 in. of plastic, this is the baby for you. There's also a wider variety of pressure-feed guns at the lower end of the price spectrum.

The other variable in choosing the gun is whether or not your compressor has a receiver tank. If it doesn't, you'll need a bleeder gun, which flows air constantly and stops the paint when you release the trigger. Where else would the air go?

Compressors that pump into a tank (and therefore have their own shutoff system) don't need a bleeder. For my money, cutting down on all that hissing and pumping while you're not actually spraying is a real benefit, but not the sort you're going to die without. If you have a receiverless compressor, it's probably not worth replacing just to avoid a bleeder-type gun. Some people worry

about bleeder guns kicking up stray dust, but I don't think it's a problem.

The business end of a spray gun is the air cap; that's what ultimately blends the air and paint and controls the spray pattern. You can get internal- or external-mix types, and they do just that: internal-mix caps blend the air and paint inside the gun, while external-mix caps combine the two just ahead of the nozzle itself. Most do-it-yourself automotive paints dry too quickly for internal-mix caps, so they plug up almost immediately. I'd go for an external-mix cap every time.

The fluid tip (which metes out paint in the proper ratio), the fluid needle (which starts and stops the paint flow) and the air cap itself all have to work together—you can't mix and match them and still expect good results. I'd strongly recommend buying a gun in which these features come fully assembled, and one that's also rated to use the paint you plan to shoot the car with. (Most automotive guns will shoot most kinds of paint, however, so if you already have a gun it's probably going to be okay.) Your friendly paint supplier will make

Self-contained turbine painting system is gaining acceptance with do-it-yourself restorers. The Eastwood Company

sure you get the correct setup, but pay close attention to all the instructions and warnings found on the labels. There will be cross-references, advice and admonitions on everything from the paint to the thinner to the primer to the gun to the compressor; take heed of all of them or you might get burned. Needless to say, there are also safety warnings galore. Take heed of these, too, or the results might be fatal. Paints are flammable and toxic; don't take chances with them.

It's also imperative that you follow the manufacturer's instructions *to the letter* when it comes to cleaning your spray equipment. Some guns don't come with cleaning instructions, however; the manufacturer presumes that you come from a long line of psychics. In this case, you should write and specifically request cleaning instructions, or check with your local paint expert to explain the cleaning of your particular gun. It's not something you can be sure of doing right just by following common sense, and the quality of your next spray is directly proportional to the quality of your last cleanup. There are so many little passages, checks and doohickeys in the gun that just a smidgen of dried paint inside can—and will—bollix up the whole works.

Your cleanup will be done with the same sort of thinner you've used in painting. Use another thinner and you risk a nasty reaction inside the gun, which can do a lot of damage and make the job all the more difficult in the end. Every manufacturer (and every spray painter) has their own routine for cleaning, but I like to start by draining the pot (you can store and reuse mixed paint, assuming it's not a chemically hardened type like Imron) and cleaning the pot inside and out with thinner.

Turbine Painting Systems

There's a new kind of spray system on the market now, and though I've never used it I'm beginning to hear good things. It's a turbine-type kit—a complete compressor, hose and gun unit priced competitively with buying all these things individually in conventional materials. Of course if you've already sunk a bundle into your own conventional compressor, this system won't be cost effective.

The compressor uses a turbine rather than pistons to supply air, and there's no receiving tank; the air flows at a relatively low pressure and the paint being used is thinned way down compared to conventional systems. The guns are usually simplified as well, cutting down on gaskets and passages to speed up the cleaning process. Advantages to this system are supposedly less overspray, less paint consumption per car and less danger of water and oil in the air supply. I'd talk to someone who's shot a car this way before trying out this system yourself.

Then I add a little clean thinner to the pot, screw it back on the gun and clean the outside of the whole affair before proceeding. That way I don't keep getting paint on my hands, which get back on the gun, and on and on.

The next step is to shake the paint pot well, then shoot some thinner through the gun with the airflow cranked way up. Remember that the thinner (and the paint still in the gun) will do nasty things to any surface you care about, so this isn't some-

This decent-sized home compressor has a receiver tank, so a bleeder gun won't be needed. Output may not be high enough to support a professional suction-feed gun, however. Check your requirements before you start to paint.

A moisture trap has to be included in any spray system to keep water and oil from entering the spray stream and fouling the paint. The Eastwood Company

thing I'd recommend doing next to a freshly shot car.

After that the gun is broken down and every thread, hole and tube is cleaned out thoroughly with a good bottle brush. Some of the sealing washers have to be cleaned up, but others should be left alone—again, the manufacturer's instructions will tell you how to proceed. Whatever you do, don't throw the whole gun into a pot of solvent. That usually damages a small but expensive sealing gland that I'd *swear* is placed deep inside the gun just to weed out amateurs.

There's also a great temptation to jam a stiff probe into some of the smaller orifices of the gun. Don't do it—you might damage the hole and change the spraying characteristics of the gun,

---

Choosing Primers

Selecting the proper primer depends on how much work you want to do once the primer is sprayed, what functions the primer should perform and what kind of paint you're applying over it. These are some primer types currently on the market:

• Pure primer: Relatively thin, this primer merely acts as a base for the paint. It won't fill in nicks or add any real qualities of its own to the paint job.

• Etch primer: This eats microscopically into the steel to give the paint a better grip. It keeps rust down a bit by preventing water from traveling under the paint.

• Primer-surfacer: Thicker than regular primer, this will fill in small nicks and sanding scratches. Two coats of primer-surfacer can be used where more might be necessary with regular primer. Primer-surfacer doesn't sand quite as well as pure primer, but the whole idea is to avoid sanding in the first place. It's chemically hardened, so what you mix but don't use has to be tossed out.

• Spray putty: Very thick and gloppy, this will fill in major flaws and blemishes. It's really too thick for most amateurs to use—it goes on a little wavy and blobby and can easily be too thick to take a good coat of paint.

• Non-sand primer: As the name implies, you don't have to smooth out this primer before applying the next coat.

• Chip-resistant primer: Again, as the name suggests, this makes a very tough base coat that resists nicks and scratches. It's good for front valances, wheelwells and rocker panels. Chip-resistant primer also cuts down on noise transmitted through the panels.

• Flexible primer: This primer is for use on rubber bumpers and other flexible parts to resist cracking. It also adds some chip resistance in wheelwells and other exposed areas.

• High-zinc primer: This primer type uses a lot of zinc to combat rust. It's good for cars exposed to the elements or just as insurance.

---

rarely for the better. When the whole gun is clean, pack it securely out of sight where kids won't be tempted to play with it, and turn your attention to cleaning up the hoses, the garage and the compressor. And oh, yes, don't forget to rinse the overspray off the dog.

The Painting Area

You're probably not going to have a professional spray booth at your disposal, so you'll have to convert your own space into something that's as sanitary and dust-free as possible. A full garage is certainly the best thing to start with, but you can also seal up a covered carport with plastic sheeting and get good results. You can even, if necessary, paint outdoors on a calm day—that's very risky, of course.

In a full garage, the first step is to move out everything that's not nailed down, especially grimy things like mowers, rag bags and old tools. Your concern is partly keeping overspray off these things and partly keeping dust out of the room. Sweep and then vacuum everything, including the walls, roof and rafters. It's a good idea to coat the ceiling of the garage with plastic sheets stapled into place, especially if there are exposed rafters or storage bins around. If there's a water heater or other flame source in the painting area, it will have to be turned off for the duration of each spraying session.

You have to strike a compromise between dust-proofing and ventilation in your spray room; since dust damage can be repaired but your lungs cannot, go for ventilation. Mount an exhaust fan in an open window and seal up the area around it with stiff cardboard or wood, held in place permanently with screws or temporarily with duct tape.

Somewhere in the room away from windows, drafts and heat, also mount a good thermometer. The paint, thinner and ratios are all dependent on certain temperatures to work correctly.

Right before you start to paint, you can wet down the floor to trap dust that would otherwise be kicked up as you walked. If the car isn't already in the area, a garden hose will do the job. (You can also wet down the walls if they were covered in plastic; beware of drips from the ceiling, however.) If the car is already in the room, use a bucket to avoid getting water on the prepped automobile. Don't make puddles, just get the floor damp enough to trap and hold any dirt.

Just before the final cleaning of the car, wipe down your compressor, hoses and gun to remove excess dust. You should also wear relatively clean, lint-free clothing when doing any spraying.

Choosing Primers and Paints

You have a lot of things to consider here; first and foremost should be the results you're after in terms of color, finish and durability.

The depth of the finish is determined by what type of paint you use, how many coats, your color sanding between coats and your post-hardened polishing job. Lacquers generally offer the deepest, most glassy shine. Enamels are a little flatter and shallower, and two-pack isocyanates like Imron and Durethane offer a deep shine but a plastic-like overall finish. Though isocyanates are actually much tougher than lacquers, they *look* softer—a look that can be glaringly obvious on a 1950s or 1960s car.

Since three paint types—lacquer, enamel and two-pack—are your main choices, let's look at them in detail:

Lacquer

Probably the current favorite of classic car restorers, lacquer is forgiving to apply. It dries quickly so bugs and dust don't have much time to settle in. Since it's sanded between coats, the painter can make sure every layer is smoothed to perfection before continuing. It goes on at relatively low pressures—about 20-30 psi (pounds per square inch)—so it doesn't take much of a compressor and it doesn't make a lot of overspray. Lacquer's biggest advantage is probably the ease with which it can be rubbed out later. An amateurish application can be turned, with lots of color sanding and polishing, into a mirror-smooth, two-foot-deep shine. And lacquer is relatively inexpensive to buy—you can afford to build up lots of coats and sand off lots of paint.

On the negative side, lacquer is pretty soft. It nicks and scratches easily and doesn't last as long as other paints. It also needs to be sanded and rubbed out; if you'd rather damn the torpedoes, hope you get the spraying right and have something that goes on glossy from the gun, this isn't the stuff for you. Lacquer is very sensitive to the surface it's being sprayed on to—it will crack and craze unless the lower coats are of just the right material. Lacquer is also a poor choice for frames, suspension parts and other components that will be exposed to rocks and stones; and since you don't want to rub out any surface that's not completely smooth to start with, all heavy castings should be done in enamel or two-pack paint as well. Finally, lacquers fade more quickly than other paint types, especially in reds and yellows.

Enamel

Enamel is a lot tougher than lacquer and a little less expensive, though neither will bankrupt you. Enamel's strong suit is that it usually goes on glossy right out of the gun. You just spray it on, let it settle and poof—instant respray. Enamel won't react with an old coat of paint below it, either. It's just the thing for giving that tired old nag one more spray before shipping it off to the morgue. If you can do a good prep and spray job, enamel may be the paint

Chip-resistant primer will help prevent nicks and rust on front valances.

for you. It's certainly faster than lacquer and less work in the long run.

The main disadvantages of enamel reveal themselves when you make mistakes; enamel stays wet longer than lacquer, so more bugs have a chance to commit hara-kiri in the paint before it's set up. Even when enamel seems dry, though, it's not really cured—it dries by evaporation but hardens by oxidation, a process that can take weeks. Therefore if you make a mistake, it might be weeks before you can go in and correct it before throwing another coat of enamel on top and trying again. Most do-it-yourself enamels can be color sanded when fully cured to remove blemishes. Spraying enamel on the car also means that the next paint job will have to be enamel as well, since other paints will react to it.

Two-packs

DuPont's Imron was the first two-pack, but now there are some competitors out there—all of them

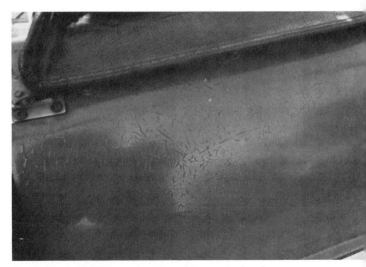

Cracking and lifting was caused by spraying lacquer over enamel without stripping the old paint first or correctly using an isolator.

more or less the same in terms of ease of application, gloss from the gun and hardness. Two-pack paints are, in many ways, a do-it-yourselfer's dream. They're tough as nails and help prevent chipping, are nearly fade resistant and tolerate chemicals like gasoline, bird droppings and even brake fluid. They go on smoothly most of the time, and most can be color sanded later to achieve a glossy smooth finish, if need be.

The main disadvantage of two-pack paints is the one that makes it virtually unsuitable for amateur use: its toxicity. These paints are called isocyanates, and the similarity to cyanide is not coinciden-

tal. Isocyanates will cause respiratory ailments and even death if all the proper guidelines on ventilation and respirators aren't followed to the letter. Other disadvantages include the high cost of these paints, the plastic-like and rather shallow finish they give and the fact that a chemical hardener must be added to each batch right before spraying. Mixed paint that's not used must be thrown away. The gun and other equipment must be stripped down and thoroughly cleaned before the paint dries or they'll be ruined beyond repair.

All automotive paint is made up of three components: pigment, vehicle and solvent. Pigment is a powder suspended in the liquid component (vehicle) to give the paint its color. (Pigment can also serve other functions in specialized paints, like rust retardation and scratch filling.) The vehicle holds the pigment together, carries it to the metal from the gun, protects it from the elements by sealing it up and adds the gloss, shine and protection of the paint job. Solvent merely makes the pigment-vehicle combination runny enough to flow through the paint gun and over the metal surface. It quickly evaporates, leaving the thickened pigment-vehicle behind to harden on the car. Solvents must be of the correct type for the paint being thinned and the temperatures being worked with. Since you can always add more solvent but never take it away, add solvent a little at a time until the proper consistency has been reached.

With lacquers, the solvent is lacquer thinner and it's mixed about 50:50 or even 66:34 with the paint. Enamels use a reducer, and much less of it. Two-pack paints dry differently from enamels and lacquers: the solvent flashes off in the same manner, but the actual hardening takes place by chemical reaction, not evaporation or oxidation.

The type (and even brand) of paint you select will determine the amount of work involved—what primers to use, how (or if) to sand between coats, how many coats are needed and so on. In general, though, the order is as follows for spraying over an existing layer: wash the car, wipe it down with wax and silicone remover, wash again with soap and water, dry thoroughly. Next, smooth out the paint and feather any edges, then clean and wet the painting area. Wash the car *again* (last time), wipe it down with methylated spirits (denatured alcohol), mask it, tack it off and go. All the wiping should be done with clean, new cloths; rags, even the ones sold in car parts stores, contain too much grease and wax for the job. (Tacking off is done with a resin-impregnated tack cloth, which picks up any dust or metal filings still left on the car immediately before spraying.)

For painting raw metal, start with a phosphoric acid wash and remove the acid completely with water or the recommended neutralizer before it dries. Wash the car with soap and water, dry it,

Picking the Color

Choosing the correct color of paint for your car can be complicated. Here are some factors to consider:

• Sticking with the current color might let you avoid painting the doorjambs, under the hood, in the trunk and about a thousand other fiddly little places. If you want to match the original color exactly, try to find a nonfaded section under the dash, inside the fuel door or underneath the door panels to use as a starting point. This will usually be much brighter and richer than the color on the rest of the body.

• Light colors hide small flaws in the bodywork better than dark colors. Black should only be applied to a car with flawless metal.

• Stick to a factory-correct color that was offered the year your car was built unless you don't care about originality.

• You can often decipher the car's original color from its build plate. More times than not, that color has nothing to do with the color the car is now.

• If going to a nonfactory color, avoid modern shades like orange and pink that may go out of date in a few years. Deep green, silver and red will never go out of fashion.

• If you're having paint mixed for you, have a few variations made of the color you think you'll select; some lighter, some darker, a few with different color ratios. Spray each onto some primed scrap metal and let them dry. From that you can choose the variation that you were after, not the one that happened to get mixed up for you at the supply house.

• Red, yellow and orange fade faster than white, silver and blue.

• Metallic paints are harder to apply than nonmetallics. They must be applied in equal depth all over the body or some areas will be more reflective than others. Metallics are also not original on many early cars.

• Spray any paint—whether mixed specially or from an original equipment source—onto primed scrap metal before applying it. That's the only way to know how it will really look on the car.

wipe with methylated spirits, mask, tack it off and go for it. Steel panels can immediately take an etching primer, but aluminum and galvanized panels should first be covered with a high-zinc primer. All primers are relatively porous and will absorb water from the atmosphere—don't let a panel sit in primer for any length of time, or it will quickly rust underneath the coating.

The Spray Job

When you're finally ready to apply primer or color coats, the pressure is on—or so it seems. In truth, the actual spraying, while critical, is not usually as troublesome as all the prep work, research and shopping trips, or as the instruction sheets might make you believe.

Always keep in mind that paint is there primarily to prevent corrosion of the metal underneath. Pay special attention to getting the paint *everywhere*—into boxes, hinge openings, cracks and crevices. Doing the paintwork yourself lets you add an extra-thick coating to these places that are often neglected at the factory. Do an especially good job of painting cowl boxes and wheelwells—these areas are where rust usually forms first.

Before you hook up anything, play with the gun for a while to get the motion of spraying down pat. You want to move the gun across about a 2 ft. section of the car at a time, bending your wrist as you go so that the gun runs perfectly parallel to, and about 6 in. from, the surface. Hit the trigger just after you start moving the gun and release it just before you stop each pass. Each pass should cover about half of the one before it and half the unpainted surface below.

Your primer coats will teach you a lot about how you'll apply the color coats. Technically, the passes with paint are usually broken up into three coats: the lightly sprayed *tack coat*, which gives the next layers something to adhere to; the *color coat*, which hides the undercoats and starts to add depth; and the *gloss coat*, which finishes the job and adds the rich luster.

Primer is much more forgiving than regular paint—it doesn't run as much and, being flat instead of glossy, takes on its proper surface more readily. Use your primer coats to explore the best order in which to cover the panels, the best way to get into nooks and crannies and the best way to hold the gun over tricky sections.

Before painting, don't forget to use body sealant in all the seams, cracks and joints where water could otherwise enter and start rust. And when you're done, go ahead and spray rubberized undercoating on any surfaces that had it from the factory.

Spray Painting

The first step is to check out the equipment, car and spray area one more time. When you're satis-fied, blow the dust off the tops of the paint cans and open one up. Stir the raw paint well with a clean metal rod. Then mix it in a clean mixing pot to specification. Check the viscosity with a viscosity cup and timer.

Filter some paint into your paint pot and attach it to the gun. Adjust the spray pattern to your liking with the gun held about 6 in. from a scrap surface and parallel to it. Move onto the car and spray. Each car can be done in a number of different ways, but the classic order of panels is: roof, door, adjoining front fender, hood, front valance, opposite front fender, adjoining door, adjoining rear fender, trunk, rear valance and opposite rear fender.

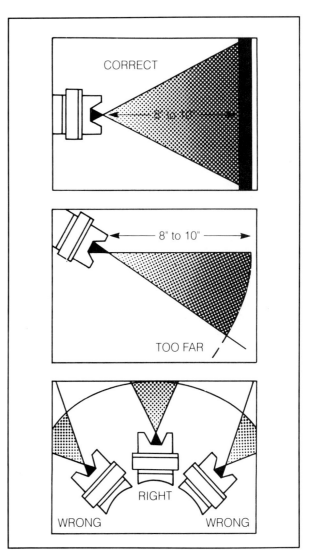

The nozzle of your spray gun should always be kept perpendicular to the surface that it is painting. If you move too close or too far from the surface, you'll get paint sags, orange-peel finishes and many other problems. Practice on a test panel before you begin your actual work, trying to lock your wrist and elbow and moving your body with the gun as you paint. PPG Industries

RECOMMENDED SPRAYING SEQUENCE

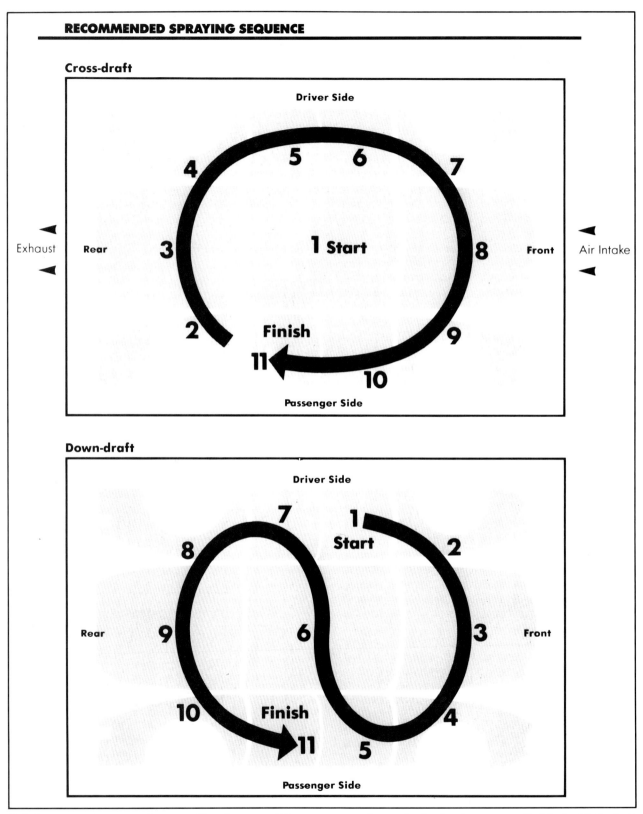

Cross-draft

Driver Side

4   5   6   7

Exhaust   Rear   3   **1 Start**   8   Front   Air Intake

2   **Finish**   9

11   10

Passenger Side

Down-draft

Driver Side

7   **1**

8   **Start**   2

Rear   9   6   3   Front

10   **Finish**   4

11   5

Passenger Side

To help you apply your paint as uniformly as possible, follow this DuPont recommendation for spraying sequence of body panels. This system allows you to fully paint each panel before moving on to the next and also should help you in timing your painting so the first panels are dry by the time you are finished with the last, so you can shoot a second coat depending on the paint system you are using. Sequences are shown for both cross-draft and down-draft ventilation systems. DuPont

You can tackle door, trunk and hood lips as you go, but most people like to do the engine compartment and trunk in separate sessions. Try to get into nooks and crannies right before shooting the panel surrounding them. And try to cover outside and inside edges before shooting the panels surrounding them. Run your air supply hose over your shoulder at all times to keep it from dragging in the paint.

Paint Safety Guidelines

When painting, it is imperative that you adhere strictly to safety guidelines such as these:
• Paint is flammable when wet and potentially explosive when airborne. Take precautions as needed.

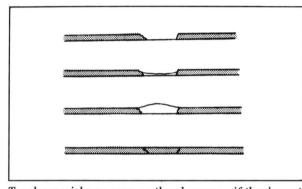

Touch up nicks as soon as they happen—if they're not rusty it's a minor job. Clean the area with wax and silicone remover and dab a little thinned body paint into the chip—it should flow just to the edges. Build up successive coats until the surface is raised a little. Sand the repair smooth with very fine wet-and-dry paper, finish with polishing compound and wax the surface. Tom Smitham Graphics

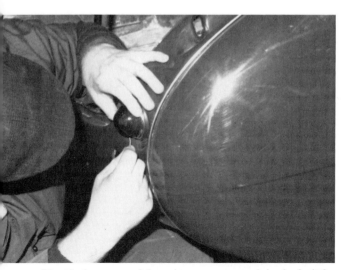

Plastic lenses and housings are surprisingly brittle; don't overtighten them when they go back on.

Relatively mild blistering was caused by contamination of the primer or lower paint coats. Water, fingertip grease or oil are the likely culprits; the panel simply wasn't cleaned properly before spraying.

Cracking caused by improper surface preparation, too many coats of paint or poor primer adhesion.

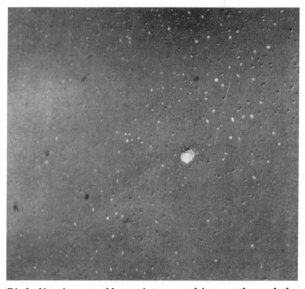

Pinholing is caused by moisture pushing out through the finish while the paint dries; the top coat is usually put on too thick and its surface hardens before the lower paint has dried completely.

• Always wear a charcoal-activated mask when working with regular paints. Two-pack paints require a genuine respirator system.

• Wear protective clothing at all times to avoid unnecessary skin exposure.
• Thinners and solvents are volatile—they evaporate readily—and their fumes are poisonous and flammable. Never leave solvents in an open container.
• Seal all paints and chemicals so children can't get at them.
• Clean up any spills immediately.

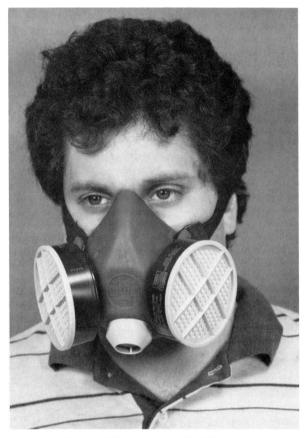

A simple charcoal filtration mask will protect you during sanding and nontoxic spraying . . . The Eastwood Company

. . . but a genuine respirator system is mandatory for working with toxic sprays like isocyanates. The Eastwood Company

4

Interior Restoration

Interiors are something of a mystery to most do-it-yourself restorers, perhaps because we're more used to working on solid metal objects than cloth, leather and plastic. But interior restoration is for the most part fairly easy work, and it's a nice change of pace; no more greasy footprints in the house, no more brake fluid dripping on your hair and no more skinned knuckles. You might glue your fingers together, but you get to do it in a nice warm basement instead of a cold garage.

Repairing Water Damage

If England were in the middle of the Sahara Desert, I could understand why the British are so bad at sealing water out of their cars. It rains in that country constantly, though, yet English cars have about the worst weathersealing around.

Any British roadster that's been driven in the rain has probably been leaked into; repairing the damage caused by those leaks isn't enough. You

Artist's airbrush covers enough area to paint small interior panel without excessive overspray. The Eastwood Company

A full interior respray can mean complete disassembly and thorough masking. Even if the whole car is stripped, mask the interior from the exterior and do the jobs in separate sessions.

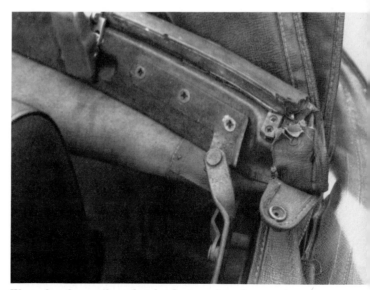

Worn header rail gasket leads to a lot of annoying leaks—water usually sprays right in your eyes.

87

Good window rubber is the first line of defense for keeping door panels from rotting. Erika Sandford

have to also repair the leak itself, or next year you'll find yourself right back where you started from.

Finding the source of a leak isn't always easy. The first thing to do is to make a visual check of the most likely areas, but water can run a long way along the inside of the car before actually dripping down on your feet. If all else fails, you can sit in the car with the windows and top up while someone else points a hose at the suspected areas.

Most leaks come from around the windows, of course. Proper adjustment of the top and windows, sound window insulation and good weatherstripping are going to be necessary to avoid future dousings. Do a visual inspection first to locate all the missing or torn rubber pieces, and make sure that the top meets the windows on all sides. Even when they're perfect, of course, some English tops and windows meet in a sort of flap-it-over-the-side-and-hope-for-the-best fashion. Unlike domestic cars, they often don't use a rigid, weatherstripped beam across the top of the window. That's all the more reason to adjust things as well as possible.

The height of the window is usually adjustable at the front and back once you've taken off the door panel. Each window is adjusted a little differently, but there are basically two variations: either the entire window regulator moves up and down, or limiting stops in the window tracks do. Either way, it will probably take a few tries to get the window adjusted properly. Put the top up while you're doing the work, that way you can just butt the window up into place and secure whatever bolts there are that hold it.

For the top, you might be able to shim up or fiddle with the rear mounting screws, and sometimes the individual bows can be loosened and

Obviously, a lot of wind and water is going to get by this weatherstripping. The weatherstripping costs next to nothing—the seats, carpets and paint that will be ruined are expensive.

Replacing cracked windshield rubber is a big job, but there's no way around it once things get this bad. Rust and mold are going to set in soon unless this gets taken care of. Brett O'Brien

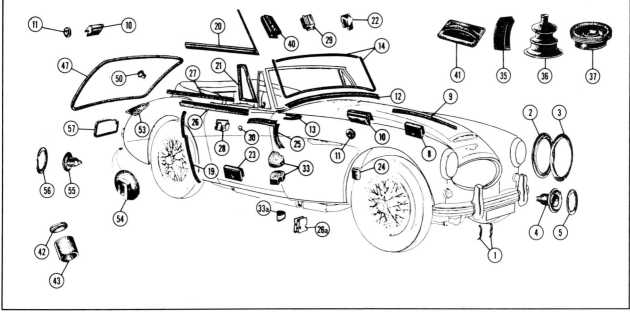

All kinds of rubber pieces will be needed. Old rubber seems minor but it harms the appearance of the car and can lead to costly rust and water damage. Moss Motors, Ltd.

played around with. Even the front clips may have some degree of movement built into them that you can take advantage of. And on cars like some later Triumphs—cars that feature American-style rigid beams and weatherstripping over the windows— your life will be made easier instantly. If the beams themselves can't be loosened and adjusted, then it's sometimes possible to go to slightly different weatherstripping that more accurately matches the windows. As a last resort, the whole top frame itself is pretty flexible; you can simply manhandle it into a more convenient location if you have to. The chances of making things worse rather than better are pretty good, of course.

The other chief place for water leaks, barring a hidden tear or a split seam in the top, is around the windshield. The most common failure is for the beading that holds the glass in place to dry out and crack, which gives water a nice pathway into the car. The crack itself won't always be apparent, and simply tracing it from the drip usually doesn't help—the water can travel a fair distance between

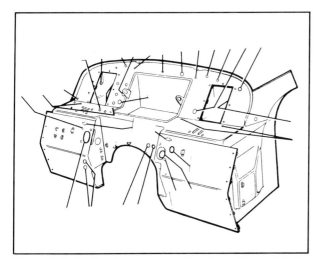

Every hole in the firewall must be plugged up with the proper grommet, sealer or blanking plate. Heat, water and toxic fumes will enter the interior without them. Moss Motors, Ltd.

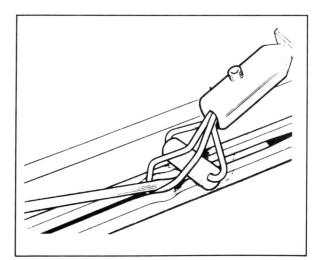

A special sealing tool is required for many MG and other windshields and backlights. The main rubber seal fits nicely into a gap in the frame, but a second spreader cord must then be inserted to finish the job.

the glass and the frame before it actually comes in. As a rule, the corners, particularly the bottom corners, are the first things to go. Quite often you'll see that previous owners tried to plug leaks with clear goo. Sometimes that works and sometimes it doesn't. There are a number of commercial sealers, most of them silicone based, that can be injected into a suspect area of the beading, but you should do just that with them—inject them *in between* the glass and beading, don't build them up on the outside. Simply slopping it on over the existing rubber usually doesn't do much good.

If the windshield frame bolts onto the cowl, check the rubber strip at the bottom of the frame and the sealing gaskets under the pillars. If one's bad a drip might seem to spout mysteriously, haunted-house style, from underneath the dash. These can be quite destructive; not only will the water ruin your carpeting, it can short out your gauges and wiring as well.

Finally, it's possible that the car is leaking through a hole in the firewall, floorboards or wheelwells. As mentioned earlier, it's imperative that all these holes are found and plugged. The proper rubber body plugs can be obtained from a parts source; most bodyshops also carry a variety of Caplugs, a trade name for various-sized rubber plugs, on hand. These are simply pressed or bonded into place, with any wires or cables passing through a hole in their center.

Holes in the floorboards have been either eaten out by rust, caused by a missing body plug, or drilled by a previous owner installing seatbelts or something else. Splitting seams in wheelwells are not uncommon in areas that were spot welded at the factory. Any rust found around a hole or split has to be dealt with properly, and then body sealant or even plastic filler has to be laid in to plug up the leak.

Cleaning and Small Interior Repairs

A surprising amount of work can and should be done with all the panels and carpets still in the car. Small tears, stains and general crud are best attacked with everything held in place where it belongs. About the only thing I'd remove would be the seats, to get some maneuvering room inside the car. While they're out, gently brush and vacuum up all the crumbs, old food and coins, spreading open the seams with two fingers to get into the crevices. Left in place, this debris will rot and ruin the material. After brushing and cleaning the seats you can get on to more serious work.

Vinyl is tough enough to handle most of the commercial cleaners on the market, but I'd still recommend starting with a solution of mild soap and water. Since the soap is doing the actual work, mix the solution fairly strong, then work it into the vinyl with a soft-bristled brush. A paintbrush works well, as will a soft shoe-shine brush.

Once the soap has been worked in, remove the suds with a damp, clean, wrung-out cloth. You'll probably have to go after a given panel a few times to get all the soap off, but resist the temptation to

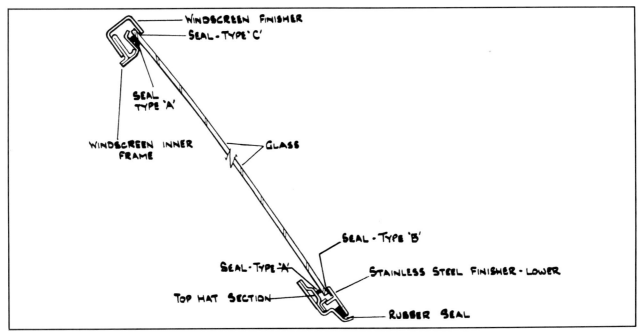

The complexity of most windscreen's internal sealing can be deceptive. Unless all the pieces are in good shape and properly located, water will find its way in. Just because a leak sprouts from a certain point, don't assume that's the only source of a problem.

saturate the cloth—water is the enemy of everything in your interior, so use it sparingly. If soap and water don't do the trick, then go ahead and use something a little stronger like a professional vinyl cleaning solution. The end result should be a clean seat or panel, but just removing the dirt isn't always enough. Some vinyl panels will look chalky after cleaning, are faded from the sun or just have a stain that's too deep to be cleaned.

I've had good luck with spray dye on pieces that simply won't clean up. The more extravagant alternative, of course, is to just replace or at least recover the entire piece. Recovering simple vinyl-covered panels is relatively inexpensive and easy, but it's something to avoid if you can. Instead of recovering a grungy-looking part, at least try to give it a shot of commercial dye and see how it comes out.

Leather panels are a lot more sensitive than vinyl ones. You should use the same procedure as already outlined, but with leather you should avoid any solution stronger than mild soap and water, unless it's one specifically made for leather automobile interiors. Connolly, the folks who've supplied leather to the British auto industry since the beginning, have a whole line of cleaning goodies that work wonders. Lexol is also good for bringing back lifeless leather—a few applications will bring the suppleness back to the material. Most commercial cleaning solutions not specifically made for leather will soak in and result in awful-looking blotches. You should also avoid oils and cleaners made for tougher leather products like boots, saddles and jackets; these are usually too much for softer automotive seats and panels.

The small hole in the shift boot is enough to let heat and fumes into the cockpit. Don't take chances—replace the boot.

This seat can be brought back to life easily. Hide Food and Lexol will restore the sound leather, while a professional or dedicated amateur can easily sew in a new side panel.

Steering column collar looks hard to remove and paint but it isn't; the central pad pops right off, revealing the steering lock nut right below, and the collar and wheel come apart with a few bolts.

Tears and Splits

Before tackling a serious cleaning job it's best to repair any tears and split seams. On rigid pieces like kick panels you can usually fix a tear by sticking the edges back down very carefully with contact cement. For upholstery work, 3M makes an excellent contact cement called General Trim Adhesive. They also make a strong glue-for-all-seasons called Super Weatherstrip Adhesive—most parts suppliers call it "gorilla snot"—that's good to have around for any job.

There are a number of commercial kits you can use to fill in any seams that still show after the tear has been cemented down. Usually these consist of a liquid goo you dab into the tear and then set firm with the heat of an iron. By placing one of the included pattern-making sheets over the repair, you can get a surprisingly good match with the surrounding panel.

Pasting and patching doesn't work as well on seats, though, which are constantly being stretched and played with. Sewing up seat tears with thread is usually not the answer, either—the repair will show and the tension on the seams usually pulls the thread out in short order. Depending on the size and location of the tear, you can either patch or sew it (a temporary fix), replace the whole seat panel (a job for a pro, but usually not a very expensive one) or install a whole new seat cover (expensive but well within the limits of the amateur's skills). Let's take them in that order.

To patch a simple tear, the edges of the tear should be brought together and supported from behind by a piece of similar seat material bonded into place with contact cement. The same goo-and-iron kit you'd use on a rigid panel will finish the job, but only for a few months. Unless the tear is on an unstressed panel like the back of the seat, pretty soon the edges will start to split again and you'll be right back where you started from.

Replacing a whole seat panel is a more complicated job, and since it means matching materials, cutting out a new piece to size and most importantly sewing it in correctly with all the seams and piping to match, it's one I prefer to leave to the pros. Somebody who's adept at sewing might want to give it a shot themselves. It's important to match the direction and type of grain exactly, and any sewing will be easier if you use button thread run across a piece of beeswax for your stitching. It's also imperative that the stitching runs through sound material on both sides of the repair—rotten old leather and vinyl will tear at the threads almost immediately.

The final option for your original parts is to put on new seat covers. New-looking seats at a reasonable price used to be something that restorers could only dream about, but complete kits have become more and more common in the last five or ten years. These days it's unlikely that a full seat-cover set won't be available for your car.

This seat cover's a goner. Embossed plastic can't be patched and you're certainly not going to get a vinyl repair kit in here!

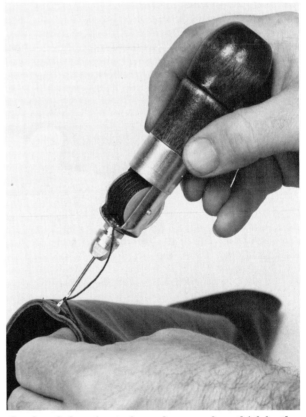

One-handed sewing tool speeds up work on thick leather and vinyl, though it might not be easy to duplicate the stitches already on the car. The Eastwood Company

With just a bit of patience and common sense, you can put on new seatcovers and really transform the interior of your car. By paying close attention to how you took the seat apart and removed the old cover, the basics of putting a new one on should be obvious. Just in case you get confused, though, it's best to do one seat at a time and use the other one for reference.

The tools for the job are pretty basic: standard and Phillips screwdrivers, a utility knife, a pair of heavy scissors and a few different pairs of pliers—for example, one set of needlenose, one standard and maybe one hog-ring; hog-ring pliers are inexpensive upholstery tools available at most any tool store.

You'll also need a good adhesive, and while any interior trim adhesive will do fine there are some more exotic alternatives. One you might want to consider is a slow-setting contact cement that lets you reposition the parts for a few minutes after they've been stuck together.

You'll also want to have some sheets of thin foam rubber around; you might have to buy larger blocks once the old seatcovers come off, but you can hold off on that for now.

Installing Seatcovers

Each seatcover fits a little differently, but for twin buckets the basics of the job will be the same no matter what car you're dealing with.

Remove the seats from the car by taking them off their tracks or unbolting the tracks from the floor. (This is usually easy once the seats are pushed all the way forward and back to expose the mounts. You might have to coax them with a rubber hammer.) Move the seats to a clean workbench or a table covered in new cardboard or towels. Separate

New seat webbing is inexpensive and makes a big difference; don't skimp here or you'll remember it every time you sit in the car.

the top and bottom sections; this often means pulling the plastic or metal trim panels off the sides of the seats.

Flip the bottom cushion over and take off any mounting hardware and track slides. While you're there, take stock of the condition of the lower seat support—if it's a rubber diaphragm type, make sure the hooks haven't ripped through the dia-

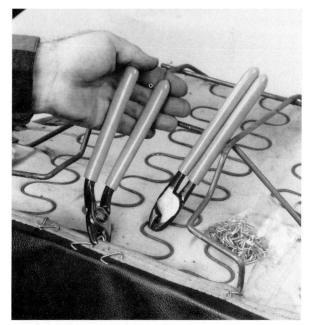

Spring-steel clips as used in most English cars let you fudge the fit later, but hog rings (shown) must be cut out and replaced if you don't get it right the first time. The Eastwood Company

---

Tightening Up the Seat Seams

Fixing loose seams is simple assuming the material on either side of the seam is intact and not rotten. You can even do the job without removing the cover from the seat. Get a curved needle from a sewing or sailing shop, some button thread in the right color for your seats and a lump of beeswax. Run the thread through the wax before proceeding—it will travel through the seat material without binding that way.

Start by doubling up the thread and making a knot at the far end. Hide this knot down in the vee of the seam and simply push the curved needle through the seats in the same manner as the original pattern. (You might have to push the needle through with pliers if the seats are made of a few layers of leather.) When you get to the end of the repair, lock the thread with a slip knot around an existing stitch, cut it and hide the remaining end down in the seam.

phragm and rendered it useless. Similarly, inspect and replace any bad spring-type seat cushions. (You'll have to replace bad supports or the seats will feel awful when they're back together again.)

Start unclipping the upholstery from the seat frame. If the clips are made of spring steel, save the unbroken ones in a coffee can to make sure you can use them again. If they're hog rings, cut through them and prepare to use new ones in their place. Gently cut through the bottom few inches of the corner seams and start peeling the old covering back. You might find that it's glued on in a number of places—if it is, work gently to avoid tearing the cushions. Stubbornly glued covers can be gently cut away from the foam rubber with a serrated bread knife.

Once the sides of the covers have been removed you'll probably find that more clips hold the top panel in place, hooked to blind wires below the covering. Poke around to find and remove the remaining clips, and pull the covering the rest of the way off.

Remove and inspect any stiff cards or wires that are attached to the old seatcover. You'll have to put them in the new one or replace them with something handmade. Lift off the seat cushions (if they're not glued down) to check the seat frame and springs for damage and rust. Clean and paint any rusted metal and re-string any springs that have come loose. You might even want to sandblast

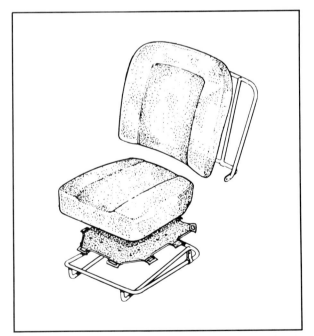

Even if a seat looks okay, your back will immediately know if the diaphragm, foam, or frame needs work. Diaphragms and foam are available for most cars, and the small investment in time and money to replace them is worth it many times over. Moss Motors, Ltd.

and refinish the seat frame—use a tough enamel to resist scratches from the seat clips.

Now turn the seat bottom upright again and take stock of the foam padding. If the old covers were torn and water found its way into the padding, the foam itself is probably ruined. To check it, run your fingernail across the surface. If big chunks of dry foam break away, the whole section should be replaced. You can cut new cushions from heavy foam rubber with a serrated or electric knife; a few inches of softer foam might be called for in the center section. Whether cutting new foam or not, add a single piece of 1 or 2 in. soft foam over the entire cushion to give it a smooth surface. Glue everything together with contact cement and let it dry completely.

Next, warm the new seatcover in the sun and under an infrared lamp *briefly*. You don't want to make it too soft or it will wrinkle later—just make it soft enough to be workable. Turn the new cover inside out, replace any card or wires and lay it in place over the cushion; fix the center clips in place and check that the seams are even and straight. Start working the corners of the seatcover down over the foam a little bit at a time. By the time they're finally all the way over, the seat will probably look a little sorry—baggy in some places and tight in others. That's alright for now. Just make sure that any piping or patterns that run along the outside border of the seat are lined up properly and everything looks straight.

Snugging the cover as you go, put a few clips in each corner of the new seatcover. This is the only tricky part of the job: You want to stretch the cover tightly enough to make it lie flat and even but not so tightly that the material will tear away from the clips the first time you sit down. It's better to be on the loose side, since you can always go back later and tighten things up. Once you start clipping down the sides of the cover you'll have to do some fudging to get a smooth and even appearance. Keep trying—eventually it will all sort itself out.

If all went well, you should have a factory-fresh lower cushion by now. If you don't, however, fear not. There's one more trick you can use to work out the little, annoying wrinkles that can be almost impossible to avoid when you do this job. Set up a steamer by attaching a piece of heater hose to the mouth of a boiling kettle. By playing this steam over (and if possible under) the wrinkles you can soften the vinyl to the point where it will smooth out all by itself. While hot it'll seem too baggy, but when it cools and shrinks back it will retain its wrinkle-free appearance. A regular heat lamp will do the same job, but not quite as well as steam.

With a couple of minor variations, recovering the top cushions will be done the same way. One difference might be that before you can take the old seatcover off you'll have to remove a stiff plate from the back of the seat by pulling out some screws or blind push clips. Another is that due to the shape of the top cushions, it will be harder to fold the cover down to the bottom of the seat. Gluing some thin plastic sheets to the top half of the side bolsters will make the job a lot easier.

If you had to remove any handles or knobs that poked through the seats there's an easy way to recreate their holes in the new upholstery: simply tap smartly on top of the old mounting point with a rubber hammer. If this doesn't cut a perfectly shaped new hole it will at least give you a template to cut out with a utility knife.

There are a few more things you might keep in mind while putting on new seatcovers. For one, this is a perfect time to attend to other bits of related hardware. You should clean and polish the seat tracks, de-rust any fasteners that need it and polish any chrome handles or bezels that came off in the process. It's also a golden opportunity to repaint the metal or plastic seat side covers, which you might never get around to otherwise.

Also try to cut away any gross excess from the inner seams of the new covers before you slip them on. Some kits are meant to be glued into place as well as clipped, while others just clip in; follow closely the instructions included with the kit. And if you have to cut holes or flaps into the seatcover anywhere, try to make a rounded cutout instead of a single slit which could tear later. Finally, apply a very light coat of white lithium grease to the seat runners before bolting them back in.

Before you go to the trouble of installing new seatcovers, it might pay to go through the local junkyards and look for a complete set of seats that are already in good condition. (Your chances will be better if there's an enclosed version of your open car, like the MGB GT or the Triumph GT-6.) Finding a good set of used seats is sometimes easier than you might guess, but finding ones that exactly match those on your car is naturally a lot tougher. The pattern, shape and material of the seats in most cars changes frequently; making sure that the seats you buy are correct for your year and model of car is up to you. The judges will definitely care if your '70 Midget has '67 Sprite seats, but the back of your pants isn't likely to know the difference.

The color, of course, can be changed with dye if that's the only thing bothering you. (Dye might last only a few years, so you could be repeating the process every now and then.) When dealing with vinyl seats, beware: some spray dyes will eat into the surface of older vinyl. It can also be hard to change from a very dark color to a very light one, although the reverse is usually no problem. Test your dye in a hidden spot first, and if any problem arises you should go on to a different brand. You can also try using leather paint from a hobby shop if there's a problem with normal spray dye. With

leather, the chances are much more remote of finding decent seats at a junkyard; still, it's worth a look.

It's possible to re-dye leather seats as well as vinyl ones, and the results can be good. With leather, it's probably better to go with liquid dye instead of a spray; leather will soak up dye much more effectively than vinyl. A number of companies make excellent leather dyes for automotive applications, but finding just the right color can be difficult. If all else fails, you can send an unfaded swatch to the original manufacturer (most likely Connolly, in England) and they'll usually mix up some dye for a price.

To revive faded leather, liquid dye is wiped onto the seats and allowed to dry. After that, a few passes with hide food and a clean towel will put the seats in amazingly good shape. Changing colors with liquid dye will take quite a few more swipes to finish the job, and the color might not *ever* be correct. New types and colors of dyes are always coming onto the market, though, so ask your parts supplier for advice if there's any doubt as to what your best choice might be.

Cleaning Carpets

British carpeting can be pretty flimsy. A threadbare carpet can be considerably improved with a liberal coating of dye to at least make the color even overall, but it will never pass for new. You can also tidy things up cheaply by replacing any vinyl or

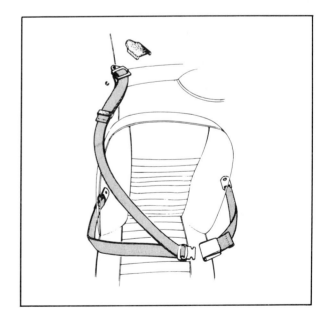

Good seatbelts are a must. Most older cars had lousy belts or none at all; replace them with later-style belts from the same manufacturer or aftermarket period pieces. Moss and other suppliers carry belts that won't get points marked off on a judging sheet. Moss Motors, Ltd.

leather edging that's come apart, which is a straightforward enough matter of cutting new edges and sewing them on with a needle and thread. Again, though, just edging old carpets won't cure what ails them—only replacement can do that.

First, though, a word about cleaning. If you're lucky enough to be starting with sound carpets, it's usually best to leave them in place for cleaning. The exception here is when they smell musty or mildewy; then the carpets should be taken up along with any padding or insulating material beneath them, and everything should be hung in the sun to dry. (While you're waiting, check the floorboards thoroughly for rust; chances are you'll find some.)

If the carpets and pads dry out and lose their musty odor, you can go ahead and clean them

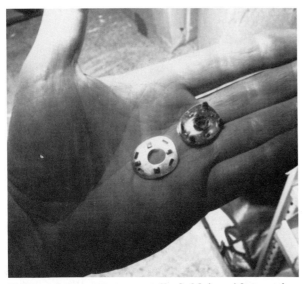

Tops and carpets are usually held in with two-piece clips like this one. The flat ring slips over the spikes, which are then folded over to hold the clip in place.

before putting them back in. If they retain the smell, though, it's best to chuck them and start all over. By this point the mildew will have seriously weakened the fibers and the carpets will fall apart soon—to say nothing of making your car smell like a locker room.

The first step is a thorough vacuuming. (You can pick up items such as dirt clods and pine needles with an old plastic brush beforehand, if needed.) I like using small rechargeable vacuums like the Black & Decker Dustbuster when just doing a routine cleaning, but for real dirt you're going to need a serious vacuum with a few different attachments. Get into every crack and crevice with a crevice attachment first, then use a small square head to clean up the flat surfaces. Don't forget to move the seats all the way forward and back to get everything out from under them, and don't neglect the parcel shelf or the vertical walls at the front of the footwells. It also doesn't hurt to rub the carpet with the palm of your hand to work grit up to the surface. Keep after it; even though it will seem like every pass of the vacuum raises another layer of dirt, sooner or later you'll reach the end. And while you're at it, don't forget to vacuum out any map pockets or console wells.

If you've bought yourself the average used car, a thorough vacuuming will take a fair amount of time and give you something less than stellar results, however. The next step is to go back in with regular household carpet shampoo and repeat the whole procedure. (Don't pour shampoo directly onto dirty rugs, or the liquid turns the dirt to mud and makes things worse than they were when you started.) Once you've rubbed the shampoo in and let it set, vacuum it out again and all the dirt should be removed. Any flaws beyond this point will call for dye.

Replacing a Carpet

It would seem that replacing an entire carpet would be a major task; well, it used to be just that. But these days almost every car has a pre-cut carpet kit available for it; while these cost quite a bit more than doing all the sewing and fitting yourself, they make the job so much easier that I'd opt for a full kit every time.

All kits, of course, are not created equal. A high-quality kit will include not only good, durable carpeting but also sewn vinyl or leather edges as original, well-cut and trimmed sections, pre-formed humps as needed, detailed instructions and all mounting hardware. Expensive carpet kits will also sometimes include things that the less-expensive ones leave out—extra sections for the doorsills or the trunk, perhaps. Factor that into the equation, and the price of a good kit is sometimes barely more than a cheaper set would have been. Besides, a cheaper kit is usually little more than a few pieces of black plastic carpeting cut out in roughly the same shape as the floor of the car. For that, you could have gone down to a carpet store, purchased a roll and cut your own panels using the old stuff as a template. (On a really rare car, of course, you might find yourself doing just that (coming up next!).

Probably the biggest tribulation of installing new carpets is getting them to conform to round sections like the transmission tunnel or wheel arches. Carpet in these areas is often just stuck down with adhesive, so trying to work the wrinkles out of it once any cement has dried is going to be frustrating to say the least. Cut out vee sections as needed and get the carpet formed up well before starting with the glue. Pre-formed sections make this job a hundred times easier, and the results will always be much better than if you tried to fit a flat carpet over a humped base. Pre-formed sections are usually made up on a steam-heated die; you can't do this at home, however.

Often even a high-quality kit will make some panels a little larger than necessary; the manufacturer wisely figures that it's better to have to cut the piece down than to discover it's too small later. Carpet can be cut with a sharp matte knife or heavy scissors, and the sort you get in kits almost always comes with a nonravel backing. If you're working with plain sheets of carpeting from a supplier, however, sometimes you'll have to coat the back in heavy glue before cutting or else the edges will start to unravel soon after you finish the job.

Installing new carpets from a kit is fairly easy. As you remove the old carpeting, of course, you should be taking notes on how it was mounted in the car. First, however, you'll have to remove some pieces of the interior just to get to the carpets. The seats will almost always have to come out, along with their runners. A center console, if it's there, will probably have to go, too. (Look for screws along the bottom edge, beneath the ashtray or console well, and around the shift boot. There will also probably be some blind clips or screws at the front where the console swoops up to meet the dashboard.) The bezel around the shift boot should be taken up, making this a good time to replace the inner and outer boots if they need it. And if the car has rear jumpseats, the bottom cushion might need to be removed before you can get to the last lip of the carpet. Back seats sometimes just screw into exposed tabs, but usually there's a springy steel wire along the bottom of the seat that pushes into clips on the floor. By gently pushing in on the bottom edge of the seat, you can free these clips and get the seat out—uncovering hundreds of old combs, french fries, coins and so on. Store the seats (and everything else) in a safe place.

Most carpets are held down with snaps or clips at the tops of the footwells, the rear bulkhead and some glue in a few hidden places. There's often a rubber beading holding things in place at the door-sills, too: these should come right up by levering a bit with a screwdriver and pulling the rest off by

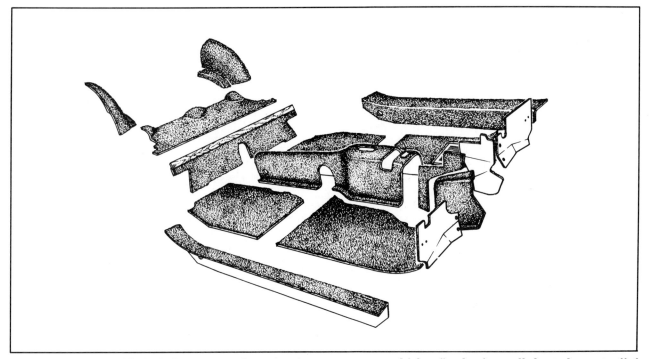

High-quality carpet kit includes pre-cut pieces, hardware, heat-formed panels and instructions. The price *may seem high at first but it usually beats the pants off of doing the job yourself.* Moss Motors, Ltd.

hand. All of these should be noted while the old rugs are coming out.

Carpets that have been glued into place will usually come up with just a bit of muscle power, but a flat putty knife often speeds things up considerably. If that doesn't do it, go in with some contact cement thinner, dabbed sparingly below the rug with a small paintbrush, to soften the glue. You can leave some of the old glue in place when putting down the new carpets, but big globs and fibers should be cleaned up with solvent before continuing.

Once the time comes to actually lay the new carpets, keep in mind that the nap of the rugs should all run the same way—that is, line up the material in a consistent pattern. Use the old carpets as templates to fit any mounting snaps in place. (Usually these are two-piece affairs where you push a spiky ring through the carpet and into a backing plate, then fold the spikes down to hold the two together.) If you don't have old carpets to use as a guide, lay the new carpets without fittings, mark where the snaps and clips should be with chalk and take the carpets back out to fit the hardware.

Hand-Cut Carpets

If a carpet kit *isn't* available for your car, you may want to make your own replacements.

The first order of business is to dig up the right carpeting in bulk. A local carpet supplier might not have what you're looking for—he'll mostly have household carpet and indoor-outdoor plastic. (I know, because my first MG came with Astroturf rugs—most unappetizing.) The weave, depth and weight of most household carpeting isn't close to the automotive grade, and usually comes without a nonravel backing. Check anyway to see if he at least carries auto carpeting. If he does, it should be cheaper than going to the next step.

The next step is getting bulk carpet from an auto parts source that specializes in interiors. Get the

---

Adding Interior Insulation

While the carpets are out of the car you should be considering your options for adding insulation. Most British cars pump considerable heat into the cockpit in this fashion, and though that's good in winter it stinks come summertime. (Holes in the firewall will also let in deadly fumes, so make sure that all those are sealed up before you even drive the thing.) Most also have some jute or padding below the carpet, but not enough to keep your feet from baking on a hot summer's day. The factory padding, of course, also does two other things: it makes the carpeting feel better, and cuts down on noise radiated into the cockpit.

The worst areas for heat leakage are the transmission tunnel, firewall and the floor above the exhaust pipe. Noise comes in more from the floorboards, through the back panel and the wheelwells. If the factory padding isn't giving you enough insulation, you can add more in a number of different ways. Ideally, there's a stock cold-weather insulation kit available for your car. Unfortunately, you'll often find that even that isn't good enough to do the job. If that's the case, you can do something about it yourself. Here are some suggestions:

The bargain-basement way to cut down on noise is common graveled roofing paper held down with lap cement. This is strictly a low-cost dodge—the stuff looks ridiculous and it's permanent; once you've tar papered the floor of the car, that's how it's going to stay. The cheap dodge for heat protection is a thin layer of household fiberglass insulation. Aluminum-backed fiberglass insulation beneath the carpeting is so simple to apply it sometimes even comes with its own glue-down backing. But fiberglass is relatively thick for the amount of protection it gives, it's

definitely not stock and ironically enough it's also very flammable. Finally, the cheapie method for adding both kinds of protection comes, as so many cheap things do, in a spray can. Regular old rubberized undercoating will do a fair job of insulating the car from heat and noise—assuming you don't mind the idea of spraying rubbery glop all over your interior.

A more proper solution is chewed rag, which is commonly found under the trade name Enduralator. This is a heavy mat made of chopped, compressed old pieces of cloth; it does a nice job of cutting down on both heat and noise at the same time. Chewed rag can be hard to come by, though—you'll probably have to get it at a professional bodyshop.

The best fix is also the most expensive: closed-cell foam. Much lighter than chewed rag, Celltite (the most common brand) is thin, easy to use and very clean—it doesn't disintegrate over time like chewed rag. Unfortunately, Celltite is neither cheap nor easy to find. Your best bet in locating some is either a rubber supplier or a bodyshop that specializes in trucks. Big rigs use yards and yards of the stuff.

Some auto supply shops also carry pre-cut insulating kits for specific cars, usually made of plastic-backed foam. This kind of material is often available pre-cut for doors as well, where it sits below the door panel and cuts down interior noise considerably.

Whatever you settle on, it's probably best not to actually fix it into place where you don't have to. (You might have to glue it to the transmission tunnel, or hold it into place with some self-tapping screws bedded in sealant.) That way you can always return the car to its stock, though noisier and hotter, form later.

---

authentic replacement, not something a lot nicer or crummier than the original. (Old advertisements and dealer handouts usually mention the OE [original equipment] carpet type.) Buy a fair amount of the stuff in case you make some mistakes in cutting. The supplier will be able to give you a good idea of how much your particular car will need.

Once your bulk carpet shows up and you're satisfied with its quality, take all the old carpeting out of the car (noting its location, hardware and trimming) and lay it flat on a large, clean surface. Use a matte knife to split open any seams or folds.

Bearing in mind that the nap of the new rugs should all run in the same direction, lay the old carpeting over the new and shuffle it around to figure out how you'll waste the least material in cutting out the new rugs. Chalk the outlines, put the old carpet to the side and cut away. Heavy scissors will usually do a better job than a matte knife. Try fitting the new carpets into the car before you recreate any seams, sew on edges or fit any fasteners—now is the time to make small corrections, not later. Once you're satisfied with the results, go ahead and finish them.

The difficult part will be recreating any preformed panels to cover complex curves—mainly the transmission tunnel. Sometimes this was done at the factory simply by veeing the carpet and sewing it back up to form an angle. That's easy enough to recreate; copy the vee and reattach the carpet in a sewn seam. To strengthen the seam, glue another piece of carpet behind the seam, back to back.

For heat-formed carpets you'll have to be trickier; in fact, you might want to let a professional do the work. A trusty upholstery shop can usually imitate heat-curved panels for an amount of money that's well spent to avoid the aggravation of doing it yourself. If you'd rather give it a shot at home, though, start by laying the new carpeting over the transmission tunnel at its widest point and hold it in place with a few globs of poster plastic—that sticky stuff that comes in a bar you tear into chunks. The carpeting has to be large enough to cover the floor a few inches on either side of the tallest point of the tunnel.

You'll probably have to do some serious veeing and even insert a triangular panel or two, but with lots of chalking, cutting, sewing and gluing you can get a transmission tunnel without puckers and obvious seams. If the car doesn't have a central console but one was optional for it, it may help to buy one if available—you can hide a lot of sewing and wrinkles underneath it.

Interior Metalwork

The older your car is, the more likely there's some exposed metal on the interior. Usually this metal is sprayed body color (which is troublesome, as we'll see), but occasionally it was painted black (making things a little easier for the restorer).

The trouble with body-color metal pieces is that they have to match the exterior color almost perfectly. I say almost perfectly because they can, in fact, be just a hair off; the result will be an illusion that the color looks a little different due to the different light inside the car. Get it more than a touch wrong, though, and the effect is just plain silly.

A not-quite-perfect match won't ever work, though, from one interior piece to the next. Freshly painted door tops will look ridiculous unless they're an *absolute* match with the painted dashboard or instrument panel. You can always give it a crack, but be ready to go on and paint everything else in the interior if the match isn't exact.

Like anything else in a restoration, painting the interior metal takes some planning. If the dash is just an extension of the cowl, you'll obviously be better off including it in a full body respray instead of trying to match one to the other. The dash vents, by the way, are easy to confuse on many cars; they must point toward the windshield if they're going to defrost it.

That brings up more problems: Do you then have to paint the instrument panel as well? What about the windshield pillars? There's no end to it, so think through how you want to proceed instead of just masking something off and going hog wild with the spray gun.

As the amount of work you plan for the car gets smaller, the bigger the job of painting interior metal gets. In other words, shooting the interior in the course of a ground-up rebuild is a dawdle—it barely slows you up. Shooting just one worn-through door, on the other hand, seems like it takes forever; you have to remove the window fuzzies, take the door panel off, mask the inside of the door or strip it out, and either mask the entire interior or take the doors off the car. One way to make things easier is to try painting with an artist's airbrush instead of a spray gun or spray can. This cuts down on overspray and makes the masking less critical, though you should still cover and protect everything in case there's an accident.

More difficult than door tops are body-color instrument panels. You'll have to remove the wheel, mask the steering column and pull out all the gauges and switches. The latter job is usually the biggest pain—labeling and unhooking all the wires is work enough, but just getting the gauges themselves out can be a major task. Most of the time the gauge is held in by a metal bar across the back that's secured with knurled nuts, but as the car gets newer the mounting methods become more and more complex. Switches are usually held in place by screw-on bezels, but the knob itself is fixed by a setscrew or locking pin.

Sometimes you can get away with loosening the gauges, removing the bezels—usually by rotating them a quarter turn and pulling—and pushing everything back behind the dash. Cover the gauges and switches with plastic bags, mask the backside of the instrument panel well, drape masking paper from the bottom of the panel to the floor and go to it. Bear in mind that you can break the gauges or wires this way if they're not supported from behind, and disconnect the battery before doing any work behind the dash. This method is riskier than complete removal, but often much faster and easier.

Aside from getting a clear shot at the parts, painting interior metal isn't much different from exterior metal. You should still make sure the surface is completely clean, you still need to deal properly with any rust you find and you'll still be smoothing out the old coat before spraying. You'll also need to strip any panels that have been worn through all the way down to bare metal—trying to feather an edge on something as confined as an interior panel is more trouble than it's worth. Since the interior isn't exposed to the elements like the exterior, you can usually get away with one coat of primer-surfacer and two coats of color.

Make sure you don't get chemical stripper on interior parts; in fact, you might want to just sand through the paint instead of stripping it. Use only fine wet-dry paper once the paint is broken through; you won't be building up a large enough number of primer and paint coats to hide larger scratches.

Respraying interior panels that came in black is a little easier since it saves the trouble of matching the paint to the body color—everything else is going to be just as difficult. Scratches and nicks in a black crackle finish present their own problems; a simple touchup won't do here. The only real choice is to strip down the whole panel to bare metal and apply a new coat of crackle black. (Crackle finishes are available in cans from most parts supply houses.) You might even be unlucky enough to face the problem of *both* finishes on one surface—early Spitfires, for example, used a crackle-black center panel mounted in a body-colored instrument panel. Thank you, Triumph!

Refinishing Wooden Panels

In every magazine article I've ever read about a new Jaguar, the author swoons over the car's real wood paneling. Why does Oldsmobile save maybe ten bucks by using fake wood in their cars? Buyers would happily cough up the ten-spot and Olds might stop getting beaten up by the magazines.

Fortunately, the wood on most English sports cars started its life in a tree instead of an oil well. Okay, maybe it went through sixteen different laminating and patching machines before it saw a car, but at some point it was growing in the ground.

Real wood panels are elegant, surprisingly resilient and, best of all for us, relatively straightforward to restore. Woodesque plastic is actually much harder to set right; make sure you know what material you're dealing with before doing anything. You might even find that your "wood" dash is really a photo-printed piece of metal. Some cars use real wood for most of the panels and fake wood for some smaller items, so check it all out thoroughly. The best way to tell the difference is to get to the back of the panel—it will be obvious whether it's wood, plastic or metal by what the backside looks like.

Real wood—whether smoothly polished or rough and open-grained—can suffer from a number of ills. If the woodwork, veneer and varnish are basically sound it's probably best to just clean the panels with a commercial solution made for fine furniture and to wax it with carnauba. This will rarely bring the wood up to a mirror finish, but some people like the look of time-worn wood in an older car. It's an element that ages gracefully and reminds you of the car's long and honorable service.

Perhaps the most common of the more serious problems is delamination; much of the wood used on auto interiors is just plywood with an attractive top sheet called a veneer glued on. Either the veneer or, less frequently, the entire set of layers starts coming apart from the effects of sunlight, water and pollution. Panels can usually be relaminated by applying clear waterproof wood glue between the sandwich layers and clamping the laminate together again. Protect the outer surface of the panel with a piece of plastic, some foam rubber and a backing board. If that doesn't work, a new panel will have to be made or found.

If the laminate is warped beyond the restorer's ability to screw it down flat again, steam can be used to soften the entire panel and then a heavy weight can press it down flat to dry. This probably *causes* delamination more often than it straightens the panel, but at this point you've got nothing to lose.

The varnish on the top of the wood can also flake off or just look shabby; there can be stains from oil and water that have soaked into the surface, and there can be physical damage like nicks, dents and burns in the wood face itself. All of these things can be repaired with varying amounts of difficulty— the question is whether you want to repair it at all or simply replace the whole panel. As we go along we'll talk about setting these things right, but for now let's concentrate on replacement.

The simplest method of fixing up real wood is to just buy a finished panel from a parts source and slap it on in place of the old one. These aftermarket panels vary in quality from the passable to the excellent, and the price is usually commensurate with the work. Replacement is the most time-effective method and, naturally, the most costly.

(Besides, by the time you've completed a frame-up restoration you could practically have grown, sawed and milled your own walnut burl; what's the rush?) But even aside from saving you some bucks, woodwork is worth doing yourself—because it's a lot of fun.

The most radical do-it-yourself solution for badly beat-up paneling is to cut new panels and varnish them yourself. Strangely enough, this can be the quick and easy method too, at least compared to stripping, repairing and revarnishing the original piece. Assuming the panel you're working on is merely a flat piece with a few holes and angles cut into it, the hardest part of the job will be finding a suitable piece of wood to work with. Luigi's Lawn, Liquor 'n' Lumber probably won't have a good solid panel or the right veneers for the job; try a local supplier of furniture materials instead. A router and a jigsaw should be all you need to cut the panel to size.

Since most wood panels are veneered, often all you need to find is that thin top layer in the right pattern—what goes beneath it can be just a piece of marine plywood. (You're certainly welcome to use a solid piece of high-quality burl, teak or what-have-you to replace a laminate, but it'll cost a lot

By the end of its run, the Austin-Healey picked up some gorgeous expanses of real wood paneling. Elegant as they are, these wood faces provide the home restorer with a whole new set of skills to be learned in their repair.
Robin O'Brien

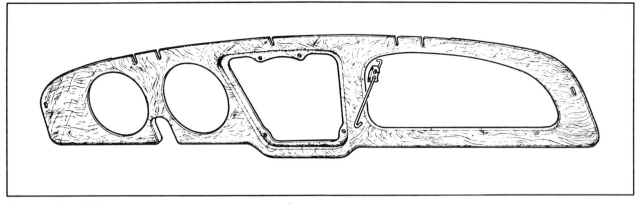

Flat wooden dashes are easy to remove, easy to repair and recreate, and very elegant. Don't skimp on this area. Moss Motors, Ltd.

more. Many older cars did, however, use solid panels—replace these with solid wood for authenticity's sake.) Curved panels or parquet-like sections, as often found along the tops of doors, will be considerably harder to recreate at home; here a replacement is usually much easier than a repair unless just the varnish needs work.

The other concern when cutting your own panels, or installing new ones that have been made somewhere else, is matching them to the rest of the interior. If the only wood in the car is the instrument panel this isn't such a big deal, but you can still get into trouble. Show judges absolutely love to point out incorrect grain and finish, to the point where you have to wonder if they're actually closet druids. Still, they often have a point—deep walnut burl on a 1952 MG TD simply isn't right; the car came with rather cheesy wood from the factory, and that's the way it should be restored.

Refinishing Existing Wood

It's almost impossible to refinish wood in place without causing more damage to the surrounding panels, so take all the wood out of the car and work it over on the bench. And I do mean *all* the wood—

a newly finished panel will make any untouched pieces glaringly obvious.

The first step is to strip off the old varnish. Some people say you can do this dry, but chances are you'll damage the veneer. I'd recommend instead using a water-based stripper to lift the varnish off chemically. There are commercial strippers designed for wood that fit the bill here, and other general-purpose strippers that are safe to use. Harsh solvent-based strippers will discolor the wood beyond repair, though, so choose something very gentle and be prepared to apply two or three coats. Lay the stripper on, let the varnish soften, gently remove it with a brush, rinse the panel and lay on the next coat of stripper.

Once the old varnish is off you'll probably find that the grain has swollen a bit and some of the pores have opened up. Lightly sand the grain smooth again with very fine garnet paper and the new varnish will fill in the pores.

On solid wood panels, small scratches and dents can sometimes be sanded smooth and feathered out to match everything else. You can also raise the dented area with a little steam from a kettle.

The alternatives are to put a new veneer on the entire piece or to try and hide the flaw with wood dough or a similar filler. If using a filler, it's important that the dough, the coloring medium and the final varnish will all work together with the wood. Get all three at the same time or one might react badly with another. Depending on your filler, match it to the color of the wood before or after it's been stained—some fillers take stain and others do not.

With damaged veneers more drastic methods are called for. Many people have had good luck with patching veneer, cutting out a small section around the flaw and gluing in a well-matched replacement piece. By cutting the patch in an elongated diamond shape and rounding off the edges, they say, an almost undetectable repair can be

Repairing Wood Splits

Splits, usually caused by a screw hole or a dent, are almost impossible to set completely right. The prescribed method is to run some clear waterproof glue into the split and then clamp the edges together. This doesn't usually do the trick, but a line of wood dough and some good sanding work might make an acceptable join in the end.

An alternative method is to rough out a vee in the area of the glued split and insert a matching wedge of veneer; finding a match is the hardest part of doing it this way.

made. The trick here seems to be that the patch will never look quite right unless the cuts run mostly in the direction of the grain.

Well, maybe other people can do this, but I can't. Whenever I've tried dropping in a new veneer section the patch looks terrible; the grain never matches, the color is usually just a hair off, and the seams are glaringly obvious no matter how well I've tried to match and shape the patch.

Dropping on a whole new veneer might give you more satisfactory results, but of course it's going to take a little longer. This is a great repair, though, for an instrument panel that some yokel cut a hole in for an aftermarket switch or gauge. Remove the old veneer with a thin-bladed putty knife and fill the offending hole with a glued-in wooden plug. Sand everything level with medium-grit dry paper before proceeding.

With the old veneer off, coat the base panel with resin glue or a nonstaining waterproof adhesive like Elmer's. Then lay on the new veneer uncut, making sure that the grain runs in the right direction and is reasonably horizontal.

Next make a sandwich around the panel with a sheet of plastic over the veneer, some stiff foam rubber over that and a sheet of wood on top. Clamp the whole thing together and let it dry overnight. When it's set, trim the excess veneer to within a few millimeters of the proper dimensions with a very sharp X-acto knife (there are also tiny hand saws made for this). Finish off the edges with a sanding block, sanding from the face of the panel down; otherwise, the veneer might lift off and ruin the whole job.

Putting a new veneer on the dashboard is a relatively simple way to repair major damage, and it has another big advantage: If you correctly cut out new faces for the glovebox and ashtray door, the grain will match and line up perfectly on those pieces. Stain and varnish the veneer as you would a solid piece of wood—all that's coming up momentarily.

Applying Wood Stains and Varnish

Mass-produced wood panels were rarely darkened by stain; usually their deep color came from a tint in the outer varnish itself. When you strip this varnish off you often find that the wood isn't an even color all the way across the panel. What's happened?

The wood itself might *never* have been a uniform color; its variations could have been hidden at the factory by blotching on lighter and darker varnishes. It's also possible that areas of the wood that lost their varnish early on will have faded much more quickly than those which kept their protective dark coating, resulting in a patchy, scuzzy panel. Alternatively, a previous owner might have

dabbed wood stain onto the panel where the varnish wore off. If this happened, when the varnish comes off the spots that were stained will remain dark.

No matter what the cause of multicolored wood might be, setting it right is simple if the variations aren't very pronounced. Usually one good dose of wood stain will bring everything back to a nice, even color; by using a clear varnish instead of a dark one, you can then get the original color back on the panel.

Really dark areas, though, should be bleached before staining. I've had good luck using nothing more than a very dilute solution of household bleach and water, thoroughly rinsed off when finished, of course. There are also commercial wood bleaches on the market you can try, most of them using some sort of acid as the bleaching agent. These, too, should be thoroughly removed before going on to the next step; water-based bleaches are much safer to use than solvent-based ones.

Once you've done all the work—if any was needed—to the wooden panel it's time to apply the varnish. This is going to take awhile, but it's as easy as laying on paint with a brush. Varnished panels can take quite some time to dry, so I like to find a box that will fit over the piece and keep dust off it while it sits and hardens. It will be days before some of the coats have set enough to be worked on.

Assuming you decided to stain the wood rather than rely on darkened varnish for color, I'd start with a clear polyurethane—as opposed to oil-based—varnish that's been cut down fifty percent with the manufacturer's specified thinner. That way the varnish will soak into the wood instead of pooling on top of it, and it will run smooth right off the brush. (You can try a spray varnish if you like, but I've always had fine results from the brush-on type when suitably thinned.)

If you haven't stained the wood, though, go to a tinted varnish to achieve the right color. Even if the wood is supposed to be blond, a little yellowish tint is needed to make the panel look like it came from a car factory instead of a lumber store.

You'll have to apply several coats with thinned varnish; at first it seems like the wood just drinks the stuff. But that's what you want—to lay on a deep, protective coat instead of a cosmetic one across the surface. After letting each coat dry, slap on another one. Eventually the pores and grains will clog and the varnish will lie on top of the wood instead of soaking into it. If the panel is supposed to be rough-grained, one more coat of varnish after the pores first clog should bring it to the finish point. Let the panel dry and fit it back on the car.

If it's a mirror-smooth surface you're after, though, don't stop varnishing until the last coat sits up on top of the wood. Then let it rest for a few days—go off and do something else.

When you come back later the varnish will be completely set up and ready for the next step. Go over the panel with very fine garnet paper (you can find it in woodworking supply stores) and remove the varnish from the very top of the wood. Once you've got a surface of good hard grain and completely clogged pores, you're ready to lay on the coats that will build up that mirror-smooth surface.

This time you'll be using thicker varnish—thin it down just enough so that the brush marks flow out, anywhere from about one-third thinner to no thinner at all. Lay on about a half-dozen coats of varnish, letting each one dry in between, and let the finished piece rest for at least another few days. The varnish won't harden completely for a couple of weeks, but it will usually be workable after three days.

When you go back to do the final polishing, start with very fine garnet paper again. This time, though, break the grit down a little by tearing the paper in half and rubbing the two pieces together. Now sand out the flaws, brush marks and dust until you have a smooth, cloudy surface—don't cut all the way through the varnish layers, of course.

If you used a polyurethane varnish you'll be able to polish and wax the wooden panel just as you would the paint on the car: start with polishing compound and finish off with a generous coating of carnauba wax. The results are quite surprising; you're likely to be smirking with self-satisfaction for days.

Artificial Woodgrain

There's always a chance that your interior wood isn't really wood at all. A few English manufacturers used woodgrain-printed contact sheets over plastic instead. Often called Di-Noc, the trade name of 3M's most famous type, this contact sheet has a nasty habit of scabbing off and tearing after a few years in the sun.

In theory Di-Noc-covered panels are easy to restore—just strip off the old stuff with contact cement thinner and lay on a new sheet. In practice, though, there are a number of problems; the first is finding the proper replacement sheets. You'd think that nobody would have bothered to make up more than five or six different imitation wood patterns, but it turns out there are probably more fake woodgrains in this world than real ones. You can

Many Austin-Healeys had simple painted dashboards instead of wood- or fabric-covered ones, making restoration straightforward and easy. The metal dash here was disassembled and then stripped, primed and repainted. Robin O'Brien

try your parts source, a furniture builder, a paint store or a plastics store to find a good selection of imitation wood contact sheets. The trouble is that even if you find the right pattern, the covering itself will probably be wrong—most of them are too thick and papery to be stretched over an automotive panel. The proper type of covering is a thin, strong, flexible plastic, and it should stick like glue once it's laid down. Regular contact paper will come off in no time flat.

Your best shot is to try to find a similar wood pattern on the side of an American station wagon or minivan. Measure the various panels on this car to make sure that one continuous piece will be long enough to do your job, and then try to weasel just that one section out of the local dealer. They'll usually try to sell you a whole car's worth, which is a waste of money unless you want the world's only TR4 Woody—it might be all you can get, though. Your friendly neighborhood bodyman might also be able to point you in the right direction if you strike out at the Ford dealer.

Another potential problem with plastic wood coverings is getting them to stick on complex surfaces. A flat panel should be no trouble, though you might have to vee a few corners. But compound curves and humps can be a bear to cover; warming the backing metal and the plastic with an infrared heat gun will help soften things up considerably.

Finally, to protect the new plastic from tears and smudges, it's a good idea to lay on a protective clear coat over the top. Clear plastic paint or wood varnish will usually do the job, but try it out on a scrap first to make sure it won't curl the plastic.

Rarer than Di-Noc is a woodgrain finish that's printed directly onto a wood-colored base, and it's a good thing this is rare, because it's virtually impossible for the do-it-yourselfer to restore. There are a few alchemists out there who can sand down the panel, lay on a new brown base and replicate the wood pattern painstakingly by hand. But this is a hard thing to master, and most of us never would. It's better to pay a professional to do the job for you or to find a replacement panel in better condition.

Gauge Repair

Most gauges are electric, but speedometer-odometers, some temperature and pressure gauges, and some tachometers work on simple mechanical principles. (The mechanical gizmos will be covered here; electric gauges are covered in chapter 7.)

Now mind you, to work on a simple mechanical principle and to be a simple piece of mechanics are two very different things. There's plenty to go

With gauges and steering wheel back in place, the Austin-Healey dash looks sharp in a dark blue paint.
Robin O'Brien

Good used gauges are fairly easy to find—they seem to be one part people never throw away. Most British gauge bezels and lenses are held in by tangs. Just rotate the bezel a quarter turn, line up the tangs and lift the bezel and lens off.

wrong, and English gauges seem to explore the possibilities—Smiths and Lucas have pushed the outside of the gauge-failure envelope since Day One.

My first MGB had chronic speedometer ailments. I now know that the problem with my speedometer had nothing to do with the gauge itself—the trouble was that the flexible cable running up from the gearbox was kinked. The symptoms were typical; the needle wavered back and forth between 40 and 90 mph while I was going down the road at 55.

To make matters worse, I lubed the dickens out of that cable and the graphite eventually fouled the gauge proper. The correct thing to do would have been to make sure that cable was snug and intact at both ends (it fits onto a drive gear at the bottom of the transmission and another at the back of the gauge) and that it wasn't kinked or bent. If that didn't solve the problem, I should have checked the cable for stretching by measuring the amount of cable coming out of the sheaf against the figures in the shop manual and stripped it out of the sheaf to look for breaks and bends. If the cable checked out, *then* I should have moved on to the less likely chance that the speedometer itself was bad.

Short of replacing an obviously busted piece, about the only repair do-it-yourselfers should undertake on a speedo is simple cleaning and re-oiling. If the works of the speedo seem to be gummed up, suspend them for a while in alcohol to dissolve the gunk, drain them well and finish them off with some aerosol hi-fi switch cleaner. (Only do this when the gauge face and the odometer wheel can be removed or protected from the chemicals.) Re-lubing should be done with just the lightest dab of clock or switch oil dripped off the end of a

Dirty bezel and lens will clean up easily and make this MGB tachometer look like new. Spin the bezel around to free up the tangs, shine up the chrome with wax or chrome cleaner and the lens with Glasswax.

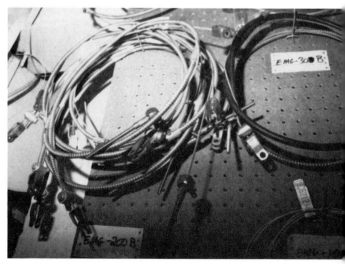

Metal sheathing makes control cables tough, but also lets them act as a ground wire if the battery strap goes bad. That can lead to fires and burnt wiring.

toothpick—anything more will simply gum up the parts again.

If cleaning the instrument and checking out the cable don't cure the problem, I'd say it's best to replace the speedometer. On really rare cars you can have a specialist look into it instead, but junkyard speedos are too cheap to pass up and they usually work fine. Drop in used gauges whole or transfer their guts to your own better-looking faces and housings.

Somewhere on the speedometer there will be a four-figure number starting with 1: that's the number of cable revolutions for every mile racked up by the odometer, or TPM (turns per mile). Matching the TPM to your old speedo will ensure that the gauge remains accurate; if the donor car came with a different set of transmission gears, a different rear end or even different wheels the odometer and speedometer won't read correctly. If you can live with that, fine; if not, these figures have to be found and checked.

If you want to change the odometer reading of your new speedometer to match that of your old one you might find the job trickier than it looks. (Rolling back an odometer just to lower the perceived mileage of a car is, aside from being dishonest, highly illegal.) Disassembling a junk speedo like your own will show you how to approach the problem, though you'll probably break the odometer in the process. You might find, however, that the odometer has some sort of security system to prevent tampered-with odometer wheels from ever lining up quite right again. If the proper odometer readings are important to you, it might be better to send out your original gauge for fixing instead of mucking around with the odometer of a replacement.

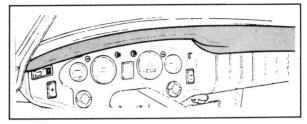

Fast and cheap fix for cracked dash is a pre-made plastic cap that fits over the top. These will never look quite right, but they're a real improvement for the time being. Getting a whole padded dash out and replacing it is a big job but the only correct fix. Moss Motors, Ltd.

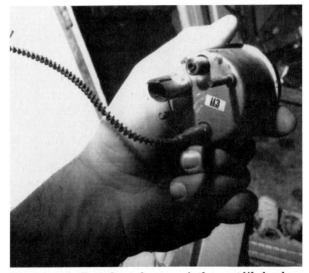

The joint of a Bourdon tube gauge is the most likely place to find a problem. The first sign of trouble is a fluctuating or broken gauge; after that, oil starts running down the back of the dashboard and onto your carpets. Chase down problems in oil pressure and similar gauges before they get out of hand and ruin something else.

What looks like big trouble on this dash pad isn't. The covering is soft leather, not rigid plastic as on later dashboards. The whole pad can be removed (there are fasteners behind the dash) and recovered at home.

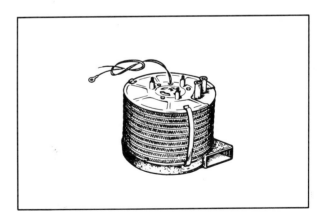

The basic heater core is like a miniature radiator. Flush it out whenever you remove it from the car and check the fins well for leaks. You can usually detect a leaking core by the smell of antifreeze in the interior. Moss Motors, Ltd.

107

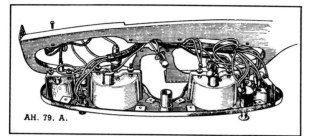

Bless Donald Healey's soul. The early Austin-Healey dashboard merely flops forward—granted, you've got to pull some recalcitrant screws to get there first—as a unit to make repairs and adjustments a snap. Anyone who's ever worked behind the rigid dash of most later sports cars will appreciate the wisdom of the design.

Mechanically driven tachs—a rare item except on very old cars—can fall victim to the same ills as speedometers. Generally those are a bad drive cable, a bad cable head at one end or a mucked-up set of works. It's also possible that the tach is getting the wrong information from its drive source, particularly if it's driven off the generator. Check for a slipping drive belt, a nonstock pulley or an incorrect drive gear.

The other type of mechanical gauges, pressure and temperature units, work on the Bourdon tube principle. The Bourdon tube is basically a flattened, flexible tube bent into something of a banana shape. As pressure increases in the tube it tries to straighten out, and that's what moves the indicator in the gauge.

A mechanical oil pressure gauge merely connects the Bourdon tube inside the gauge to a pressurized part of the oiling system through a long (usually copper) tube. Mechanical temperature

gauges work a little differently, the system being closed instead of open. At the engine side, a bulb filled with ether sits in the appropriate engine fluid. As the fluid heats up the ether boils and expands, raising pressure inside the Bourdon tube and straightening it.

Both types of gauges are susceptible to a few maladies. The Bourdon tube itself is remarkably tough—I've never seen one break. But the feed line from the engine to the gauge often develops cracks or loose fittings that let the ether or oil leak out and render the gauge useless. On oil pressure gauges, simply solder up the leak or fix the fitting and the gauge should work again. On temperature gauges, you're pretty much stuck. Most people can't lay their hands on a few ounces of ether at a moment's notice, and that's just as well. Ether, on top of being able to knock you out cold while you work with it, is positively explosive if the fumes come into contact with flames or a red-hot burner. And since you need to boil the sensing tube to get the new ether in, I'd say forget the whole thing—spend the money for another gauge instead of burning down your house.

Cosmetic repairs on gauges may or may not be easy. It can make a world of difference to just take the bezel and lens off the gauge and clean them up. Chrome bezels will respond to chrome polish; the lenses will clean up with Glasswax. Separate the two before cleaning or you'll get a slimy ridge of wax that has to be removed with cotton swabs. Plastic lenses will respond nicely to motorcycle visor polish.

The faces can be harder to resurrect. The easiest thing will be to pirate new faces off of some salvaged gauges. Rare gauges can present you with a real problem, but you might be able to find replacement face decals from your parts source—just stick the new decal over the old face and you're home free. If you can con someone into letting you borrow a good gauge from their car, it's also possible to make a full-size black-and-white photo of the good gauge's face and fit it into your own unit. You'll have to have the printer dodge out the needle in the darkroom. You might even have to recreate the faces by hand. Transfer type by Letraset or a similar manufacturer will help.

Door Panels

The door panels seem to be the first thing to go on a lot of cars. People kick them open, the backing cracks, the armrests get tired, the trim disappears, and water drips down the window channel and the whole door rots like an old banana. No matter what the cause, you can expect door panels to be on your "things to do" list.

How does the panel come off? If some thriving culture of mold has made its home inside the door panel, you can usually rip it off like wet newspaper.

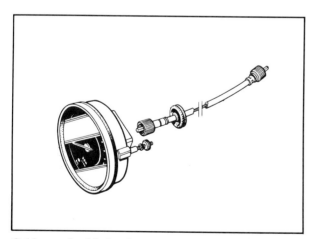

Cables and cable heads are more likely to go bad than mechanical tachometers and speedometers themselves. Make absolutely sure that the problem doesn't lie in those places before replacing the more costly gauge unit. Moss Motors, Ltd.

If things aren't that bad, though, you might have trouble figuring out where to start. On old cars it's simply a matter of removing the chrome-capped screws around the edge of the door, but newer cars don't make it so easy.

Even getting the window cranks and door pulls off can be a trick. Sometimes they're just held in by a setscrew, but more often than not there's a devilish circlip holding the thing in place. It works like this: A splined rod passes from inside the door through the panel. There's a groove cut around the end of this rod, and two corresponding channels cut into the back of the door handle or window crank that fits over it. The handle goes on the rod, then a circlip is snapped over it so that little tangs rest in the two channels and pinch into the groove. To make absolutely certain you can't remove the window crank without a special tool, most cars have a spring-loaded plate between the crank and the door panel that covers up the circlip.

There's no satisfactory way around these things other than getting the proper removing tool. This is a piece of flat steel that's been cut out to just the right size to push the circlip back off. The handle then falls off or, powered by the backing spring, rockets across the garage and disappears behind the water heater.

A twist on this theme is a retaining pin that slides through a hole in the handle and rod and is held in place by a spring-loaded escutcheon similar to the one already mentioned. This one is actually a little easier to remove—a helper can use two flat screwdrivers to hold the escutcheon back while you simply drive the pin out with a very small drift. Occasionally these pins are tapered, so you may have to go at it in both directions before getting it out of the hole.

The same door panels that feature these diabolical handles usually also use hidden clips to hold the panel to the door frame. These are simply press-fit at the factory, and a little leverage with a large, flat screwdriver should snap them back out. Gently slide the screwdriver between the door frame and panel, then move it along until it meets a barrier—that's the first clip. Lever it up and keep repeating the process. If the backing panel is old or rotten, of

The Banjo-style steering wheels of many of the earlier British sports cars—including this Austin-Healey—are very stylish and very difficult to restore. Epoxy can be used to fill in cracks in the rim, sanded over and then painted. If further restoration is needed, you may be better off looking for another steering wheel or hiring the job out to a pro. Robin O'Brien

course, it's just as likely that the clip will stay in place and you'll break through the panel instead. There's little you can do about it beyond being as careful as possible and using a special clip-removing tool instead of a screwdriver—your parts supplier will point one out for your car. If you're cutting a whole new door panel, it's no big deal if the clip breaks through the panel. If not, you may have to replace the clip in a stronger part of the backing panel and drill a new hole to fit it in the door frame. Don't forget to coat the new hole with a good coat of paint before putting everything back together again.

Often the armrest screws into the panel and then into the door frame itself—you'll have to remove that to get the whole assembly off. Other times there's a padded section at the top of the door that comes off first by removing the screws at either end. This, incidentally, can be removed and recovered all by itself if it's the only thing ailing the door panel.

Just the sort of door panel a do-it-yourselfer loves. The top rail and the panel itself were recovered in no time flat using the original backings and fixtures. You won't find many simpler jobs.

Once the panel is removed you can take stock of what you have. If the backing itself is sound, you'll just have to recover it with new vinyl or leather held on from behind with adhesive and/or staples. On the simplest cars, those with a door panel that's basically a covered piece of wood, this is a breeze.

Most of the time, however, the backing itself will also have to be replaced. You can go to the same compressed cardboard material the panel was originally made from, or a thin sheet of marine plywood. Plywood is a lot stronger than cardboard and should last considerably longer, but make sure the added thickness won't keep the door from closing properly. You might need slightly larger clips and screws as well.

Recovering Door Panels

The easiest upholstering job in the world is recovering a simple door panel like the one on classic Allards and Aston Martins. These are merely covered and padded pieces of wood with a few screw holes drilled into them. The procedure is as follows.

Remove the panel from the car. Lift the cover from the backing by pulling up its adhesive and/or staples. Peel it off the backing board and if it is sound, save it for later. If not, trace it out and recreate it in stiff card or marine plywood. Don't forget to re-drill any mounting holes *precisely*. If clips are used to hold the panel in, you'll need to drill two holes: one big enough to fit the head of the clip through and a smaller, adjacent hole to hold the clip in place.

Next, trace out the backing panel on the backside of your new covering and cut out the pattern leaving a few extra inches all around. To add a nice, puffy surface to the finished panel, add a layer of upholsterer's linting between the covering and the backing board. Cut it exactly to the size of the board. Then lay the covering face down (on a

Occasionally a door panel will be made in two distinct sections: an inner assembly is fixed inside the frame and then an outer panel covers the rest of the door.

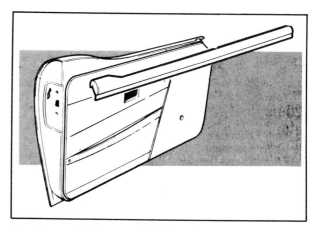

Topping rail takes most of the abuse on many door panels. They're easy to replace and repair. Moss Motors Ltd.

smooth and clean surface preferably protected by towels) and fold it over the edges of the backing board. You'll probably have to cut some vee sections out around the corners to make the covering lie flat; only cut them to within about ½ in. of the outer edge.

Fix the covering to the back of the board with contact cement and staples. Start in the middle of a straight section first and work to the corners, making sure to pull the covering tight enough to prevent any wrinkles but not so much that it stretches unduly. Repeat the procedure on the opposite edge of the board, move on to the other edges and attack the corners last. At the corners, secure the middle and then work out to either side, veeing the material as needed.

Using a *very* sharp awl, poke through the screw holes from behind. (A word of caution—not all the holes in the door panels necessarily had screws in them originally. Here's where cross-checking with the old panel can save you some heartache.) Alternatively, fit the new clips into place as needed and remount the panel.

Of course, it's never quite that easy. Even the simplest panels usually have some piping around the edges. Okay, buy enough piping (from an automotive interior supply house, a parts store or a regular upholstery shop) to go all the way around the door panel and staple it into place over the folded lip of the new door covering. (All the staples used in securing door panel material and trim must, of course, be short enough not to poke through the other side of the repair. Apply them with a staple gun.)

But let's say, just for the sake of argument, that you *don't* happen to be driving a 1925 Bentley—not that it wouldn't be nice. Cars of the 1940s and later usually have a large opening in the middle of the door panel that's a combination storage pocket and grab-chain recess. (Grab chains, for those of you who've never used one, simply mount at the far end of the door on one side and the door opening mechanism on the other.) To deal with this kind of opening mount the cover first and deal with the cutouts later; otherwise the covering might tear in the middle while you're doing the initial stretching.

Open up the area covering the hole with a pass of a matte knife, and then carefully cut back in straight lines to the corners of the opening. Here, too, you want to cut only far enough to leave the slit about ½ in. behind the folded-over finished product.

Simple storage bins behind the door panel can be recreated using heavy card stock folded and glued together. Cover this box with felt flocking and staple it to the back of the door panel. More complicated boxes can be repaired with new flocking or purchased as reproductions.

As the cars get newer and the door panels

Except for moisture-induced waves at the bottom, this door panel is okay. Since it's embossed plastic and would have to be replaced instead of re-covered, it's worth trying to fix the waves down to the frame with additional blind clip or even hidden zip-ties, then leaving it be.

become more and more complicated, the sewing and fiddling needed to recreate them becomes a bigger job. To make seams and pockets across the panel itself you're going to need a good sewing machine—one strong enough to go through a few layers of vinyl or leather. Many home sewing machines can't do it, so look for an industrial-strength machine in the local want ads or buy an obsolete one from an upholsterer or drapery shop. There are a surprising number of them sitting around gathering dust. Sometimes they've been retired because the needles and thread are no longer available, though, so look into that before you make out a check.

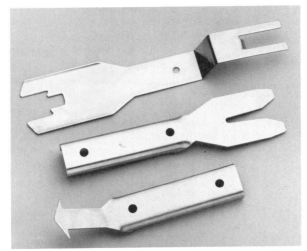

Some life-saving door panel tools. From top: handle cir-clip remover, door clip lifter, chrome trim remover. The Eastwood Company

111

The open center of this panel shouldn't slow you down much. Just stretch the new covering on as before and slit open the cutout afterward. The cuts must stop at least ½ in. from the edge of the opening, or they'll show when the material is folded and fixed to the back of the panel.

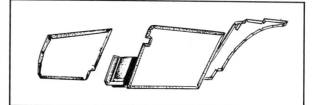

The rear of a rigid panel that has received a home recovering might look a little rough, but who cares? It's hidden completely once the panel is back on the car; just make sure you cut plenty of vees into the new cover so the front surface looks good. Moss Motors, Ltd.

No matter how complicated a sewn door panel gets, the procedure for recreating them from scratch will still be the same; use the old one for a template, cut open any seams to see how it all fits together and go to it. You might find that some of the more complicated pieces aren't worth doing yourself. A local upholsterer can make up elasticized pockets and the like for so little money that you'd be silly to sew your fingers together trying to do it on your own.

On many later sports cars it's simply impossible to recreate a door panel from scratch; heat- or electrically-embossed plastic panels will just have to be replaced with recreations, NOS or junkyard parts. You can always try, of course, to recreate the embossed pattern with real stitching and vinyl or leather. The result will probably be of higher quality than the original, but it won't be stock.

Embossed plastic door panels usually have another feature that's impossible for the do-it-yourself restorer to repair: vacuum-chromed plastic trim. The chrome often comes off these strips over time, leaving the exposed plastic in glaring white or (why do they *do* this?) electric blue. The only practical remedy here is replacement, though if no replacement parts are available there are mail-order houses which specialize in rechroming plastic pieces.

Some other things in the interior simply aren't worth fixing—it's better to replace them outright. At the top of this list should be rigid-plastic covered parts made from stiff foam, like many armrests and dashboards. On these pieces, a plastic covering that's more brittle than flexible is fixed directly to the foam backing. When the covering splits or falls off, the piece is reduced to junk—you can't separate the covering without destroying the foam below, and even if you could it's not likely you'd be able to reproduce the complex curves in regular

vinyl or leather. There are kits of all sorts that are supposed to repair cracked dashboards and the like, but I have yet to find one that works. Usually you slop on some liquid goo much as you would when repairing a regular tear in vinyl, and iron on a patterned finish to set up the repair. The trouble is, the repair rarely lasts more than a month or two before it splits wide open again.

An alternative would be to glue in a piece of matching vinyl; even if the repair lasts, though, the chances of making it invisible are slim. Fortunately, it costs the manufacturer a fair amount of money to tool up to build a piece like this, so a car thus afflicted should be common enough to make spares available. If you're holding a split armrest from a Peerless GT and raising an eyebrow right now, the piece is probably a proprietary component from a larger manufacturer. In the case of a Peerless, I'd bet the armrest is shared with a production Triumph.

Window Mechanisms

Almost all the window cranking mechanisms (called *regulators*) fitted to British sports cars work the same way. The window crank turns a geared rod, which meshes with a much larger gear—usually only a half-circle of a gear, actually—attached to a long arm. As the gears turn, the arm is raised or lowered; the end of the arm has a roller that fits into a channel at the bottom of the glass, so the window moves up and down while you turn the crank. Simple.

Usually a spring is included in the works to provide some balance for the weight of the window, and the window itself rides up and down in two weatherstripped channels. Windows can also ride on side or bottom rollers.

It's remarkable that such a simple principle can give you something that's such a pain to fix. Repairing the regulator itself is time consuming; getting the glass, the rollers and the regulator in and out of the door without shedding a quart of O-Positive is another matter. Even though the regulator itself is held in place with just a few bolts, it often seems that there's no way all those parts will come out through the holes of the inner door. They went in, though; you just have to figure out how. Once you've removed the door panel you often have to take out the glass—in fact, unless the door is lying flat on the ground you almost *have* to take out the glass. There may also be a few extra braces on the inner door that have to come out, or some trim strips at the top of the door.

The most common failing with the regulator assembly is probably at the roller on the far end of the arm. This can wear out, fall off or freeze solid; the result will usually be a window that works reluctantly. Difficult but working windows can also be caused by too much lubrication or a broken spring. The teeth on the window crank or the large gear can also wear or break off, giving either no action at all or jerky winding of the window.

All of these ailments can be fixed individually if the proper replacement parts are available. The regulator itself is usually riveted together, but by drilling out the rivets a repair can be made; if there are no repair parts available, of course, it means replacing the whole unit. If you do have repair parts, pack the area where the gears mesh with heavy grease before riveting the unit back together again.

Assuming you have a helper to hold the glass in place while you make the repairs, reinstalling the regulator should be a lot easier than taking it out. You already know how it goes in, and the vulnerable parts of your hands should be coated in a protective layer of bandages by now. Clean all the moving parts and roller tracks with kerosene and apply a thin film of white lithium grease to keep them moving properly. (Avoid thinner lubricants like gear oil or WD-40, which will dry or drip out in a short time.) It's always a good idea to fit every-

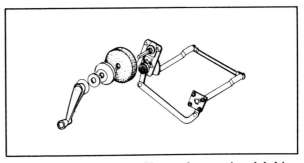

Window regulator assembly needs occasional lubing with a thin coat of white lithium grease. Trouble is usually in the joints and rollers instead of the mechanism itself. Moss Motors, Ltd.

thing back together before tightening any single bolt down—you'll need to adjust the window before you're done.

The only other type of window mechanism you're likely to find is the cable-and-pulley setup. This is almost the exclusive domain of Italian sports cars, however, and I won't go into any great detail other than to say that their method of operation and repair is very obvious.

The only area that might give you trouble is trying to fabricate your own cable. I've found it much easier just to give the dealer a few dollars and start with the factory replacement rather than fighting with an oversized cable from somewhere else. If you must cut a cable to size, however, it's the same procedure as cutting a choke or accelerator cable; use one blow of a cold chisel instead of snips or shears, and preserve the end of the cable with a dab of solder to prevent fraying.

5

Engine, Transmission and Drivetrain Restoration

The engine is the heart of a restoration. It has to look right, perform right and sound right, and it has to *keep* doing all those things for a respectable amount of time without attention.

More than any other single factor, the engine will determine whether or not you enjoy getting out and driving your car. If it's not reliable you'll never quite feel at ease behind the wheel. If it's not as powerful as it should be, you'll never feel you're getting all the fun you're entitled to. And if it doesn't make great noises under all conditions, you're simply missing a huge part of the fun of owning a classic sports car.

There's a lot to know and do with engines. This chapter will give you some background before you start out on your own with an engine rebuild manual in hand for your particular car.

To Rebuild or Not to Rebuild

Is a rebuild necessary? For some people, those with lots of experience and practice, an engine

rebuild is something to approach as a matter of course. If they get a car with a lot of miles on the block they'll just go in and rebuild the thing to head off any problems later.

For everyone else, a rebuild is something that's best left off unless it's really needed. A poor-running engine isn't necessarily going to need anything more than minor tuning and fiddling to bring back to life. In general, an engine with good oil pressure, good compression on all the cylinders, no real thirst for oil and no untoward operating noises isn't one I'd be tempted to open up.

These flaws can also be dealt with individually sometimes, rather than in the course of a full rebuild. A surprising number of major-sounding repairs can, in fact, often be made with the engine in place and the rest of the components undisturbed. Timing chain repair, piston and ring replacement, oil pump work, major bearing replacement, an entire valve gear rebuild—all of these jobs can usually be tackled with the engine *in situ*. The question is whether it would be faster and easier to do it that way, or if the time spent pulling the

Now here's a lovely sight—there's not much in this MGA engine bay, but what's there has been cleaned and finished well.

A nice selection of Lotus and Jensen-Healey dohc parts at a swap meet. These parts will cost a fraction of OEM replacements, but might need some machine work to be brought up to snuff.

114

engine would be offset by the time saved on the job itself. (Once the engine is out of the car, though, the temptation is almost irresistible to rebuild absolutely everything—even if you only needed to replace the oil pump.)

A full rebuild is called for when something major needs attention and many other things are at or near the same point. And in the end, if one major component has failed due to wear and tear, the others are probably getting there as well.

Okay, just for argument's sake let's assume the drivetrain needs a complete overhaul. If you're a halfway decent wrench, doing it yourself will be one of the most entertaining and educational parts of the restoration. Engines, which seem quite mysterious and imposing if you've never opened one up, will never confuse you again.

If you're still struggling with your tool kit, though, there's no shame in looking at a few alternatives to a home rebuild. The most costly would be to simply tow the car to a trustworthy professional, drop it in his parking lot and say "do it."

There are a lot of in-by-eight, out-by-six engine rebuilders out there, and in no way should you get mixed up with one. After a complete rebuild by a cheapie shop about the best you're likely to wind up with is an engine that runs like a slightly tired original. A competent rebuilder, on the other hand, will be able to make an engine that's tighter and stronger than it ever was from the factory. (You can farm out things like porting, balancing and blueprinting to a specialist and get the same results yourself.)

Finding this master rebuilder will be the hardest part of the job. Seek advice from others who have good examples of your car, talk to the local clubs and have a look around any shop before you give them your work. It should be clean, orderly, well lit and modern.

Finding the money to pay this rebuilder without getting arrested for armed robbery will be the second hardest job. A thorough rebuild of even a simple engine can easily cost $3,000 or more. Something more exotic like a Jaguar or Aston Martin engine can cost three times that amount.

The second most expensive alternative is to buy another engine complete and preconditioned from a supplier. These usually come in short-block form; the head, manifolds and accessories are not included, and have to be reconditioned or purchased separately.

By the time you factor in tool rentals, machining costs, parts, mistakes, chemicals, gaskets and so on, a preconditioned short-block might not be that much more expensive than a home rebuild. (If your time is worth something to boot, or if you manage to injure yourself during the rebuild and factor in the medical bill for a broken finger, you might actually come out ahead with a preconditioned job.) Of course, you might also find that a preconditioned block for your car costs the equivalent of a small house in Idaho—it all depends on the machine.

In any case, a preconditioned block isn't a good answer on all fronts. First and foremost, it robs you of one of the most fun jobs of the restoration. Besides that, many times a preconditioned block just isn't up to the standards of one you've rebuilt yourself. Everything will be done correctly, make no mistake, but without the very fine tolerances and top-quality components that you would lavish on the engine yourself through undying love and enthusiasm.

A preconditioned engine will also be obvious if anybody matches the numbers of the engine and frame. The engine won't be original, but that's not too important with most British cars—yet. In the past, it wasn't important with Corvettes, either, but matching numbers now adds a considerable premium to those cars.

A step down in cost from installing a preconditioned engine is that old home rebuild. Here the advantages are those mentioned already—fun and education—plus the possibility of saving some dough and the satisfaction of knowing that you've done it all yourself.

Probably the cheapest option when the old engine is too tired to continue is a salvage swap. You can find used replacement engines from private parties, parts cars or junkyards. It's possible to find a high-quality rebuilt engine in a wrecked car, but I'd be more tempted to buy a sound original unit—you never know how well a rebuild was performed unless you were the one in charge of the project. If you're going to buy a parts car anyway, getting a decent engine in the bargain might tip the scales in favor of a certain car.

Junkyard engines are the riskiest of all, but also the cheapest. A local yard near my house has a blanket "any engine for $200" rule, and that means the *whole thing*—heads, manifolds, alternator, carburetors, the whole shooting match. You just can't

---

Draining the Fuel Tank

Before you park the car, run the gas tank to almost empty; then move to a well-ventilated area before opening the drain or lower hose connection. Catch the fuel in a glass container, and if it's clean put it in another car.

In its drained state, the fuel tank is more dangerous than it was when it was full—it's fuel vapors you've got to watch out for more than the liquid stuff. To purge the tank, fill it completely with water while allowing the vapors to escape; once you're done, drain it again and allow to dry. While the tank's empty, consider putting some slushing compound or other sealant inside.

You can flip the engine over easily on a stand and you won't be bent over during your work.

beat a deal like that; the accessories alone are worth it. Unfortunately, for every sports car that comes to the yard there are 400 Chevettes and Pintos to wade through. The sports car engines that do make it are rarely in good shape, but occasionally folks get lucky.

Hybrid V-8 Power

One other option that's at least worth mentioning is swapping the original engine for something from another car. There are prefab kits to help you fit a Buick V-6 to a TR-7 or TR-8, an Olds or Rover V-8 to an MGB (à la the MGB V-8 once available in Europe) or even something as nutty as a small-block Ford V-8 to an E-Type. Since you can coax 300 horses or more out of these domestic engines, the possibilities are amusing—or maybe terrifying is a better word—to contemplate.

It's not likely such a swap would be easier or cheaper than just putting the right engine in the right car and leaving things the way that God and British Leyland intended. Still, some pretty hairy cars can be the result, so if you're particularly adventurous and just a little bit screwy, this might be the thing for you.

The Home Rebuild

All in all, the preferred method for engine replacement is to rebuild the engine yourself and farm out some of the machining and checkout work to professionals. If that's the course of action you plan to follow, there are a few things to bear in mind.

Rule #1: The success of the rebuild will be determined primarily by the cleanliness of the operation. All the parts and the work area have to be absolutely spotless—any little grain of grit or metal that makes it into the finished product will quickly eat away the sterling insides of your newly refurbished powerplant.

Rule #2: Oil all moving parts before reassembly unless specifically told not to. You'll be using assembly lube throughout the rebuild (which is supposed to protect the parts until the oil starts flowing from the pump) but don't trust that alone. Drizzle clean oil on the crank journals and bearings before locking things down. Wipe oil into the bores before reinstalling the pistons. Pour oil over the timing chain and gears before sealing them up under their cover. And every time you apply oil, wipe up any spills and wash your hands thoroughly to avoid violating Rule #1.

Rule #3: Get familiar with the process of the rebuild before you even walk into your garage.

Professional parts washing tank is handy but not necessary. They often show up used at garage closings and swap meets.

A close-fitting tray like this one will keep parts from getting lost at the bottom of a soaking tub. Pick them up at tool stores or swap meets.

Study your shop manual and your rebuild guide as though you were about to be tested for a Ph.D. on the subject. Take notes, read the material twice, think up reminders—there are things you'll come up against that you'll need foreknowledge to handle.

Rule #4: Always defer to the experts when in doubt. In truth, there's actually a middle ground to strike here; it won't do to have your local expert tire of your calls when you're halfway through the rebuild. On the other hand, if you can't remember just how that thrust washer goes in, ask someone. There are going to be things which just aren't covered in the best of books.

Rule #5: Try and avoid invoking Rule #4 by using Rule #3 and carefully documenting the disassembly.

Rule #6: Always buy guaranteed parts when possible; don't buy them too far in advance, though, or you might find the guarantee has expired before you get a chance to install and test the unit.

Engine Cleaning

If a full rebuild is the order of the day, your immediate concern is to get the old monster out of the engine bay. The first job is to clean everything in the engine compartment up to hospital-sanitary conditions.

The fastest and most thorough way of cleaning the engine and bay is by professional steam cleaning, which is also the easiest thing on identification plates and other metal parts, though it can dry out hoses and insulation. (Have the rest of the

You've got to hand it to Triumph on this one—lift-away hood of Spitfire really makes things accessible.

car—underbody, wheelwells, rear axle and so on—steamed while you're at it.) It used to be that steam cleaners were hard to find, but lately there's been an upswing in steam services that will do the job right in your driveway. (They usually muck up the driveway in the process; move the car to the street if you have to.) Look in the Yellow Pages to see if this service is available to you.

If you can't steam clean the engine, you might try a coin-operated car wash with an engine degreasing wand. These wands shoot a fairly caustic brew of cleaners under pressure; I don't recommend them for restored cars, since they tend to blast off decals, leave the paint chalky and just generally

Pressure wand combines garden hose and soap feed tube to mimic coin-operated engine sprayer at home. The Eastwood Company

This vintage Lotus Elan rests on high-quality jack stands—even the kids aren't likely to push it off.

It often seems like there's just no way an engine will come out of a tight bay. Pulling off all the intake and exhaust goodies makes it easier, but great care may be needed to avoid damaging the surrounding sheetmetal, no matter how far down the engine is stripped.

chew up the engine compartment. If the engine is coming out for a rebuild anyway, though, it's unlikely that this kind of damage will matter to you. Just be sure to quickly and thoroughly wash any splashed cleaner off the exterior of the car and the glass. Protect the ignition and carburetors from the solvent and water you're about to shoot all over the engine. Several heavy-duty freezer bags, held in place with rubber bands and duct tape, are about the best thing to use, and it doesn't hurt to put some clean cotton rags under the distributor cap and into the carb throats to soak up any overspray

Long engine brushes help work gunk and scale out from water and oil galleries. Hot tanking and flushing are the first steps. The Eastwood Company

that makes it that far. You should also clamp a sheet of plastic under the caps of the master cylinders to prevent water from fouling up the fluid. Don't forget to undo any of these things, but especially the master cylinder protectors.

A gentler but slower alternative is to use proprietary engine degreaser at home; this won't be quite as simple a procedure as the back of the can leads you to believe. The first thing to do is to scrape away as much of the grease, dirt and debris as possible with a wooden probe, a dull putty knife and a stiff wire brush. Make sure to remove as much slag as possible *dry*. Engine degreasing is an environmental nightmare in any case, but this will help a little. The slag should be stored & disposed of as mentioned in Appendix V. Right before putting the bags on, warm up the engine for a few minutes to soften the grease as much as possible. Take great care to protect paint, rubber and glass outside the engine compartment, then spray or brush on the goop liberally.

There are any number of spray- and brush-on degreasers formulated for engine compartments. A new one called Grez-Off is my current favorite. It works quite well and lasts about as long as four cans of aerosol degreaser (Grez-Off is a pump spray). Coat the engine and surrounding area liberally with cleaner and let it work in for about five minutes. Rinse it off with water from a squirt nozzle and take stock of what you've done; most likely, you'll have removed all the grease from the accessible parts of the engine and left big nasty slabs further down where you can't easily reach them—behind the starter, in the strengthening webs and so on. Using more degreaser, try to work up the remaining grease with a small wire brush or toothbrush, then spray on even more degreaser, wait a few minutes and rinse them again. By now most of the engine and bay should be surprisingly clean.

Removing the Engine

The next step is to take stock of what needs to come out and off before the engine can be removed. Your rebuild book will point out specifics, but usually the radiator and oil cooler (where fitted) are the first things to go.

The hood will also have to be removed at some point, and now's as good a time as any. To make aligning the hood less of a hassle later, most people scribe around the hood hinges with a sharp point before loosening them. If you don't want to damage the paint like that, you can make a mark in permanent felt pen or simply take precise measurements of the hinges' relation to the sides and back of the hood. (If you do scribe the hood, don't forget to touch up the scratches later to prevent rust.) Before you loosen the bolts, protect the cowl with a heavy blanket; that way if the hood slides back the damage will be minimized.

Put the hood in a protected, out-of-the-way place and cover it with blankets or towels. It's best if it can be laid out flat; propping it up against a wall is risky. It's also a good idea to inspect the hood latch and release cable; if the cable breaks later, it can be a real bear to open the hood again. The cable must be in good shape, as must the clips holding the housing in place—if those break, the cable can't travel far enough to spring the latch.

Ancillaries that stick out from the engine like carburetors and the distributor often come off. Removing the exhaust and intake manifolds may be more trouble with the engine in the car than it's worth, but check and see. Whether taking the exhaust manifold off the engine or loosening the header pipe from the rest of the exhaust system, the nuts will be frozen. Soak them with penetrant for a few days prior to loosening them. (Consider stainless-steel fasteners when you reassemble the exhaust system.)

On cars with extremely heavy engines (not the sort you're likely to come up against here), it's sometimes a good idea to remove the head to lighten the load. That's mostly up to you, although some cars don't offer a very good lifting point for the engine once the head is off.

Most front-engine, rear-wheel-drive cars also give you the option of removing the engine alone or in unit with the transmission. I'd usually recommend the latter; it makes aligning the clutch easier when you put everything back together and lessens the danger of breaking the transmission's first motion shaft on installation. It also makes it easier to renew the clutch plate and throwout bearing, which should be changed as a matter of course. Still, removing the engine alone is a simpler job; it's lighter and there's not nearly as much fudging and fiddling involved to get everything clear of the car. You're also less likely to put something through the firewall or windshield of the car.

Whatever car you're working on—and whether you're pulling the engine alone or with the transmission attached—most things will be the same during removal. After cleaning, drain all the fluids from the car: oil, coolant, power steering fluid, brake and clutch fluid. Free up all the wiring and piping and hoses that connect the engine to the rest of the car, and don't forget heater hoses which might be hidden at the back of the block. (It never hurts to tag the drained components with a wire tag marked "empty," though it's better still to simply follow a thorough fluid checklist before finally starting up the engine again.)

No matter how well you've drained all the fluids, some will remain and leak out all over you and the car. Be ready with rags and jars to deal with the mess. You'll also, of course, have to drain the fuel lines before you can get on with the job. Open the lines at the fuel pump or the lowest point under the car and catch the fuel in a clean glass jar as it comes out. You can clamp off the fuel line before the pump if you'd like, but it's safest to drain the whole tank now and be done with it.

Take the opportunity of having the engine in the car to remove the main dog bolt (it bolts through the timing cover in line with the crank, in the middle of the main lower pulley) from the front of the engine. Stick the car into high gear, chock the wheels, set the brake and give the bolt a few good shoves with a long socket, an air wrench or an impact driver. (It's occasionally reverse-threaded, so take care to turn it the correct way—your manual will warn you if the threads aren't standard.)

As you disconnect the wires, label each one well instead of relying on your memory and the sometimes faulty color coding. Also, gently fold and tuck each wire, especially big ones like the starter cable and the main ground strap, out of the way against the fenders and firewall as you go.

Check to make sure that the oil-pressure gauge pipe and water-temperature sender are removed and tucked safely away. Also see to it that throttle and choke cables, heater valve cables where fitted, and all the vapor and fuel lines have been disconnected.

If the transmission is coming out you need to get under the car to disconnect the first U-joint in the driveline and any electrical connections like back-up lights and automatic transmission switches. Also remove the clutch slave cylinder and tie it up under the car so it doesn't dangle from its hydraulic piping. Depending on the car, the shift linkage itself or the whole remote shifting assembly may have to come off before the transmission can be removed.

Dealing with Air Conditioning

If your car has air conditioning you'll have to jump through a few extra hoops before pulling the engine. The best thing is to take the car to a garage and have the air conditioning system properly vented; freon, the big daddy of the ozone-eating C-F-C family, is what fills the system. But professional venting doesn't only help the atmosphere; the escaping freon will be extremely cold, and will shoot all over your hands the instant you crack open the first air conditioning lines.

While the air conditioning system sits idle and empty it's extremely susceptible to dirt and water getting inside. This will quickly ruin the system, so seal up all hoses and parts immediately in tight plastic bags. (You can often find plastic caps to seal up the compressor and receiver fittings at a plumbing supply store.) Before you can operate the system again, have it evacuated and recharged professionally.

If the gearbox is staying in, remove all the bolts holding the bellhousing to the engine only after securing the front of the transmission with a jack stand (to prevent the transmission from resting on the engine by its first motion shaft). You may also find that the starter has to be removed before the two pieces will come apart.

Also make sure that semirigid connections like the speedometer cable and mechanical tach drive have been removed. When you're absolutely certain that all the wiring and pipes are free, loosen the engine and transmission mounting bolts a few turns and get ready with the crane. Steering columns and boxes generally remain in place until after the engine is gone. Take a look at the steering and suspension chapter before tackling them.

A good engine hoist is absolutely essential. Some people try to make do with a block-and-tackle mounted on roof beams or even a tree limb, but this seems unnecessarily dangerous to me, as well as excessively hard to work with. A decent hoist should be stout, roll easily on its wheels, and its hydraulics should operate smoothly and predictably. Buying one is impractical for most people, but renting is a very inexpensive alternative.

With the gearbox left in the car, pulling the engine is usually a pretty simple job, though at least two people will still have to be there to help guide the engine and operate the hoist. Taking the gearbox out with the engine does complicate things; it's best to jack the rear of the car way up to give you a better angle to work with. Either way, cover the windshield and firewall with heavy blankets or linoleum to offer it a measure of protection in case of an accident.

The most common method of slinging the engine is to mount two plates on diagonally opposed head bolts and connect them together with a chain. Choosing just the right link of the chain to lift with the hoist is critical, as that determines the angle the engine will take once it's lifted off its mounts. It usually takes a few tries—fitting, lifting, letting back down and refitting—before the ideal link is found. You can also support the whole unit with specially made nylon straps that fit all the way around the engine. These can be a little dicey—I'm not crazy about them.

Once the hoist begins to take some of the weight of the engine, remove the engine and transmission mounting bolts. They should come off cleanly and without binding. If they don't, then the engine is probably not very well supported by the hoist. Lift the engine a little bit to break the seal of the mounts, then let it down again while you make any necessary adjustments to the chain and the hoist position.

Now comes the trickiest and most dangerous part of the job—actually getting the engine out of the car. You'll need at least one set of hands to guide the engine past the firewall and bulkheads while another person operates the lift. It will take a few tries, and at first it may seem like the unit simply isn't going to come out. Don't worry, it will eventually. If the engine seems to be hanging up at any time, lower the hoist a bit and discover the problem; don't try to force things.

The danger, of course, is that you suddenly find yourself in charge of many hundreds of pounds of metal suspended in midair. Not only can the engine fall on something, or worse somebody, it can crush hands and limbs between itself and the firewall or fenders. The most common injury of the job is getting a hand caught between the top of the gearbox and the transmission tunnel. This is often more scary than harmful; if you keep cool and shove the engine back down while *immediately* removing your hand, you might get away with a few bruises and a case of the shakes.

If the engine decides to do something nasty while it's suspended, your first reaction will be to try to grab it—and that's where you run into trouble. It's usually best to just sit there and watch it happen; there's not much you can do except sacrifice part of your body in a vain attempt to stop it. Pick a spot to maneuver the engine from that's not likely to ram into anything else—in other words, hold on to the oil filter mount instead of the main pulley.

It's usually easier to lift the engine free of the car and roll the car backward instead of rolling the hoist and engine away. As soon as the engine is free of the car, lower it as close to the ground as possible before moving the hoist. The chances of tipping (and getting hurt in the process) are minimized.

Most engines can be gently laid on their sumps on a sheet of wood, or better still a pallet, though aluminum oil pans might not appreciate this treatment much. Eventually, you'll want to lay an inline engine on one side so it doesn't fall over later; check to see if anything on the side will be damaged first. If not, let it slowly roll over as you lower the hoist to the ground.

As soon as you can, separate the engine from the transmission and mount it on a suitable stand. You can do a lot of work on the ground, but a stand makes all jobs easier and some simply possible. The transmission should be moved to a safe place and kept covered until you're ready to deal with it. Both items should be cleaned and degreased completely as soon as possible.

Once the engine is secured to the stand you'll start breaking it down. The shop you locate to do the various machining tasks—overboring the cylinders, boiling out the head and block, checking bearing true and so on—will let you know just how far to go at each step. Generally, you'll take nearly everything apart: the cylinder head, the oil pump, the pistons, rods, crank, cam, rockers, pushrods, lifters, bearings, timing gear, engine plates, oil seals. Everything goes.

Disassembling the Engine

There's no way to cover everything fully here; at this point you should be immersed in your shop manual and rebuild guide and this book should be on a warm shelf inside the house. But it never hurts to talk about some general guidelines and tricks; these might even help you decide if engine rebuilding is the right thing for you.

On an overhead-valve (one that uses pushrods and has valves in the cylinder head) engine, removing the head is usually a simple matter. Undo the cylinder head nuts (some of them will also hold on the rocker shaft) in the sequence listed in your manual a few at a time. As the rocker assembly comes off, don't lose any parts and keep them in order on the shaft. The head may need some convincing to break its seal with the block—use a rubber mallet to shock it free if needed. You'll also want to pull out the pushrods before proceeding;

keep them organized so they can go back in in the same order. To get the pushrods out without accidentally bringing a lifter along with them, break the seal between rod and lifter with a little sideways snap on the rod.

For overhead-cam (one or two camshafts will be on top of the head) engines, the job's a little trickier. Usually the first thing to do is release the cam chain tensioner at the front of the engine. Then free up the camshaft sprocket (usually keyed to the shaft) and wriggle either the sprocket or just the chain away. The head bolts may be doing double duty as camshaft bearing bolts, so you might find yourself removing the cam(s) even if you didn't want to at this point. There will be a method described in the manual for noting the proper valve timing to make reassembly easier—follow it.

The flywheel usually comes off easily by simply folding back the retaining tabs, loosening the bolts and pulling off the wheel. You'll have to hold the crankshaft in place first, though, usually with a piece of hard rubber between it and the block. That means removing the oil pan to stick the wedge in.

The oil pan shouldn't present any problem as long as you're sure to remove all the bolts holding it in place. Don't whack on the pan with a rubber mallet unless there's no other way to break it free of the block. Occasionally there will be a pipe from the oil pan to the block held in with O-rings; gently slip

Engine-block petcock makes draining the coolant a breeze. If your block doesn't have one, you'll have to drain it by loosening the lower main hose.

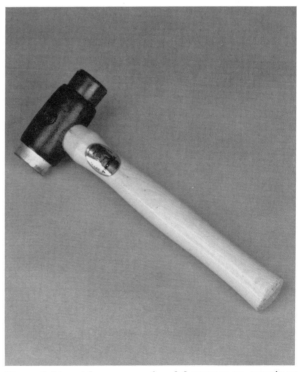

You might need a copper-faced hammer to convince recalcitrant main bearing caps that they do indeed want to go back in the engine. The Eastwood Company

121

this out while the pan comes off, and install new O-rings on either side before bolting things back together.

The timing gear and chain can be a real bear to get off. Just getting to them is often a hassle, involving the removal of a lot of junk before you can even pull the timing cover. Having loosened the main dog bolt beforehand helps considerably, but the main pulley is one tough number and you'll often need a puller to remove it. Once the timing cover is off, usually the best method for removing the gears is to lever the gears off simultaneously with two suitable irons per gear and the chain in place. (Watch this one—it varies a lot from car to car.) To check the timing chain for stretch, hold it parallel to the ground, side plates down, and look for sag. There shouldn't be any to speak of.

Removing the crankshaft usually makes getting the pistons out a whole lot easier, but the reverse is also true—remove the pistons and the crank's a simpler job. Most pistons will push up through the block once the head has been removed, though you'll probably have to break down a carbon ridge at the top of the cylinders first. By the same token, get the crank out of the way and the pistons will come out the bottom with ease. There's no "right" order for most engines.

All the reciprocating parts connected to the crank or operated by the cam have to be kept in order unless they're all going to be replaced. That means that the proper piston has to go back into the proper cylinder with the proper connecting rod secured by the proper big-end cap, and everything must be facing the proper direction—in other words, *keep everything straight!*

Getting the crankshaft out—once the timing gear, pistons and other ancillaries are removed—may or may not be easy. Often you'll find the main bearing caps are stuck in so tightly that it seems you need dynamite to shift them. What you'll really need is a special slide hammer that's made to screw into tapped holes in the caps. Don't try to lever the caps out with a screwdriver, which will chew up the bearing surfaces and ruin them.

Some people like to pull the crankshaft out with the pistons and rods still attached, then break down the assembly on a bench. That just might scratch up the cylinders, though, so it's probably best to undo the connecting rods before removing the crank. Put the caps back on the rods immediately, making sure that they're facing the right direction.

As parts are removed they should be cleaned, inspected and properly tagged. Cleaning engine parts will be easier if you're lucky enough to have a professional-style parts washer in your garage. Very few people do, of course, so the next best thing is probably an old stock pot filled with some commercial cleaning fluid. (Kerosene will also work,

but both are flammable and dangerous to leave lying around.)

Grimy parts can be left to stew in the cleaner for a few hours, but you don't want to forget anything down at the bottom. An old lobster pot—the kind with a close-fitting screen at the bottom of the pot—works like a charm. Once the grease has softened, scrape it away with a plastic-bristled brush and wipe down the part with a clean rag. Some parts of the engine will require intense soaking, others very little; never immerse a distributor or other electrical part in cleaning fluid.

The flywheel will probably be in good shape, although any dust on its surface is likely to be asbestos. Wipe it down with a kerosene-moistened rag rather than blowing it off. While you're there, check the flywheel carefully for cracks, chipped teeth around its edge or discoloration due to overheating. The flywheel should also be checked for minimum thickness—any flaw or an overly thin flywheel means a new one should be found. The flywheel must withstand considerable centrifugal force in operation; a failure could lead to a virtual explosion of shrapnel.

The hardest pieces to clean might be those in and around the combustion chambers. These will usually have acquired a lovely layer of heat-tempered carbon. Fortunately, carbon build-up can be more or less removed with a wooden scraper and a gentle wire wheel attached to a drill.

One of the more difficult jobs you might face is removing the cylinder head studs from the block. There are special stud-removing tools you can use, but the home remedy is to fit a nut a little way down the stud, thread another nut on top of it and unscrew the stud by turning counterclockwise on the lower nut while forcing the upper nut downward with a little clockwise pressure. Once the studs come out, check the threads carefully and see that the stud isn't bent, the threads aren't damaged in the least and the threaded section of the stud hasn't stretched; extreme stretch shows up as a taper in the middle of the threads. Try to run a stud nut all the way down both sets of threads. If it binds or hangs up anywhere along the way, the stud should be replaced.

On some engines it's also very common for the studs to chew up a few threads in the block. If this happens, the hole will have to be cleared and possibly retapped before the rebuild is completed. You might also consider applying a little sealer to the bottom threads before reinserting the studs—not locking fluid, but a pliable corrosion protectant.

Examining the Top End

Once everything is taken apart and pretty well cleaned up, it's time to check on the state of the pistons, bores, head and crankshaft. The most important checks are also the easiest; use your eyes and fingernails to check for scoring or localized wear in all the bearings and on the crank journals. The pistons should be inspected for scoring or heavy discoloration at the crown, and for cracks or loose-fitting gudgeon pins (usually called wrist pins in American garages) underneath the crown. (When reassembling the engine, it's critical that the gudgeon pins are in good condition and correctly mounted.) Cracks in the head or block should be looked for throughout; often they'll appear as a stain or line of color in an odd place.

If a serious flaw is found during inspection—not just a crack, but also seriously worn bores, a chewed-up crank, bent webs or anything else that will cost a lot to correct—on most cars it's easier

A ghastly but not uncommon sight under the rocker cover of an early Austin-Healey engine. The accumulation of crud over the number one and number two cylinders is probably the result of clogged oil passages in the head, which perverts the blow-by system and leads to heavy deposits in the top end. This whole head is going to need reworking—just cleaning off the grime won't do a thing. Robin O'Brien

Keep rocker gear assembled on its shaft to avoid losing parts or getting them out of order.

Cams themselves are generally pretty tough. The lobes and gears should be checked, but expect problems instead in the block's cam bearings.

Double overhead camshafts, as on this 4.2 liter six-cylinder Jaguar E Type, will considerably complicate cylinder head teardown and head gasket replacement due simply to the number of components.

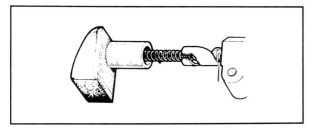

To tear down double-overhead-cam heads, the cam chain must first be slackened, which means locating the tensioning slipper and relaxing it. The tensioner shown (MGC) is typical, but all kinds of different units are used. Often, unfortunately, the tensioner is hidden down in the guts at the front of the engine and is almost impossible to get to.

into your car for the trip home. Of course, any salvaged part will have to be checked out thoroughly before the purchase to ensure that it doesn't share the same flaws as the one you've already got.

At the same time, if the original block is important to the car—if it has a significant history or a replacement is too hard to find—just about anything can be done to set it right again. Even a gaping hole from a thrown rod can be fixed, for a price; this kind of work is only practical if the value of the car will be significantly increased by retaining the block it came with.

Examine the valves, especially the exhausts, closely for pitting, cracking or burned-away edges. If you have a spring compressor and can disassemble the head (by compressing the springs and removing the two retaining cotters), examine the valve guides by inserting the correct valve back in the head without its springs and trying to wiggle it

and cheaper just to go looking for another piece. Junkyard blocks can be had for a song, not counting the hernia you might get trying to lift the thing

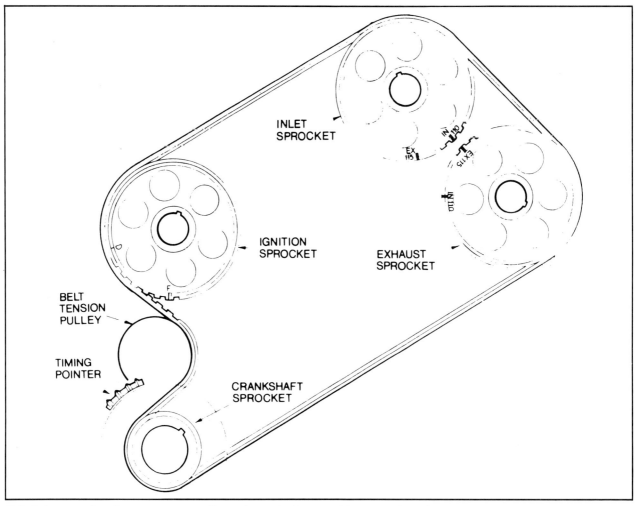

Belt-driven overhead cams are generally easier to deal with than chain-driven ones. This Lotus layout uses a reasonably accessible sprung pulley, which means your biggest problem ought to be the simple matter of matching all the timing marks back up when you finish.

back and forth in the bore. There shouldn't be any play. Slight pitting of the valve seats can be polished away, but larger pits will mean new seats must be installed in the head—a professional job. Valve sealing can be easily checked by pouring some solvents into the ports with the valves and springs in place and letting the head sit for a few minutes. The more fluid leaking past the valves, the worse the seal.

As long as you have the head off and the rest of the engine needs rebuilding, it's probably a good idea to fit new valve guides regardless. This is usually a matter of pressing out the old guides with the appropriate drift and pressing in new ones. The new guides must protrude through the head to exactly the same depth as the old ones; it's best to do every other guide in the first pass, using the old guides and a straightedge to set their positions. Then you can go back and do the other guides, using the new ones to position the straightedge.

There's growing controversy over the value of replacing the stock guides and exhaust valves with ones of bronze and Stellite, respectively, and hardening the valve seats. (These are supposed to compensate for losing the protection of lead in the fuel.) This certainly can't hurt, but recent studies have shown that the danger of running unleaded fuel in older cars has probably been exaggerated. On the other hand, making the valves and guides stronger than stock is a good idea regardless of whether you think unleaded gas will harm the head or not. Think of this as insurance against future engine problems and select or reject it accordingly.

You can grind in replacement valves or clean up minor pitting of the valve seats yourself with valve-grinding paste and a lapping tool (basically a dowel with a suction cup on the end to hold the valve by its face). Smear a little paste on the seat, install the valve and spin the tool between your palms. It's best to use all new valves, though old valves can certainly be reused in a pinch, providing they still have plenty of seating area and "meat" left on them. Whether the valves are ground in at home or in a shop, it's imperative that all the paste be removed before the engine is put back together. If any paste gets into the oiling system, you'll be rebuilding the engine again a lot sooner than you'd like.

Valve springs shouldn't give you much trouble, but they're cheap enough to replace that it's always a good idea. Tired valve springs will lead to valve float at high revs and a loss of power; serious float can also do a lot of damage, since the piston might contact the valve at the top of its throw.

Most cylinder heads are rather prone to warping. In theory, you can check for warps by placing a straightedge across the bottom of the head in different places and trying to fit a feeler gauge beneath it. In practice, though, it's best to have this checked over professionally—even a minor warp will lead to lots of blown head gaskets, which can in turn lead to more serious damage. The block itself should be checked for warping as well, particularly on BMC engines (MG, Mini, Sprite and so on). While the shop is checking for warpage, have them Magnaflux the head. This will show up any cracking that might cause trouble later.

Reconditioning a head can certainly be done at home, and your rebuild book will tell you how to go about it. Basically you're looking at new valves, guides, seats and springs, all correctly mounted and properly tested. It's a pretty exacting business, though, so you may want to leave the whole thing to a pro—the money you pay may be worth it in the end, in both performance and reliability. (You can also find preconditioned heads for a price; the same cautions apply to these as to preconditioned engine blocks.) While you're thinking of it, check the rocker assembly carefully for scoring of the shaft, broken spacing springs or worn rocker arms.

While on the subject of the head, it's possible to get some relatively inexpensive performance gains in this area while leaving the engine technically stock. Polishing and smoothing the combustion chambers and intake ports (and the intake manifold while you're at it) may or may not give you a noticeable boost in horsepower—it depends on how well this was done at the factory originally. Matching the intake ports to the intake manifold can also give a little power gain. Theoretically, all this work can be done at home with a small rotary file and some emery paper. In practice, though, I'd leave it to an expert; there's too much chance of messing things up instead of making them better.

Done correctly, the combined effects of polishing, port matching and possibly planing the head (to increase compression) or reshaping the combustion chambers (to aid breathing) gives a good boost of power to an engine that remains externally stock. You can, of course, go quite a bit further in this direction; the basic key to improving performance is getting more air in and out of the engine with every revolution. The catch is just that: you have to get more air in *and* out of the engine. Just attacking one side of the problem won't help, unless the engine is already unbalanced by design.

There are endless internal modifications of a more or less serious nature that can be undertaken to boost flow and therefore power. Most of them, though, will require some sort of external cue like larger carburetors or aftermarket exhausts to work as they should. Substantially upping the output also substantially ups the loads inside the engine; you'll need to beef up the rest of the parts to handle the extra work.

Examining the Bottom End

Moving on to the block itself, check the bores visually for scoring and especially brown patches.

Deep scoring makes this flywheel a write-off.

Brown patches will point to localized hot spots, the result of either overtorqued cylinder heads or a blocked water jacket. The ridge at the top of the bores will give you a fair idea of the overall state of the cylinders. This ridge is beyond the range of the rings, so it remains pretty much true to its original size and shape while the cylinder walls below get worn away.

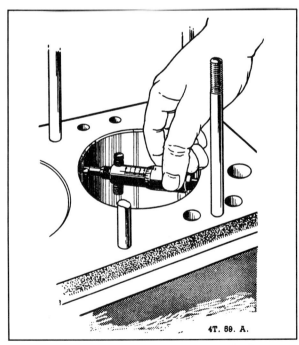

Checking the cylinder bore with an internal micrometer will show up any ovality; bores that are oval beyond tolerances must be either re-lined, re-sleeved, or bored out wider and fit with appropriately oversize rings and pistons.

Before you can do this, though, you'll have to clean away the carbon ridge that's probably formed at the tops of the bores. (If the pistons are staying in place—say you're just changing a head gasket or working on the head itself—leave this ridge alone.) The best method for removing the carbon is to lap away at it gently with some worn emery paper that's been soaked in kerosene.

Once the carbon is gone, feel the depth of the ridge first with your fingers. If it's really big (say a half a millimeter deep or more), the block is going to need reboring or resleeving and you might as well consult with a pro to see if the block's worth saving. If it's smaller, though, you can check the bore diameter with an internal micrometer or a comparator gauge. The bore should be checked against factory specs or simply the unworn ridge. Take measurements at the top, middle and bottom of the piston's range, making a check in each place and then another at the same spot with the tool turned 90 deg. Keep all these figures written down on a table for later reference.

A Homespun Bore Wear Check

Since most of us don't just happen to have a comparator gauge lying around and almost nobody will rent a precise instrument like this, a low-cost alternative to check bore wear is to use a new oil-control piston ring, an old piston and a feeler gauge. It's either that or let a professional do the job.

1. Fit the ring squarely into the bore at the unworn upper ridge. Make sure it's square by pressing against it with the piston from below.
2. Measure the end gap with a feeler gauge, and write it down.
3. Push the ring down into the upper range of the piston's travel. Ideally, it should rest right where the top ring would sit at Top Dead Center (TDC). Square it again.
4. Measure the end gap and record measurement.
5. Repeat the previous step with the ring in the middle and Bottom Dead Center (BDC) positions.
6. Divide the largest increase in end gap (from factory specs or the unworn ridge) by pi. That's the amount of bore wear.

Cylinders under about 3.5 in. in diameter generally need reboring if they show more than about 0.010 in. of wear. Larger cylinders can tolerate about half again as much, say 0.015 in., but the exact figures will be listed in the shop manual for your particular engine.

You might find yourself turning the problem of worn bores into a blessing; the cylinders can be opened up and fitted with larger pistons and rings for a slight increase in displacement and power. The alternative on badly worn cylinders, resleeving, may or may not be a big deal with your engine.

Simply finding a better block might still be the answer.

Cars with worn press-in cylinder liners will be simple to repair, but the new liners must be carefully checked before going on to the next stage of the rebuild. Basically this is done by offering up the liners without their sealing rings and making sure that they spin freely by hand. If not, there's a problem somewhere (probably at the bottom where the old sealing ring has left crud in the block) that needs looking into. Once in place with the proper rings, the liners should stand above the line of the block evenly all the way around, and each should stand out the same distance.

Next, turn your attention to the crankshaft. First check to see that the dog threads are okay, the keyways are good and that there's no discoloring due to stress or heating on any of the journals. If the crank passes these tests and no obvious scoring is evident on the journals or bearings, go ahead and check the journals for size and ovality with an external micrometer and a Plastigauge. (This is a deformable plastic rod that's slipped over the journal, which then gets its cap bolted back on and tightened down to torque. Take the cap off, pull out the flattened Plastigauge and compare its width with the chart enclosed in the kit. That tells you how much clearance there is between the journal and its bearing.)

If the journals are more than 0.002 in. out of round they'll need grinding, and if too much metal is missing—either due to wear or grinding—you can fit oversize bearings in minor cases. (A machine shop will have to grind and polish the journals to size first.) Stiffer medicine is called for when the clearances are too wide to be made up with oversize bearings; metal spraying will build the journals back up (as will shield arc welding), and then a good straightening is called for. The journals can then be professionally polished back to the proper size. None of this work should be bothered with until you're sure a better crank can't be found for less money.

Another important check is the oil pump. This has lots of potential flaws in the gears, the end float and the cover-gear clearance—check them all against factory specs and repair or replace a pump that fails. The relief valve and spring should be tossed and replaced every time you rebuild the pump; be prepared to reset the relief valve to the proper pressure once the engine's been broken in again.

Check the camshaft visually for signs of excessive wear, and inspect the bottoms of the lifters as well. It also pays to take a micrometer and measure each lobe of the camshaft for overall height, then compare it with its intake or exhaust brethren. A big variation between lobes (say a few percent or more) means the cam will have to be replaced. Also check the distributor (and any other) drive teeth on the shaft for sharpening or chips, and make sure that the sprocket keyway isn't bent or chewed up. Finally, have a look and feel at the cam bearings and journals; trouble on the cam itself is rare, but it's best if new bearings are installed and finished by a professional. Bad cam bearings, either shell bearings or those integral with the block, are often the cause of low oil pressure. (Shells will be dissolved by hot tanking and you'll have to replace them regardless.) Pay special attention to any thrust buttons or spacers that come out with the cam—they should be replaced with new ones.

Lifters are an expendable item; replace them whether they look okay or not. Many people feel the same way about pushrods, but these can at least be checked by rolling them across a known flat surface like a pane of glass. Any bent or suspicious-looking rods are history; keep the remainder in the proper order so they can go back in the same way they came out.

Finally, give the pistons a once-over to see if they're in any shape to go back in the engine. Generally, if the bore has not been altered the old pistons can be reused if need be. Don't separate them from the connecting rods unless you have a good reason to suspect something wrong; these parts are often best left alone.

Sticking gudgeon pins, scoring of the piston skirts, serious discoloration on the crown or any cracking are warning signs that the piston should be tossed. Piston ring clearance (end and horizontal) should be checked with the new rings in place and the grooves nicely cleaned out—too much clearance will mean fitting oversize rings or new pistons. If there is a clearance problem, it will almost always be confined to the top ring.

If new pistons are to be fitted you might find the gudgeon pins nicely frozen in place; boiling the piston in water will usually free things up. Follow the manufacturer's directions for fitting and securing gudgeon pins to the letter. Piston rings, by the way, should be replaced as a matter of course.

Rebuilding the Bottom End

It's now a few days, weeks or months since the teardown started, and I hope you've been enjoying yourself in my absence. Somewhere along the way you've chosen a good method to really clean out the head and block.

A great alternative to cleaning the head by hand is bead blasting, which you can do yourself at home with the proper setup. If not, just take the whole head to a specialist and let him have a go at it—the results will pay for the expense many times over. For surfaces that are to take paint later, abrasives like fine silica or aluminum oxide should be used. These will micro-etch the metal and give the paint something to latch onto. Unpainted surfaces

New flywheel should last forever if the clutch disc is changed regularly.

should be shot with a gentler media like glass beads or steel shot. (Shot blasting will also relieve stress in, and therefore strengthen, reciprocating parts like connecting rods.) Exhaust manifolds and other crusty pieces are also candidates for blasting. All blasting and cleaning should be done before any machine work.

Cleaning the block by hand is a nightmarish job to be avoided. These days there's no doubt that having it professionally "boiled out" (also called hot

Professional-style hone breaks down glaze from cylinder walls; it's the best way to ensure good ring seating on a rebuilt engine. The Eastwood Company

tanking) is the only way to go. This process not only gets all the goo off the outside of the engine, but clears the oil and water galleries as well—a necessary part of the rebuild. Make sure that all the casting plugs have been removed before boiling. When you get the block back, spray aerosol carburetor cleaner through all the galleries and pressure wash them with hot water and detergent. Rinse all that gook back out with a final blast of clean hot water. (Hot tanking might dissolve some aluminum parts, especially ID plates. Talk to your shop about what needs to be removed before dropping off the block.)

Before launching into the reassembling process, make sure that all your gasket surfaces are up to scratch. *Never* reuse a gasket or seal you could replace, especially the critical ones like the rear mains. You want to first remove all the crud like old gasket bits and sealer from both surfaces—a razor scraper is the weapon of choice. A really smooth and true surface is the only way to keep leaks at bay; no amount of Jiffy WonderGoop Sealer is going to make up for proper preparation. Clean but don't polish the mating surfaces; they should be smooth but not shiny.

A complete range of gaskets is available for just about any car these days; if you do come up against a gasket that's not available, though, one can be made from a roll of gasket material on your bench. The best method is to lay an appropriate sheet of gasket material over the part in question and to tap out a form with a small rubber hammer. You can then cut the gasket to size with scissors and an X-acto knife.

Once the pistons, crank, rods and bearings are all ready to go back in the engine, try them out by fitting the rods to the crank, lightly oiling the bearings and torquing the caps. The pistons should rotate around the crank freely and hang below it by their own weight; they should also be firmly in place and not offer any wiggling or vibration when jiggled to and fro. The first things to go back into the engine are usually the pistons, of course, so you'll have to disassemble the whole rig as soon as it's been checked out.

Next, check the piston ring gaps by fitting the oiled rings into the bores all by themselves. The end gap should be measured and brought into tolerance in the manner specified—usually by filing one end of the ring away. When the gaps are correct for a given piston install the rings, remembering to offset the gaps as specified to avoid giving the oil a straight shot into the combustion chambers. Wipe lots of fresh oil into the bores and prepare to stuff in the pistons.

A ring compressor makes all the difference in the world at this point, and while you could force the pistons in without one, it's a dangerous and frustrating job. Usually it's easiest to fit the pistons from below; leave the rod bearing shells out for the time being, or if the bearings are in unit with the rods, loosely fit the end caps to protect them. This will be especially important if the friction between the compressor and the rings is enough to make you force the pistons in with the shaft of a light hammer.

If you do have to force the pistons in, stop immediately if one freezes up on its entry to the block. Usually this means you've got a ring hanging up on the way in, and you've got to pull the piston out and check the rings for damage before proceeding. (From here on you'll be using assembly lube left and right, but don't forget that extra oil.)

Once the pistons are in, clean and dry the rod bearing housings and fit in the shells. Make sure that these go in the right way, in the right direction and in the right housing. Dribble oil generously over the shells right before the crank. (You may have to attach the flywheel bolts before the crank is lowered into the block. If you forget, they'll be almost impossible to fit later.)

Fit the main bearings and gently and evenly lower the crank into place; try to avoid turning it once it gets close to the block, which might dislodge a bearing shell. Fit the upper thrust washers in next. Finally, fit the main shells to their caps and lower them in along with the lower thrust washers. If the main caps are a very tight fit, you might have to tap them into place with a copper hammer. Don't use wood or a rubber hammer here; the fragments coming off can get into the works and cause problems later.

Lightly torque the main bolts and make sure the crank is moving smoothly and freely. If it is (and you've covered all the other steps required so far by your manual), torque the mains to spec as indicated and rotate the crank once again—it should still spin freely and well.

The next step is to fit the rods to the crank. The procedure is basically the same as it was for fitting the main bearings and the crank to the block. Use lots of oil, defer to the manual for torquing specs and procedures and don't forget to use all the proper retaining goodies that should be there. Finally, at the risk of sounding like a broken record, make sure the right piston is in the right bore using the right cap on the right rod and that everything is facing in the right direction. Once each piston is fitted, give the crank a few turns and check that everything's spinning okay.

Shoving the cam back in on ohv cars should be a simple matter. If the timing gears look good you can use them again, but the timing chain should be replaced unless you know it's very new. Generally, you must fit the chain to the gears first, align the timing marks punched on them and fit the whole assembly to the crank and cam as a unit.

You might find the oil seal in the timing cover rather difficult to get in place—go gently on it or the cover will bend and leak later on. Once it's in, hold the gasket on the cover with sealing compound and then ease the crank pulley through the main seal; rotate it a couple of times to center it, then put the pulley onto the crank with its key. Once that's in place, torque the timing chain cover in stages and at diagonal bolts to avoid warping.

For ohc cars, it's probably going to be much easier to leave the front covers off until relatively late in the game. Once the head is back on and the cams are in place, then you can go back and fit the cam chain or chains, set the chain tensioner and rubbing block, and cover everything up. All ohc cars require slightly different rebuild procedures, so go by the book and the notes you made on disassembly.

Fill the oil pump with fresh, clean oil before putting it back into position. (On some pumps you can prime the system before starting the engine with a special adapter fit to a drill; this drives the pump gear from outside the engine. On others, you'll have to pull the spark plugs and crank the engine until

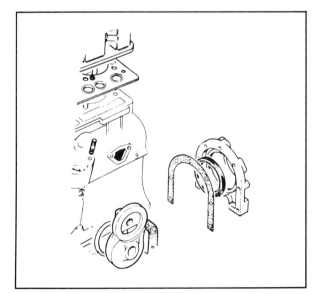

All-important rear main seal prevents oil from leaking onto clutch face and ruining the assembly. If it goes bad in operation the engine, transmission or maybe both will have to come out. Moss Motors, Ltd.

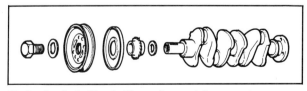

Main dog bolt (far left) can be a nightmare to remove. Leave car in top gear, chock the wheels and go after the bolt with lots of leverage or an impact driver. Moss Motors, Ltd.

you get oil pressure before trying to start the thing.) Make sure that the pump's pickup screen is clear.

When fitting the flywheel, make sure it seats all the way before torquing it and locking it into place. You must also make sure that the flywheel is properly located. Sometimes the only indication of this will be a mark at the edge of the wheel (usually ¼ on four-cylinder engines or ⅙ on sixes) which must point straight up when the number one cylinder is at TDC. Finally, add the water pump and you're ready to reunite the head after refitting the cleaned studs to the block. (Give the water pump a critical eye and replace it if you have any doubts; aluminum water pumps especially have a very short life span.)

The head gasket should, of course, be new, and there will be a proper top and bottom. Don't use any gasket goop unless specifically instructed to, and don't let the gasket snag on the studs while settling it down. Dribble a touch of clean oil into the

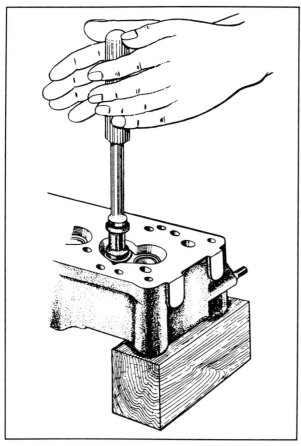

Lapping in valves with a hand grinder is easy work. A small dab of grinding paste quickly cuts down the valve and seat as you run the grinder between your palms—a suction cup holds the tool to the valve.

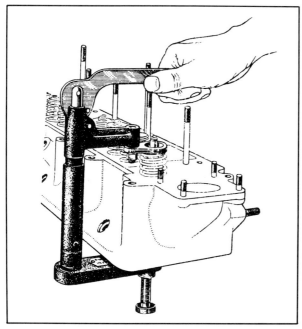

Spring compressing tool is vital to valve work—there's no other way to get the locking cotters off.

Scum, carbon and oil fouling can be cleaned from combustion chambers with wooden scrapers and wire wheels. Bead blasting will do the job faster and better, but costs money.

cylinders one last time and ease the head on. The manufacturer will have published torque specs and sequence—these must be followed precisely to avoid warping the head and blowing out the gasket. (Follow any instructions for retorquing the head after the engine has been run awhile; steel heads should be retorqued hot, while aluminum heads must be cold. If there are no retorquing instructions but you're not told *not* to do it, retorque the head after the first 100 miles of operation.)

Special heat-proof manifold gasket can't be replaced by a hand-cut job. Most gaskets can, however.

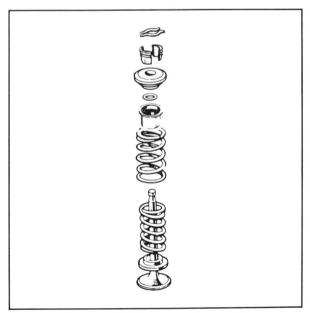

Valves, springs and locks are pretty much throwaway items in a full rebuild. They might be okay, but why take the chance? Moss Motors, Ltd.

Rebuilding the Top End

With the head on, tackle the valve gear assembly. On ohv engines this should be a simple enough matter of submerging the lifters in oil before slipping them into place, dropping in the pushrods, fitting down the rockers and shaft and sealing up any lifter gallery plates with the appropriate gaskets. (This is one place you might consider using a little pliable gasket sealant, as the gallery doors inevitably weep oil once the engine is back together. Use it sparingly, however; any sealant that finds its way into the oil will play havoc with the valvetrain, especially if hydraulic lifters are used.)

Follow the factory specs closely when setting the valves. It's imperative that the valve lash is set only when the valve in question is fully closed—that is, resting on the base of its cam lobe rather than a ramp or peak. The manual will tell you when that occurs by pointing to another valve that will be fully open at the time. Usually this follows the Rule of Nine for four-cylinders—when number one is fully open, set number eight; when number four is fully open, set number five and so on. For sixes it's a Rule of 13—either way, the procedure will be the

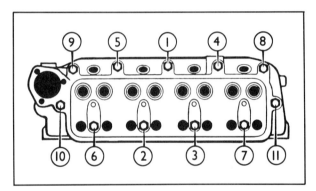

Proper cylinder head torque sequence must be followed at all times. This MG head is typical, but your sequence might be a little different. Moss Motors, Ltd.

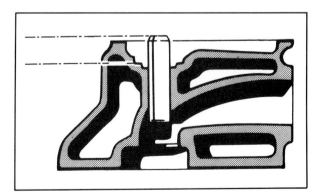

Valve guides must all protrude the same distance from the head. Measure them individually and against each other. Moss Motors, Ltd.

same. When you're sure the valve you're working on is closed, loosen the lock nut on the rocker, turn the adjusting nut or screw until the proper feeler gauge *just starts to drag* between the valve stem and rocker arm and tighten the lock nut again. Check

the clearance once again, and if it's okay proceed to the next valve.

It pays to set all the valves, then turn the crank over by hand a few more times and do the whole procedure again. You'll inevitably catch a few valves that are pretty far off even though you thought they were okay the first time around. Once you're satisfied that the upper end is complete and properly set up, pour a substantial amount of oil over the valves, rockers and down the pushrods (use a quart or so) and fit the rocker cover and gasket. Avoid sealant here—you'll be taking the rocker cover off frequently, and gasket sealer will make the job harder than it needs to be.

Setting the ignition timing can be a real pain if your distributor doesn't use an offset drive. For regular gear drives, about the best thing to do is to put the number one cylinder at TDC (Top Dead Center). TDC is found by aligning the timing marks and seeing that both valves are closed, or by sticking your finger over the number one plug hole and checking for the compression stroke; when you feel it pumping up, set the cylinder to the top of its throw and there you are. Then wire up the distributor cap properly and align the rotor with the number one lead on the cap. Drop it in, making sure that the gears aren't offset to the point that the rotor moves a fair amount off the lead once it's in place. Double-check the ignition timing before moving on—you want the engine to start immediately so oil is pumped through it as soon as possible. Be

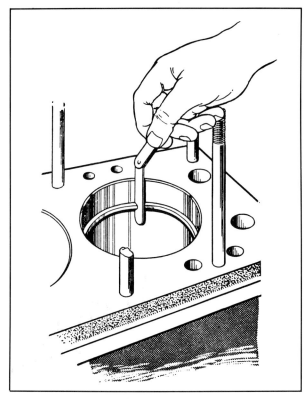

Measuring ring gap is a simple enough matter; make sure the rings are square in the bores by tapping them in place with a piston, then check the end gap with a feeler gauge. Improper gap causes too much or too little oil along the cylinder walls.

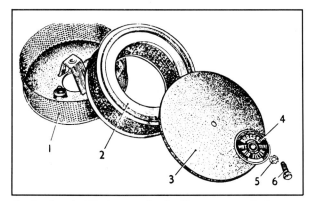

Early Austin-Healey mesh air filters come all the way apart for easy cleaning. A little soap and water will tidy up the outer sleeve, but the inner mesh element needs a good soaking in solvent. Properly cleaned filters are cheap life insurance for your engine.

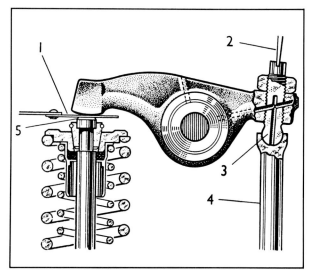

Simple Austin-Healey valve adjustment requires that you slacken off the locknut holding the adjusting screw (3) in place—something the manual neglects to mention. Feeler gauge (1) of proper thickness should just drag between rocker and valve stem (5) when clearance is perfectly set. Hold the screw in place while you tighten down the locknut, then check the clearance again when you're done.

particularly careful not to get the distributor 180 deg. out of whack; the rotor will be pointing to the number one lead when that cylinder is actually finishing its exhaust stroke.

Painting and Refinishing

Painting the engine can be done with the parts separate or all built up—I prefer the latter. You can do the block and head satisfactorily with brush paint, the surface of the metal being rough enough to hide the brush marks, but what's the point? Spray cans of high-temperature paint in the right color will do the trick as well. Before proceeding, of course, make sure that any open holes and ports are well masked off with tape or cotton rags. You'll probably have to go back later and scrape or sand some paint off of the gasket surfaces for the manifolds and other parts.

There are two neat tricks that will make the painting easier; first, a thin film of petroleum jelly on the casting plugs will keep the paint from adhering to them; unpainted plugs were stock on most,

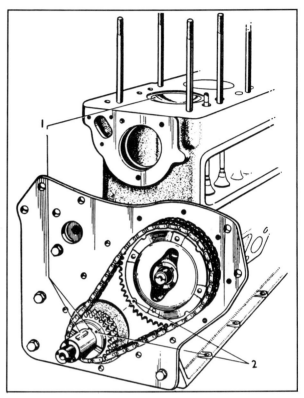

With piston number one at TDC (1), the timing marks between crank and cam sprockets must line up perfectly (2). If something's not right, you have to catch the problem and fix it now—the engine will never run otherwise.

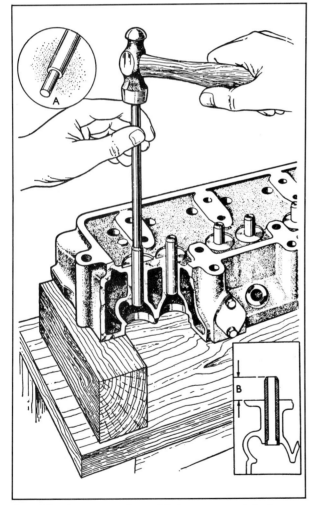

Punching in a new valve guide is as easy as it looks, to a point. The first catch is to have the right drift (A) for the job, and the second is of course to ensure the proper clearance between head surface and guide. With those caveats in mind, though, just pound 'em on in gently.

The aluminum valve cover and Monza-type oil filler cap on this Austin-Healey were polished to top off the engine and add the finishing touch. A lot of research went into getting exactly the right shade of blue-green engine block paint as well. It's the details that count in a proper restoration. Robin O'Brien

133

High-temperature manifold paint may not be stock on your car, but it cleans up the engine compartment considerably.

Heat-resistant pads on hood keep paint from blistering up above. They must be replaced if they're removed for painting or cleaning.

Refinishing the Engine Compartment

Before the engine comes out you should have decided if you'll be refinishing the engine compartment. If so, you might as well remove all the ancillaries from the fenders and firewall before pulling the engine to avoid damaging them at that time. All the wiring, relays, tanks, fuse blocks, hood bumpers, weatherstripping, everything must go. Photos, notes and tags must be used throughout the disassembly process.

Be especially careful when removing hydraulic lines; if they're bent out of shape they'll be hard to fit back in later. The lines themselves should be cleaned with mild steel wool, flushed with kerosene and protected with a shot of clear coat if desired. (Stick a little cotton in the very ends of the line to mask off the insides.) Seal hydraulic lines tightly in plastic and store them out of the way so they don't get crushed later.

Most decals in the engine bay can be removed and replaced with reproductions later. ID tags and the like can usually be removed by gently drilling out their rivets. (When you reattach them, it's easiest if you peg one corner with an un-popped rivet while riveting up the other sides.) ID tags are easy to damage and important to preserve—clean them gently with soap, water and a soft brush at first. If that doesn't do it, move on to gel toothpaste applied with a finger. If you wear the paint off the plate you'll have a devil of a time reapplying it correctly.

With the engine out, before you can start smoothing out the paint in the bay you'll have to go over it many times with degreaser, silicone and wax remover, and soapy water. Use lots of toothbrushes to get into the nooks and crannies, and when you're finally done rinse everything well with a strong stream of water. Blow out all the cracks and crevices with compressed air to get all the water and chemicals back out before you start painting.

Mask all the holes and cracks in the engine compartment from behind (especially those in the firewall) right before you get ready to spray your first primer coat. Check carefully for missing captive nuts; braze these back into place now, because you won't get another chance.

Small dents and flaws can be filled and sanded as usual, but high-build primer might be worth considering if there are lots of little nicks in the old finish. The rest of the car, of course, must be completely protected from the paint being shot in this area. Remove any support bars before spraying, and think about unscrewing the tops of the fender and cowl, if possible, to keep paint from building up in the seams and making a sloppy finished product.

It can be a real pain to color sand complex shapes like the engine compartment and firewall, so consider a glossy-from-the-gun enamel or two-pack finish for the whole car if this job is part of a total respray. The engine compartment will usually be painted body color, but sometimes part or all of it will be a gloss- or satin-finish black. Don't forget to spray the underside of the hood if it needs it, but try cleaning it up first with lots of degreaser, wax and silicone remover and polish.

Once the engine bay's been cleared out, you'll have to decide whether or not you'll also remove the front suspension. Often that's the best way to get really good-looking results, but lots of careful masking may get the job done. Rough suspension parts can be built up and smoothed nicely with a few coats of high-build primer; use enamel or two-pack paint for the color instead of softer lacquer, which will chip off quickly; beware of painting or scoring bearing or bushing races; and seal up exposed aluminum pieces with clear coat instead of priming them and spraying them silver.

but not all, cars. (By the way, try to knock the new casting plugs in place with one solid rap on a wooden drift when you fit them.) Second, the rocker cover should be painted separately and more carefully on a bench, since this surface is smoother than the rest of the engine and more obvious once the hood is up. (You'll have to smooth and beat it into shape if it's rough.) One good way to get the right look is to protect the rocker cover with newspaper and slip it into place while you're painting the rest of the block (to mask off the top end). Once the rest of the engine is painted, pull off the rocker cover, remove the paper and spray it carefully on its own. Again, high-temperature paint is the order of the day.

Exhaust and intake manifolds usually respond well to blasting before installation, and there are some very good super-high-temperature paints on the market you can use to color the exhaust manifold (though this won't often be stock). These generally need the high heat of a working engine to cure fully, so you might want to save this job for later. Get the engine back together and running, then take off the manifold, paint it and bolt it back on to dry completely.

Getting the engine back in the car should be no easier than getting it out; if nothing else, you now have a clean and probably painted engine compartment to worry about scratching. Install your new motor mounts loosely before dropping the engine back in to make mating easier. Clean all the splines you encounter with fine steel wool and kerosene, then apply a little oil to help them slide into place.

As everything under the hood goes back together, keep an especially sharp eye out for lines, wires and hoses that should be replaced before you're finished. Fuel and emissions lines are especially important, as a leak in one can cause a major fire.

Once everything's back in order, refill all the fluids except the coolant immediately. (Use all new fluids, never reuse the old stuff.) You'll start pouring pure water in the radiator the moment the engine first fires, and switch the heater on to fill its core as well. (Don't use antifreeze at first, in case there's a leak somewhere. When you're sure the engine's tight, drain about half the water out and fill the system back up with high-quality antifreeze.)

Now as you can imagine, the last 10,000 words or so are a long way from the instructions for a complete engine rebuild. They should be a good start, but as I said at the beginning of this chapter, you'll need a whole lot of outside material and help for this job. Start with a good shop manual, a good rebuild guide and a good network of machinists and experts to answer questions as they crop up.

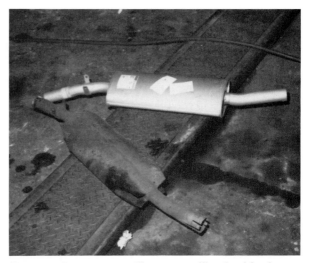

Some replacement mufflers are affixed with clamps instead of welding—a real aid for do-it-yourself repairs.

You generally think of the exhaust system as a noise suppression system, but it's main function is keeping carbon monoxide and other nasty gases away from you and your passengers. It also affects the performance of the car: a well-designed exhaust manifold helps ease gas out of the combustion chambers, while a badly made one impedes the flow.

British exhaust systems are particularly fragile: not only do they corrode like any others, they're invariably the lowest point on the car and constantly getting banged and beaten up.

Check your existing exhaust system for leaks by starting the engine and covering the rear of the pipe with your hand (do this while the engine's still cold). Any big leaks will be obvious from puffing noises under the car.

Leaks in the exhaust system can be deadly, so this isn't an area to mess around with. There are some proprietary goops and patches that will seal up leaks more or less effectively for a while, but don't turn to these unless you absolutely can't afford a new exhaust piece. If you do make a repair in plaster or a similar material, try to support it with a sheet of aluminum held in place with exhaust clamps. Very small holes may be suitably patched with exhaust putty, but anything larger than ⅛ in. won't stay fixed for long.

Any aftermarket exhaust system probably ought to be the same shape as the factory unit, although those weren't engineered particularly well themselves. Most "performance" exhaust systems are noticeably noisier than stock, so let the supplier know how much engine noise you want to hear when you're done.

Aftermarket exhaust systems often come piecemeal through the mail and must be welded together in a couple of places. You can do this

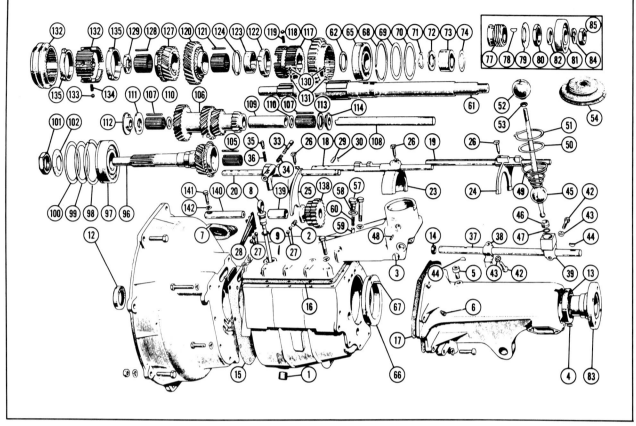

Inside the average gearbox. This should give you a hobby for a while. Moss Motors, Ltd.

Transmission System

By transmission, I mean getting torque and power from the engine to the rear wheels—not just the gearbox *per se* but also, and perhaps more

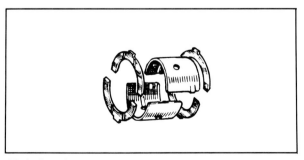

Main bearings and thrust washers should be replaced every time you rebuild the unit. Make sure new thrust washers are installed correctly—with the bearing metal facing outward. Moss Motors, Ltd.

importantly to us, the clutch and rear end. I won't go into the principles of torque and the need for different gears, as I think they're pretty obvious to anyone who's ever driven a manually shifted car. Instead, I'm going to talk about what can go wrong in the transmission system and what the do-it-yourself restorer can realistically expect to do about it.

Clutch

There have been any number of automotive clutches used through the years, but the only one you're likely to come across is the single dry-plate variety. The clutch, of course, gives you the ability to connect and disconnect the engine from the rest of the drivetrain. In the case of the single dry plate, that's done in a simple fashion that's harder to explain than understand. At the front of the transmission, a disc with pads of friction material (similar to that used for brake pads) around its rim is splined to a shaft that ultimately carries power to the rear wheels. It's free to slide back and forth on this shaft, but the splines force the shaft to turn when the disc itself rotates.

One side of this disc faces the engine's flywheel; the flywheel, of course, is rigidly locked to the crankshaft and always turns at engine speed. On the other side of the disc is something called a *pressure plate*, a ring of metal that's the same size and shape as the friction surfaces of the disc. The pressure plate is forced against the disc by springs inside an assembly surrounding it, the *clutch plate*. The clutch plate is rigidly bolted to the flywheel, and the pressure plate is securely connected to the clutch plate.

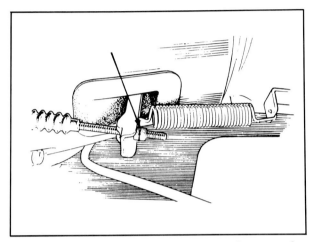

At the first sign of clutch slippage you need to get under the car to see if the clutch is merely out of adjustment or if the trouble is more serious. The only way to tell is to see if there's still room for adjustment along the clutch rod, and the problem goes away after an adjustment has been made. Usually a pair of locknuts (arrow) determine the engagement point of the clutch by moving the clutch fork up and down the clutch actuating rod. With a cable operated (Jensen-Healey, shown) or mechanical linkage clutch (Austin-Healey and others), moving the fork further down the rod makes the clutch disengage later, preventing undue slipping. On the more common hydraulically operated clutches, move the fork further up the rod to do the same thing.

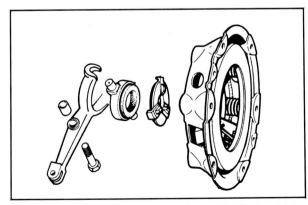

Throwout bearing and release lever (left) should be replaced at the first sign of trouble; once you're in there working you want to tackle these jobs while you can. Moss Motors, Ltd.

So just to make it clear, the clutch plate and pressure plate are in effect one piece with the flywheel; they rotate at engine speed at all times. But floating around inside there is the clutch disc, which, if you were to pull back the pressure plate so it didn't clamp the disc against the flywheel, could sit perfectly still while the flywheel, pressure plate and cover plate rotated on either side of it.

Normally, of course, the strong springs between the clutch cover and pressure plate don't allow that—they sandwich the clutch disc so tightly that it must spin at the same speed as the engine. And since the disc is rigidly splined to the rest of the transmission system, that forces the rest of the driveline to spin along with it.

The springs between the pressure plate and the cover plate can either be lots of simple coil springs or, more commonly these days, a single cone-shaped diaphragm spring. In the former case, when you push in the clutch pedal it forces levers in the clutch plate to pull the pressure plate away

Glazed friction surface indicates a worn or overheated clutch disc. The disc and possibly the pressure plate will have to be replaced. At best, a glazed disc makes smooth engagement difficult, at worst it can lead to premature failure of the pressure plate and flywheel.

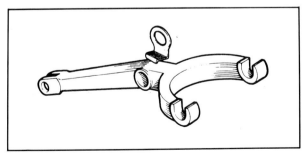

Release lever and pivot should be checked for damage and wear; a flaw here makes clutch action unpredictable.

The three release levers of a coil-spring clutch plate can be replaced individually if needed.

from the clutch disc. In the latter, pushing on the clutch ultimately forces the inside of the diaphragm spring in, which bends its outer edges out and releases the pressure on the disc.

Now a few things are needed to make all this work in practice. The clutch pedal usually needs some kind of linkage, either hydraulic or mechanical, to transmit its motion down to the area of the clutch; these systems are no big deal for the do-it-yourselfer to figure out. Once that motion has been carried down to the right place it pushes a large *release lever* back and forth to move the levers in the clutch plate or the inside of the diaphragm spring. (This lever mustn't be bent and its pivots can't be oval or worn.) But there's also a bearing between the release lever and the diaphragm spring or levers in the clutch plate; that's commonly called a *throwout bearing*, presumably because that's what you ought to do with it every chance you get.

Replacing a throwout bearing is in and of itself a pretty easy job. Getting to it is another matter; since it's buried deep down between the engine and gearbox, one or the other of those pieces must be moved out of the way. Every time you have easy access to the throwout bearing you should replace it, unless it's very new indeed. (Simple carbon disc bearings can be inspected visually, while ball-race bearings can be spun in the hand and checked for roughness or disassembled and checked by eye.) Even if the bearing appears good, though, it's better to change it while you can instead of waiting until you have to. (Sometimes you can view the throwout bearing through an access panel in the bellhousing, but usually you have to split the engine and transmission.)

The linkage between the pedal and release lever must of course be up to snuff. Cables obviously can

Corroded pressure plate can be professionally skimmed —within limits. Remove too much metal and the part can fail dangerously in use.

Clutch slave cylinder is often the source of poor clutch action. Bleed and inspect it annually.

stretch or break, and should be kept well lubed with graphite or the specified lubricant; the hydraulic variety is subject to the same ills as hydraulic brakes, which are covered elsewhere. Both types should regularly be checked for crud and corrosion at their various pivots, which should be lightly coated with white grease or the specified lubricant.

Your manual will give you specific lubricating and adjustment instructions for clutch free play and so on, but basically you just want two things: Before the pedal is all the way to the floor the clutch should be well disengaged, and before it's all the way out the clutch should be completely locked up. These adjustments are usually made in an obvious fashion with threaded fittings and lock nuts. While you're under the car, check that the hydraulic line to the clutch salve cylinder isn't leaking or "ballooning," both of which will short-circuit the effectiveness of the system.

The clutch disc itself is simply a consumable item, and it will last anywhere from 10,000 miles to the whole life of the car, depending on the driver, the use it gets and the power of the engine. The more you slip the clutch—that is, the more time you spend with the clutch not fully engaged or disengaged—the sooner the disc will wear out. Obviously there's a lot of friction in the system, and the hotter the disc gets the faster it wears. Therefore, the first few seconds of slipping are much less destructive than the following seconds; make your shifts as quick as you can while keeping them smooth. Intense heat generated by prolonged slipping will damage the material around the disc as well—the springs, plates and even the flywheel.

Excessive slipping can also be caused by incorrect clutch adjustment—the clutch never quite locks up—or a worn disc. Both of these are a recipe for more damage to the other components, so the clutch adjustment and wear must be checked out. (You can usually identify a slipping clutch early on; the engine will rev faster than the car accelerates even though your foot's off the clutch.) The opposite condition, where the clutch never quite disengages fully and makes smooth gear selection difficult, can be caused by improper adjustment, sticky disc faces, sticky disc splines, a worn clutch plate or a worn disc.

Once you get to the disc itself, measure the thinnest section of one piece of lining; if it's 2 mm or less, the disc is too worn to continue. (The thinnest section is almost always on the flywheel side of the disc—it's hotter there.) Also look for missing chunks or strips, loose rivets or uneven coloring, particularly brown or black patches. Discoloration indicates the lining has burned or been fouled by oil (usually leaking from the rear main seal of the engine), and must be replaced. Check the inner splines of the disc for damage or rust. Light rust

Clutch alignment tool locates disc properly while the rest of the clutch assembly is tightened down. The disc should slip right onto the gearbox's first motion shaft after alignment.

can be removed with a fine file, but as long as you've gone this far you might as well toss the old disc regardless and install a new one. (Remember to wash the protective coating off the disc with soap and water and dry it well before installation.) The disc might also have springs around its center or spring steel leaves between the pads; these must be unbroken and unbent.

Inspect the pressure plate and clutch plate, though problems in these components are relatively rare in normal use. The springs should not be discolored due to heat, any actuating levers must not be bent or worn and the cover can't be warped or bent. (These things can often be replaced individually if need be.) While you're looking through the clutch, clean up any dust with a kerosene-moistened rag. It probably contains asbestos particles, so don't just blow it away. Also clean the splines on the first motion shaft with fine steel wool and kerosene if they're dirty.

Juddering and shaking when you let out the clutch usually point to oil fouling, although warping or heat damage to any of the parts will give you the same results (as will something like a worn U-joint, broken motor mount or unbalanced driveshaft). Check for warping by looking for uneven wear of the metal surfaces and by trying to get a fine feeler gauge between the component itself and a good straightedge. Warping, scoring or damage to the flywheel or pressure plate can often be repaired by skimming the parts at a machine shop, although there are limits to this. The parts must remain thick enough (a spec will be given) to withstand the heat and force on them or they'll fail— come apart at high revs and blow through the bellhousing like a grenade. If there's any doubt, replace a clutch part instead of repairing it. Deep scoring, which usually totals the part, is caused by allowing the clutch disc to wear down to its rivets.

When you're fitting a new clutch disc, it's got to be aligned by guiding it along a special tool (a different one for each car) that fits through the disc and into a central bearing in the flywheel. (You can theoretically do the job without this tool, but you'll be fighting it for hours and hours.) Once the alignment tool and disc are in place, tighten down the clutch cover in gentle stages at diagonally opposed bolts. That holds the disc in place until it's slipped over the first motion shaft of the gearbox on reassembly.

Most clutches are balanced to the flywheel and engine, so you can't just bolt them back up any old way. There's usually a mark from the factory on the clutch plate and flywheel to align, but if not, make your own with permanent marker before taking things apart. If you're bolting up a new clutch plate or using a new flywheel and there aren't any marks, you might have to take both pieces to a machine shop for balancing—consult your parts supplier to be sure.

Gearboxes

Your reaction upon first opening up a gearbox should be something along the lines of "Egad!" If your transmission behaves properly—that is, doesn't make a lot of noise, changes gears without undue crunching and the shifter doesn't rattle or hop out of gear—for heaven's sake, leave it alone.

And before you're convinced the problem is in the gearbox, inspect and adjust the external linkages as outlined in your manual. The procedure differs from car to car, but generally it involves nothing more than gaining access to the linkages, looking for loose or worn connections, taking a few measurements and tightening everything back down when any failure has been corrected.

If you're really curious, drain the oil from the box and look for metal chunks or lots of filings. You'll probably find a few random filings, and despite their implications I'd recommend pretending you didn't see them. Larger pieces or heavy filings mean you've got a problem you'll have to deal with. First, take a peek inside the gearbox by removing the inspection cover. Look for worn or chipped teeth on the gears, worn selector forks (the little levers that slide the gears around) and shafts that are loose in their bearings. If you find any, you're faced with a clear choice: Get out the manual and follow the laborious instructions for replacing the bad parts and measuring, adjusting and trueing everything again; find a good transmission specialist; or get yourself a better gearbox.

None of those is a particularly appealing prospect. Internal transmission work is complex, exacting and seems annoyingly arbitrary, while going to a specialist might mean you'll be putting his kids through college. Locating a better replacement box may not be easy or cheap.

Due to the very nature and variety of gearbox repairs, your own manual will guide you step-by-step through the process. The only suggestions I can add are remember to clean the gearbox thoroughly before starting, start with all the right tools and keep everything in order. You'll have a much easier time with selector forks and detents than synchronizers, shafts, bearings or the gears themselves. The gear selectors are pretty straightfor-

It's a tight fit inside most gearboxes—get one piece out of alignment and the whole unit's often shot.

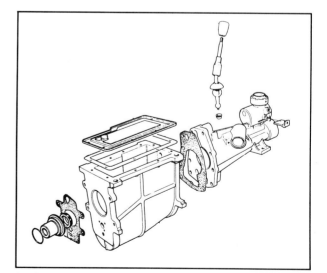

Leaky gearbox is usually caused by bad gaskets, some of which are easier to replace than others. Check any vent breathers first and make sure they're clear. Moss Motors, Ltd.

ward, but for anyone working on gears or synchros, those of us about to rummage through the junkyard for another gearbox salute you.

Salvaged gearboxes are often inexpensive, and therefore my favorite alternative. If you can't get one with a guarantee, though, you could well be putting in a little money and a lot of time for nothing; aside from visual inspection, there's no way to know just what you're getting. Gearboxes also come with a number of ratios; a used box might not have the same gears as your old one and you might not like the new selections. (On the other hand, you might come across that rare, heavy-duty, close-ratio MG four-speed you've always wanted and pick it up for $100.)

You can also buy a new or preconditioned gearbox from a supplier, though that's usually rather expensive compared to having your own box repaired professionally. The advantage, of course, is that everything will work like new. Paying somebody to fix a worn selector fork won't do anything about the whining second gear or the worn-out synchros.

Gear Selector Repair Tips

For minor gearbox repairs, you don't have to be the sort whose idea of a good time is decoding Soviet spy messages to enjoy doing them. Worn selector forks or detents often cause the stick to chatter or hop out of gear. If that happens, check for the following:

If the selector forks aren't attached to the transmission cover or the removed part of the case, they'll slide back and forth on rods next to the main gearshaft.

Remove the interlock mechanism (which prevents more than one gear going in at a time) from the selector assembly to gain more access to the area.

Most selectors use ball-and-spring detents that must be removed before the forks can be attached. Don't lose these pieces, and watch for the ball or spring rocketing from its hole when you release its cover.

If the selector rod is positively mounted in the gearbox case, you'll have to remove it by releasing the retaining bolt or lock at the far end.

Inspect the selector rod, forks and fork bearings for wear or scoring; replace any unit found defective. Also inspect the ends of the fork where it contacts the gear or synchro; the pads should be smooth and polished but not deeply scored or worn. Inspect the mating surface on the gear or synchro for damage if the fork is bad.

Rear End

In referring to the rear end I mean the final drive gears and the differential, which are built in unit with each other and, for our purposes, might as well be thought of as one piece. (This section will

Most British overdrives are operated by a solenoid mounted alongside the unit itself. The contact points at the bottom of this solenoid must be clean and set to the proper tolerance or the overdrive won't engage. Robin O'Brien

only talk about front-drive, rear-engine cars. If you have a Mini or a Jensen FF, most of this will apply but you'll have to excuse the terms and locations used.)

The first job of the rear end is to translate the high driveshaft speed from the transmission into lower wheel rotation speeds, usually at a reduction rate of between 3:1 and 4:1. Since the rotation has to be turned 90 deg. anyway, this is a simple matter of fitting a small gear driven by the driveshaft to a larger one connected to the rear axle shafts. (Yes, even in a "solid axle" rear end there are in fact two shafts, one to each wheel. It's just that with a live axle these shafts ride in a hollow tube shared by both wheels; in an independent rear end, the shafts are free to move about up and down on their own.)

The second job of the rear end is to provide differential action: allow one rear wheel to turn at a slightly different rate than the other if needed. I recently wrote a book about all-wheel-drive sports cars, and the technical side of how and why differentials work still gives me a headache. To spare us both, take two things on faith—around a curve the outside wheel must travel a farther distance than

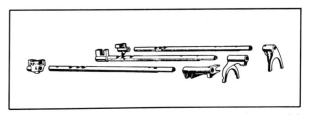

Selector forks and rods can be handled by a careful do-it-yourself restorer. Parts alone may cost more than a salvage gearbox, though. Moss Motors, Ltd.

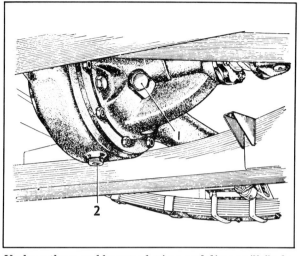

Under a thousand layers of grime and dirt you'll find a rear axle filler (1) and drain plug (2). Since you don't know how long the old oil has been in the car, replace the rear-end fluid the first time you get the chance.

the inside one, and the arrangement of gears in the differential allows this to happen.

Live rear axles need to be inspected for leaks from the seals at the ends of the axle (stains will appear on the brake backing plate or the end of the axle). Independent units give you more things to go wrong; the flexible couplings must all be tight, the rubber mountings for the differential housing should be uncracked and any sliding splines should be cleaned and lightly greased whenever the assembly is apart.

Rear ends can be of the regular (identified by the drive being taken in at the axle centerline) or hypoid (the drive coming in below the centerline) variety. The only reason you should care about this is that a hypoid rear end is subject to higher loads; its failure rate is a little worse, its adjustment more critical and it needs a special heavy-duty hypoid gear oil.

As with transmissions, rear ends are rather tricky to repair and adjust, and finding a better unit is always a tempting option. Having a profes-

The entire live rear-axle assembly comes off pretty easily, though it weighs a ton. Whole rear axles may be available used for not much money, which will save you a lot of mucking around with axle seals, differential, pinion gears and so on. Rear-axle ratio may not match your own, though, which will change overall gearing of the car.

New axle shafts will rarely be needed unless the splines of the old one are chewed up by a differential failure.

If a U-joint is old enough to have spider webs on it, it's old enough to be replaced. U-joints should be inspected for looseness annually and replaced on most cars every 50,000 miles; on others, particularly those with independent rear suspensions, their life is shorter.

sional do the work is also worth considering. To him, the expensive part of the job is often removing the unit from the car; pull it yourself and deliver it on a platter and the repair might not be too expensive.

The rear end's gears carry the highest torque loads of any in the car, so they tend to be the first ones to complain. They're surprisingly resilient though; on some British cars a tired rear end may whine lightly and happily for 100,000 miles or more. On others, the whine quickly becomes louder and the unit soon fails. Leaks from the rear-end gaskets or the axle seals are usually caused by failure to clean out the breather on top of the differential housing. This lets pressure build up in the unit when it gets hot.

The differential also fails from time to time, particularly on cars with limited-slip differentials. The limited-slips you'll encounter on a classic sports

car use locking pads, ramps, balls or pucks to restrict the free motion of one wheel somewhat in relation to the other. These add-on devices are all subject to wear and tear.

Taking the rear end apart almost always entails removing it from the car, taking it to a bench and removing all the bearings with the proper drifts

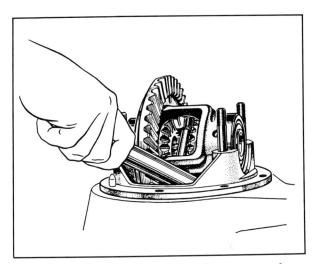

Once the securing clamps are all undone, you can lever the differential unit right out of the housing. It's best to use a stout wooden lever to avoid bending the differential case or unit.

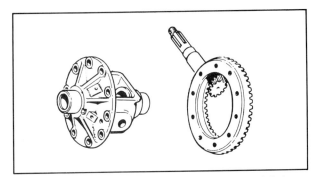

Ring and pinion gears (for final-drive ratio, right) are fixed solidly to differential cage (for differential action, left). Pinion is adjustable front to back, while ring gear-differential assembly can be moved from side to side. Moss Motors, Ltd.

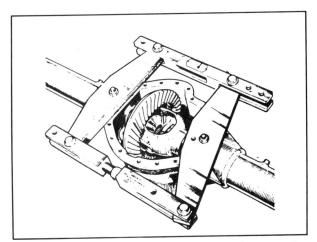

A common tool on live-axle repairs is the spreader shown here, which opens up the mechanicals ever so slightly to allow the innards to pass through. You'll be hard-pressed to do without it.

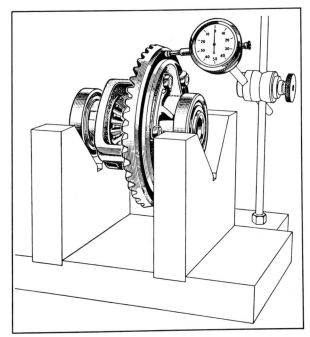

Crown wheel runout should be checked with a dial indicator; you probably won't be able to see any problems by eye. A crown wheel that's outside the acceptable limits specified in the manual is best discarded for a better unit.

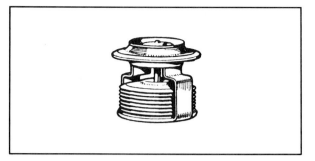

Alcohol-filled bellows thermostat will fail in the open position; if the car starts running cold this is the first thing to check. Wax capsule thermostats usually fail closed, leading to overheating. Moss Motors, Ltd.

and pullers. (The limited-slip hardware can occasionally be fixed *in situ.*) Before you do this, though, you might want to take the opened differential to a pro and ask for his opinion. He might tell you to bolt the cover back on, stick it back in the car and ignore the noise.

If you do have to go farther in, the bearings themselves should be inspected for wear and corrosion and replaced if any is found. The gears, however, are almost certain to have some damage to them, slight discoloration if nothing more, and this needn't be terminal. Usually there will be some noticeable sharpening of the teeth, some pitting of the mating surfaces or some wear at the gears' front edges; if serious wear or chipping is found, obviously the gears will have to go. But with less-definite wear, it often pays to take the gears to a trusted professional and get a second opinion. Often, the gears can be reused despite their appearance.

Oil cooler in the nose of this vintage racing Jaguar helps keep oil (and overall engine) temperature down under tough conditions. Mike Lamm

Whether the gears have failed or not, if you've pulled the bearings you'll have to replace and reset the whole shooting match. This is definitely a go-by-the-book job, but the basics are the same from car to car. The differential support bearings (which locate the differential and ring gear from side to side) are set either with threaded adjusters or shims. In the latter case, the shims are first fit oversize, a measurement is taken and then they are reduced to spec minus a hair to allow for squishing after installation.

Getting the pinion gear and ring gear to mesh correctly can be a hassle; this one's really best left to a pro with the proper tools and jigs. In theory, the manufacturer only lists a shim, a collapsible space or a torque spec to set the pinion gear's distance and therefore its mesh with the ring gear. A few additional checks to ensure that the ring gear is located where it should be finishes the job.

In practice, as the rear end gets old enough to need attention these figures aren't all that accurate anymore. The best home remedy is to apply some oiled-down engineer's blue (a coating fluid that shows where parts are contacting each other) and to set the pinion adjustment by eye.

The engineer's blue will show where the gears are meshing; inspect the ring gear teeth and adjust the pinion gear until the mating occurs about halfway from the back of the tooth and ends about a quarter of the way from its front. The mating must also take place exactly in the middle of the tooth's height—that is, evenly between its peak and valley.

Cooling System

If you're one of those dozen or so loons still driving around in an air-cooled Berkeley, skip all this. For the rest of us—everyone who's ever raced a temperature gauge to the top of a hill—a review of the cooling system is in order.

Technically, the cooling systems should also be thought of as a lack-of-cooling system. Everybody's familiar with what happens when the engine gets too hot. But when the engine doesn't get *hot enough* much more subtle, but no less insidious, damage can occur.

An overcooled engine will make less power and get worse mileage than one that quickly warms up to operating temperature; it will also have a shorter life span. Gases formed in the combustion chambers condense into acids and find their way past the rings and into the oil. Fuel can condense before entering the combustion chamber and also filter down to the oil. And the minute amount of water that condenses every night in the crankcase might not get hot enough to boil away and be carried off through the crankcase ventilation system.

All of these impurities will hamper the effectiveness of the lubrication system and result in increased engine wear.

The principle of liquid cooling is quite simple, and the practice is pretty straightforward as well. All you have to remember is that heat—energy—is passed from one object to another; whatever gives up the energy becomes cooler and whatever receives it becomes hotter.

Inside the engine are a number of hot spots—the combustion chambers and exhaust ports are the biggies. If you just started up an engine and let it run without any method of cooling, the intense heat (energy) at these spots would quickly flow into the surrounding pieces and warp or burn them. It would also quickly scorch any oil in the area.

By flowing liquid over these areas, though, most of the energy is absorbed by the liquid instead of the metal and oil; the liquid then flows on to the radiator, where the energy is passed to air flowing by. The cooled-off liquid is recirculated for another lap and the process starts all over again.

To actually make the system work there must be coolant, a water pump, a radiator, water galleries in the engine block and head, hoses, a thermostat and a cooling fan.

The coolant should be a mixture of water and quality antifreeze. A good antifreeze doesn't just keep the water from freezing, it also raises its boiling point (in the old days antifreeze could actually *lower* the boiling point, but that kind is gone from the market) and inhibits corrosion in the cooling system with special additives. These additives don't last forever, so the entire system should be flushed and refilled with fresh water and antifreeze at least every other year. Many radiator shops suggest using distilled water instead of tap water; this costs a bit more, but it will cut down on scaly deposits over time and maybe save money in the long run.

Water Pump

The water pump, which forces coolant through the system, is one of the system's weakest links. It simply doesn't last that long, so you can expect to replace a few while you own your car. Almost always driven by a fan belt off the main engine pulley, the water pump normally pulls cool water from the radiator and forces it through the block (and heater where fitted). Some pumps are fitted with a clever hole in their face; this starts weeping coolant when a pump failure is imminent. (Although, this might also just be a leaky transfer hose.) Other pumps simply let you find out the hard way that they've given up the ghost.

A water pump that's about to fail often gives some warning by emitting sick-sounding grinding noises. On pumps with a fan bolted to their nose, try rocking the fan back and forth; if it moves appreciably, the pump has either already failed or will shortly. The main cause of water pump failure is incorrect belt tension. If the belt's too tight, the

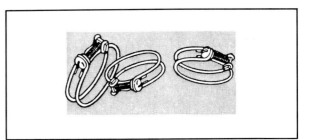

Dual-wire hose clamps may be authentic but they just don't work all that well. Replace them with band clamps unless you're showing the car. Moss Motors, Ltd.

bearings are quickly destroyed; if the belt's too loose, the pump just doesn't pump. There should be about ½ in. of free play in the average fan belt.

Most older water pumps can be rebuilt with new packing and bearings. I've found that these parts are getting almost impossible to find, however. (The repair isn't always successful, either.) If the parts can't be found—or if a new or rebuilt pump is available for not much money—I'd recommend replacing it rather than trying to fix the old one. Even an old pump that takes to a home rebuild doesn't seem to last as long as a replacement.

On rarer cars, however, you can save a lot of money by rebuilding the pump yourself. If you can find the parts and have access to the right tools, go ahead and do the work as outlined in your shop manual. This is basically a straightforward job with one or two exceptions: it will make things easier if you have a puller to remove the water pump impeller from the shaft, and a press can be helpful when fitting everything back together. You might also encounter a bushel basket of free ball bearings

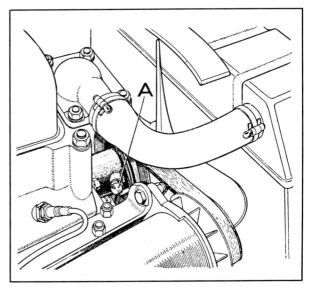

Older water pumps usually need some kind of supplemental lubrication, either through a grease nipple or an oiling hole as shown.

Heater valve is a frequent source of leaks; cleaning the threads and wrapping them in Teflon tape often solves the problem. Lubricate the cable and valve annually.

that rain out of the pump the moment you take it apart. Do the work over a metal pan to catch them all.

Radiator

The radiator is kind of the workhorse of the cooling system, and usually a tough enough piece of goods. Failings common to radiators are leaks—usually showing up as rust-colored streaks running down the fins—and blockage. Blockage on the outside of the fins is easy to spot and correct; old bugs and tar and dirt and oil merely clog up the outside of the radiator and hamper its ability to pass heat from the coolant to the surrounding air. This can be fixed by gently wiping the fins with kerosene—don't bend them, they're quite fragile—and then

Poorly soldered radiator fins are likely to leak again soon.

using a stiff plastic brush and lots of soapy water to remove the remaining crud. You can blow out any junk left behind with a gentle stream of water or compressed air. (Incidentally, too much paint will hamper the fin's abilities as well, so never apply more than a coat or two over the radiator during the restoration.)

Blockage on the inside is harder to detect but probably more common. Rust and scale quickly form in the cooling system and it loves to get caught in the narrow passages of the radiator. A good test is to completely drain the radiator, remove the bottom hose and quickly pour a gallon of water into the top. It should come out at the bottom immediately without backing up.

If it doesn't, you'll have to clean out the inside of the radiator. Minor deposits can be removed with a commercial flush-and-fill kit powered by a garden hose, but most of the time it's best to take the radiator to a professional shop to be boiled out. Even this doesn't always do the trick, so you might also consider trying to find another radiator in better condition.

Leaks can often be soldered; I'd let a professional solder holes in the fins because the job is harder than it looks. Cracks around the header tank and hose takeoffs can be fixed by a do-it-yourselfer using an appropriate solder. There are also a number of chemical goodies you can pour in the radiator that are designed to stop the leak from the inside; these pour-and-patch solutions make me nervous, though. Even if it stops the leak, what *else* is it going to stop? I can't bring myself to use them.

Radiator hoses are simply expendable items that should be changed every couple of years without fail. They can tear, split, blow out and harden over time—the latter perhaps being the most dangerous, since a hardened hose can transmit vibration to the radiator and damage it. Try to use pre-formed hoses when you can find them; they're easier to work with, don't constrict the water flow and simply look better. Since preformed hoses aren't always available, though—some cars didn't even use them when new—try to at least get a hose with internal wire support for the top and bottom mains. These will last longer and resist kinking better than plain hoses.

Pulling off an old hose can be a real pain since they like to freeze onto their mounts, but if you have a new hose in hand you can just slit the old one and peel it off. When you first buy a car I'd recommend changing *all* the hoses immediately. That means not just the mains but especially the smaller feed hoses and heater lines, which are harder to reach, and therefore probably older and weaker, than the main ones.

When fixing up a new hose don't overtighten the clamps; as soon as the new clamp bites into the rubber, stop tightening. Unless the car is going to be

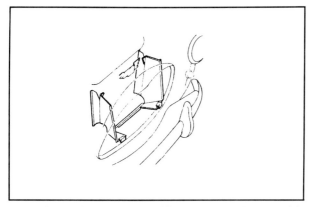

If radiator shroud came with the car, make sure it's there and in good condition. Shrouds can make a big difference in the car's cooling ability. Moss Motors, Ltd.

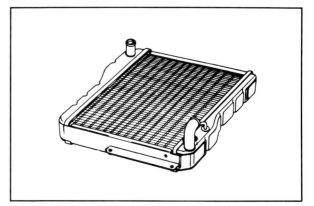

Radiators usually get blocked in all those small fins. Water from a garden hose should travel from top to bottom without backing up. Moss Motors, Ltd.

shown, I'd recommend replacing the old dual-wire clamps with the modern steel band type. (In your carry-along safety kit, toss in a few of the new plastic press-together hose clamps and some duct tape. I don't have enough experience with plastic clamps to say you should use them all the time, but late at night on the side of the road they're a whole lot easier to put on than metal clamps. Duct tape is used to temporarily patch a blown hose—it works like a charm for a few hours.)

The thermostat is going to be another big source of woes. Normally sitting in the engine under the top main hose connection, it regulates the flow of water from the block into the top of the radiator. When the engine is cold, the thermostat stays closed and water is routed straight back to the water pump. As the engine warms up, the thermostat opens and re-routes the water so that it flows through the radiator before being allowed to return to engine. Operating temperature is reached much more quickly this way; many people remove the thermostat if the car shows signs of overheating, however, and foolishly leave it out. If your car tends to stay cold for a long time after starting, check to see if there even *is* a thermostat in place.

Early thermostats are of the bellows type: alcohol inside a set of metal bellows boils and expands with heat, eventually pushing open a valve that allows water to flow past it. Newer thermostats use a temperature-sensitive wax capsule instead of alcohol and bellows, but the operating idea is the same. Both types of thermostats will fail after a while, and both can be tested the same way. Pull the thermostat out of the car by loosening its housing; this can be tough if the housing bolts have rusted into place, so use WD-40 on them before you start. Taking off the housing will also probably dribble water all over the engine, so unless you don't mind some added slop under the hood it's a good idea to drain the block and radiator about halfway. Most English engines have petcocks in

both places; if not, loosen the lower radiator hose enough to let some of the water out.

Once the thermostat is out, suspend it in a pan of cool water on the stove. Then heat the water slowly and see if the thermostat opens as the liquid approaches the boiling point. You should also suspend a thermometer in water to check on the exact temperature of opening and closing—the rated opening temperature is usually stamped on the base of the thermostat itself. If a thermometer isn't available, though, you can usually just eyeball it; the thermostat should start opening before the water reaches a rolling boil.

Thermostats must be placed back in the engine the correct way—with the temperature-sensitive device pointing down into the block. The thermostat housing gasket must also be in good shape; you're probably best off replacing it every time you pull the unit out.

Next up on the hit parade is the fan, which pushes or pulls air through the radiator to enhance the transfer of heat. The fan is traditionally made of metal and mounted on the end of the water pump nose. (This sort of fan constantly turns and robs the engine of power even when additional cooling isn't needed, so some variations have been developed for later cars.)

The only real problems with simple bolt-on fans are a crack in the metal (which can lead to a dangerous fly-off at speed), bent blades, bad rubber or Nyloc bushings, or backward installation. (The blades should be installed, of course, so that they draw air through the radiator instead of trying to push it forward from behind.) This most basic type of fan is often balanced to the water pump, so mark the relative positions before removal. If you forget, there will usually be some marks already there— dimples in the pump and pulley that must line up, or a hole drilled through the fan that corresponds with a dimple in the pulley behind it. Inspect the bushings carefully and replace any that are brittle

147

or cracked. These are another big cause of water pump failures.

Two twists might be added between the fan and water pump to keep the fan from turning when it isn't needed; in one, electric elements inside the fan connect and disconnect it from the spinning pulley on commands from a temperature-sensitive switch. These fans can fail to work properly if the electrical connections inside them or the switch get corroded or break. Other fans use a clutch filled with a temperature-sensitive viscous fluid that locks up when the engine gets hot. Viscous fans are virtually bulletproof as long as none of the fluid leaks out. To avoid this, don't rest them face or backside down. Both types of automatic fan can be checked simply by starting the engine and watching to see if they start spinning once the car is thoroughly warmed up.

Auxiliary electric fans can also be used, either from the factory or added after the fact. These will either push (from the front) or pull (from behind) air through the radiator—it doesn't matter which—and can be controlled manually by a switch on the dash or automatically by a thermo-switch in the coolant flow. Check the automatic variety the same way you'd check a viscous fan (by eye), and just flip a manually controlled fan on to see if it's working. If either type has failed try to first jump power, and ground directly to the fan motor. If it still doesn't spin the trouble is in the motor itself; if it does spin, the trouble is in the ground, switch or wiring.

An element of the cooling system that's usually overlooked is the pressure cap. By pressurizing the liquid in the cooling system the boiling point is raised and the engine can operate safely at a hotter—and more efficient—temperature. A pressure cap merely closes off the system until a preset level of pressure is reached, at which time it opens and lets some fluid (and pressure) escape. Usually an overflow tank catches the escaping fluid and the engine is allowed to suck it back up when things cool down.

The only thing likely to go wrong with this system (aside from a leaky overflow tank) is that the rubber gasket on the bottom of the cap tends to crack and break up with age. Check this visually and replace the whole cap if the gasket is suspect.

You can also get the cap itself pressure tested at a garage if you suspect it doesn't work even though it looks okay. It will cost about as much as a new cap, though, so I rarely bother.

The same garage can also pressure test the entire cooling system, and this might be a better investment. If the cooling system loses pressure after it's been pumped up on the test rig, it indicates a leak somewhere. An external leak should be relatively obvious unless it's in the heater core. (The core is a real bear to get to on most cars, so leaks often go unnoticed.)

If there are no signs of an external leak, chances are the head gasket is letting some of the coolant pass into the combustion chambers—the proverbial "blown" head gasket. This should show up quickly on a professional test rig; run the engine briefly and it will rapidly pressurize the cooling system. Other at-home indications are an oily scum floating on top of the coolant with the engine turned off, small white bubbles running in the coolant while the engine is on or water in the crankcase oil. Bad compression readings on one cylinder also can point to a blown head gasket.

Unfortunately, overheating is not always caused by a fault of the cooling system itself—two tuning adjustments can also be responsible. If the initial engine timing is retarded too far or the automatic advance gadgetry isn't working quite right the engine will run hot enough to outstrip the capacity of the cooling system. An overly lean mixture will do the same thing, and the ultimate cause of overheating is identical in both cases; the combustion charge is still burning after the exhaust valve opens. The super-hot gas passes through the exhaust ports rather than being confined to the combustion chambers, which are better able to absorb the heat.

Improper lubrication can also lead to overheating—the wrong grade or level of oil will do it. It's also not uncommon for newly rebuilt engines to run a little hot during their break-in period—not too hot, of course, or the brand-new engine can be ruined before it ever gets set up right. In short, make sure that the timing, fuel mixture and lubrication are all correct before tracking down a hard-to-find cooling problem.

6

Carburetor Restoration and Tuning

Everything I've said up to now about making sure you can get things back together after you've taken them apart goes double, *triple*, for carburetors. Even the simplest carbs have about three jillion little pieces to keep straight.

You not only have to document how everything comes apart, you have to be very gentle and patient in the disassembly. I went over to my friend Joe's house once to help him rebuild a Carter four-barrel, and got there just in time to see him pull the top off the carb and tip the whole thing over. About seventy little balls rained out and rolled down the driveway, picking up speed as they went down the

gutter and out to sea. I took Joe into town to buy a new carburetor.

Discretion is the better part of valor with carburetors, particularly if your car runs fine already. The two schools of auto repair—the "Everything must be taken apart and checked to be reliable" school versus the "If it ain't broke, don't fix it"

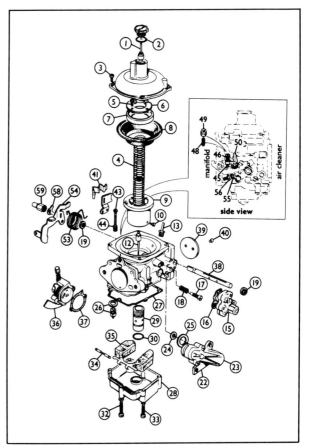

Your average Stromberg CD carburetor. Pay close attention to the condition of the main diaphragm (part number eight); it can't be torn, crimped, cracked or eaten away by solvent and fuel. Moss Motors, Ltd.

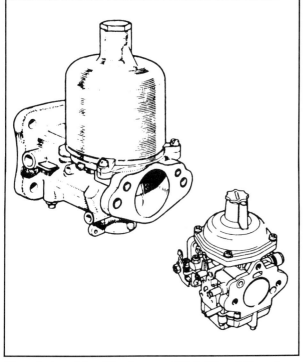

Most obvious identifier between SU (left) and Stromberg (right) is the SU's much taller dashpot. Moss Motors, Ltd.

149

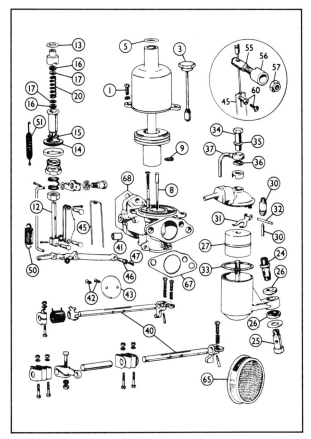

Early SU might look a little daunting from this angle, but it all goes together sensibly—assuming you keep the assemblies straight as you go. Moss Motors, Ltd.

Uni-Syn synching tool can be adjusted for overall air-flow by spinning the central block in and out.

school—really come to loggerheads here. The sensible course of action is usually somewhere in between; on a simple SU I don't mind tearing the whole thing down. With the four-barrel Holley sitting menacingly atop a TVR Griffith's engine, however, I'd rather clean and adjust the accessible parts and leave the internal workings alone, if possible.

Some components, like automatic choke housings, should be left alone as a matter of course. Your shop manual will indicate which items to avoid doing exploratory surgery on.

Tune-ups are a constant happening with British carburetors, and not a cheap one if you're paying someone else—sooner or later you'll have to learn the job yourself. As daunting as carbs seem, they soon lose their mystery and you'll actually *enjoy* working on them.

There are two distinct types of carburetors on English cars, *fixed jet* (Weber, Holley, Solex, Carter, Zenith) and *variable jet* (SU and Stromberg). You have to handle them two different ways.

Fixed-jet carburetors, which are relatively rare in this field, are more complex but they need much less attention. In general, as the engine speeds up and the demand for fuel and air increases, different holes and jets come into play inside this type of carburetor. But it doesn't matter whether you understand their principles or not: Clean, inspect and adjust a fixed-jet carb to specs and it will work—that's all there is to it.

Variable-jet carburetors, which are much more common on English cars, are another matter. These are simpler, and it's a good thing—you really have to know how these monsters work if you ever want to make them perform. Carburetor theory is covered later on in this chapter, and if you've got SUs or Strombergs under your hood you should study that section carefully.

Carburetor Rebuild

Tune-ups, which can usually be done with the carburetors on the car, are one thing, but carb rebuilds are something else entirely. To make sure

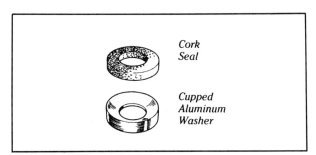

Cork Seal

Cupped Aluminum Washer

Cork gasket and aluminum washer prevent major leaks underneath older SU carburetors. The cork adapts to the washer and must always be reassembled with the convex side down. Moss Motors, Ltd.

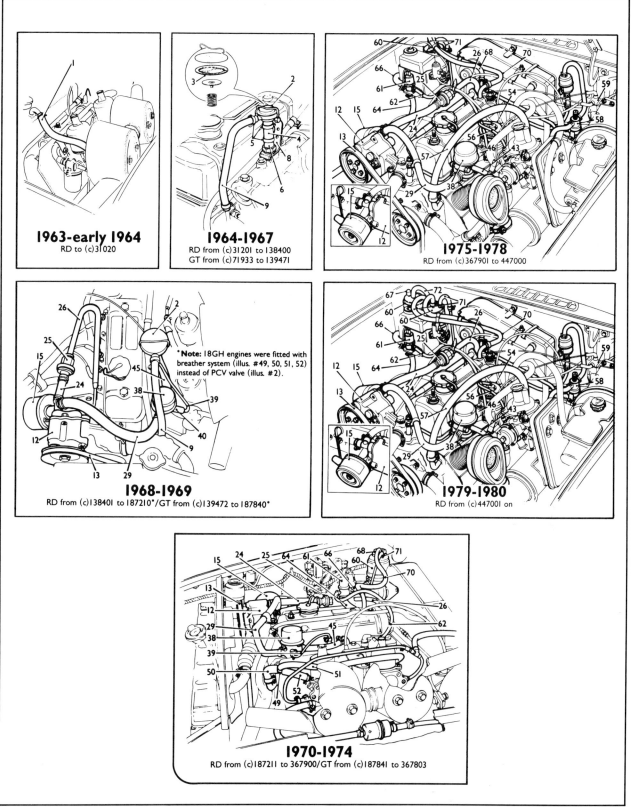

1963-early 1964
RD to (c)31020

1964-1967
RD from (c)31201 to 138400
GT from (c)71933 to 139471

1975-1978
RD from (c)367901 to 447000

Note: 18GH engines were fitted with breather system (illus. #49, 50, 51, 52) instead of PCV valve (illus. #2).

1968-1969
RD from (c)138401 to 187210*/GT from (c)139472 to 187840*

1979-1980
RD from (c)447001 on

1970-1974
RD from (c)187211 to 367900/GT from (c)187841 to 367803

Smog equipment became more and more complex—and troublesome—as time went on. Obviously, this is a big factor in deciding what year car you're after. (In general, the less smog equipment, the easier the maintenance and the higher the horsepower.) Find out what sort of smog tests are part of your state's registration system and whether the buyer or seller is responsible for the equipment. Moss Motors, Ltd.

a tune-up's going to work, I like to rebuild the carbs on any newly acquired car at least once.

Rebuilding means taking apart the carburetor, checking out all the parts, cleaning everything thoroughly, resetting everything to specifications and replacing any parts that need it. Under the "parts that need it" heading should be included as many gaskets, washers, O-rings, springs and check valves as you can lay your hands on. That means starting out with a rebuild kit.

A rebuild kit consists of replaceable parts deemed necessary by a supplier, based on his experience of what parts usually need changing—just buy the kit and swap the bits. When buying rebuild kits, though, remember a few things: Give as much information to the salesperson as possible, including year, make and model of car, and the carburetor brand, type, size and serial number. For cars with multi-carburetor setups, don't forget to mention whether you need a kit for the front or rear carb (or the middle if you've got three), for all of them or whatever.

In practice, you'll probably have more bits in the kit than you need, since one kit may serve a number of different carbs. You might also find that your kit *doesn't* have some of the things you'd like to replace, especially the float needle and seat, main needles and carburetor-to-engine mounting gaskets. The mounting gaskets are almost mandatory, so get them if they're not included. The float needles will need replacing soon if they don't right now, so buy those too. (If you don't use them right away, seal them up and keep them in the car; they'll probably save your neck later.)

On really beat-up carburetors you might have to replace big items like bodies or dampers. These items can cost big bucks new, so a trip to the junkyard might be in order, but be careful; many carb bodies and parts *look* alike without actually *being* alike. You'll have to give any swap-meet or junkyard carbs a thorough going-over to make sure they are

indeed correct for your car. (Even if they are, internal parts like jets and needle diameters might be different.) Finally, a used carburetor body might have exactly the same problems—and more—as the carb you're replacing.

Before you can rebuild a carburetor, of course, you've got to get it off the car, which can be harder than it looks. Once you get the air cleaners off, the first thing to do is to loosen the throttle cable, choke cable, return springs and so on. The same goes for the interconnecting rods that link multiple carbs together.

Removing the Carburetors

I suspect the English auto industry hired one engineer to do nothing but figure out the exact position that would prevent people from using ratchets or box-end wrenches to remove their carburetors. Another genius came up with the bright idea of making the nuts themselves out of an easily rounded alloy of something like aluminum, brass and wet Kleenex. And in a scheme worthy of the Nobel Prize for physics, someone else made the studs so long that the nuts won't come off without first pushing the carb halfway down the threads. Perhaps the idea here was to ensure that the threads would stay well lubed with the mechanic's own knuckle blood; whatever the reason, monkeying the carbs off the engine can be a real pain.

If the carburetors stick to the engine but you're sure all the nuts are loose, then they've probably fused to their gaskets. Simply jiggle the carbs around until they come free—don't bend the studs or bolts holding them on, of course, and don't whack them with anything solid. Most carburetors are aluminum and don't take kindly to physical abuse.

Once the carbs are off the engine they're duty-bound to spill gas and oil down your sleeves, so beware. Tip and rotate them over a pan to catch whatever comes out.

Before taking anything else apart, clean the outside of the carburetors *thoroughly*. You can use a

Interconnecting rods needn't be removed for tune-up; just slack off the nuts on the connectors.

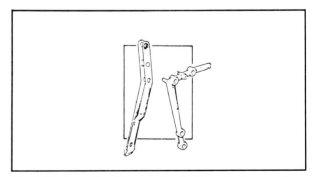

Choke linkages tend to round out at the pivots over time, leading to imprecise jet location and rich mixture. Replace them if they're not up to snuff. Moss Motors, Ltd.

soaking bath on fixed-jet carbs, though many variable-jet units have rubber diaphragms and O-rings that can be damaged this way. Alternatively, use solvent and toothbrushes, aerosol carb cleaner or both.

Once the outside is cleaned up it's time to dismantle the carburetors. Remember, the idea is to get the inside of the carb cleaner than it was when you started (carburetors are extremely susceptible to dirt and grit in their innards). Make sure you have a clean, smooth surface to work on, but not newspaper. Paper soaked with gas and oil falls apart, has lots of creases for parts to roll down and tends to hide bits and pieces beneath it. (I also lost an O-ring for hours once when it landed in the cereal bowl of a Froot Loops ad.) I'm much keener on clean, smooth plastic coverings or a very clean wooden workbench. Best of all is a metal baking sheet with sides, because the lips on the side will catch any parts that are making a last-ditch bid for freedom.

Once the actual disassembly starts, work in sub-assemblies; dismantle, inspect, clean and rebuild each one before moving on to the next section. Bear in mind that many carb parts will fit back on the unit any number of ways, but only one will be correct. This is particularly true of linkages, suction chambers (the big cups on top of SUs and Strombergs) and so on. I like to make a small scribe across both pieces in a hidden area so I can line them up correctly again later. Since this is a bad idea on a show car, you can also write down the relation of any markings to one another. On a Stromberg dashpot, for instance, you might make a note that the "m" in "Stromberg" lines up with a certain bolt or wire on the engine.

Another thing to watch is the location of the screws you remove. Ten screws might look the same from the outside but be different lengths. It's easiest just to put the screws back in their holes once the pieces come apart. When that's not possible, make a drawing or a cardboard template to hold the screws in their original relationship. You can do the same thing with a piece of styrofoam.

The natural place to start disassembling many carburetors is the independent float bowl. The purpose of a float is twofold: One, it shuts off the fuel flow when the bowl is full, which keeps the fuel pump from pressurizing the system and bollixing up the works. Two, it sets the level of fuel in the carburetor jet, which is something we'll get into later on. Accept for now that the float has to be properly adjusted for the engine to run correctly.

The bowl usually needs a good cleaning and the float should be checked to see if it lives up to its name. If it has a leak, of course, it won't rise to shut off the fuel flow when it's supposed to. You can shake the float and listen for sloshing inside, although sometimes solder in a metal float will

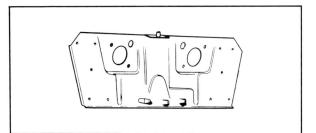

Stamped heat shield behind many carburetors is famous for cracking. It's there to keep fuel off the hot exhaust pipes and heat away from the carbs, so replace it if damaged. Moss Motors, Ltd.

make the same sort of noise. If there's any doubt, immerse the float in very hot water—a leak will show up quickly as bubbles.

Leaky plastic floats need to be replaced. Metal floats can be patched with solder: boil the float out, drain it, clean the hole, then cover the leak with a *minimum* of solder. Sand down the repair as best you can with fine paper; the float shouldn't weigh much more than it did originally. Test it again before putting it back in the carb, or save yourself a lot of trouble and find a new one.

On a fixed-jet carburetor, slowly work through all the chambers, openings and jets looking for scars and swapping old parts for new. Aside from inspecting the emulsion tube for cracks and damage, checking air control screws for scoring and inspecting all the linkages, there's not much else to look for on fixed-jets. All the parts should be thoroughly cleaned and anything that's scored or bent must be replaced.

The next thing to attend to is the all-important float needle and seat. If the needle is worn, or if dirt or crud is found anywhere in the assembly, the needle won't close entirely and the engine soon gets flooded with gas. If the valve *sticks* closed the

Out of sight, out of mind—it's a pain to pull most English airboxes off to check the filters, but it's necessary at every oil change.

engine starves, which is no better. The assembly should move freely; the needle must drop down as soon as the float drops, and close off tight when the float is pushed up. With the top of the float bowl off the carburetor you can check both of these things by blowing through the tube that brings fuel into the carb and pushing up on the float. (You might have to put your finger over an exit tube to the next carb or a vent hole—you'll find the right combination on the second or third try.) Finally, you'll need to set the float to the correct height if it's adjustable. Follow the instructions in your manual or rebuild kit—and defer to the former if there's a discrepancy.

A worn needle valve—usually it will show as a ring worn into the needle about midway up its taper—always needs to be replaced, as does its seat. If a replacement needle isn't handy, though, you can usually extend the old one's life by polishing the ring with rubbing compound. (Make sure all the compound is removed before putting it back together.)

With the float chamber taken care of, the next subassembly depends on the carburetor. Look at the dashpots of variable-jet carburetors next. The dashpot should be unbent, the inner surface and piston must be clean and unscarred and only the most minimal corrosion can be removed before scrapping the assembly. (Most manuals say there's no rescuing an even slightly corroded assembly, but if you're already resigned to losing the unit, try smoothing the bore with some very fine emery paper soaked in kerosene.) The piston itself should be as good as the dashpot, and if you have any reason at all to suspect these pieces, do a drop test.

Turn next to the main needle, which is fit to the bottom of the piston. Remove it by loosening—slackening, as the English would say—the setscrew sunk into the piston body, and let it slide out. (Some carburetors have spring-loaded needles, so be sure not to lose any parts that come out with the needle itself.)

Once the needle is out of the piston, a visual check often confirms your worst fears: any scraping along the needle's shank relegates both the needle and the carb's main jet to the scrap heap. (Occasionally you'll come across a needle that's so badly scored you wonder how on earth the car was running in the first place.) If the needle looks okay, though, it just needs to be checked for true. That's simply a matter of rolling it across a flat surface and making sure that it's not bent. The tip of the needle shouldn't wiggle as it's rolled or else it's a goner.

Once the needle checks out, turn to the jet—the tube assembly that the needle slides in and out of. Without removing it from the carburetor—or on SUs its connection to the float bowl, either—inspect the pipe between the jet and the float bowl for leaks. The seal on the float bowl side is usually haphazard at best, so be gentle with it and keep it under close watch. SU jets should slide smoothly in and out of the carburetor body, while Strombergs are usually fixed in place. Both types should be free of any scoring inside and out.

Next move on to the linkages. The throttle link should operate smoothly, and the butterfly inside the carb shouldn't hang up on any surfaces. The choke linkage should move freely a little ways, then progressively engage the choking mechanism—usually by lowering the jet itself, though many chokes work on different principles. (If the choke levers or clevis pins are worn and oval, the choke won't work correctly and can let the car run too rich, eventually diluting the oil and causing all kinds of grief. Chokes and their mechanisms are more important than they seem at first.) All the springs (especially the carburetor-to-engine return springs) must be clean, unbroken and unstretched. Any plastic clips or joints must be unbroken.

The spindles that run through the carburetor are also a major source of woe. The shafts and bushings that hold them will wear out over time, and when air starts entering the carb through these openings it makes tuning almost impossible. Grab each spindle gently with pliers and look for signs that they're not quite tight in their bushes. You can also check the spindles by shooting some aerosol carburetor cleaner at them while the engine is running. If the engine coughs or stumbles, the bushings are bad.

All older carburetors probably have some wear in their spindle bores, and new spindles alone might cure a minor problem. But if the spindles move around noticeably they'll need to be rebushed. Occasionally a carb came with plastic or metal spindle bores that could be replaced, but generally the spindle rides in the aluminum carburetor body itself. In that case, rebushing means that a machine shop drills out the old bores, puts in new bushings and reams them to size. This isn't an inexpensive proposition, nor is it one most shops can do: the drilling has to be done independently from one side to the other, so getting the holes to line up perfectly is difficult.

In the end, you usually have to send the carbs out to a mail-order shop that specializes in the job or simply find better carb bodies. (Volvo dealers used to rebush SUs regularly—old Volvos used SU carbs—so you might try one of them, too.)

Finally, give the carburetor body a critical eye. Cracks and dents usually mean the carb has to go. A crack all the way through the carb body makes the unit a goner, unless it's so rare that you can justify the heavy machine shop costs needed to fix it. Likewise, a dent that changes the shape of a venturi or float chamber or interferes with some moving part relegates the body to the scrap heap— or the core exchange pile.

While you're going through all these steps you should be looking for dirt and crud; it needs to be eliminated from all surfaces, especially the little passageways where it likes to accumulate. Usually a good shot with aerosol cleaner will do the trick, but sometimes you'll have to go in with a soft brush and really put some effort into it. Unless it's absolutely necessary, don't go poking around in a passage with a metal wire, which almost always enlarges the hole and changes the flow characteristics of the carburetor. About the only time you'll need to physically ream something out is on a very old carb that's been sitting full of water—there will often be milky fluid in the carb and a lot of white stalagmites all over the place. These are darn near impossible to get out of small areas, though you can clean them off flat pieces with fine emery cloth soaked in kerosene. A badly corroded carburetor is almost always a goner, but it doesn't hurt to try to rescue it; you'll only be out a little time.

Mating surfaces between parts should also be checked for true, and you can usually get away with doing this by eyeballing it—if something *looks* warped it should be checked with a straightedge. Parts out of true usually have to be scrapped, but occasionally they can be ground back into shape with emery cloth or fine sandpaper stretched over a flat surface like a piece of glass or marble. (No, most people don't keep marble slabs on their workbenches.)

A much more common occurrence is a little chip or scratch in a mating surface that lets air leak in or fuel leak out. Very small scratches will be covered up by a regular gasket, but larger problems need more drastic solutions. Depending on how big a hole needs filling, there are different gasket-in-a-tube products to do the job. They should be compatible with exposure to fuel, of course, and your parts supplier will direct you to the right one if you bring in the part in question.

While I'm on the subject of gaskets, I should point out the importance of knowing which ones you can and can't remove from the carburetor. Replace as many as possible, but before you go merrily ripping them off the carb make sure you've got a replacement! Try your darndest not to ruin any gaskets while you're first disassembling the carb—there'll be plenty of time to ruin them later. Even the best kits seem to be short a few gaskets that you think they should have. Once you've slated a particular gasket for execution, however, it's imperative to get

---

Air Filters

Unless you don't mind frequent engine rebuilds, make sure your air cleaners are in place and working. The slick unfiltered velocity stacks you always see on racing cars might improve performance, but the guy who put them there *expects* to tear the engine down every few hundred miles. Any sand and dirt that get sucked into the engine will scrape up the cylinder walls, valves and rings, totaling the engine in short order.

Any air getting into the engine has to pass through the filters first. Paper filters need to be replaced when they get dirty or performance will suffer, and wire mesh filters need to be cleaned and oiled often or they stop doing any good.

Most early sports cars use mesh filters. Mesh isn't quite as effective at removing dust from the intake air, but if they're clean they work well enough. To keep them working right follow these suggestions:

Toss the whole unit into a solvent bath to sit for an hour or two. Then agitate the bath long enough to dislodge all the dust, papers, cat hair and general crud accumulated inside. Tip the filters out and drain them, then prop them up to dry. Coat the elements with fresh engine oil. Once you've dripped out and wiped away all the excess engine oil—twirl them around your head if you don't mind spraying a little oil everywhere—put them back on the car.

You might be tempted to scrap the original filter system for a number of reasons, most of them legitimate. Paper filters trap more dust than mesh, so some people make the change for that reason. Others find that the paper elements designed for their car went out of production sometime in the Dark Ages. But some people go to a nonstock filter in the hopes of improving airflow and therefore performance. If the new filters provide as much protection as the old ones that's fine, but don't expect any miracles. Many stock engines wouldn't know what to do with increased airflow if you stuffed it in with a GMC supercharger; the added "boost" of low-restriction filters isn't likely to make any noticeable difference. It could well be enough to require you to retune your carburetors, though, setting them just a hair richer.

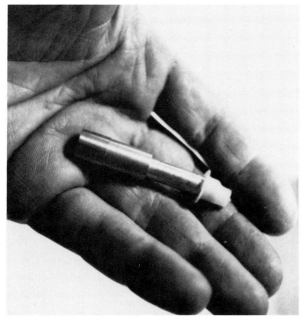

Main jets must be replaced whenever a flaw is found with the main needle.

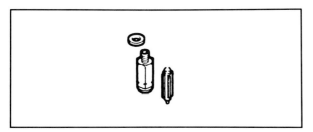

Float needle and seat should be inspected frequently; change them both if there's any doubt about the condition of either part.

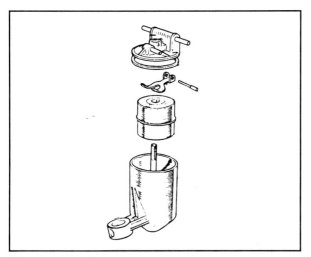

Float level is adjusted by bending the fork above the float to spec; it's the same principle on all adjustable floats you'll come across. Moss Motors, Ltd.

all of it off. That often means going over the gasket surface with a razor blade, which is an easy way to nick the surface, cut yourself and force grease into the wound all at the same time.

A lot of carburetors (and fuel pumps) use one or more diaphragms made of rubber, plastic or even coated paper. These should be changed if they're included in a rebuild kit, but otherwise just make sure that they're not torn or cracking. Diaphragms are surprisingly tough, and usually they're okay even in an older carburetor. Exposure to carb cleaner often ruins them, though, so give them a critical eye.

Other ancillary bits will have to be dealt with as you find them. Spring-loaded automatic chokes—relatively rare on English cars—should be sanitized by shooting in some cleaner. (Don't take them apart, as the springs have a bad habit of throwing little bits of the mechanism in your face.) Bent or broken return springs should be replaced. Corroded external pieces should be cleaned and spray-sealed or painted if you're going for a quality restoration.

Carburetor Reassembly

When putting the carburetor back together it has to be rebuilt *exactly the way it came apart.* (Unless it was put together wrong by the last guy, which is a nightmare you'll only solve by close inspection of the manual and diagrams.) The gaskets have to be right side up. Bent washers have to go on with the convex side pointing the right way. Nuts and screws and spacers have to all be put on in the right order.

As you're putting everything back together, give all the moving parts a light coat of oil and make sure they work smoothly. Oil the O-rings to seat them properly, and check that needles and jets are moving freely and not hanging up anywhere. Finally, remember that any screws or bits that are hanging in the airflow—the screws that hold the throttle disc to its spindle, for example—are going to cause a lot of grief if they come loose. A piece of metal that flies into the engine usually takes a cylinder with it, so take advantage of any locking method the screw came with originally. Usually spindle screws have splayed ends, but use a teeny dab of fuel-proof locking compound just to be sure.

Carburetor Theory

Oh, the words people use to describe SU carburetors! The letters stand for Skinners Union, but the other acronyms that have been suggested are universally unprintable. To many, these devices operate on a terrible, mystical plane of physics that doesn't apply anywhere else in the galaxy.

The thing is, SUs are actually the simplest, most basic carburetors in the world—which is one of the reasons I'm going to use them as my examples here.

The other is that chances are good your own car uses SUs or principally similar Strombergs, both of them variable-jet types.

SU carburetors use an absolute minimum of parts, moving and stationary, to do an amazing amount of work in an extremely clever way. They are simple, basic devices whose actions depend in no way on dark incantations, wings of bat or eyes of newt—which is just as well, since you'll be fiddling with them for as long as you own your car (and because Moss Motors stopped selling newt's eyes when Jensen-Healey folded).

But before any carburetor can make sense you need to know a few basics: The first is that engines run on a mixture of air and fuel, at a ratio in the neighborhood of 14.7:1 by weight.

Let's say that 14.7:1 is an ideal mixture for our engine; all the oxygen in the air and all the gasoline in the fuel is consumed with each firing of the spark plug. (The ideal ratio is also called the *stoichiometric* ratio.) A ratio like 16.0:1, which would leave some oxygen unburned, would be called weak. A mix of 13.0:1, which would leave some gas unburned, would be called rich.

Strangely enough, you don't always want a perfect mixture. On cold starting you want to stuff a really rich mix into the engine for a little while, mostly because cold fuel doesn't atomize well. Similarly, a slightly weak mixture gives better mileage when cruising down the road, and a slightly rich mix is called for under acceleration. So the carb needs to supply different mixtures at different times, and an incorrect mix at any time means

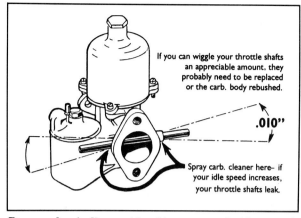

Damaged spindles and bushings are endemic to variable-jet carburetors, and they'll show themselves with these tests. Moss Motors, Ltd.

trouble. Too weak a mixture causes overheating and pinging, while too rich wastes gas, pollutes the air and fouls up the spark plugs.

The ony time you want to deviate far from 14.7:1 is on that first cold start, and that's the only time that most variable-jet carbs need some kind of mechanical add-on to meet the engine's demands. By pulling the choke, you artificially increase the area through which fuel can get to the engine. Everything else, like the slightly weak cruising mix and the slightly rich acceleration mix, is done automatically.

Here's the basic idea: You have a horizontal tube connected to the engine on one side and open at the other. As the engine turns it sucks air in through the tube. (Actually, atmospheric pressure

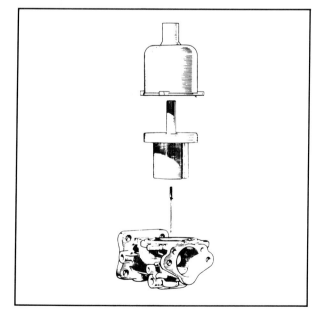

The piston sliding in and out of the airflow is the main fuel metering device; the needle attached below it is the fine-tuner. Moss Motors, Ltd.

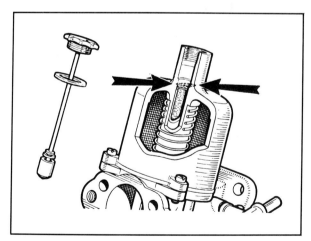

The oil level inside SU dashpots is critical to the carburetor's performance and varies from model to model, though most pre-1965 units (shown) have the oil level flush with the horizontal lip of the dashpot. No matter which carb you're dealing with, it's important to find the appropriate measurement and stick to it; every week the carbs will need topping up.

Mechanical fuel pumps rarely give problems as long as the filters are clean. Check them by removing HT lead from the coil, holding a jar under the output hose, and having a helper crank the engine. Pump should put out a regular flow of fuel with every revolution.

pushes the air in, but only guys with pocket protectors and slide rules will fight about it.)

In the middle of this tube is a piston that moves in and out of the airstream: it almost blocks it off completely when the engine's just ticking over, and moves farther and farther out of the way as the engine speeds up. The whole idea is to create a *venturi*—a tube with a restriction in the middle. If you pass air through this tube you'll get an area of low pressure at the restricted point (as proven by physicist G. B. Venturi, who probably had a pocket protector, a slide rule and lots of free time on his hands).

The faster the air flows the lower the pressure at the restriction gets, and you can see where this is all going. The piston in the SU carb moves out of the

Lower electric fuel pump joint is right where rocks and crud can damage it. This is the most common source of under-car fuel leaks.

158

way as the engine (and therefore airflow) speeds up to keep the low pressure at the restriction fairly constant. (Variable-jet carbs are also called *constant-depression* carburetors for this reason.)

There's a hole right at this low-pressure spot, and that's where the fuel enters the airstream. The hole is actually the top of a tube called the *jet,* and the jet is connected to a bowl full of gasoline. Again, you can say that the fuel gets sucked in here or you can say—since the bowl's at atmospheric pressure and the jet is open to a point of lower-than-atmospheric pressure—the fuel gets *pushed* in here. No matter how you look at it, the result's the same.

Now, then. Since we're keeping the pressure on the jet constant by moving the piston up and down, something's got to give us more fuel as the engine speed—and therefore the amount of air entering the engine—increases; otherwise, the proper ratio of air to fuel would be lost. Variable-jet carburetors make the necessary corrections by putting a tapered needle on the bottom of the piston to *slide in and out of the jet.* The higher the piston goes, the less the needle blocks the jet and the more fuel is allowed into the airstream.

Why does the piston move up and down? The piston rides up and down in an enclosed chamber called a dashpot, and it makes a tight seal between the dashpot's upper and lower chambers. The dashpot is vented above the piston to the engine side of the tube, while it's vented below the piston to the atmosphere side of the tube. When the engine is running, there's less pressure on the engine side of the tube and the piston gets pushed up by the higher air pressure underneath it.

But the really neat tricks are the simple ways small variations in the mixture are created. For example: Fixed-jet carburetors use pumps, diaphragms, balls and levers to provide an extra squirt of gas under acceleration. That's fine until they get all gummy and stop working, which in my cars, at least, takes about a day and a half.

In the SU some oil is added between the piston and the rod that keeps it centered in the dashpot; that oil also slows the piston's rise a little. Sure, that constricts the jet, but more importantly it *decreases*

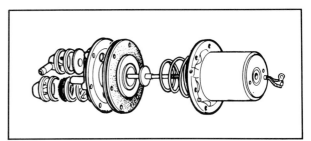

Fuel pump diaphragm rarely goes bad; don't open up the housing until after you've checked the points, lines and filters. Moss Motors, Ltd.

the pressure on the jet—more fuel flows into the airstream even though the opening isn't increased. The result is a temporarily richer mixture when you crack open the throttle; a few drops of oil do what some carburetors need eight different parts for.

Now if all that seems confusing, just remember there are two things that control the fuel flow: low pressure from the venturi size, and restriction from the needle in the jet. Of the two, the pressure differential is more important. The needle is just a fine-tuning mechanism.

Making Variable-Jet Carburetors Work—The SU

Once you know how variable-jet carburetors are *supposed* to work, you can learn how to *make* them work. Before getting into actual tuning of the carbs, though, you have to make sure that everything else is on the up-and-up mechanically. That means setting and measuring and inspecting everything that can be physically checked first—including not just the carbs but the points, igniton timing, tightness of the intake manifold, spark plugs and valve clearances. All these should be done first, since you can inspect them visually—you can *see* if they're right. Once you get to tuning the carbs, you'll be doing it

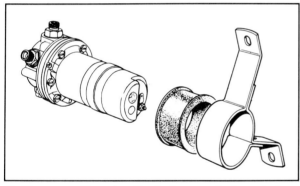

Rubber mounting ring for fuel pump isolates it from shocks. The ring is cheap (and the pump expensive) so replace it if it falls apart. Moss Motors, Ltd.

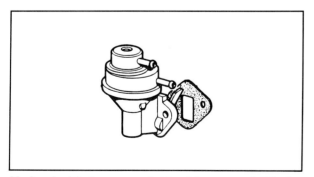

Mechanical fuel pump gasket is a big source of oil leaks. Some sealant doesn't hurt here.

Mixture Variations and Carburetor Adjusting

Three major factors can drive you to replace the innards of a carburetor—temperature, altitude and internal engine modifications. Excessively low air temperatures or airflow-increasing mods will force you to run a richer mixture than normal at all rev ranges. Variable-jet carburetors offer special needles and jets for these conditions, while most fixed-jet carbs offer modified jets for all occasions. Thicker damper oil or stronger piston return springs may also be specified to enrich a variable-jet carb mixture. (The stock damper fluid for SUs is 20 wt. straight oil, which can be found in motorcycle shops as fork oil if you can't locate it anywhere else. Strombergs use regular motor oil.)

High altitudes and excessively hot air temperatures may force you to change needles or jets to attain a leaner mixture.

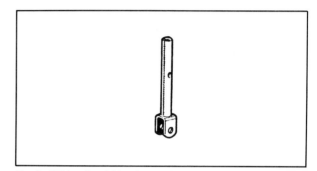

Early SU jet should be checked for deep scoring along the shank, one of the big causes of leaks with this kind of carb. Moss Motors, Ltd.

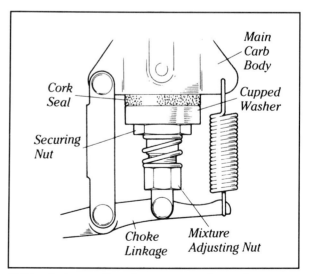

Getting in to move the mixture nut can be a pain on some carbs; remove the choke linkage and spring for the time being. Moss Motors, Ltd.

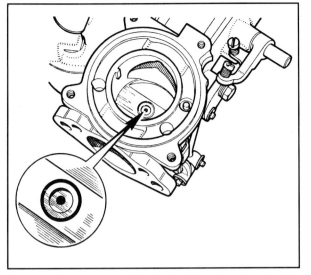

Jet centering means just that; the jet must not be offset in the carburetor body or it will bind with the needle and throw everything off. Refer to the text for centering tricks with your particular carburetor.

by ear and eye and inspiration, so you'd better make sure everything else is ready to go.

The first few tune-ups are confusing. Soon enough, though, you'll be able to field strip and tune a set of SUs blindfolded.

Single-Carburetor SU Tuning

The single-carburetor tuning procedure isn't much different from the one for multiple carbs, except that you only have to do it once and you don't need to do any carburetor synchronizing:

Pull off the air cleaner, start the engine, let the car get up to temperature and shut it off. (If you can't even start the miserable thing, set the initial idle and mixture as follows and try again.) Disconnect the choke cable.

Back the throttle adjusting screw off completely, then turn it 1½ turns past where it starts to move the throttle and leave it there. Move the jet up until it's level with the bridge or, failing that, as high as it will go. (To get a good look at this you'll probably have to push the piston up out of the way.)

Push the piston about halfway up, then let it go. It should drop to the bridge with a rather startling "click." If it doesn't, something's wrong; either the jet's not centered, the main needle and jet are bad or the piston and dashpot need work, in that order. You'll need to fix the problem before proceeding to the next step.

Lower the jet by turning the adjusting nut two full revolutions. Start the engine and set the throttle adjusting screw so the engine turns over at about 800 rpm. (Many cars are simply too tired to idle at 800 anymore, so settle on 1000 if you have to.) Move the jet adjusting nut up or down until (as every manual ever written in England calls it) "the fastest idling speed consistent with even running is obtained." That means the fastest idle you can get before the car starts popping and missing. Always remember that moving the jet and needle apart enriches the mix—moving them closer together leans it out.

Readjust the idle speed to 800 rpm. Now comes the fun part. Raise the piston one or two millimeters with the lifting pin on the side of the carburetor, or use a screwdriver if the lifting pin is frozen. If the mixture is too weak the engine will die off; if it's

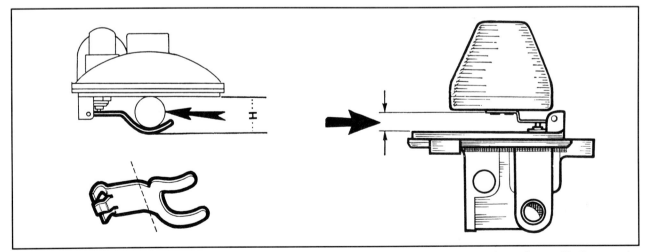

Two types of float level adjustments are used on most SU carburetors. Earlier units with a floating fork (A) are measured by inserting a drill bit of the proper diameter between the fork and the fuel chamber lid while holding the assembly upside-down; the bit should fit perfectly when the fork rests completely on the needle. Later units (B) with an integral bowl and fork can be measured with a bit, micrometer, or ruler; simply bend the fork until the proper clearance is reached.

too rich the revs will rise a fair amount; and if it's just right they'll rise slightly and then settle back almost to normal.

You can also judge mixture by what's coming out of the tailpipe. Black smoke and an even misfire indicate a too-rich setting. An unpredictable miss indicates a weak mixture. And the sound of a correctly tuned engine doesn't need describing—it simply sounds great.

Play with the mixture until correct, then reset the throttle adjusting screw one more time if you need to. If you did, check the mixture once more; it should still be okay but you might have to play with it a little more. It could take a few rounds of stair-stepping between mixture and idle speed before the carburetor idles properly and the engine gets the proper air-fuel ratio.

Replace the choke control cable with about a millimeter and a half of free play. Then have a friend pull out the choke until *just before* it starts to move the jet or choke disc. At this point you should be able to control the engine speed with the fast-running screw on SUs—the one that acts as a stop for the choke linkage on the carburetor. Set it so that the engine idles at about 1000 rpm, then push the choke back in.

Top off the dashpot with 20 wt oil, just below the hollow guide rod on dust-sealed carburetors (the ones without a little hole in the dashpot cap) and just above it on nonsealed ones.

The car should idle at 800 rpm, the exhaust should be clear and melodious, the engine should accelerate nicely with a stomp on the gas and all should be right with the world. If not, though, it doesn't mean there's something wrong. Don't be surprised if you have to go through the whole procedure another time or two before getting it right.

Multiple-Carburetor SU Tuning

The first step for multiple carburetors is a little different. After disconnecting the throttle and choke cables, slacken off the nuts on the rod that connects the carbs together until the actuating links spin freely.

Proceed for multiple carburetors as you did for single ones—just do everything twice or, heaven forbid, three times—until you get to the point of setting the fast-running screw. Now you get into the entertaining business of carb synchronization.

To synchronize multiple carburetors you'll need either a Uni-Syn or similar synching tool, or a 3 ft. piece of rubber hose. Stick one end of the hose up to your ear and the other up to the throat of a carburetor. You can pretty accurately gauge the airflow by the hissing noise you hear.

Start the engine with the carbs about 1½ screw turns off the throttle stops. Stick your Uni-Syn or rubber hose up to each carb and check its airflow.

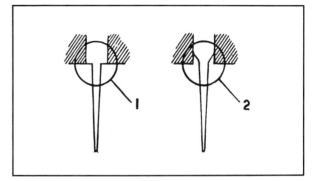

Non-sprung SU needles should be located with their shoulders flush with the bottom of the piston; with the much rarer slope-shouldered needle, align the bottom of the piston with the very end of the slope.

In the Uni-Syn a small ball will rise up and down in a clear tube indicating flow—the higher it goes, the more air is being drawn into the carburetor. You can adjust the scale itself by screwing the center block of the tool in and out. With a rubber hose, the louder the hissing, the more air getting to that carburetor.

On dual-carburetor setups, speed up the slow carburetor to match the fast one, then back off the

---

Electric Fuel Pump Woes

The electric fuel pumps used on most English cars are a bit iffy. If you like, you can usually swap them for a nonstandard rotary pump from another manufacturer.

Stock electric pumps usually fail in the following ways:

Pump Quits

You'll just notice that the pump stops clicking all of a sudden, or doesn't *start* clicking when you turn on the ignition. The wiring and connections are probably bad; if not, give the pump a sharp pop with a copper hammer. If the pump starts again, the points inside need cleaning. (If the pump doesn't start up again, it could still be the points.)

If the points aren't the problem, try loosening the fuel line at the first carburetor; if fuel starts flowing again, there's probably a stuck needle valve in the carbs. After that, check all the fuel filters and the lines for clogging, another big problem.

Pump Won't Quit

There's either a leak in a line somewhere, especially at the joints on the pump itself, or a needle valve is stuck open. In the latter case, fuel will dump all over the engine and tip you off immediately by the smell (or flames leaping out from under the hood!). There's also a slight chance that there's an air pocket in the fuel line. Purge it by pumping fuel into a glass jar from a disconnected line at the carburetor.

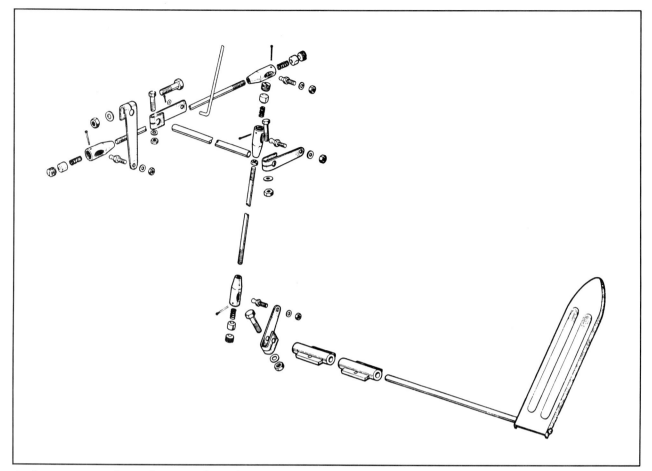

As important as the carburetors themselves are, the linkages should not be neglected either. All these pieces are subject to binding and failure. A good day's work is to pull the entire assembly apart and replace every washer, spring, and clamp. Sticky linkages can have you chasing carburetor demons that aren't really there.

same amount to achieve a normal idle. Repeat the procedure until both carbs draw the same amount of air. With triple setups, match the fast and slow carbs to the one in between.

Keep doing this until the carburetors seem to be drawing about the same amount of air and the idle is correct. Check the mixture of each carb again with the lifting pin or a screwdriver, and reset as needed. Check the airflow again and reset

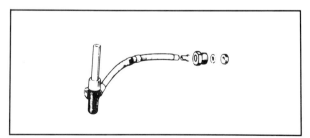

One-piece jet and tube from some SUs makes a lousy connection at the float bowl; go easy on it. Moss Motors, Ltd.

as needed. Keep going in this cycle until you've achieved a normal idle, all carburetors are drawing evenly and the mixture of each one is correct.

Reconnect the throttle links and blip the engine up to 2500 rpm. Let it run there for a few seconds, drop it back to idle and check the cars once more. They should still be functioning as you set them—if not, go back and give them another crack.

Reattach the choke cable and ensure that the choke on all carbs moves at the same time; correct any errors. When the chokes are set evenly, adjust the fast-running screw as on a single-carburetor setup.

SU HIF Carburetor

The later HIF carburetors were cobbled up in response to tightening emissions regulations, and consequently they're a bit more complicated than the older models in construction. (The biggest visual tip-off is that instead of a separate float bowl, the float bowl makes up the bottom of the carburetor body—hence the HIF name, for Horizontal Integral Floatchamber.)

HIFs use a disc choke which needs an occasional cleaning, but the mixture level is much easier to set than that of older SUs—it's just a simple screw. All in all, I don't mind the HIF one bit. While it might seem different externally, adjust and tune it as you would any other variable-jet carburetor.

Stromberg Carburetor

The other common variable-jet carburetor on English cars is the Stromberg. The Stromberg works in the same fashion as the SU, with a few notable differences in construction. The two biggies are a much smaller dashpot and piston assembly (possible because there's a diaphragm inside that makes a positive seal around the piston) and the integral float chamber on the bottom.

There's no clear advantage to the SU over the Stromberg or vice versa, although each has its adherents. In general, English car makers used whichever type they'd gotten used to, although politics sometimes came into play as well. Triumph changed over from SUs on the early TR-4s because SU was affiliated with the rival BMC company—it didn't change the car's performance one whit. Setting the mixture on Strombergs is usually simpler than on SUs, but often requires a special tool.

Some things to remember about Strombergs: On some units, the main needle leans inward, and it has to be put back in this way after disassembly. On others, while a special tool may be specified for adjusting the main needle, you might be able to get away with using a 0.125 in. Allen wrench. Stromberg Type CDSEs also need a special tool to remove the jet.

Don't mess with the jet of a Stromberg if it's sealed to the body by a plastic plug (usually with a

Balance tubes between multiple carburetors should be unclogged and tight.

Centering SU Carburetor Jets

On all SU HIF carburetors and the newer HS models with spring-loaded needles, don't worry about centering. But on earlier carbs, it pays to lift the piston and drop it to check the jet centering. If the piston falls with a loud click, you're fine.

If not, you'll have to center the jet.

On H-type carbs, remove the adjusting nut spring and loosen the locking nut, screw the adjusting nut all the way up and take the damper cap off the top of the carburetor. Stick a pencil down the dashpot and lightly press the piston down while holding the jet hard against the adjusting nut and tightening down the lock nut. Replace the adjusting spring and try the piston drop test again—repeat the procedure if necessary. If you can't center the jet after two or three tries, inspect the carb body, piston, dashpot, needle and jet for damage.

On HD-type carbs, loosen the locking nut just enough so the bearing will turn. Hold the jet up and push the piston with a pencil as before; tighten the lock nut, and check for the click as before.

For HS carbs without spring-loaded needles, remove the adjusting spring if there is one, loosen the locking nut and screw up the adjusting nut fully if it's got one. Center the jet by pushing the piston in as before, tighten down the locking nut and recheck the assembly.

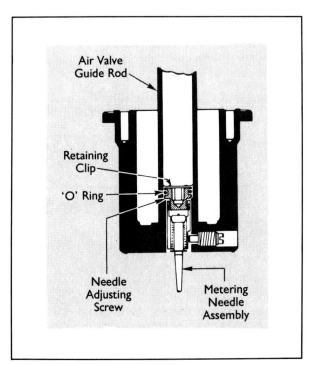

Lots of oil loss occurs in Strombergs with adjustable needles when the sealing O-ring goes bad. The service manual says not to mess with it, but careful handling will get the O-ring changed without damaging the rest of the carb; you've got nothing to lose. Moss Motors, Ltd.

brass cap covering it up). Just leave it be unless it's leaking fuel, in which case you'll have to dig in there to change the O-ring. And pay close attention to the condition of the main diaphragm—it should be clean, pliable and completely free of tears, pinholes, cracks, squish marks and so on. Roll it around between your fingers, try to see light through it and tug lightly on the edges. If there's any doubt about the diaphragm, chuck it and get a new one. If the diaphragm's okay, though, clean it off with a new rag and throw it back on. (Some rocket scientist at Stromberg made the diaphragm out of a rubber that's weakened by gasoline, so don't use any solvent stronger than denatured alcohol on it. When you're putting the diaphragm back in, incidentally, make sure that it's sealed all the way around and tighten the screws in small increments to prevent squeezing one part more than the others.)

As with SUs, Strombergs with fixed main needles need their jets centered from time to time. Jet centering on Strombergs with fixed needles is done basically the same as on SUs. Hold the piston down with a pencil and screw the jet up until it contacts the piston, then tighten the jet holder. Back the jet off three full turns and check its centralization; drop the piston and listen for the click.

Tuning Strombergs is again very similar to tuning SUs. The only differences of note in construction are the actual location of the idle screw and the interconnecting linkages; these change from model to model but are quite obvious on inspection. And rather than using idle speed as a guide to choke tuning, with Strombergs you just have to see that the fast-running screw is off the choke cam when the engine is tuned, warmed and the choke is fully off. Strombergs may have adjustable jets or needles to set the mixture, and a special tool may be required for either one; the idea is again the same as on the SU, though. Increasing the distance between needle and jet (lowering the jet or raising the needle) enriches the mix; decreasing the distance makes the mixture leaner. Some Strombergs also have an idle trimming screw on the side of the body; this fine-tunes the mixture. As the engine gets older, it will have to be slowly turned in until it's completely closed off. Basically, the trimming screw is something you won't need to worry about unless you rebuild your engine.

Newer Strombergs came with an automatic choke. I try to stay away from these if possible, but if they don't work there's no choice but to go in and play with them. Usually, a simple cleaning with all the parts in place will either cure the problem or reveal a broken piece. Don't remove the bimetallic strip (the coiled spring inside the housing) under *any* circumstances. You can check its operation, though, by dipping the whole assembly in hot water. The strip should start to move quickly, pulling in the tapered needle as it goes.

Tuning Fixed-Jet Carburetors

Though fixed-jet carburetors were almost universal in the American automotive industry before fuel injection came along, they've always been relatively rare in the English world. A fixed-jet carb usually has more parts overall than a variable-jet, but fewer moving parts. They generally require fewer tune-ups, too, and those facts are almost certainly related.

Tuning a fixed-jet carburetor should be a simple matter of setting the idle with the throttle control screw and adjusting the mixture with the volume- or air-control screw as specified in your manual. (Turning an air-control screw clockwise makes the mixture richer; turning a volume control screw clockwise makes it leaner.) Weaken the mixture until the engine begins to run with an unpredictable misfire or threatens to stall. Then enrich it, carefully counting the turns of the screw, until the engine begins to go off song again—this time the misfire will be regular and predictable. Back the screw off to a point halfway between the two and you should be pretty close to the ideal idle mixture. Making a half-turn either way might make the engine run smoother and faster, so experiment with small adjustments until, you guessed it, "The fastest idle speed consistent with smooth running is attained." You'll probably have to reset the throttle screw once more to get the proper idle speed back.

Unfortunately, just getting the idle mixture correct is usually not enough. Solex, Zenith and Weber carburetors all use different fast-running adjustments, accelerator pump mechanisms and so on. Setting these carbs to spec isn't hard, but you'll have to consult your shop manual, or better still a book dedicated to your carburetor type, to learn the complete procedure.

Weber Carburetors

The hottest fixed-jet carburetor—probably the hottest carburetor, period—you're likely to encounter is the Weber. It's not that the carbs themselves inherently flow more air or fuel or anything else, it's just that Webers are infinitely and easily adjustable, they have an excellent reputation and they're made to extremely high standards. (That's often reflected, of course, in an extremely high price.)

Unless your English car is an exotic like a Lotus or an Aston Martin, a Weber is going to be an aftermarket addition, which might cause some headaches in setting it up. Fortunately, it's easy to change jets and while you might be fiddling for a long time, you'll get it right in the end. If all else fails, the initial settings can be made by a specialist, who can teach you to do the work next time in the process.

Just adding Webers to your car may or may not make a big difference in its performance. To really take advantage of a Weber (or, for that matter, any aftermarket intake system), you might have to also install a free-breathing exhaust system and do some work to your cylinder head. A reputable parts supplier will discuss the realistic benefits of installing Webers on your car as it sits right now.

There are so many different downdraft Webers that even beginning to classify them is a major undertaking. Most English sports cars use sidedraft carburetors, though, and there are only two sidedraft Webers: the DCOE and the DCOF. (Actually, there's also a single-barrel OC model, but those are more likely to turn up in museums than under the hood of your car.) Identifying Webers is easy; after an ID number, a group of letters like DGV, IDA, DCOE or so on will tell you the carb type.

Weber DCOEs are something of the standard of the industry in British sports car modifications. If you plan to improve your car's performance in a major way, it probably pays to get familiar with DCOEs and their clones from Japan. DCOEs are remarkably easy to work on, and intentionally so: Weber made them so that they could be quickly tuned and modified at the track. Lift off the top cover and you're right at the float and jets; from this position, just about everything on the carb can be quickly removed, inspected and replaced.

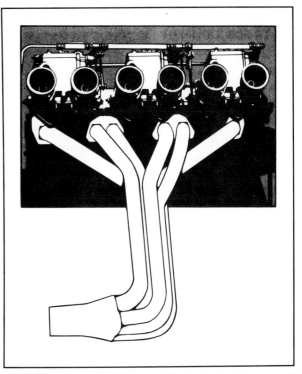

Imposing triple-Weber setup will give fantastic power if internal and exhaust modifications can make use of it. Moss Motors, Ltd.

7

Electrics Restoration

You've probably seen the T-shirts at British swap meets: "Joseph Lucas, Prince of Darkness," or "Why do the English drink warm beer? Because they have Lucas refrigerators?" British electronics have a lot in common with British carburetors—they are much maligned, rarely understood and frequently on the fritz. They are also, however, pretty darned basic.

You don't have to be an electrical wizard to work on them; in fact, it might actually help if you're not. You can spend hours pulling amperage readings out of a system before determining what's wrong and trying to fix it, but it's often faster to just go in, fiddle around and try to solve the problem on a much more basic level.

How Electrical Systems Work

At the risk of telling you what you already know, let's start out by getting one thing straight: The key to it all is a complete circuit. Using a battery and a

To properly finish the electrical restoration of this Austin-Healey, replacement wiring that matched the original was used. The end result was a concours-quality restoration. Robin O'Brien

light bulb as an example, you'll only get the light to turn on if one end of the filament is soundly connected to the battery's negative pole, and the other to its positive pole. Electricity flows freely through metal and water, but it's blocked by rubber, plastic, air, dirt and most other things. Materials that electricity flows through easily are *conductors*; those it can't travel through as well are *insulators*.

Anything that prevents electricity from flowing from one pole to the other will cause an electrical system to fail: a broken wire, a burned-out filament, corroded contacts or a switch that stays open (the metal contacts inside the switch don't touch each other). If there's not a complete path of conductors from the battery to the light and back, forget it. If the circuit is complete, though—don't worry for now about proper watts, volts and amps—the light will illuminate.

Electricity is also lazy—it will take the easiest path from pole to pole that it can. If you took the same lighting circuit and added another wire bypassing the bulb (creating a *short circuit*), it would flow around the bulb and the light would stay off. Now you get into *resistance*; electricity will flow through the filament of the bulb if it has to, but it's easier to flow through big, fat metal wires. When you make electricity work hard, like forcing it through a filament, is when you get something out of it. If it has to spin a motor or light a bulb to get back to the other pole it will, but you have to give it no alternative.

Now all circuits—for our purposes, anyway—must have some resistance in them for safety's sake. If they didn't, the electricity flowing freely from pole to pole would not just be a waste, it would heat up the battery and the rest of the circuit, causing a fire or even a battery explosion.

In automotive circuits, the idea of a wire to the job site and another one coming home is the same with one minor twist: instead of running return wires all the way back to the electrical source, the unit is *grounded* to the car itself. In other words, the entire car acts as one big return wire. Power flows out through a wire, into the unit where it does its work, and then into the body or frame of the car to return to the battery. The battery's ground pole—usually the negative terminal—is just connected to the frame. (If the main ground wire is loose, it can cause the ground circuit to be carried by something like a choke or heater cable. If these cables are hot to the touch, that may be your problem.)

Now you have to add a few more things to the circuit to force electricity to do what you want it to. One, of course, is a switch. This simply breaks or completes the circuit at the appropriate time, usually by connecting and disconnecting two pieces of metal.

Another is a fuse, a piece of metal in the circuit that burns up if it gets too hot. If a wire becomes frayed and touches a ground before it reaches the unit it's supposed to power, there's no resistance anymore and you might have a fire on your hands. Before the wiring or battery can get that hot, though, the fuse burns up and breaks the circuit.

The first thing to check when an electrical system fails is the fuse. Inspect the circuit and isolate the cause of the blown fuse before popping in a new one and considering it fixed. Look for frayed wires, melted insulation and short circuits in the unit itself.

In practice, English cars do seem to just blow fuses spontaneously sometimes. Some people will throw in a new fuse right off and see if that cures the problem for good, for a few days or for a few seconds. Inspect the circuit beforehand, but if no obvious cause is found go ahead and try a new fuse. If that one blows, you'll know you've got a problem on your hands. Whatever you do, only replace an old fuse with the correct amperage replacement—

the fuse is there to prevent damage and fire in case of a bad short. Putting in a heavier duty fuse in the hope it won't blow out is asking for trouble.

Fuses and batteries account for the majority of the electrical problems you'll encounter. Check regular batteries with a hydrometer once a month; inspect the main terminals twice a year and replace if needed. Fuse boxes should be disassembled and cleaned once a year, and spare fuses should be carried in the car at all times.

Beyond the battery and fuse box, probably the most common cause of electrical failures is a broken circuit due simply to corrosion or crud—dirt and especially corrosion are great insulators. The first thing to do if an electrical part gives you grief is to simply clean up all the terminals in the circuit with emery paper (fingernail emery boards work very well) and then hook everything back together again. Most of the time that's all it takes to make the fix.

6 Volt and 12 Volt Systems

Back in the good old days before lots of power accessories and high-compression engines, most auto electrical systems worked on 6 volts. (Volts are a unit of electrical measurement roughly equivalent to water pressure—the higher the voltage, the easier it is for the electricity to push through a source of resistance.)

There's really nothing wrong with 6 volt systems, but you have to use the proper wiring, bulbs, and accessories when working on them. (To get the same amount of electricity through a wire with 6 volts the wire must be bigger than it would be for 12

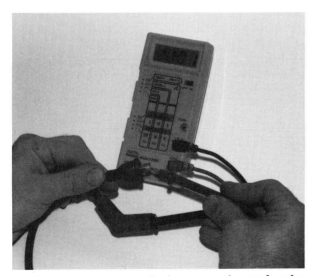

Multi-tester made especially for automotive work; volts, ohms, ignition dwell and even engine speed can be read. The Eastwood Company

This little chip in the taillight can lead to all kinds of grief. Water will get into the assembly and destroy the terminals, wiring and even start rust on the body. Small fix, big potential for trouble.

volts—just as you'd need a bigger pipe to flow the same amount of water through at a lower pressure.) Use thinner 12 volt wiring on a 6 volt system and the electrical goodies will perform sluggishly (for lack of juice) while the circuit itself will get extremely hot (from too much resistance).

It should be obvious which kind of system your car uses, if not from the manual or just common knowledge then from the battery itself. In addition to having "Six volts" written prominently across the top, 6 volt batteries usually use three filler caps while 12 volt batteries use six.

Some Healeys, MGs and the like with 12 volt systems actually used two 6 volt batteries wired in series, apparently in an attempt to make things more confusing and expensive when they failed. If you get tired of fighting with the two six-volters, it's

okay to drop one small 12 volt battery into one of the trays and use that instead. You'll have to bypass the old tray entirely, of course, to make a complete circuit.

Positive Ground and Negative Ground

Older English cars are usually positive ground ("positive earth" in England), which as you'd guess means that the positive battery terminal is attached to ground and power goes out to the electrical parts in wires from the negative terminal.

Later English (and nearly all other) cars are wired negative ground. It doesn't really matter one way or the other, as long as you know which type your car uses and stick to it.

The accessories must also be capable of operating on the proper polarity (ground type). It's vital that charging and jump-starting be done by attaching the charger or cables' *ground* terminal to your own; don't blindly hook things up negative to negative and assume that's the same thing.

There's usually a plate like this in the engine compartment of an English car wired up negative ground—the "normal" way to Americans. Positive-ground cars usually don't mention it. Moss Motors, Ltd.

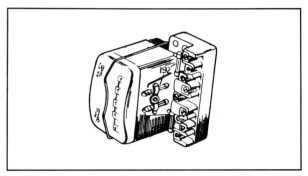

Failing voltage regulator (control box to the Brits) will mimic all kinds of other maladies: low battery, broken generator, short circuits. Some, like this one, need to be cleaned and adjusted periodically. Moss Motors, Ltd.

A terrifying wire junction. A lousy tape splice has been made at the bottom, wiring is missing its insulation as it comes out of the harness and things just plain look ready to burst into flames. Tackle this kind of thing before it causes problems, not after.

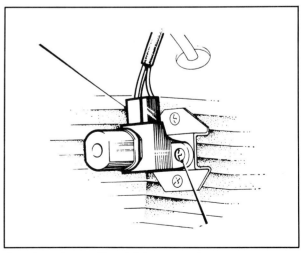

A major source of headlight woes—floor-mounted dimmer switch is right in the path of leaks and dirt. Usually just the outer terminals get corroded. Moss Motors, Ltd.

Occasionally, you'll find that you'd like your older English car to be wired up negative ground so you can fit newer accessories, an alternator instead of the original generator, a stereo and so on. There are kits available from parts suppliers to help you do the switch—it's a fairly easy job.

Electrics Troubleshooting

Once you've cleaned all the contacts and quickly checked the wiring, the next trick with electronic troubleshooting is to try to keep breaking down the problem in half until you isolate the flaw. (On simpler circuits you should be able to trace the wiring by sight, but it never hurts to consult the wiring diagram in the manual first. Most circuits power a whole lot of different things at the same time, and the trouble could be in more places than you'd expect. Get familiar with the diagram and learn how the current is *supposed* to flow before you figure out how it actually *is* flowing.)

Using a test lamp or multi-tester, check to see if power is making it to the unit itself; if it isn't, you know the problem lies farther back between the power source and the unit. Pick a fuse box or switch halfway along that part of the circuit to try to cut the problem in half again—see if power is making it that far. Keep at it until you've narrowed the trouble down to a single area or component.

Electronic diagnosis only asks that you be very thorough and systematic. The system can always throw you a few curve balls, but by being careful with your methods you should be able to catch them quickly. Just keep an open mind as to what kind of peculiarities might be interfering with your systematic approach.

Let's take a simple electronic failure—a taillight that doesn't come on—and examine how to go about fixing it. As you'll see, there's nothing particularly difficult about the process, there are just some twists and turns and variables that can confuse you along the way.

First, turn on the taillight so that it would normally light up. Make sure that the bulb itself is working by trying a new bulb in the same place. If the second bulb also doesn't light, you can assume the problem is somewhere else. (A curve ball would be if *both* bulbs were bad, but don't expect this right off. If the power and ground seem to check out later, you'll look into this possibility.) Clean all the bulb, socket and terminal contacts and try again.

Next, check for power coming into the taillight assembly. Attach one lead of your test lamp to the base of the light socket and the other to a good ground. If the test lamp lights up, you know electricity is making it that far and the trouble is in the ground circuit. If adding a ground wire cures the taillight, check the assembly's ground connection—usually the back of the lamp just touches the body. If there's a separate ground wire, trace that back and check for continuity at its ultimate destination.

Once you're sure you have power coming in and good ground going out, put the bulb back in. If the taillight still doesn't work, you're looking at an internal fault—either both bulbs were bad or the socket itself is faulty.

If power *isn't* making it to the assembly, go back to the taillight switch and check that out. If power *is* getting to the switch but not coming out the

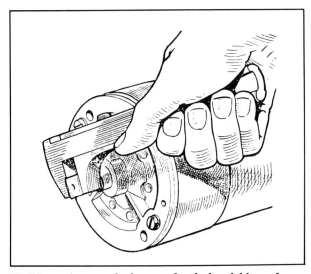

Wailing noises, smoke from under the hood, blown fuses, strange discharge readings, and melted wiring are the hallmarks of a pinion gear that's stuck in mesh with the flywheel. (Simply put, the starter doesn't let go again after it turns the engine over.) To disengage a suspected pinion gear, grip the end of the starter armature with a stout wrench and give it a good twist. Disconnect the batteries to avoid accidentally bridging two high-tension terminals with your wrench.

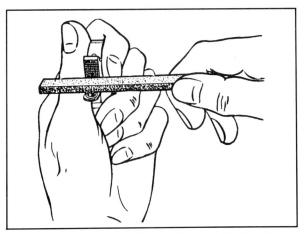

An emery board or fine file, carefully wielded, will true up the distributor contact points. Indications of badly-aligned points are pitting, pockets of discoloration, or a weak spark.

other side when the switch should be on, the switch is bad. You can replace it or, if you're lucky, take it apart, clean up the contacts and springs inside and put it back together.

If power isn't making it to the switch, go back to the fuse box and check the wiring going both in and out. Power going into the fuse but not out the other side means a bad fuse, even if it looks good. It could also be a bad fuse block connection. If power isn't getting to the fuse block, trace the wiring back—well, you get the idea. As you can see, the basic principle is quite simple; the application of it takes a bit more ingenuity.

Electrical components more complicated than lamps and switches often fail internally; that's obviously the case when a unit that's getting power and making a good ground still doesn't work. You'll have to decide for yourself, depending on the cost and ease of finding a new one, whether or not you want to go in and try to fix the unit. Often it's worth taking the thing apart regardless. If you're already resigned to replacing it, you've got nothing to lose.

Once inside the unit, you'll often find visual clues to the damage, like burned wiring, char marks or a broken connection. To check it further, it will help considerably if you can get a schematic of the component, but that's not always available. With motor assemblies (that includes starters, alternators and generators) try to find strong continuity between the body of the component and its internal magnets or coils.

Some continuity is often normal, however, so you'll have to go a few steps deeper and check the

unit's resistance with a multi-tester. The specified resistance may be listed in ohms, but you're interested in the specified amperage. Lower resistance (a short, in other words) will show up as higher amperage than normal across the unit.

Ohms, obviously, are a unit of measurement for resistance, and as long as we're at it we might as well cover the relation of volts, ohms and amps. (Amperage, measured in amps, is a unit of measure roughly equivalent to volume over time; with water, the measurement would be cubic feet per minute (cfm)—it's usually called *current* in electrical work. In equation form, it's volts (pressure) = amps (volume/time, or current) x ohms (resistance). So if you're putting the same voltage into a unit but the amperage has increased above normal, the ohms have obviously decreased. Decreased ohms means decreased resistance, and decreased resistance is merely a fancy way of saying "short circuit."

You may find yourself removing internal pieces of the failed component to check their insulation. It's often possible to reinsulate magnets and coils with a professional electrical tape—the heavy fabric kind, not the plastic stuff you get at the supermarket. By and large, though, it's easier to locate a replacement part than to do anything but an obvious repair on most components. If that's impossible and you can't find the fault yourself, you can hire an automotive electrical specialist to do the repair. Most of the time you can find one locally, although many are listed in classified ads like those in *Hemmings Motor News* and *Cars & Parts*.

Wiring Diagrams

Use wiring diagrams, but don't always trust them.

You almost can't get by without a good wiring diagram. On the other hand, each car seems to be wired a little differently from the one that came down the production line before it, so the chances aren't very good that your car uses the exact color coding and wiring paths as the general diagram. Fortunately, most of the systems that cause all the trouble—fans, lights, wipers and so on—seem to be the same from car to car. It's the little doohickies like overdrives and power windows that seem to part with the diagram most often.

Finding the right diagram is one of the best arguments for getting a good, authentic factory manual. Obviously, if there's one diagram included in a book called "MG, 1929-1975" it's not likely to do you a lot of good. A good diagram will not only show you how to trace a circuit you're currently working on, it'll also give you a good idea of how the car's wired up in general—do the wires usually change color when they go through a junction block? Are there sometimes inline fuses under the hood? Do a lot of components use separate ground wires instead of grounding to the body or frame?

Windshield wiper motors feature a motor assembly (left) that can be tough to sort out, but also a mechanical assembly (right) that's easy to repair by sight.

A wiring harness monster, laying in wait for unsuspecting victims. This could best be described as a project; the easier, more sane route would be to purchase a replacemnent.

You'll be a lot happier if you take your wiring diagram down to a print shop and make a few enlargements of it before proceeding. These are easier to read, you can write all over them and if a copy gets lost, who cares? Keep one copy clean and safe on file and use it as a master. Correct it as you go through the car and discover discrepancies along the way.

Wiring Harnesses

Wires themselves almost never go bad. The connectors come loose and get corroded all the time, but the actual wires will only fail when the insulation has been rubbed off—you should be able to see it visually. It's very rare indeed for a wire to fail inside a wiring harness; that's about the last possibility you should consider.

Still, you *might* just find that your car has been mucked about so much that it's easier to replace the whole wiring harness and be done with it. This is in no way a minor undertaking, however, especially if you haven't stripped the car down to its last few nuts and bolts in preparation for a complete rebuild.

A complete harness swap is usually only a good idea when somebody else has been making guerilla repairs for so long that you can no longer make heads or tails of what wires lead where. I once owned a Triumph "repaired" in this manner—a tangle of color-coded wires went into a huge junction block on the inside of the firewall and came out the other side. It took me a couple of days to realize that the colors coming out of the firewall had absolutely nothing to do with the ones going in.

By and large, the work involved—and the room for error—in installing a new harness makes it a job

to avoid if you can. On the other hand, it can take a tremendous amount of time to chase screwy wiring all over the car—considerably longer than it might take just to start again from scratch. It's your call.

You'll have to specify *exactly* the make, model and year of your car, along with any options like factory radio, overdrive, automatic transmission and so on, to the harness supplier. You should also only consider a high-quality harness; the cheap ones are worse than starting with a spool of wire, scissors, some tape and doing it yourself. A high-quality harness will use the same color coding as the original item.

Even if a whole harness is available for your car, which they sometimes aren't, it's not going to be perfect. It'll have a few extra wires somewhere, a few missing and it probably won't be the right length in all places. Furthermore, the connectors and clips are rarely all just the way you'd like. You'll have to lay the new harness out next to your old

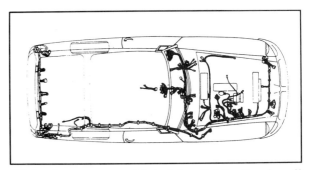

Wiring harnesses aren't to be taken lightly. Tagging all those wire ends is a job in itself. Moss Motors, Ltd.

171

one and make repairs and replacements before fitting it—add and subtract wires as best you can to match the harness that's come out of the car.

You might find adding wires inside the harness impossible, but you can often get away with wrapping them along the outside carefully with black gaffer's tape. Pay special attention to places that have obviously been rewired on the old loom, and take note of wires whose colors don't match. If there's a discrepancy, consult your wiring diagram and defer to it when working up the new harness.

The old clips and connections can be put onto the new harness where needed, but make sure to clean them well beforehand. Always try to solder new clips in place instead of just pressing or

---

Lucas Color Coding

Lucas came out with a more-or-less unified series of wire color codes before World War II. Sometimes these codes are helpful, but relying on them too much can get you in more trouble than just tracing things from their source. Even when the factory diagram is correct (which is not always), the coding seems to have just been ignored from time to time.

The basics of the wire coding system, however, are as follows, with solid colors listed alone and solid colors with stripes listed as solid color/ striped color.

Brown: Main feed from battery without fuse or switch protection.
White: Ignition circuit. Also components powered off ignition switch without fuse or switch protection.
Green: Components fed through ignition switch *with* fuse or switch protection.
Blue: Headlight.
Red: Taillight and side marker.
Black: Straight ground.
Yellow: Generator connections wired through ignition.
Brown-yellow: Generator to voltage regulator.
Brown-blue: Ignition switch to voltage regulator.
White-red: Igniton switch to starter solenoid and starter switch to starter solenoid.
Green-purple: Brake lights.
Blue-white: Headlight high beams.
Blue-red: Headlight low beams.
Red-white: Dashboard lights.

Lucas also instituted a standard color coding for fuses, although other manufacturers don't go by it. The Lucas fuse codes are a color printed on paper, listed here as print color-paper color.
Red-yellow: 5 amps.
Green-black: 10 amps.
Black-light brown: 15 amps.
Black-pink: 25 amps.
Black-white: 35 amps.
Purple-yellow: 50 amps.

---

squeezing them on, and secure them with shrink tubing. (Shrink tubing is a plastic material that shrinks around the connection when you heat it.)

You can also raid a junkyard for extra connectors, but ask the yard owner first. They often get peeved if you trash the whole electrical system just for two bucks' worth of fasteners. You can also pirate wires and subharnesses from scrap cars; check them for continuity before installation.

Before you can change a harness, of course, you've got to yank the old one out—often easier said than done. Make good drawings of how the old harness fits in the car before you even start pulling it, marking down the clips and grommets it passes through as you go. Finally, note every single connection for color and source. Before you're finished you'll fill up quite a few pages.

When you're done taking notes, disconnect all the fasteners and unclip the harness from the engine compartment. Gather up the entire harness and gently pry out the grommets that hold the various wires in place through the firewall. Then move on into the interior of the car and do the same, and keep working back until you're done. Draw the wiring from the rear of the car into the interior, gently wind it up on the floor and pull everything from the car out through the engine compartment or interior.

Getting the new one in might be tougher. Depending on the car, it's often easiest to secure the main harness to the floor of the interior and feed it forward and back as needed. You may find a *little* soapy water or WD-40 helps ease the harness through the firewall and the floor, but dry the wiring and connectors off well immediately afterward.

All the sealing grommets and clips should be reinstalled exactly as before. You'll find that laying in the new harness isn't all that tough if your notes and modifications were 100 percent accurate. Since that's rarely the case, though, there will be a lot of additional time spent jockeying back and forth between the old harness, the new one and the diagrams to figure out where everything goes.

One problem you're likely to find is that you'll need a *fish line*—a stiff piece of metal wire used as a leader—to pull the harness through floorboards, up window pillars and into other difficult places. It helps to tape up the ends of a fish line-guided set of wires to keep them from catching as they pass through holes.

Avoid running the wiring close to a heat source like the exhaust system, radiator, clutch assembly or even the heater core. And remember that no matter how careful you were when laying the new harness in, you're going to have to run down at least a few electrical glitches—it's just the nature of the job. Remember that the problem might be in the wiring, but it might also be in the component being wired up.

Temperature sending units are basically one-piece affairs—no user-serviceable parts inside.

Six-volt batteries are getting hard to find. Moss Motors, Ltd.

One more thing: You *can* go to a specialty shop to have the whole car rewired from scratch with the proper codes and wire gauges. This is a very costly alternative, though, so it's only practical on an extremely rare and valuable car.

Replacement Electrical Components

A shop teacher at my old high school used to have a pet peeve. "*Never*," he would say, "*EVER* buy electrical parts from a junkyard." Naturally, we'd be in the back row snickering like fools, because we'd just rewired Millard Johnson's whole pickup truck with ten bucks' worth of used parts and it worked fine.

In the end he was probably right, though. For one thing, Millard's truck would cough at regular intervals from that day on. But he was also right because you usually don't know if an electrical part will work at all, and for how long, just by looking at it.

It used to be that you couldn't get a guarantee on junkyard parts, but that's not always the case these days. It's more common, in fact, for *new* electrical parts to be unreturnable now. And even if a used part isn't guaranteed, you'll often find it so much cheaper that you could buy six or seven for the cost of a single new one. A new Jaguar alternator probably runs a few hundred bucks at the dealer, and a little less from a mail-order house. If a salvaged one costs $30, you can guess where I'll head.

Electrical components can be difficult to clean, so if show-quality appearance is important you're usually better off buying new ones. If you're cosmetically spiffing up an electrical part, avoid getting cleaners, dust or paint inside it. Also be careful not to destroy any decals or tags on the unit. If you do buy an electrical component new, bring the old unit down to the shop and compare it to the replacement closely since it's probably not returnable. Mail-order houses' return policies vary, but generally you can send electric parts back if they're still sealed in their original plastic.

Generators can be bought new or used, or often repaired at home. Usually they either need just a lubing—some oil on the felt washer or some high-temperature grease under the lube cap—or new brushes. Fitting new brushes is usually a matter of pulling out the long bolts holding the generator together, taking out the old brushes and fitting or soldering on new ones. While you're there, clean the commutators with fine sandpaper and alcohol. If they need to be undercut, proceed as directed in your manual. (Usually you'll have to make sure that the grooves between commutators are a given depth all around.) More complicated work is possible, but it's rarely a good alternative to just finding a better unit.

Alternators, on the other hand, are a lot harder to repair; you're usually best off replacing them and giving up the old unit for the core charge. About the only thing you can do besides any listed tests in your manual is to make sure that the alternator drive belt is tight enough to spin the unit. Each alternator can be tested with a multi-tester in its own way. Make sure to test the alternator before replacing it, or you might find the trouble was actually somewhere else.

Starters, too, are often easier to replace than repair. You'll probably find that the honking big screws holding the coils to the walls of a starter or generator housing won't shift no matter how hard you try; take the component to an electrical shop and they'll free up the fasteners for you.

The same electrical shop can also probably fix whatever is ailing the component, albeit likely for more than it would cost to simply get another one. If originality is important, though, or if a replacement simply isn't available, these shops do exist. Make sure to point out any nameplates, stamping or tags that must be preserved when you drop off the component for servicing.

Often, just the solenoid of the starter goes bad, or the return spring for the pinion gear breaks and the starter refuses to unmesh with the flywheel. The teeth on the pinion and flywheel ring gear must be in good shape or the starter will at best spin free of the engine; at worst, flakes of the teeth will get into the oiling system and cause a world of damage. Flywheel ring gear teeth can be replaced only by a machine shop with the proper equipment, or the whole flywheel can be tossed out and replaced with a better one. Worn flywheel teeth can also keep the starter from disengaging once the engine kicks over. (A stuck starter can sometimes be freed temporarily by turning off the car and rocking it back and forth in top gear.)

Batteries

One thing you don't want to mess around with is your battery, which will give you no end of grief if it's not up to snuff. I strongly recommend replacing a suspect battery with a high-quality, time-guaranteed replacement.

A good battery is well worth the $30 or so it costs over a real cheapie, which will mimic all sorts of other, more costly electrical woes and probably cost you more money in the long run through false repairs.

A battery that won't hold a charge needs to be replaced, but first make sure that there isn't a light or some other small circuit that's staying open and draining the battery artificially. A malfunctioning

Rear-mounted batteries are often out in the open where a good shot from a stone can puncture them. A wooden or plastic protective case might help here, but it should be well vented so fluid and gases can escape.

A great $1.99 investment. Battery terminal cleaner can save all kinds of money by keeping perhaps the main source of electrical woes, cruddy battery terminals, at bay.

The twin 6 volt batteries on this MGB have been replaced by a single 12 volt unit. Real racers will place the battery like this—on the passenger's side—to even out the one-up weight of the car, but the rest of us can use whichever side is more convenient.

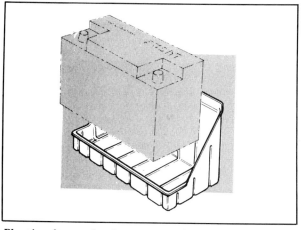

Plastic aftermarket battery tray isn't stock, but it cuts way down on the damage leaky batteries do to sheet metal. Moss Motors, Ltd.

generator-alternator or voltage regulator will also cause a battery to behave as if it's on its last legs. Before replacing the battery, follow the charging system tests outlined in your shop manual with a multi-tester.

Most garages will try to sell you a new battery if you have starting problems with your car. It's more common, though, for the problem to be elsewhere. Check the starter, battery cables and switches before buying a new battery. The fastest way is to borrow a good battery from another car and bolt it up temporarily.

A few tips to long and happy battery life:
• If you don't have a maintenance-free battery, check the water level in the cells once a week; top it off (to just a hair over the inner plates) with nothing but pure, distilled water.
• Keep batteries well charged—once they've drained completely they'll never be the same. On a car being stored, either hook up a trickle charger or remove the battery, store it in a warm, dry place and charge it up once a month.
• Charging batteries create lots of explosive gas. Charge them only in a well-ventilated area away from open flames and heat.
• Battery acid is strong enough to eat your clothing and seriously irritate your skin. Wash your hands and any part of your body that comes in contact with the battery with soap, water and baking soda.
• Baking soda and water will neutralize battery acid on the battery itself, concrete, metal or your skin.
• Keep the terminals clean with a wire terminal brush and impregnated-felt washers designed to reduce terminal corrosion.
• When jump-starting a car, always make sure that the cars aren't touching and the batteries are connected first ground to ground (that's not always going to be negative to negative on British cars, so watch out). Incorrect jumper cable routing can cause serious mechanical damage and serious injury from exploding batteries, so be careful with this job. Don't just go by colors—a red cable doesn't mean the person who installed it knew what he was doing.
• Avoid side-terminal batteries. Not only will you have to go to new battery cables, side terminals are fragile, hard to jump and charge and just a general pain in the neck.

Starter System

Most owners manuals give you a table of trouble-shooting tips to narrow down problems and causes. Unfortunately, they're often written for people with the IQ of a summer squash. Under "starter" might be a dozen symptoms that all boil down to the same thing: the battery, the starter, or something in between them is busted. Now go take a multi-tester and figure out which one.

These guides are helpful, but it's important to know how the system works so you can plan your own attack. Almost all failures can be traced to something easy like a dead battery, broken wiring, a blown fuse or a bad connection. Those are the things to look for first.

When you hit the starter, it opens a circuit that lets current pass to a solenoid on top of the starter motor itself. When that solenoid is activated, it moves the starter's pinion gear into mesh with teeth around the edge of the flywheel and, a split-second later, completes a much higher current cir-

Starter pinion (left) and flywheel ring gear teeth should be inspected carefully. Faulty teeth need immediate replacement.

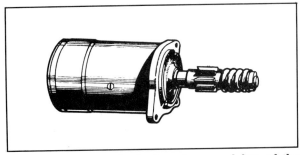
Older starters can be broken down and lots of the smaller parts are straightforward to replace, particularly the main gear and spring. (The newer ones are pretty much sealed for life.) Moss Motors, Ltd.

175

cuit that gives the starter motor the juice it needs to crank over the engine.

If the pinion gear or the flywheel teeth are chewed up, the starter usually works but it doesn't spin the engine. If the solenoid is bad nothing seems to work, and if the starter itself is messed up you can usually hear the solenoid kicking in but all that happens next is that the rest of the electrical system goes dim. Some cars use a starter relay under the hood, and if this goes bad it will mimic a number of other starter problems. Try jumping past the relay by bridging its contacts with an insulated screwdriver. (Make sure the car is in neutral and the brake is on so you don't run yourself over in the process.)

Charging System

Starting the car takes a fair amount of juice from the battery; for the next couple of minutes, the voltage regulator lets electricity flow from the generator (or alternator, as the case may be) into the battery to top it off again. All the time the generator-alternator is turning it should be making electricity; the voltage regulator decides when and how much of that electricity should go into the battery, which will be ruined by too much charge as

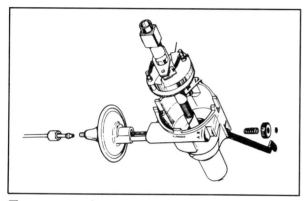

The vacuum advance mechanism (left) points in the direction opposite the distributor's rotation—in this case the distributor spins counterclockwise. Moss Motors, Ltd.

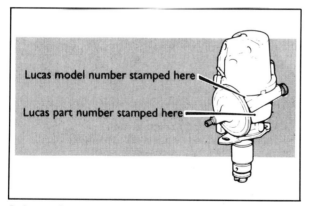

Information you'll need to know when ordering new distributor goodies. Moss Motors, Ltd.

Distributor mounting plate doesn't need to be taken out to adjust or remove the distributor—just loosen the through-bolt. Moss Motors, Ltd.

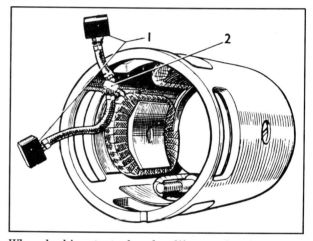

When checking starter brushes (1), trace the wiring back to the point at which it meets the field coils (2); the most likely place for a short circuit is right there. If the insulation is frayed or broken the whole system fails.

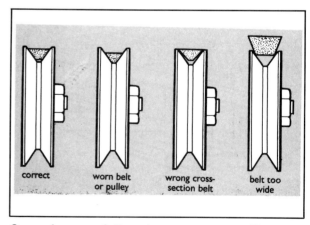

One main cause of alternator or generator problems and failures is simply incorrect belts or tension. (Tension should leave about half an inch of up-and-down play in the belt; too loose and the unit won't make power, too tight and it's quickly ruined.) Use this guide for selecting belt width. Moss Motors, Ltd.

quickly as too little. The ammeter or voltmeter tells you how much electricity is being put out by the generator at all times. You might notice that right at idle the generator isn't spinning fast enough to

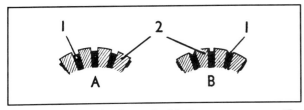

put out the full 13.5 or so volts it's supposed to. That's usually normal if it's the case.

While the car's traveling down the road, the generator supplies the electricity for the lights, motors, ignition and so on. The battery's reserves should only be drawn from when the generator isn't turning out enough juice to cope with it all—during starting, perhaps when every accessory on the car is in use, or at a low idle. When this is the case, the voltmeter, ammeter or discharge light will tell you what's happening. If the meter or light indicates that charging is not occurring under any

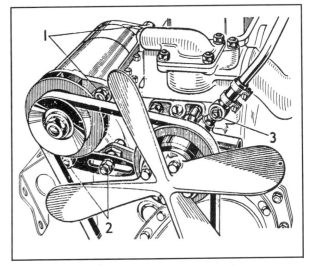

Commutator can be cleaned with fine emery paper. The insulating sections (1) must be evenly and cleanly cut between the metal segments (2). If they're worn unevenly, cut them down carefully with a fine carborundum stone or file.

Low generator/alternator output is often no more serious than a loose belt. Both mounting bolts must be slackened and re-tightened or the belt will never be tight.

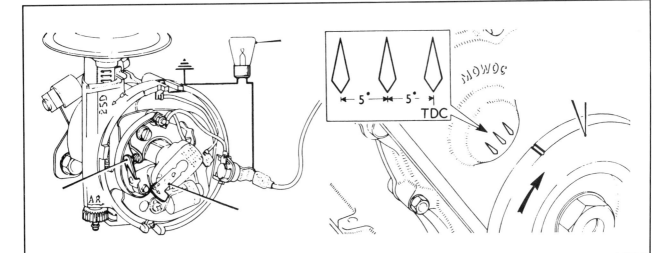

Basic wiring for the static ignition setup outlined in the text. The key is to make sure the engine is at TDC before starting, or you've got an even chance of starting 180 degrees out of phase. Once TDC is reached, you can correlate static timing with the ignition advance marks

on the crank dampener to get it right where the book tells you it ought to be. When the test light lights the contact points have just opened, so set the dampener where it ought to be, rotate the distributor until the light just lights, and there you are.

circumstances other than the ones listed, the charging circuit should be inspected and repaired immediately.

Ignition System

Occam's Razor more or less says that if two equally plausible explanations for an event are given, the simpler one is correct. That's almost always true with British cars, which will need about twenty hours of carburetor and electrical fiddling for every hour of heavy-duty repair. Concentrate on these things first on any car that

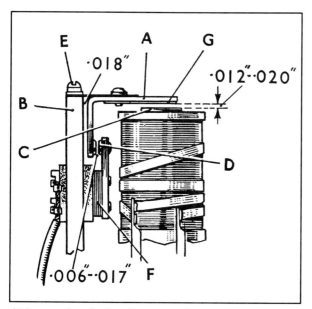

Older mechanical voltage regulators have internal clearances that must be maintained to deliver proper electrical system charging. The clearances are usually okay and this doesn't often fix a problem, but it's free and easy to do—give it a quick look before getting too fancy deeper in the car's electrical system. (Before going into these with a feeler gauge, disconnect the battery!)

The rotor looks okay under the cap of the MGB distributor. Mike Hohn

Coils usually work for about 50,000 miles and then slowly give up the ghost. The best check is to swap them for a better one and see if that helps.

Clean up the cap contacts with emery paper and wipe the dust out with a rag and a little kerosene. Most of your ignition problems will start and end with the cap, rotor, points and condenser. Mike Hohn

doesn't run quite right. Most are old and simple enough to abide by the Mechanic's Repair Litany:

"Is it getting spark?"

"Yep."

"Is it getting gas?"

"Yep."

"Well, geez, it should run."

Get fuel and spark right and it usually will. If the fuel pump's pumping (check at the main line to the carbs), the carbs and valves are set to spec, and the distributor and ignition goodies are all new and working, ninety-nine times out of 100 the car will run fine.

Getting Spark

As soon as you acquire a car, turn your attention to the ignition system. You can go piece by piece once you're familiar with the machine, but for now follow this procedure:

First, pull out the plugs and make sure that they're the right ones for the car and in good condition. Now throw the plugs in your spare parts drawer and buy *new* ones. Gap them to spec by either gently levering the electrodes open with a

Underneath the rotor there's usually a felt pad that needs an occasional drop of oil; that keeps the distributor shaft lubed. Mike Hohn

Locating a Dead Cylinder

If the car doesn't seem to be running evenly even though all the hardware looks in order, try to find a dead cylinder. Start by pulling one plug wire at a time with a pair of well-insulated pliers. Do this at the engine, not the distributor, and never even get *close* to the main coil wire of a running car unless you want to get the living daylights zapped out of you—maybe literally.

Each time you pull a plug wire, you should be able to hear a distinct worsening of the engine sound. If you find a cylinder that doesn't affect the engine whether hooked up or not, there's the offender. The first thing to do is to swap that spark plug wire with its neighbor and try again. If the problem cylinder moves with the wire (about a 50 percent chance), there's your culprit. If it doesn't, try swapping spark plugs (about a 20 percent chance). If that doesn't do it, check the valve settings on that cylinder (5 percent). Still no soap? Try changing the distributor cap (say another 5 percent). About now you're expecting to need a new cam, right? Wrong—chances are the carb feeding that cylinder simply isn't working right or there's a vacuum leak in the intake system, especially if the dead cylinder is at the far end of the engine (about a 17 percent chance). Only the last 3 percent of the time will the problem be more serious internal engine damage.

Points gap is ready to be measured when rubbing block sits on highest portion of the cam. Mike Hohn

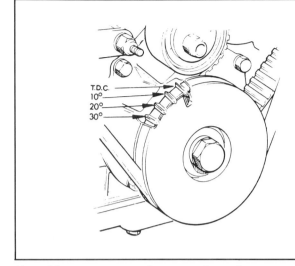

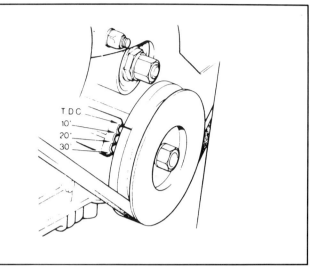

Two of the more common degree marks on dampeners or engine plates. You'll probably have to remove a lot of sludge to see them clearly, and a little chalk rubbed into the markings makes the whole job much easier.

penknife or gently tapping them closed against the ground, until the proper feeler gauge or wire just begins to drag in the gap. Stick the plugs back in, but don't overtighten them—just go finger-tight and then maybe a revolution or two farther with a plug wrench.

Take off the distributor cap and rotor. Clean the cap with kerosene inside and out and look closely

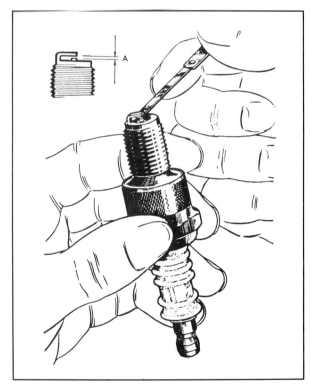

Plugs are correctly set when the proper ring just begins to drag in the gap.

Somewhere among all that equipment there's a timing mark on the main pulley of this Rover V–8. The timing light senses pulses from the first spark plug wire and illuminates the mark at precisely the right moment; the strobe effect shows where the timing is set.

for cracks in the body and especially around the contacts. If you find any, chuck the cap and replace it. Also look for seriously worn contact points, and again toss the cap if you find some. Come to think of it, toss the cap regardless—throw it in the spares pile if it looks okay or the garbage otherwise.

Inspect the rotor for pitting or lots of wear. If you find any, throw the rotor away. If you don't find any, introduce the rotor to its new friends in the spares box. Seeing a pattern here?

Take the points and condenser and escort them forthwith to their brethren spare parts. Install new ones, making sure to wire up the condenser the same way the old one came out. (The condenser wire fits underneath the plastic insulating bush, not on top of it; it makes contact with the points.) You'll notice that the points are spring loaded, and that they open and close as they ride on peaks on the distributor shaft. Park the shaft so that a peak is hitting the rubbing block of the points (in English, that means put the car in gear and roll it until the points are fully open). Set the points gap by loosening the locking screw and levering the points around with a screwdriver until the proper gap is achieved with a feeler gauge. Tighten down the points and check them again with the gauge.

While your head is stuck down by the distributor, make sure that the wiring to the distributor isn't frayed or broken. The thin wire from the coil to the distributor is a constant source of woe. Also take off the vacuum advance hose going to the distributor at its far end and suck on it—you should be able to see the distributor move a little bit as you do so. If not, the vacuum advance mechanism needs work or the hose itself is clogged or broken.

The coil is almost never bad, but just to be sure I like to sneak one from a car I know is working and stick it in. If you can't hijack one, buy a spare. You can constantly swap the two whenever you have ignition problems to eliminate that part of the equation. Coils should be changed every 50,000 miles regardless.

Make sure the battery's juiced up. If it's got enough kick to crank the engine quickly, it's got enough to start the car.

There are a few ways to set the ignition timing, but only one of them works if the car itself isn't running. (The initial and other gross timing adjustments will be made by loosening the distributor base and moving the whole unit; fine-tuning can be done later with the knurled knob on the base of Lucas distributors.) Basically, this is done by turning the engine until the correct point on the main pulley (something like 8 or 9 deg. BTDC [Bottom Top Dead Center]; it will be listed in the manual) lines up with the timing pointer. Connect a test

Slightly offset distributor drive makes reinstallation easy. Geared drives are much harder; make sure the rotor doesn't move off the number one lead when you push the distributor home. Mike Hohn

---

Getting Wired

To properly wire the spark plugs you'll need to know four things: the car's firing order, the number one piston, the direction of rotation of the distributor and the way the manufacturer numbers the plugs. Inline engines are almost always arranged with the front cylinder as number one; vee engines are all different, so consult the shop manual.

The rule of thumb for determining rotation is to look for the vacuum advance cylinder. The rear of the cylinder will point in the direction opposite of rotation; of course you can always kick the engine over with the distributor cap off just to be sure.

The fixing order on most four-cylinders is 1-3-4-2, which means that after the number one plug is wired you'll go in rotational order to the number three plug, the number four and so on. To find the number one plug lead, set the engine to TDC (as outlined in chapter 5) and the rotor will be pointing right to it.

A bad voltage stabilizer frequently causes multiple gauge failures. Moss Motors, Ltd.

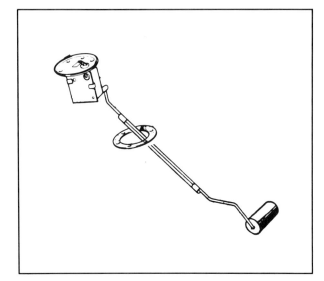

Leaky float or bad sending-unit ground are the normal causes of fuel gauge errors. Moss Motors, Ltd.

lamp between the contact points terminal on the side of the distributor and a good ground. Turn the ignition on and rotate the distributor housing until the test lamp lights—that's the correct ignition timing *at idle.* It doesn't tell you anything about how well the automatic advance goodies are working.

Another way is to use a timing light, which will tell you not only the correct timing at idle but also the timing as the engine speeds up. (This is made easier by rubbing some chalk into the timing marks on the main pulley to make them show up better.) Of course, the car has to be running for this one.

The third way is simply to road test the car. Set the timing as far advanced as it will go before the engine starts to slow down (it will speed up as the timing is advanced a good deal, then finally start to drop off). Then back it off a hair, let the car get up to temperature and drive up a hill in a high gear. Keep backing off the timing until the thing stops pinging and there you are. Of course this method is a little tough on the car and again, the car has to be already running.

Electric Gauges

There are two main kinds of electric gauges, the bimetallic-strip variety and the magnet-iron type. The former occasionally, and the latter almost always, uses a voltage stabilizer before the instrument itself to control excessive needle wavering. These stabilizers, which are usually hidden away in the wiring to a number of gauges, often burn out. If several gauges go out at once, the stabilizer might be at fault—disconnect its output wire and check it with a multi-tester. The other obvious cause of multiple gauge failure is a blown fuse; other interior goodies are often powered off the same circuit as the gauges, so the short may well be in the horn, turn signals or a similar component. Some gauges also need to ground through their cases to the dash panel. If the gauge or its mounts are loose, that can cause the gauge to fail.

As with their mechanically driven brethren, electric gauge faults are usually not in the gauge itself. More often you'll find a problem in the wiring, ground or sending unit. The gauges sometimes do

go bad, though, and once you've checked out the rest of the system you might have to crack one open and have a peek. Also in common with mechanical gauges is the typical cause of internal problems—layers of dirt and crud inside the gauge itself. Electronic gauges that should work but don't often will respond to nothing more than a serious blasting with aerosol switch cleaner.

Bimetallic strip gauges, which take a few seconds to warm up once you start the car, are darned near impossible to repair except for resoldering any broken wires or contacts inside. (For all gauge work, the wiring inside is minuscule and a suitable soldering gun extension should be made up. Wrap a fine copper wire around the tip of a regular soldering gun about ten times, and pull the end of the wire free of the gun. That should get you a fine enough point to do the detail work needed inside the gauge.)

Magnetic iron gauges, which pop to life the instant the key is turned on, have one more element that can be brought back to life by a do-it-yourselfer. Again, you'll have the best luck if all you're doing is resoldering a bad connection, but the magnetic coil replacement inside these gauges can also be corrected. Magnetic iron gauges operate by swinging a piece of iron connected to the gauge's needle back and forth with varying magnetic fields. The force of the field is related to the amperage getting to the gauge, but also to the position of the coils that generate it. If these have managed to get out of whack, you'll have to go back in and secure them in place. It will take a few tries to get the coils where they're supposed to go, and the only way to really check them is to mount them, fix the gauge back in the car and see if the readings it gives you seem accurate. Usually, moving the coils breaks the fine wire connecting them, so the last step before sealing the gauge back up should be inspecting and repairing this connection. (Most ammeters and voltmeters, by the way, are this type of gauge, and if they fail completely they often take the rest of the electronic system with them. If you experience a massive electronic failure you can't explain, check out this gauge. If it's bad, replacing it might cure the whole car.)

As I said, though, the problem is most likely not the gauge itself. Fuel level, electric tachometer and temperature sending units go bad much more often, while the most common cause of all is simply a short or broken circuit between the power supply, the sender and the gauge itself. As with anything else, start at the gauge and check for power; if you don't find it, troubleshoot the break in the circuit back to its cause. It's often the sender.

Fuel level senders are especially flimsy, and they're easy enough to fix at home once you get the darned things out of the tank. That can be a dangerous proposition, so make sure you don't cause any sparks while pulling the unit, and quickly tape over the hole in the tank when you get the sender out.

With the fuel level unit out and away from the tank, turn the ignition on, attach the sender to a ground and slowly move the float up and down; the fuel gauge should move with it. If it does, either the float is broken, the sender isn't grounding properly to the tank or the tank isn't grounding to the car. On rubber-mounted tanks make sure the ground strap is in place. If the float is full of gas, you can boil it out and repair it with solder as you would a carburetor float. (See chapter 6 for details.)

Floating senders vary the amperage sent to the gauge by moving an arm across a thin conductive wire. The closer the arm gets to the end of the wire the less resistance there is, so the higher the amperage to the gauge. This wire often breaks or simply gets covered up in scum; check its continuity, repair any breaks with solder and clean the

surface of the wire and arm with very fine garnet paper. Finish it off with aerosol switch cleaner and bolt it back up.

Repairing the inside of a temperature sending unit is almost impossible, and the units themselves are so inexpensive there's little point in trying. Before replacing the sender, though, remove it and clean the threads and body completely. Stick it back in and try the gauge again—often just scraping off the scum fixes it. Since these senders ground to the engine, sealing goo or Teflon tape often keep them from working.

Electronic tachometers come in two different forms, though both may be suitable only for a certain number of cylinders, a certain polarity and have a fine adjustment knob on the back. The first type, usually found on upscale older cars, were actually like big voltmeters. A small generator, often mounted on the back of the cam but sometimes behind a belt-driven accessory, ran to the tach which merely measured the current. Test these setups with a multi-tester on the AC voltage scale; reading the DC voltage will give you all kinds of screwy numbers. Start by bridging the terminals on back of the generator and reading the output there; it should equal a certain number of volts per 1000 rpm. Your manual ought to tell you the exact figure, but it's usually in the neighborhood of 10 volts per 1000 rpm.

If the generator checks out, pull the wires off the tach and see if the juice is getting that far. If not, obviously the connections or wires are to blame. If electricity is making it to the tach, the unit is bad and you're in trouble. Once the contacts and terminals are clean, there's not much that can be done about it.

Later electronic tachometers sense the impulses in the ignition system and translate them into an rpm number. Yes, once more, the wiring and contacts are much more likely to be at fault than the inductor or instrument. If not, however, replacement will be far and away easier than repair.

8

Suspension, Steering and Brakes Restoration

It's easy to just assume that your old sports car never *did* corner like a Lotus Esprit or soak up bumps like a Bentley Mulsanne. Well, you're right—it didn't. But it probably did ride and handle a lot better when it was new than it does today. Steering

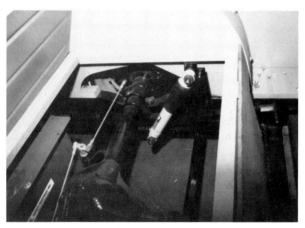

Very simple shock mounting on a Morgan—two bolts and a couple of bushings.

Entire Triumph TR-7 front and rear suspensions drop down to be worked on (or, in this case, thrown away and replaced).

and suspension systems are like anything else—they *cannot* be ignored forever and still be expected to perform.

So many different setups and methods are used for steering and suspension that this section is merely an introduction. Where there are general rules, tips and facts I can give I will, but unlike some, this is not an area to go blindly poking around in. It is *critical* to fully understand the suspension, steering or braking system you're up against before turning the first wrench. No two are attacked the same way: most of what you need to know will have to come from your own manual and from others who have worked on your type of car.

Suspension Work

The first major hassle of this kind of work is simply getting everything apart. You'll encounter nuts held on with superhuman torque, lethally spring-loaded assemblies, and bushings that must have been pressed in by Vulcan himself. But the most common problem, and possibly the easiest to defeat, will be ball joints. Unless you attack these the proper way, even the simplest suspension work can be impossible.

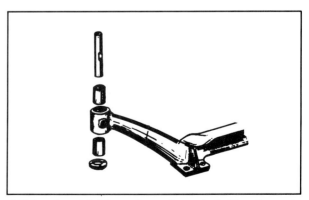

Solid axle with king pin main swivel. The theory is simple, but getting the bushes and pin out can be tough. Lots of heat is the order of the day. Moss Motors, Ltd.

184

Ball Joints

The wrong way is to remove the top nut from the ball joint and start whacking away on the tapered bolt with a hammer. About the only thing you're likely to get is beat-up equipment, a trashed joint and a pair of sore arms. In the old days, mechanics developed a variation of this method that actually worked; they put a heavy hammer in back of the hole around the tapered bolt and whacked on the front of it with a lighter one, shocking the joint apart. That's still a practical alternative if you're stuck in the middle of nowhere with nothing but two hammers and a steering rebuild on your agenda. But if you can get to a tool store, there are much better ways.

A tie-rod end separator will make your life infinitely easier. There are three kinds: those that lever the joint apart, those that wedge or pull it with a screw puller and those that wedge the joint apart with brute force. The first two alternatives are probably the safest to use, as they're less likely to damage the rubber boots of the ball joint. They're slower than the last alternative, though, and sometimes hard to maneuver.

Strangely enough, I find myself using the bonk-and-wedge variety almost exclusively. The tool itself looks like a 15 lb. sharpened tuning fork that's more murder weapon than repair item. After loosening the retaining nut on top of the ball joint (always leave it in place at the top of the threads to protect the end of the tapered bolt), slip the ends of the separator between the upper and lower arms and bang away with a heavy hammer. If you take care not to damage the rubber gaiter and its retaining clip, there's really nothing wrong with this method.

Once a ball joint is separated, before you remove the lock nut and unscrew the joint from its rod it's imperative to accurately measure its location. You can use a tape measure or actually count the exposed threads, but jot down the figures so the system will go back together in about the same relationship as before. Also jot down the angle of the joint—if it's about 10 deg. left of vertical, say, when on the car. On rods with ball joints at both ends, both joints should be threaded an equal distance down the rod, and on cars with a matching rod on the opposite side of the suspension, the length of both rod and joint assemblies must match *exactly* from side to side. (Dual-jointed rods often use reverse threads for one ball joint, so remember that as you take apart and reassemble the piece.)

After any disassembly or adjustment, the car should be professionally aligned and checked for caster and camber. Accurate measurement before disassembly gets it close, though, and make the professional's job easier and less costly—to say nothing of letting you drive the car to the shop safely.

It's obvious how the main swivel mounts on this front suspension; there's a ball joint at the top and a simple peg-and-race down below. Getting these fasteners off, however, can be an exercise in true ingenuity and muscle power—consult a pro who has already done the job.

New ball joints aren't necessarily perfect. Wiggle the joint around in your hands and check for uneven tightness or binding.

Assuming that the suspension components themselves aren't bent or damaged (which should be immediately apparent on close inspection), the main trouble spots will be ball joints, bushings and the main steering swivels. Bushings, either rubber, metal or a combination of both will be covered momentarily, but for now let's worry about the main swivels.

There are three kinds of main swivels you're likely to encounter, probably in the following order: ball joint, pin and screw-in. If most steering swivels have been regularly lubed and looked after throughout their life, they should be okay and easy to deal with. If not, they can test your patience. Consult your local one-marque wizard for advice on this or any other frozen suspension piece; as he's likely to have come across the problem—and hopefully a solution—already. (Most suspensions, in fact, will cause at least a few panicked phone calls to the local club for advice. There *always* seems to be a problem somewhere.)

If a main ball-joint type swivel needs minor adjustment, you can sometimes fit in a few shims to tighten it up. That's a factory adjustment rather than a home remedy, though it's safer in the long run to toss the old joint and replace it. Removing the swivel is generally straightforward enough: separate the ball joint from the stub axle assembly, unbolt it from the suspension arm and go to work. (That sounds much easier, of course, than it's likely to be.) One thing to watch out for is the bushel basket worth of shims that most of these systems use to keep the suspension in line; they all have to go back on in the right place and right order to set the suspension up correctly again. You should also make sure to support the stub axles on something other than the brake lines while the work is being done. Screw-on swivels should be attacked the

same way, though you might have to apply some of the lessons learned in the following king pin discussion as well.

Older sports cars (like MGs through the TC) used a king pin front end that was set into a solid beam axle, and newer cars often use a pin set between two suspension arms. Of the two, solid axle suspensions might be more straightforward but harder to deal with. Often the best thing to do is drop the whole axle off the car and prepare to tackle the king pins on a bench.

Once the solid axle is secured to the bench, drive out the main pin; usually you can screw the securing nut up to the top of the pin's threads and whack the whole thing out with a big hammer and a steel punch. A little heat from a butane torch or very soft welding flame will help considerably, however, and possibly prevent shock damage to the beam axle.

The hard part comes next—removing the phosphor-bronze swivel bushings from their races. Again, some localized heat and Schwarzenegger-style blows with a drift should drive them through. Watch out for the occasional tapered bearing, though. These, of course, can only be driven out in one direction.

Independent pin suspensions at least give you the alternative of buying an entire built-up suspension section to replace the one you're working on if the pin and spindle simply won't come apart. On notoriously difficult units, the lower arm, pin and spindle can often be replaced en masse instead of fought with individually.

Bushings

If bushings are causing your grief, you can buy an extractor or build your own. To make one, you'll need a piece of heavy pipe with a slightly larger inner diameter (ID) than the race, a long bolt and

Age needn't ruin bushings—despite the cobwebs, these antisway bar bushings look fine.

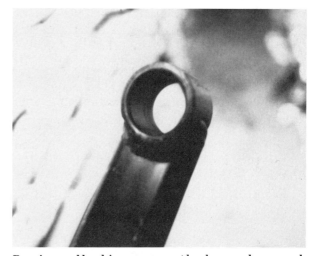

Bearing and bushing races must be clean and unscored. Don't damage them if you're forced to deform a bushing on removal.

nut, and two heavy washers with holes just big enough to fit the bolt through. One washer should have an outer diameter (OD) larger than the pipe, and one should have an OD just smaller than the race's ID. The smaller washer fits between the bolt head and the bushing, the pipe goes on the opposite side of the race and the larger washer fits behind the pipe and is held in place by the nut. Obviously, by tightening the nut and bolt you can slowly draw the bushing out.

Occasionally, you'll come up against a metal or metal-and-rubber bushing that simply won't respond to coaxing, even from an extractor. For these you need the heavy artillery—drills, reamers and saws. Pure metal bushings can be reamed to a larger and larger size until only a very thin shell

remains; this can then be crimped and deformed with a fine awl or punch until it can be removed. It's very easy to score the outer race this way, so you have to go gently and carefully through the process.

The method for removing rubber bushings with a metal inner and outer ring is a little easier: Take a fine hacksaw blade, stick it through the bushing and mount it into a saw. Then saw out a small strip from the inner sleeve, collapse and remove it and cut away the rubber in a similar fashion. The

Passenger's side front lower wishbone bushings; these look rather tired but they're probably still doing their jobs. On the driver's side, though, is an indication of where they're headed—missing and deformed rubber will need replacing, and this joint's a real bear to open up.

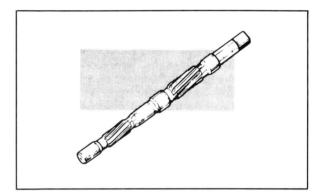

Hand reamer (shown) or professional reamer will have to do a job on most metal bushings before swivel pins can be fitted. Moss Motors, Ltd.

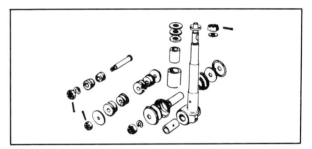

The actual swivel pin mounting and hardware make perfect sense. An expert on your car will tell you which parts can be separated and which ones ought to be replaced as a unit. Moss Motors, Ltd.

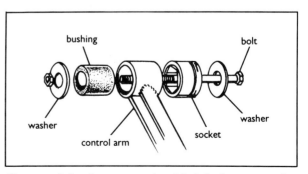

Homemade bush extractor is a big help for suspension work. Moss Motors, Ltd.

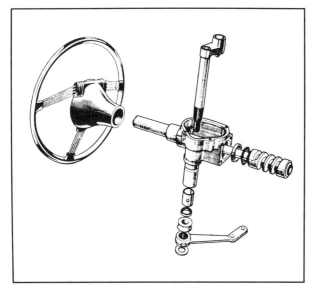

Classic steering box layout. Turning the column moves the peg on the shaft up and down the threads of the worm gear; the drop arm connected to shaft turns rotation into steering motion. Moss Motors, Ltd.

remaining outer sleeve can be deformed with a punch and removed.

Simple rubber bushings are easy to remove once you can get *at* them. (There always seems to be about 800 bolts torqued by Superman to remove first.) Putting in a new rubber bushing can be a little trickier; once the inner race is clean and dry, try a little soapy water to help ease the bushing through. Most rubber bushings can also be lubricated with brake fluid, but some cannot—check with the manufacturer before dousing them. (Protect any painted surfaces from the brake fluid, of course, which will eat right through the coating.)

Putting metal bushes back in can be no less of a hassle than taking them out. The procedure can be made a lot easier by heating just the outer race before you drive the bushing in with a suitable drift. Let the bushing and race cool completely before reaming or pressing in a new component.

King pins and other bushings often need to be reamed to size before the rest of the parts go back in, and this is a critical procedure. You can use a hand-reamer (sometimes a special reamer is needed from a parts supplier), but enlarge the hole in very small steps and use a proper pilot to ensure alignment. You can also turn this relatively inexpensive job over to a pro, who'll use a precision machine reamer.

Steering Racks and Boxes

Steering mechanisms simply wear out, and you'll often come across a unit that needs rebuilding or replacement. But before you despair, make sure the trouble doesn't lie somewhere further down the line—in the steering column, track rods, ball joints or main swivels—and that it can't be merely adjusted away. And to head off further problems, make sure your steering box or rack is properly filled with fluid. All steering systems need fluid, but some don't even have a hole to add it. Check in your owners manual for the proper fluid and refilling instructions. Rack and pinion units must also have complete, untorn boots to last.

Most steering mechanisms are adjustable by either a screw, bolt or shims. The adjustment will be made by finding the best compromise between free play and binding; more precisely, it's finding the point of adjustment that brings the steering closest to, but just shy of, tightness somewhere in

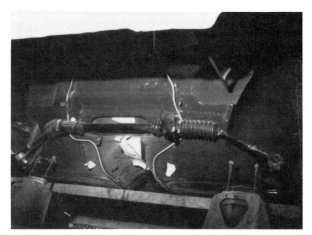

The track rods on either side of this steering rack must be exactly the same length; length is set by threaded cups and lock nuts on ball joints.

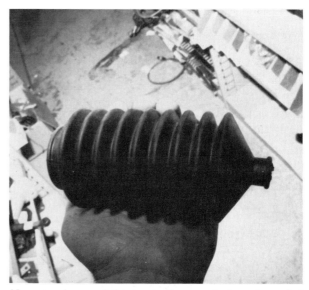

New steering rack boots can be a pain to put on, but they're necessary if the old boots are leaking. To keep the alignment as close to correct as possible, count the threads on the ball joint cups before removing them to slip the boot on.

its travel. (Tightness is also occasionally caused by hardening of the grease in the main swivels. On some cars, you can melt this out with heat and replace the grease.)

The best way to check for tightness is to jack up the front of the car so that both wheels are off the ground but the suspension is compressed. Then tighten down the steering in small steps until the first signs of binding crop up to a helper spinning the steering wheel from lock to lock; back off just a hair and that should be the best adjustment possible. Take the car out for a test drive as soon as you're done just to guarantee that there aren't any tight spots.

If the adjustment didn't cure the steering and the trouble doesn't seem to be elsewhere, the main unit is going to have to come out of the car. This can be more of a job than you'd imagine. The things to remember are (a) you'll probably have to remove a lot of ancillaries and ball joints to get to the mechanism, (b) many older mechanisms are built in unit with the steering column and have to come out with it and (c) these one-piece units usually have lots of horn wires and other doohickeys that have to be dealt with before removal. One-piece units

Entire steering column may come out with ancillaries attached. Leave the steering head assembly in one piece if you can.

will also dribble oil out the column while you're trying to remove them, so take the proper precautions. Finally, if you have to separate the drop arm or steering column from the unit itself, mark the relative position with a light punch or scribe before disconnecting it. (Use a dab of paint or correction fluid if the car is going to be shown, and remove it later.)

Don't ever whack on a steering column or drop arm in an attempt to free it from the unit; use lots of heat, gentle leverage and penetrating oil instead. All steering columns are quite fragile, and on later cars they are actually *designed* to collapse—a worthwhile safety feature, but one that makes this job rather tricky. Fortunately, collapsible steering columns seem to be of the independent, rather than in-unit, variety.

Once the steering mechanism is out of the car, take off the top cover or bottom plug and drain out the oil. (You may find that lots of parts come off with the cover, so be ready to catalog them as you go.) Then reassemble the unit briefly and clean the outside completely with kerosene.

Steering Wheel Removal

This is probably as good a place as any to say a few things about removing and replacing the steering wheel.

• Always mark the wheel-to-column relationship so that things go back the same way they came apart. Use a light scribe or marker in a hidden area.

• Most wheels are simply pressed onto splines on the column and held down by a big central nut; once the nut is removed the wheel should come off with some judicious back-and-forth rocking. If it doesn't, try to find any hidden mounting bolts or screws, and failing that resort to a steering wheel puller.

• Be gentle with fragile banjo-type steering wheels, wheels made of Bakelite or similar brittle plastics, wooden wheels and those with horn buttons out around the rim. The wiring for the latter must be completely freed up before the wheel is removed.

• While you have the wheel off, take the time to clean the horn button and contacts. You might also have to bend some of the springier contacts back into shape if they've flattened out over time.

• Secure any wires running through the column in place with tape or clips. If they fall down into the column you're in for some tedious fishing to retrieve them.

• Beware of switches and doodads (particularly the turn-signal canceling pin) that are exposed when the wheel comes off. These are usually fragile and a devil to replace.

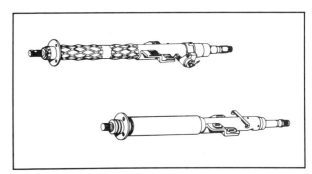

Collapsible steering colum housing (top) will be much harder to wrestle out of the car than solid variety (bottom). Both should be left alone if possible; steering gear will come out without removing column on these units. Moss Motors, Ltd.

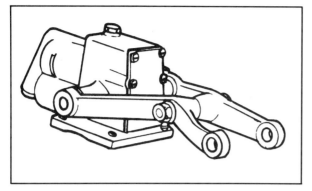

Lever shock that also acts as upper suspension arm is of course more expensive and harder to replace than regular shock. Keep it topped off with fluid and it should last a good long time. Moss Motors, Ltd.

The actual disassembly of the unit will be outlined in your manual, but bear in mind that you're looking for a few suspect things: broken ball bearings (these are mostly free balls in tapered races, which will fall out of the unit en masse as you disassemble it—watch out), worn or cracked gears, pitted mating surfaces and worn shaft bushings. Replacement of damaged parts is really the only answer, and you'll find that some of them simply aren't available anymore. You can go to a specialist for new ball bearings, and a machine shop can usually ream out old bushings and press in new ones; replacing other parts is strictly a check-and-see proposition.

As you reassemble the unit, you'll find that a dab of thick grease will hold the ball bearings in place long enough to press the races and cups back together. Other pieces like rods and gears are very finicky as to proper placement and torque loading,

Small rocks will occasionally get into spring pans (circular hole in lower A-arm) and make funny clicking noises. Dig them out carefully with a small screwdriver.

so follow the manual exactly if you want to make things better rather than worse. Without going into a lot of detail over all the various types of steering boxes, let me just say that those on more expensive cars like Jaguars, Astons and Bentleys use a lot more parts and are much harder to deal with than those on their cheaper brethren. I'd be tempted to let a specialist work over a recirculating-ball or hourglass box rather than trying to fight with it myself.

Rack-and-pinion steering, which is what you're going to be dealing with on most later sports cars, is attacked in more or less the same disassemble-and-check fashion. With the rack out of the car and cleaned up, unclip the rubber gaiters (after preparing for the oil which will dribble out in the process) and remove them. (The following steps will be performed differently from car to car, but the order is usually the same.) Center the rack in the housing by measuring both exposed ends until they're equal. If there isn't already a line or punch indicating the pinion shaft's relation to the rack at this point, mark it with a small dab of paint. (I wouldn't go pounding on these pieces with a punch, as they're often quite fragile.)

Next, remove the pinion shaft (being careful not to damage its bearings or oil seal) and inspect the pinion gear for broken teeth, excessive wear or a ridged or sharp surface across the teeth. If these are found, the gear and probably the main rack as well will have to be replaced. Look at the pinion shaft bearings with a very close eye.

Also check the ball joints at either end of the track rods. They should stand up under their own weight instead of flopping over by themselves, and must move smoothly through their entire range of motion. Their overall tension is sometimes adjustable with shims, but a joint that sticks in some places and moves freely in others will have to be replaced.

Next, remove the rack itself from the pinion side of the unit, after fighting with whatever bearings and seals you find blocking the way. Inspect the rack for the same flaws you looked for on the pinion gear. When it comes time to assemble the whole mess back together, the manual must again be carefully deferred to for setting preload, pinion float and other variables.

Springs

You'll encounter one or two of the five main springing mediums on your car: leaf springs, coils, torsion bars, struts or rubber-hydraulic. Whichever sort your car comes with, they contain a *lot* of pent-up energy. A spring under stress can easily break a bone or worse. Be careful with them and take steps to ensure they are decompressed gently and safely. A spring needs to be dealt with either because the unit itself is bad or because it has to come off before some other work can be tackled. In either case, extreme care is the order of the day.

Leaf springs—usually but not always multiple leaves fixed together—are the most common variety, so we'll start with them. The normal layout is to have one at each end of a live rear axle, with the spring attached to the underbody ahead of and behind the wheels. The front of the spring generally pivots on a fixed pin and the rear inside a movable shackle, which allows some fore-and-aft movement as the spring is compressed and released.

That's far from the only layout, however. Early Sprites and Jaguar sedans used a quarter-elliptic spring, which is half a traditional leaf rigidly mounted to the car on one end and the axle on the other. Older cars used full elliptics—two regular leaf springs, one flipped over and joined at both ends with the other, and occasionally a vehicle uses one or two transverse leaf springs on a car with independent suspension.

Leaf springs occasionally suffer from outright breaks, but more often they just lose their springiness. The car settles lower to the ground, some of the ride and handling quality is lost, the suspension bottoms frequently and, if let go long enough, the exhaust pipe gets ripped off by anything bigger than a cigarette butt.

Removing Leaf Springs

Fortunately, removing and installing leaf springs is usually easier than you'd expect. Occasionally you'll need a special tool like a spreader for the job, but a quick check in your manual will clear up any confusion. You'll need at least two good jack stands and a two-ton rolling hydraulic jack. Here's the regular method for removing leaf springs from the rear of most cars:

Chock the front wheels. Jack up the rear of the car until the wheels are free of the ground. Support the car *securely* on axle stands and remove the jack, then unbolt the wheels.

Using a piece of wood to protect the assembly, lift the rear axle slightly from the differential with the jack. Loosen the shock absorbers from their lower mounts. Then raise and lower the rear axle until the springs seem to be unloaded. (You can usually check this by looking for some slack at the rear shackles.) When the springs seem to be completely unstressed, start loosening the U-bolts or mounting plates that hold the axle to the springs.

The tension on the mounting bolts will give you a good idea of how well the spring has been unloaded. Once they seem to be coming off smoothly, support the axle with jack stands at both ends and release the mounting bolts all the way. Don't let the axle hang from its rebound straps if you can avoid it. (By the way, replace any broken rebound straps at this point.)

Remove the retaining nut (or cotter pin, or other security device) from the pins holding the spring at the front and rear pivots. Drive out the pins one at a time—with heavier springs a helper should hold them up while you do this—and pull the spring out from beneath the car.

Reinstallation is basically done in the reverse order. The only catch is that you might have to raise or lower the axle a bit before you're able to bolt things up.

Once the spring is off the car, inspect it carefully for broken or worn leaves, cracked clips or a loose center bolt. These can all make the leaf bounce back suddenly in your hands and cause an injury. Once you're satisfied the leaves are basically sound and held together well, clean them up with kerosene and a stiff brush.

If you went to the trouble of removing the spring it must have needed work—most of this should be left to a professional. About the only things a do-it-

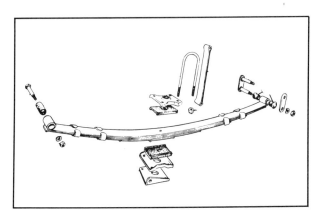

Typical rear leaf spring. Shackles at the back allow fore-and-aft movement when the spring is compressed over bumps. Moss Motors, Ltd.

Quarter-elliptic rear spring on early Sprites mounts in a box inside the rear bulkhead. Though the box sometimes rusts, the springs themselves are pretty sturdy.

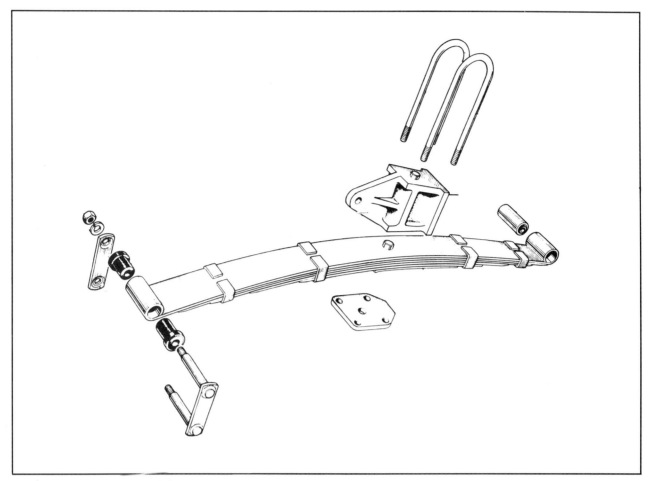

Don't let the reversed bow of this early Triumph spring fool you—it's attacked exactly like the more common version. Moss Motors, Ltd.

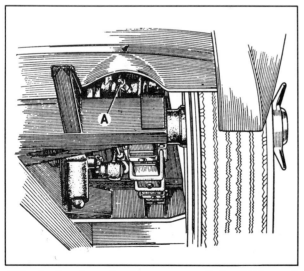

Older leaf springs often have a grease fitting (A) located below the car that needs intermittent attendance. Neglect to lube the spring and squeaking quickly gives way to broken leaves.

yourself restorer can do are swap a broken leaf, replace damaged clips and renew worn-out bushings.

If you must disassemble the spring to replace a leaf, you'll find that the individual clips are either bolted or riveted together. Before removing one, clamp that part of the spring securely in a strong vise; you can then get the clip off and *gently* expand the vise to take up the tension of the free leaves. Clamp up the spring again to install the new clip.

Replacing bushings is a straightforward job assuming the car has rubber bushes; if it has rubber-and-metal (Metalastik or Silentbloc) bushes or pure metal ones, the job will be more difficult. (Consult the bushing discussion earlier in this chapter if you have problems.) On some rubber-and-metal spring bushings you'll need to use an appropriate drift of steel pipe to press in the outer metal ring without deforming the longer inner one.

The more serious and common work, that of fixing a sagging spring, should be left to a specialist who can heat and re-arch the unit back into shape.

These shops are getting increasingly hard to find, however; if one can't be dug up locally, there are a number of mail-order shops listed in the enthusiast magazines which can take on the job. Re-arching an old spring is usually, but not always, cheaper than replacing it with a new one. Still, you should check out all the options before pulling the old one off.

When the time comes to remount the springs, fit the front end first and snug down the nut holding the retaining pin. (Don't tighten it all the way, yet.) Support the axle on the jack stands, remove the stands and lower the axle a couple of inches. Loosely mount the U-bolts or retaining plates that tie the spring to the axle, then maneuver the axle and spring up to where the rear shackle pin can be fitted. (This may be where your special tool comes in.) Fit the rear pin. Tighten down the axle-to-spring mountings all the way and reattach the shock absorber. Don't tighten the pin retaining nuts until the car is back on the ground and has been gently bounced up and down a few times—and don't forget to tighten them up after this, either. Finally, after about fifty miles of driving it's a good idea to get back under the car and retorque all the nuts and bolts; they may have loosened up noticeably as the spring settled back into place.

Next come coil springs and their close relation, struts. These are probably used on the front suspension of your car if not the rear as well. I recommend that you look at the factory literature for your specific car rather than to try and cover a few different systems. You'll find that the coil springs, spring-and-shock combinations and struts on every car are tackled differently, and each can be very dangerous if handled incorrectly.

How Tricky Can Coil Spring Work Be?

If you're well informed by your manual, installing coil springs isn't all that tricky. If you're just shooting in the dark, it can be downright impossible to know how to proceed.

For example, the entire rear suspension of the XKE comes off to make work on the springs—to say nothing of the differential, axle shafts, brakes and bushings—easier. The springs and shocks will, however, also come out by themselves with a lot of effort.

The front suspension of the Sunbeam Alpine is similarly easy to drop down, but here it's easier just to remove the springs alone.

And the spring-and-damper unit of Triumph Spitfires drops off as a unit, but everything else stays on.

No matter what type of car you have, you'll usually need some type of coil spring compressor to safely and correctly get the darned things off. Often this will be a pair of long, threaded shafts with opposing clamps at either end. These tools must be clean, straight and complete before you use them or serious injury can result. The regular method is to hook one clamp on a coil toward the top and another on a coil toward the bottom, and to tighten them together until the spring is compressed enough to remove. (One trick I've learned is to place some high-quality locking pliers just downhill of the clamps, to prevent the compressors from walking slowly down the springs.)

Torsion bars are less commonly used for springing, but E-Types and others still will pit you against them, usually on the front end. Torsion bars don't really wear out; they go out of adjustment, however, and will affect the height and handling of the car when they do.

Torsion bars are usually quite simple to adjust, and won't need replacing unless they've been accidentally damaged. You'll have to find the figures and procedures for your particular car: Everything from tire pressure to suspension loading to a full or empty fuel tank will be part of the equation.

Even though most torsion bars are the same from right to left, once installed they can never be

Corroded coil spring can be shot-peened to remove crud and relieve stress, but a new spring would be safer and possibly cheaper.

Copper hammer and wheel wrench are an essential part of the tool kit if your knockoffs don't have ears.

Rough outside of this knockoff cap makes you wonder how the threads look in back. (The cap and its spindle were mounted on the wrong side of the car, so I suspect it's made a few high-speed fly-offs—knockoff caps are threaded for the left or right side of the car only, to keep the rotation of the wheels from loosening them at speed.)

swapped with those on the opposite side of the car. Torsion bars also can affect camber, caster and other adjustments when they're played with, so have the car professionally checked once any work is finished.

Changing shock absorbers is a similarly marque-specific operation. On some cars it's simply a matter of jacking up the car, removing two bolts and going to it. On others, particularly those where the dampers also act as upper suspension arms, it's a much bigger proposition. Topping off leaky lever shocks will add to (but not spare) their lives, and go ahead and change any shocks that need it—the difference in ride and handling is well worth the effort. Make sure that all mounting bolts and bushings are in good shape.

Steel Wheels

Factory steel wheels are basically bulletproof, though they can be subject to cracks around welds or the lug area and a good shunt can bend the outer rim, causing a tire to seat poorly or blow out at speed. Steel wheels should also be checked for flaws on the inner sealing rim and stretching of the lug holes. You might also want to jack up the car and spin the wheel against a solidly mounted pointer; this will show up any gentle warping or bending.

Argh! To get this hub off means undoing the cotter, loosening the retaining bolt and taking the wheel bearings off with it. Elizabeth Gardiner

Spoke Wheels

Spoke wheels are more troublesome. A spoke wheel that runs true (tested against the same sort of pointer as used before) and has all tight spokes should be left alone. To test the spokes, tap each spoke with a pencil or light screwdriver to check its condition. A sound spoke will make a light metallic ring, while a bad one will merely click. A do-it yourselfer can handle replacing a few broken or loose spokes with new spokes and a spoke key (available from parts stores), but if a lot of the spokes seem bad or are rusting at their ends the wheel should be taken to a specialist.

To keep the wheel from freezing onto the spline, take it off twice a year and clean the knockoff splines with fine steel wool; lightly coat the splines with lithium grease before affixing the wheel to the car. (To keep grease from oozing out along the spokes, coat the spoke heads in the hub with silicone sealer.)

Also check the condition of the wheel spindle and its mountings, the inner splines and the knockoff cap—a failure here could be disastrous.

If any of these things are found, the wheel's a goner. Beyond that, there should be little or no worries with them.

By and large, spokes are a hassle: they're rather fragile, hard to keep clean and expensive to repair. Still, they look so good I'd rarely consider an English sports car without them.

You can still find good spoke wheels in junkyards for surprisingly little money. A few months ago my father, who's never owned a Triumph in his life, picked up four perfect Spitfire wheels for $50 simply because he couldn't bear to see them go to waste. He later traded them in on some equipment for his MG, so everybody was happy in the end.

Tires

If new tires are on your docket there are a number of decisions to be made. Tires are priced on a pretty straightforward scale of cost versus quality, but on most older sports cars you quickly reach a point of diminishing returns as the cost of the tire goes up. Many older cars simply don't have the suspensions to take advantage of the sticky modern tires. (In fact, many older suspensions can't handle the added loads imposed by wider, stickier rubber. Talk to a club or parts specialist before getting too aggressive.)

You also have to consider what benefits you're being asked to pay for; tires can feature long life, extremely sticky rubber, all-weather tread designs,

The classic wire wheels on this MG TF require special attention for proper restoration. Tearing down and rebuilding the wheels can be time consuming and costly; you can often save money if you do it yourself and then hire a professional to true the wheels. Note that origi-

nally these wheels were only painted, as were the wire wheels on many other British sports cars. It was rare that the wheels were chromed, as they often are on over-restored cars.

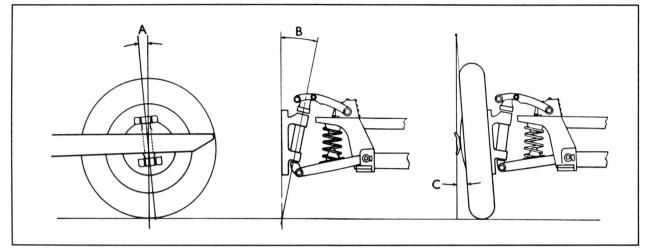

Defining caster (left), pin inclination (middle), and camber (right). (The latter two are obviously intimately related, and on most cars the correct location of one gives you the correct location of the other.) Caster and camber determine qualities such as oversteer vs. understeer, tire wear, and steering self-centering; proper adjustment is key to safe and predictable handling.

a quiet ride or any combination of all these things. Some are at cross-purposes: longevity and low noise are generally the inverse of stickiness.

Decide what kind of use you expect from the car before buying its tires. For gentle Sunday tooling in a 1960 MG Magnette you might as well get a quiet, unaggressive tire that will last more than 10,000 miles or so. For serious autocrossing with a TR-4, stickiness is more important and a high-performance radial is the only way to go—with appropriate beefing up of the suspension, of course.

You'll also be faced with a choice between cross-ply and radial tires. Radials are generally thought of as superior these days, but they don't behave the way old-fashioned cross-plies do and you might want to consider the differences. In the most general terms, cross-plies will be a little quieter than radials, shorter lived, slightly smoother over the road and offer much less grip. Since gentle, low-speed powerslides are one of the charms of some older sports cars, you might consider fitting cross-plies on them instead of radials; radials stick

Translating Tire Sizes

Before buying any tires, make sure the seller knows the *exact* size and type of the wheel and the *exact* make of the car. Most everyone knows it's foolish to buy a tubeless tire for a set of wire wheels, but it's easy to get confused over sizes and ratings.

The system by which the tires for your car were originally rated is probably long dead. You have to know how to translate those figures into today's nomenclature.

Older tires were generally rated with numbers like 5.50-15. That represented tread width in inches minus wheel diameter in inches, a system that at first seems more logical than the one used today.

Modern designations, which include much more information, are along the lines of 165/80SR-15. The last number, 15, still refers to wheel diameter—so far so good. But the first number, 165, means the tire's *total* width, not tread width, in millimeters (mm). Add about a half inch to your old tire's tread width in inches, divide that by 0.039 (which is the number of inches per millimeter) and round out to the nearest number divisible by five. (In this case you'll get 150.) With the 5.50-15, so far you've got 150/ and -15, so you're halfway there. (Actually, you're not—you'll probably find that nobody makes a tire as skinny as that anymore, and you will have to go up to at least 155 mm.

The /80 of the modern designation is merely the tire's *aspect ratio,* its width versus the sidewall height—in this case, it's 80 percent. Most older sports cars used about an 80 series aspect ratio, so this tire will be about the same size as the one originally slated for it.

If your suspension is up to it, you can go to a 10 or 20 mm wider tire for more grip if you keep the same overall height. There's a formula for figuring overall height: (aspect ratio × overall width × 2) + (wheel diameter in millimeters) = height. But generally going up 10 mm in width while going down 5 percent in aspect ratio gives you about the same overall height.

The *S* stands for a speed rating (S tires are safe up to 112 mph, T to 118, H to 130, V to 149 and Z for 150 and above), and *R* simply means the tire is a radial.

up to a higher speed but break away more quickly when they do let go.

Brakes

Brakes are one thing you don't want to mess up. If the car doesn't run, that's bad enough. But if it doesn't stop, you're in a whole lot of trouble.

There are all kinds of things that can affect the braking system of the car; many of them don't actually cause the brakes to fail. Instead, they slowly cause the brakes to become less and less effective. After a while, the driver loses the ability to stop the car quickly enough to make driving safe.

Brake Hydraulics

If you ask me, hydraulic brakes shouldn't work. The whole notion of them seems wrong: If some hard-luck prospector came up and tried to sell me on the idea, I'd say he was crazy. But the young prospector who invented the system, Malcolm Loughead, turned out to be right. Here is part of a conversation I had with him.

Malcolm Loughead: (Loughead explains the system) "You fill a cylinder up with fluid. Then attach a pedal to a piston inside the cylinder, and when you push the pedal in, the piston pushes the fluid out a pipe."

Me: "Yeah, yeah, I'm with you so far . . ."

Loughead: "Okay now, four other cylinders, at the other end of the pipe, they fill up with the fluid. And that pushes pistons stuck in them out!"

Me: "Okay, and then . . . ?"

Loughead: "And then . . . you hook those pistons up to brake shoes, and use them to stop a 3,000 lb. car going sixty miles per hour!"

Me: "Man, how long have you been out in the sun . . . ?"

Malcolm Loughead was quite sane, however. This system for hydraulic brakes was so successful that,

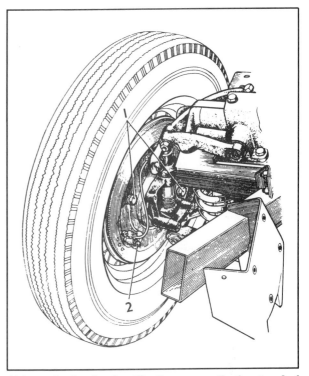

Older twin-shoe brakes like the ones on the front end of an Austin-Healey must be adjusted in tandem. There are two adjustment bolts (1) and only setting one of them drastically reduces braking capacity.

with a few notable exceptions like Ford and Bugatti, it quickly wiped rod- or cable-operated brakes off the market. (The hydraulic system worked just as well for actuating clutches, too—the principles and procedures outlined here for brakes are exactly like those for hydraulic clutches.)

Here's an unsavory sight; this rotor's a goner.

Corrosion and fluid spots on calipers are often a tip-off the unit can't be saved.

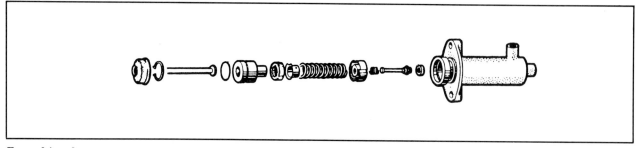

Everything that comes out of the master cylinder must be checked against the parts included in the rebuild kit. Moss Motors, Ltd.

When the Loughead name was changed to Lockheed, that was the name of the very successful brake and aircraft corporations that soon followed. I've come to simply accept that hydraulic brakes work, and though I still don't really like the notion, I must say I approve of it as long as nothing goes wrong. Unfortunately, things do go wrong, primarily due to neglect: the longer a car has sat idle, the more trouble its hydraulic system will be.

There are a lot of things that can happen to a hydraulic system; all of them are pretty easy to rectify, but also potentially very dangerous unless you fix them right away. Regular maintenance of the hydraulic system goes a long way toward avoiding brake problems, and it's a simple matter. Check the fluid level in the main reservoir every 1,000

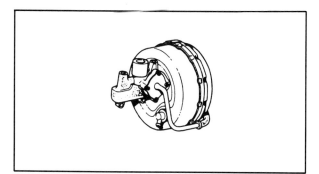

Vacuum booster can suck up brake fluid and send it into the intake manifold; you won't see a leak. Moss Motors, Ltd.

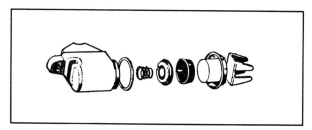

Wheel cylinder has fewer parts to replace than master cylinder. If the piston freezes inside, try forcing it out with compressed air. Moss Motors, Ltd.

miles, or once a week, to make sure the system isn't leaking. Have a look at the pads and shoes every few thousand miles. Twice a year do a visual inspection of all the hoses, pipes and cylinders to check for cracks, leaks, rust and chafing. Change the brake fluid every eighteen months or 20,000 miles; totally flush the old stuff and replace it with clean, condensation-free fluid. And bleed the brakes properly at the first sign of sponginess at the pedal.

Those simple steps will greatly extend the life of the fragile rubber cups and precision cylinder bores that the hydraulic system depends on. It will not, however, make them immortal. Every other fluid change (or every three years, whichever comes first), you ought to replace all the rubber in the system and inspect the cylinder bores while you're doing it. If any scoring or corrosion is found in the bores, the cylinder must be replaced. Brakes will simply never work right with a less-than-perfect cylinder somewhere in the system.

Rebuilding a hydraulic cylinder is usually inexpensive when compared to replacing one, assuming you have a drill, a hone (about $10-15), a good-looking cylinder and some spare time. It's worth a crack. Usually the rebuild will take, but sometimes not; there's just no predicting it.

A rebuild kit from your parts supplier will generally run about $12. Before buying a rebuild kit, though, make sure the bore at least seems okay—there's no point in buying a rebuild kit if you're also

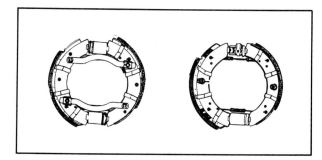

Dual-cylinder drum brake (left) gives you twice as many rebuild chores as a single-cylinder unit (right).

going to buy a whole new cylinder. Cylinders from a junkyard are available, but very often will be corroded themselves. Inspect it well if you want to go this route, but I'd advise against using *any* salvaged hydraulic parts.

If a rebuild looks possible, spread out the internals of the old cylinder before breaking the plastic seal on the kit and make sure that the new parts are correct. If not, you can return the unopened kit for an exchange or refund.

Be very careful when testing a rebuilt cylinder. Try it out first on the bench by pushing in the piston and sealing off the output holes with your fingers; if no air seems to be getting by the piston, go ahead and stick the cylinder in the car. After bleeding and adjusting the brakes, start out carefully and slowly on the test drive. If the brakes aren't 100 percent correct, take the car off the road *immediately* and do the repair again—this time with a new part.

Rebuilding a hydraulic system is usually a straightforward job. The first indication of trouble will often be a loss of fluid; a spongy pedal might also mean a rebuild is in order. If the cause of the leak can be found, the first order of business is of course to remove the offending part. If it's a cylinder there's your candidate for rebuilding. It might be a broken hose, pipe or fitting, though, and those should simply be replaced. But brake problems are *usually* the result of an individual cylinder failure. (Multiple cylinder failures can occur, however, due to moisture or grit in the fluid, lack of use, lack of fluid or incorrect fluid type.)

Master cylinders are the most complex piece of the hydraulic system. Simply getting them apart can be a real pain; often there will be a circlip or spring washer that secures the guts inside the cylinder. Circlips are best removed with the proper circlip pliers, although some fudging with needle-nose pliers and jeweler's screwdrivers will also do the job. Even then, the piston assembly may resist removal; the only thing to do is to lightly tap the open end of the cylinder against a solid wooden object until the parts come free. If all else fails, some compressed air shot through the output hole ought to free the piston and seals. If any little doodads are left in the guts of the cylinder, a soft wooden (never metal) probe might have to be poked down into the cylinder to free them up. Some cylinders use a number of securing devices besides circlips to hold the piston in, so check the manual before proceeding.

Master cylinders also consist of a fair number of bits and pieces that will make perfect sense as they come out but are very confusing when you try to fit them back in. Make good notes as the piston comes out, taking care to also mark down which direction all the cups, washers and springs are facing.

A successful rebuild will be determined by the condition of the cylinder and how clean you keep everything in the process. As soon as the unit has been removed from the car and drained, clean the outside thoroughly with the brake company's official cleaner or hot soapy water. (Solvent or thinner will damage the rubber inside the cylinder. Once the guts are out you can go to town with aerosol solvent, but make sure that all of the residue is washed away by brake cylinder cleaner before proceeding to the next steps.)

Lay the cylinder on a smooth, clean surface and arrange the internals in their original order next to it. Compare the parts of the rebuild kit against those of the original. The one-way valve at the far end of the assembly may not match exactly, but the rubber pieces should. If the old rubber seems to be swollen up a lot larger than the new pieces you might be in trouble. That can indicate some contamination, like the use of an incorrect fluid type. The rest of the rubber in the system, including all the hoses and seals, may have to be replaced.

Remove the rubber seals by squeezing them enough to fit a small Phillips screwdriver underneath and prying them off the piston, making a great effort not to score the plunger. Lubricate the new seal with fresh brake fluid and slip it on—you might think at first that the rubber won't take that much stretching, but it's very resilient. Once everything is back together the way it came out of the cylinder, lube it lightly with brake fluid and slip it into place.

Identifying Hydraulic Leaks

Check the following areas first when tracking down the source of a hydraulic leak:

Inspect the master cylinder for leaks ahead of and behind the firewall. Master cylinders usually mount with a couple of bolts on the firewall, which will be accessible with more or less fidgeting. You'll also have to bash your head against the pedals a few times while removing the brake actuating rod from the pedal. Usually there's a cotter or nut securing the swivel pin.

Leaks at drum brake wheel cylinders often show up as moisture on the bottom of the brake backing plate. Wheel cylinders must be attacked by first removing the wheel hub, which is covered in the section on replacing linings. Once you've gained access to the cylinder, remove the hose, the securing bolts or clips, and gently pry away the brake shoes. The cylinder should come out.

Leaks at disc brake calipers will be evident as fluid at the bottom of the caliper, the hose or on the edge of the disc. Calipers are usually held on to the front spindles by some large, easily seen bolts. Remove the bolts and the hose and you should be able to get the thing off.

Finally, run your fingers all the way down all the pipes and hoses to feel for leaks in hidden areas.

Wheel cylinders have fewer parts to worry about, but getting the darned things out can be a real hassle. The first problem you'll come across is simply removing the brake drum. Naturally, you start by properly raising the suspect wheel and supporting the car with stands and chocks.

Before any drum will come off, the emergency brake must be released. It's important to have the car in gear and well chocked so it doesn't roll off the jack stands. You might also have to back the brakes off by turning the four-sided bolt or star wheel adjuster on the backing plate. (Clean the adjuster's threads regularly and coat with an anti-seize compound.)

Sensible automotive engineers designed the drum to press right on over the lugs and be held into place by the road wheel. On one of these cars, just removing the wheel and gently bonking the drum

---

Potential Hydraulic Repair Trouble Spots

Before you do any hydraulic work, be warned of a few potential trouble spots:

• Metal brake lines are *extremely* fragile. Make every effort to keep as much strain off of them as possible.

• Always take advantage of any locking nut you find (a back-up nut that holds the line in place while you remove the fitting).

• To minimize fluid loss, clamp a sheet of plastic under the master cylinder cap before opening any lines.

• Lube any fittings that seem stuck or rusted. If the fitting doesn't spin freely it can kink or crack the brake line as you try to take it off.

• Don't bend a metal brake line out of the way any more than necessary; it has to line up perfectly with its joint again later, so getting it back on can be an absolute nightmare if it's bent out of shape.

• Thread all fittings gingerly by hand before tightening them with a proper hydraulic wrench. Run a little Teflon tape over the threads to prevent any leaks.

• Brake fluid is an extremely good paint stripper, so take great pains not to let any of the fluid drip on a painted surface. If some does accidentally, dab—not wipe—it up immediately with a clean rag. Go over the area again with some soapy water on another rag, rinse it well and throw both rags away.

• Cars with power brakes will occasionally lose lots of fluid without showing any obvious signs of leakage. There's a chance that the fluid is actually leaking into the brake power booster and finding its way through the vacuum pipe into the intake manifold; this will befuddle you no end unless you know to check it out. Look first into the vacuum lines for signs of fluid. If none is present, you can also open up the vacuum booster itself to have a look.

---

with a rubber hammer a few times will bring it right off.

That was too practical for some English designers, though, so they locked the drum down with monstrous setscrews. By wielding a giant screwdriver and a fair amount of muscle, the screws can be removed. Since the drum usually freezes into place with this system, though, it takes some pretty prolific rubber hammer work to free them even with the screws off.

Finally, some companies saved a few bucks by making the brake drum one piece with the hub— the assembly that carries the outer wheel bearing races and rolls around the axle. On this layout you could bonk away with Thor's hammer and achieve nothing but a sore wrist. Instead, you have to take off the central dust cap, wipe away all the grease, remove the cotter pin and retaining nut, slide off the grease seal and draw off the drum-hub combo with the wheel bearings in tow. (Since you set out to do some brake work and this forces you to do a wheel-bearing job in the process, I think we'd all rather have paid British Leyland the few bucks in the first place.)

Under no circumstances should you try more serious artillery than a rubber hammer when removing bake drums. The most common drum-removal method for first-time mechanics is to try prying the drum off by levering on the backing plate. Since the backing plate is made of something just this side of tinfoil, all this does is trash the plate—*don't do it.* The other mistake people make is to get tough with the drum and try to whack it free with a metal hammer. If you're lucky, all this will do is bend the drum a bit and make it rather dangerous to use. The drum can also crack, however, which you'll probably discover as a complete loss of braking as you try to avoid a school bus. In short, the only thing that should be whacked on with a metal hammer is a few brake designers' noggins.

Getting back to the wheel cylinders, once the drum has been removed—hopefully without liberal doses of dynamite and expletives—you'll find the wheel cylinder held into place by a spring-clip arrangement, setscrews or some nuts, studs or bolts. The removal method should be obvious regardless.

You'll probably have to lever the brake shoes off before removing the cylinder, and the brake hose or pipe will definitely have to be taken off. Once everything's freed up, take the cylinder out and rebuild it following the same guidelines as for master cylinders. One thing you might find is that the pistons simply refuse to be shifted from the cylinder. You can usually free them up by giving the cylinder a shot of compressed air through the fluid hole. If that doesn't do it, the whole cylinder might have to be replaced.

Pull out and examine the bleed screw while the cylinder is on the bench; clean it up completely or replace it with a new one. If you're fitting a new cylinder, you might find that a bleed screw isn't included—salvage the old screw or replace it. Don't put Teflon tape on the threads of the bleed screw, it will foul the first time you try to bleed the system. Instead, coat the threads with an anti-seize compound.

Disc brake calipers don't allow you as much rebuild potential as drum brakes. Basically, you can't split open a caliper—it just never seems to work right again. Nor can you do much about scoring in the cylinder walls, you simply have to chuck the old caliper and get a new one. Again, this isn't something I'd recommend as a junkyard part. Calipers stop working mostly out of neglect, and the ones in a junkyard are probably in worse shape than the ones on your car.

A caliper can have one, two or four pistons. Each piston can have leaky fluid seals, grungy or torn dust covers or be frozen into its cylinder. All will cause erratic braking and accelerated pad wear. If one of these things shows up during a pad inspection or replacement, you'll have to remove the caliper. Before doing that, though, you'd be well advised to free the pistons from their bores. Once the pads are taken out, this can usually be achieved easily by slipping a piece of wood between the disc and one piston and pumping the brakes a time or two. Once the opposite piston is far enough out to grab with pliers, slip a thinner piece of wood between the exposed piston and the disc and push out the other one(s). Then drain the fluid, disconnect the pipe or hose from the caliper and pull off the retaining bolts that hold the caliper to the car. Lift the caliper out, clean it off and bring it to a bench. Most calipers have retaining rings that hold the piston dust covers in place, and that's the first place to start. Calipers are all different, though, so you'll have to go to your manual for the teardown and reassembly procedure.

If the pistons still won't come out of their bores after you've pushed them halfway with the brake pedal, force them the rest of the way with compressed air. Once they're out, inspect the cylinder bores carefully for scoring or corrosion. If any is found, the caliper is a goner. Replace as many of the rubber seals, clips and retaining rings as possible if you're trying to save the caliper. You should only have to go into the calipers once every five or ten years—they're generally very hardy—so make everything as new as possible before locking it all down again.

Drums and Shoes, Discs and Pads

Ultimately, these are what stop your car. The drums or discs (the rotating pieces) spin with the road wheels, and when you mash on the brakes it

shoves shoes or pads (the friction material) into contact with them. Nearly all of the energy of the car moving down the road must be passed from the rotating pieces to the friction material, into any surrounding metal and on out to the atmosphere. That's a lot of work, and the parts involved slowly destroy themselves in the process.

Brake shoes and pads are the sacrificial elements of the system; they're designed to accept most of the wear and be replaced frequently. The discs and drums also wear, but at a much slower rate; if you change friction material religiously, you

Simple emergency brake linkage is adjusted with threaded rods. Most systems use cables with adjusters either on the cables themselves, their sheaths or threaded rods at the ends of the lines.

201

Brake shoes usually just rest in slots in the wheel cylinder's pistons. They're held there by spring pressure.

The only common cause of disc and drum failure is leaving the friction material in too long.

Brake shoes are generally shot when the thinnest section of their linings has worn to about 2.5 mm, or when the lining is almost worn down to the rivet heads. Pads must be replaced when they've worn to within 3 mm of their backing plates. Pads and shoes should wear evenly, and if they don't you'll have to go in and figure our why. On disc brakes, there is usually a fault in the caliper such as a sticky or frozen piston. On drum brakes, usually the actuating mechanics are installed improperly. It's also common for one piston of a dual-piston wheel cylinder or caliper to freeze up, or for one cylinder of a dual-cylinder drum brake to fail.

Under no circumstances should the lining be allowed to wear away through to the backing or rivets. Many pads have an additional feature that makes checking them easier—a groove cut down the middle. If the pad is worn past the depth of the groove, it needs replacing. Some shoes, similarly, may have markings on one side to indicate their minimum acceptable thickness.

might make it through the car's entire life on the original, untreated shoes and discs.

Friction material is made up of organic and inorganic compounds that are compressed into pucks and bonded to a metal backing plate by glue or rivets. As the material wears down, the metal backing moves closer and closer to the disc or shoe. Let it go too long and metal-to-metal contact occurs: Braking efficiency falls off dramatically, noise is increased and the discs or drums get chewed up.

As for pads and shoes, the manufacturer will specify how frequently you should pull the wheels and drums to check on the linings (usually 10,000 or 12,000 miles). I'd recommend cutting that figure down to 3,000 miles. Inspecting the brakes frequently lets you catch worn goodies and leaks before they do too much harm.

Changing pads is usually simple. A couple of pins and/or springs are generally all that hold the pads

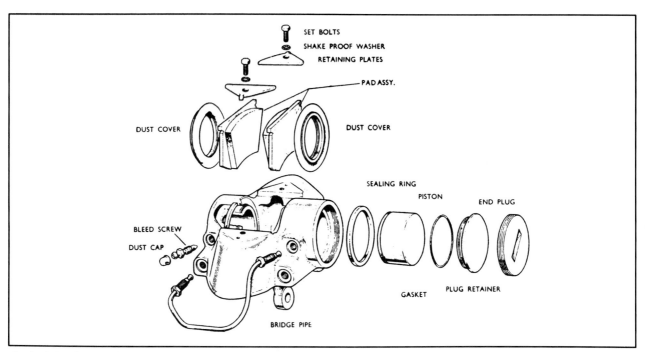

Typical brake caliper with a twist; end plug makes getting to piston possible from rear. Moss Motors, Ltd.

in and you shouldn't have to remove the caliper from the car. The general procedure is to remove the cotters that hold the pad retaining pins, slide out the pins and lift up the pads along with any anti-rattle plates or shims. (This will get the pads out on most brakes, but some of the Bendix and Girling/Dunlop calipers fitted to rarer cars are pretty wacky. Again, go to the book.)

While the pads are out, inspect the caliper's dust covers and piston surfaces for damage. Clean up the disc with fine emery cloth if it needs it, and also emery down any pitting found on the caliper around the dust covers.

To get the new pads into position, first open up the master cylinder and lay some rags around it. (The next step could push some fluid up and out of

Brake lube behind the pads of disc brakes prevents squealing—most of the time. If pads or rotor become glazed, squeal can be brought down with gentle sanding of rotor and pad faces. Moss Motors, Ltd.

Drum and Rotor Checks and Repairs

Whenever you have a brake drum off, look it over to see if it's still usable.

Begin by inspecting the drum visually for cracks. Look for corrosion and deep scoring along the swept surface; if any is found, the drum can probably be skimmed professionally. There are limits to how much skimming can be done. The drum has to remain thick enough to absorb and dissipate the heat of hard braking. Drums should also be checked for distortion (ovality) and belling (bowing of the swept surface) professionally.

If the drum turns out to need replacing, you can try to find another one in a junkyard. This will be dirt cheap, but make darned sure it doesn't suffer from the same problems as those of the old drum. New drums are relatively expensive, so it probably pays to spend some time looking around for a used one.

Discs brakes are even easier to check than drums. Remove the road wheel and check the disc for deep scoring. Light scoring can be removed by having the disc turned professionally, but deep scoring will total the disc. Heavy deposits of rust can ruin the disc, but light rust can be removed by spinning the disc while holding a flat-bladed screwdriver against it. The disc can also be ground professionally.

Spin the rotor between the pads and check for wobbling, indicating a warped disc (run-out). (Loose wheel bearings can also mimic the effects of excessive run-out, so check those before removing the rotor.) A disc can only be warped by about 0.01 mm before it needs replacing. Check all around the disc with a micrometer for uneven thickness. The maximum accepted variance is about 0.01 mm.

A disc that's slightly warped or uneven can be ground professionally. In general, you've got about 1.25 mm of surface that can be ground from the original thickness of the disc. This figure changes depending on the car, however.

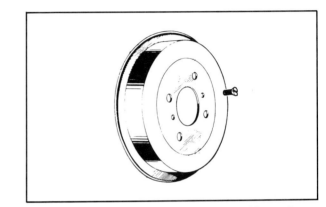

Setscrew holding drum to hub can freeze with age. Large screwdriver and lots of pressure is the answer—an impact driver might crack the drum. Moss Motors, Ltd.

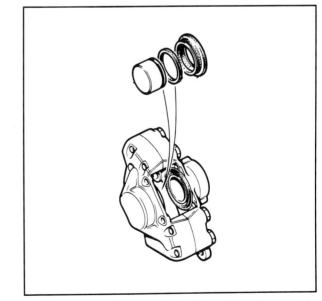

Split this typical caliper in half and it will probably never work again. Leave the unit in one piece and remove the pistons from the middle. Moss Motors, Ltd.

Another handy twist to the caliper; hydraulic housings separate from base for service. These are very eager to leak after reassembly, so don't remove them unless you have to. Moss Motors, Ltd.

the cylinder, and you don't want it ruining the paint under the hood.) Gently lever the pistons back into the calipers, either with a special tool designed for your particular brakes or a screwdriver pressing against a flat piece of wood. An alternative method, if you don't want to risk your underhood paint, is to lightly loosen the bleed screw on the caliper and fit a clear bleeding hose and jar. As soon as the pistons are pushed back into the calipers, tighten the bleed screw again. You might have to go back and bleed the brakes later.

When the pistons are fully retracted, coat the backs of the pads with anti-squeal brake grease and slip them in along with their shims and springs. Make darned sure you don't get any grease on the pad's face or the disc, as it's almost impossible to remove again. When both brakes have been dealt with, pump the pedal a few times to seat them, fill up the master cylinder again and road test the car.

The only difficult thing about changing shoes is taking all the notes needed to get everything back together the way it should go. It's best to do one brake at a time. That way you can refer to the

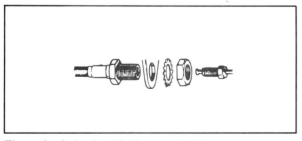

First take the hydraulic line out while holding the brake hose lock nut with the appropriate wrench. Keep holding the lock nut when you attack the brake hose mounting nut later. Moss Motors, Ltd.

opposite brake as a guide if you get confused. Otherwise, there are only a few things to tackle: one is the spring-loaded rod-and-cup fastener running through the middle of the shoe. You have to push down the head of this thing, twist it and remove it before the shoe comes off. There's special tool you can buy to grab onto the head of this monster, but pliers will work just as well; the real trick is to put your finger behind the backing plate and hold the *far side* of the rod in place while you play with the head.

Shoes often look like they'll go in a few different ways, but usually you have to get the proper left and right shoe in place and right side up for the system to work. The same goes for all the springs that clamp the shoes together. They might go in a number of ways, but only one is correct—the way they came out.

You'll probably have to back the brake adjusters off quite a bit to get the drum back on over the new shoes. To readjust them once the drum is back in place, turn the adjuster until the shoes just come into contact with the drum. Then back the adjuster off just until the wheel spins freely again—usually no more than one or two clicks. With self-adjusting drum brakes, back the car up slowly and gently press the brake pedal. (Remember that knockoff wheels will unscrew themselves in reverse, so don't back up too fast before the car has had some road time.)

Pipes and Hoses

Brake pipes can, in theory, last forever. They're very fragile, but are rarely under enough strain to do them in. Corrosion, rattling and overzealous repair work are the things that will kill them.

Corrosion is partly out of your hands. You can keep the insides of the pipes clean by changing the fluid often, and you can keep the outsides clean where you can get at them. But the side pressed up against the body will rust merrily away and there's not much you can do about it but keep an eye on things.

Rattling is easier to control. Make sure that the pipes are snug in all their securing clips and replace any clips that are missing or broken. If there are rubber bushings holding the pipes in place, make sure they haven't cracked or fallen off.

Finally, you have to avoid damaging the pipes while you're repairing something else. The two main ways to ruin them are out of ignorance (bending them to get at something they're blocking) and by trying to remove a fitting that's frozen to the pipe. Before starting any work, fittings should be lubricated and cleaned if they're the least bit rusty. Cover or plug the ends of any remaining pipes and cylinders to keep out dust and grit while you work.

If you don't have good reason to suspect a pipe of leaking, I'd leave it alone. Heavily rusted pipes can be checked by scraping off some of the surface corrosion with a flat knife; if the underlying metal is sound, again leave it alone. If it's not, the pipe is probably going to need replacing.

If a pipe does turn out to need replacing, a replacement might come new from a parts house, used from a junkyard or have to be made up from scratch in your garage. New, pre-bent pipes are the best if they're available—give the supplier all the relevant information such as marque, year and model and there's rarely any problem. Used pipes are risky at best but, Lord knows, very inexpensive. You have to be careful that used pipes aren't gummed up on the inside, corroded through on the outside or supplied with the wrong fittings for your car. Frankly, I'd say used brake pipes are a bad idea.

Some new pipes are only available in straight lengths, and even when installing pre-bent pipes you might have to twist them around a bit to match the originals. Never do this between your bare hands—the pipe will crimp and break long before it gets close to the original dimensions. Instead, use a bending tool or, for gentler curves, a suitable piece of wood or metal as a form. Get it right the first time; re-bending a single area of pipe is a sure way to crack it.

Making your own pipes won't often be necessary, but if it is, the work is actually kind of fun. You'll need a few special tools: a former, a flaring tool and a rotary pipe cutter. I'm not going to get into this too deeply, except to say that making up hydraulic lines is well within the abilities of the home restorer. Cleanliness and patience are all that are required beyond the proper tools and correct materials. The pipes themselves can be made of steel, copper-nickel alloy or copper, but whatever material you choose should be designed and approved specifically for brake work.

Copper is rarely going to be the original, factory-approved material, but I've found it perhaps the easiest and most forgiving to work with. (If possible, brass fittings should also be used to avoid future rusting and seizure.)

In brief, you start by cutting the copper to the correct length with a rotary pipe cutter, never a hacksaw. Flare one end of the pipe with a flaring tool and slip on the fittings for both ends from the other side. Flare up the other side and you're ready to start forming the pipe. The difference between a professional-looking job and one that works okay but looks lousy is getting the right angles in the pipe the first time. Once the pipe is bent it will never be quite straight again, so go carefully to avoid a wavy, shoddy-looking result. Copper fuel and vapor lines are made the same way.

Flexible brake hoses are relatively short-lived compared to pipes—you have to keep an eye on them. The effects of temperature, moisture, pollu-tants and especially sunlight are all harmful to the rubber and fabric used.

The best check is simply a visual one. Get access to the hose and bend it around, run it between your fingers and wiggle it back and forth. Flaws will show up as fine cracks or possibly traces of moisture. The ends of the hose are particularly fragile. Finally, have a helper give the brake pedal a good stomp and watch for swelling or ballooning of the hose. If any of these flaws are found, new hoses are in order. (It usually pays to *carefully* inspect the hose on the other side of the car if one is found to be bad. They seem to go out in pairs.)

Used hoses are out—always go with new ones and make sure the fittings are correct before continuing. If you're a real go-fast type (and originality and cost are not objects) consider fitting braided-steel brake hoses. These are a little tougher than traditional hoses and they make the brakes a little tighter and more precise.

The danger when installing or removing flexible hoses is that you'll crimp or bend them by not using the lock nuts provided. Once a new hose is installed and fastened finger-tight, let the car back down, rock it on the suspension and turn the wheels from lock to lock a couple of times. Check to make sure the hoses aren't crimping or chafing, then tighten them up just enough to be snug and not leak.

Bleeding

Brake bleeding will be needed because air has gotten into the system or because the fluid is old and needs to be changed.

Air is compressible while fluid is not; therefore, any air in the lines will prevent the motion of the brake pedal from effectively traveling out to the wheels. Air enters the system through a leak anywhere along the line or, more commonly, because the owner lets the master cylinder go dry. If there's no fluid in the reservoir, the pickup hole sucks in air and the whole system is useless.

Air in the lines is usually detectable by a spongy brake pedal, particularly one that firms up after a

---

Different Kinds of Brake Fluid

While DOT 3 (standards set by the Department of Transportation) brake fluid—the most common—will indeed absorb water from the atmosphere, the newer DOT 4 and DOT 5 fluids will not. That's all well and good in brand-new cars or completely new braking systems, but the fluid types are not always compatible with each other. If you have an older car using DOT 3 fluid, you shouldn't necessarily switch over to DOT 4 or DOT 5 immediately. Consult with a professional who knows your car before making the switch; it might entail replacing all the rubber in the system.

few quick pumps. Poor braking response can also point to air in the system, as can excessive pedal travel. (These are also symptoms of brake shoes out of adjustment.)

Changing the fluid regularly is necessary because brake fluid absorbs water from the atmosphere, and it simply gets gritty and mucky over time. If water is absorbed in the fluid two nasty scenarios can follow. The first is simply internal corrosion and degradation of the lines, cylinders and seals. The second is perhaps even more insidious: vapor lock. If the water in the fluid gets hot enough to boil, it creates a pocket of steam in the middle of the brake lines. One moment you'll be driving down the road with fine brakes; the next they won't work at all.

Fluid should be changed completely every year and a half or 20,000 miles just to be on the safe side. Always use the same brand of fluid if you know what was in the car to begin with. If not, flush the system, change the fluid and stick with one brand from then on. Often the owners manual will specify a particular type of fluid, usually the proprietary stuff made by Lockheed or Girling. English brakes will only work right with certain brake fluids, like Castrol LMA. Follow your owners manual recommendations or those of a professional shop.

When flushing out old fluid, you can simply push out the old with the new or, perhaps better, flush through a proprietary cleaning fluid first and then push out the cleaner with the new brake fluid. (Sometimes manufacturers will recommend simple methylated spirits [denatured alcohol] as a cleaner.) If any cleaning fluid is used, it must be *completely* flushed out before the car is put back in service.

Bleeding is a simple but annoying and time-consuming job. It's at least a two-person affair, even if you're using a so-called "one-man" bleeding kit, which I strongly recommend. The critical thing is to make sure the master cylinder doesn't get drained completely. That will mean starting all over again.

Each manufacturer will ask you to bleed the brakes a little differently. Usually this is just a matter of pumping the brakes in a certain rhythm that, quite frankly, I doubt makes much difference. Still, following their instructions can't hurt, so look in the book before going to it.

Brake Bleeding Procedure

The general procedure for brake bleeding, and the one I use unless there's a strong suggestion for another method, is as follows. On cars with all drum or disc brakes, start at the farthest wheel from the master cylinder and work your way in to the closest one. On cars with both disc and drum brakes, do the discs first and then the drums, start-ing each time with the one farthest from the cylinder.

First, fit a proper brake wrench around the bleed screw of the wheel farthest from the master cylinder. Put a slight dab of brake fluid onto the screw as a penetrant and let it sit for a few minutes. While you're waiting, top off the master cylinder with fluid and connect a clear plastic hose tightly to the bleed screw. Lay fluffy rags all around the reservoir and place the cap gently back on top.

Submerge the far end of the hose in a clear jar with fresh brake fluid at the bottom. (Throw this jar away when you're done instead of recycling it. Brake fluid is that toxic.) Have your helper gently pump the brakes a few times and then hold the pedal to the floor. Crack open a bleed screw. Fluid should come out with each stroke; if it doesn't, try opening the bleed screw farther. If fluid still doesn't come out, there's a problem farther up the line that needs inspection.

When you start getting fluid out of the system, it should at first be dirty and full of air bubbles. After a few more pumps your helper should push the pedal to the bottom of its throw and hold it there. Close the bleed screw and top off the master cylinder. Repeat the procedure until the air bubbles disappear (for a regular bleeding) or the fluid runs clear and clean (for a fluid change).

A one-person bleeding tool will make things easier. The tool fits securely over the bleed screw while a regular plastic hose is usually an iffy fit at best, and it prevents air from reentering the system through an open bleed screw if the far end of the hose comes out of the bleeding fluid. You can even, as the name suggests, do the job alone—it will mean a lot of sliding back and forth under the car, though, so it's a real pain.

Bleeding brakes is actually fastest when done as a three-person job. One person works the bleed screws, another pumps the brakes and a third constantly watches and tops off the master cylinder. When done this way, you can run all the fluid in the world through the system without having to stop every few pumps, secure the bleed screw and check the fluid level in the reservoir.

When the bleeding seems complete and all the bleed screws are tight, have your helper stomp on the pedal vigorously four or five times while you check all the bleed screws for leaks. Adjust the brake shoes. The pedal should now be hard without having to be pumped up, and it shouldn't slowly work down toward the floor under constant pressure.

Let the system sit for a while and then try the pedal again. If it seems to have stayed hard, you probably did things right. If not, you'll have to go through the whole procedure again. The second time around, though, there will be much less air in the lines and things should go much more quickly.

9

After the Restoration

Okay. You've just finished restoring the nicest MG Midget or whatever in town—now how are you going to keep it that way? The answer is proper storage, regular maintenance, quick repair of anything that goes wrong and good cleaning techniques.

General Body Cleaning

Maintenance cleaning should be done with an eye toward gentleness over all else. Frequent use of harsh abrasives and alkalis will cause the car to deteriorate almost as quickly as not cleaning it at all. You can decide how often to clean the car on your own—dust settling across it will probably drive you to frenzied cleaning without any prodding from an arranged schedule.

The body is the biggest cleaning job, although not the most time-consuming by a long shot. Before you go out with a bucket full of water, though, it pays to realize just what makes a deep, smooth shine. What you see on the car isn't really paint. It's a sandwich of color pigments suspended toward the bottom, a hard clear layer sealing the pigments in and a rich coat of wax protecting the clear layer.

The finish is constantly under attack. Chemicals in pollution, road film, bird droppings and dust will react with each layer and damage it, as will sunlight and even water. The wax is a sacrificial coating—it doesn't last forever, and it shouldn't. The idea is to let chemicals and sunlight destroy the wax instead of the paint below it; so when it disappears, for whatever reason, it has to be immediately replaced. This is important to remember when it comes to washing and cleaning, because you can inadvertently remove the wax layer without knowing it, leaving the paint itself vulnerable.

For cleaning light dirt and dust off the body, I've always gone against just about all the experts and advocated using no soap at all. Plenty of water and a very clean sponge are enough to float the dirt away with a minimum risk to the wax coating. Most detailers feel that soap lifts the dirt particles and prevents them from scratching the body, so I

should at least talk about the kinds of soap that can and can't be used on automotive finishes.

A number of commercial preparations for body washing are available, and all the name brands seem to do what they claim—remove dirt without stripping wax off the car. What you should *not* use are the following home tricks I've heard espoused from time to time:

Powdered soap: Usually too alkaline for auto finishes, and even a tiny particle of undissolved soap can scratch into the paint.

Shampoo: Looking at the back of my usual shampoo, I'm not even sure if I want to use the stuff on my *hair*. Citric acid, ammonium xylenesulfonate, methylcholorisothiazolinone and "masking fragrance"?

Dishwashing liquid: Most contain a good amount of degreaser, which will eat away wax as readily as it cuts through spaghetti sauce.

Spray cleaners: Lemon Brite, 409 and so on not only can remove wax but actually attack the paint itself.

After detailing an entire V-12, the owner of this Jag can be forgiven for showing off a little.

Soft, natural brushes and lots of cool, soapy water will reach into cracks and crevices a cleaning sponge misses. The Eastwood Company

One of the main reasons I don't like soap is that it simply violates the first rule of car cleaning: Start with the gentlest method possible and only move onto something harsher when that fails. If plain water fails, move on to soap. If the soap fails, move on to a bug and tar remover. If that doesn't work,

If very fine steel wool and alcohol don't salvage your windshield, there's heavier artillery available. Chemicals and wheels are available for do-it-yourself use, but many auto glass shops will do the job for not much money. The Eastwood Company

Let small crevices go too long and this is what you get: stainless and aluminum trim does corrode eventually. An annual detailing would have prevented this. Brett O'Brien

208

you might have to actually rub the stain out with polishing compound.

Rarely will you have to go beyond soap, however, and whether you decide to use auto soap or just plain water, the way you put it on the car is critical—overdo it. You want to not only free up any dirt and dust particles, you want them to float off the paint, not be scratched into it. Give the car a serious dousing before starting in with a very clean, very wet sponge or wash mitt.

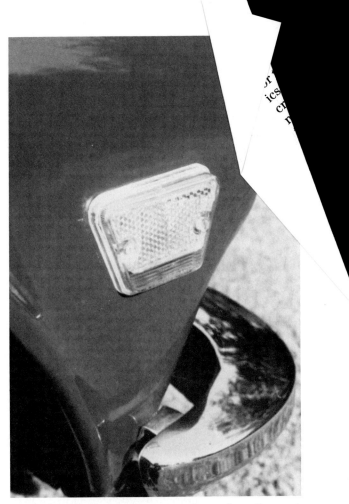

Motorcycle visor polish is perfect for plastic-faced insignia like this Triumph badge. There's really no other way to clean up the faces.

Get inside light housings every so often to clean them out; sealing gaskets must remain in place to prevent electrical and rust worries. Erika Sandford

Genuine chamois is still the drying rag of choice. Keep chamois cloths clean and they should last for years. The Eastwood Company

Plastic wheel covers tend to get gray and dirty over time. The proper respray is satin, not gloss, black plastic paint. Mike Lamm

onges should be large enough to hold lots of
er; natural sponges are far and away the best
the job, but some of the higher quality synthet-
will do if you can't see spending $20 on any sea
eature that doesn't come with tartar sauce. Wash
itts are also good to use, although I'd shy away
from the synthetic wool ones—they seem too
coarse to clean without scratching. Pure cotton
chenille mitts are best. Mitts don't hold as much
water as sponges, so it's even more critical to keep
them clean and wet. Some people also swear by
terrycloth towels for the initial cleaning, though
others feel they're too rough.

Once you've completely gone over the car with
your sponge or mitt and loosened all the dirt, rinse
it off with plenty of cool water. High-pressure spray
nozzles carry dirt farther and faster than a steady
stream from a hose, but an open hose makes fewer
droplets so the car's easier to dry.

Drying off the car is another matter where
experts disagree on procedure. Many people use
soft terrycloth towels here, too, but I don't trust
them. I'd stick with the old standby, a genuine
chamois cloth that's kept clean and wrung out
frequently. Synthetic chamois and the rubberized
fakers that look like cellulose tortillas are next to
worthless. You'll probably need at least two chamois cloths to do a car, one that holds a lot of water
for the rough mop-up work and a finer, thinner one
for the finishing work.

Most chamois cloths come soaked in softeners or
soap when you buy them, so let them sit in a bucket
of water for a few days and wring them out well
before the first use. When dry they should be stiff as
a board, not soft and flexible. Naturally, you want
to wet them and wring them out immediately
before use.

Dry the car from the top down, paying particular
attention to glass and brightwork. Blow into any
cracks and crevices that might hold water—rain
channels, rearview mirrors and so on—or they'll
leak later and make water spots.

Wear clothes that won't scratch the paint; no
jewelry, watches, buttons, belt buckles or metal
rivets. Gray sweats make a great car-washing suit,
except that they usually soak up enough water to
make you 20 lb. heavier by the end of the job. Some
detailers actually wear soft cotton aprons over
their clothes; it's worth thinking about if the neighbors don't laugh too much. Avoid tennis or deck
shoes that soak up water and dirt from the driveway and carry them into the interior.

The bitter enemy of a good washing is heat and
sunlight. Find a solid patch of shade—not under a
sap- or bird-laden tree, of course—and choose a
cool part of the day for the job. If you get side-
tracked on a difficult cleaning job, keep coating
the rest of the car in water until you can get around
to removing it.

When cleaning a really grungy car, you might
consider the effects of grease and crud on your
driveway before you start out. A self-service car
wash can be worth the time if your cleaning job
looks serious. The high-pressure wands at these
places do a number on dirt in the wheelwells and
grease under the hood, but they can also chip paint
and remove decals unless you use them carefully.

Detailing

Less frequently than the general washing you'll
want to do a thorough detailing. This takes care of
all the neglected corners and doodads that have
been accumulating crud over time. Detail cleaning
is really not that hard—it's mostly a matter of finding the right tools to get into the odd places a
regular sponge misses. You'll also attend to the
insides of several parts; remove the side-marker
lights, for example, and clean them inside with
soap and water. (Don't forget to reinstall the
weather gasket, which keeps water out of the
housing.)

Soft, natural paintbrushes are probably the most
valuable tools for detail cleaning. By cutting down
the length of the bristles you can make them rigid
enough to get into tight spaces, and by wrapping a
few layers of duct tape around the metal base you
can keep it from scratching the paint. Usually two
brushes—one about 2 in. wide and one about ½ in.
wide—and some soapy water will be needed to
clean the chrome trim, window channels, light
assemblies, emblems and grilles. A few soft-bristled
toothbrushes are also handy, especially for removing stubborn wax from tight corners and plastic
lenses. (Cotton swabs will clean out crud from
around emblems and trim strips, but they sometimes don't reach into the very edge the way a

*You can bet a lot of cotton swabs and toothbrushes gave
their lives for this bit of TR trim, but it was worth it.*

toothbrush can.) A reasonably stiff plastic-bristled brush can be a big help in removing dirt and grease from fine-grained surfaces like vinyl tops and textured steel wheels. All of these tools should only be used with plenty of soapy, cool water to prevent scratching.

All the brushes you buy will have to be kept in a condition proper for their intended job. As the brushes get more and more disgusting you should rotate them on to rougher and rougher work—first the body, then the interior, then on to the engine compartment and finally to the trash.

Clean the glass as you would anything else, but extremely dirty windows can be brought back with diluted ammonia cleaner and crumpled newspapers, or #000 steel wool and rubbing alcohol in extreme cases. Perspex (plexiglass) windows and most plastic emblems respond nicely to motorcycle visor polish.

When delving into the guts of the car for detailing you can start using more and more serious cleaning methods than you could for the paint and interior, but the rule is again to start off with the gentlest method and to work up to harsher means as needed. I'd start with soap and water on greasy mechanical parts and extras like the jack and tire iron, work up to a commercial spray cleaner (car fans swear by Simple Green) and finally try a spray degreaser on really heavy deposits.

Storage

For a car that's used regularly, keep it in a garage. I'd estimate that storing a car outdoors cuts the life of the paint and chrome and rubber at least in half. A covered carport is better than nothing, but a full garage is simply the best way to go.

There's a lot of controversy over car covers; some people won't get near them and others keep a cover on their car even inside the garage. The consensus seems to be that if you have a cover on your car outdoors, it darned well better be a good one. It must be waterproof yet breathable—otherwise water condenses under the cover and leads to rust and chalky paint. It must also fit the car well enough not to be blown around by the wind and scratch the finish.

As for using a cover indoors, it seems counterproductive. The purpose is to protect the car from dust, but the effects of dry indoor dust are probably negligible compared to the scratching you can do simply by removing and replacing the cover. If the car's going to sit undisturbed for very long periods a cover indoors might make sense, but if you're going to pull it off every month or two I don't think you're doing the paint any favors.

For long-term storage—say more than a month—you'll have to prepare the car fairly well. (Even for storage of a week or more you should disconnect the battery while the car sits. Always disconnect the ground terminal first.) The best thing you can do is to take the car out and drive it every couple of weeks, putting ten or twenty miles on it and getting the engine and transmission up to operating temperature. Don't just warm up the engine; this does nothing for the rest of the car and often the engine doesn't get hot enough to boil out the condensation and blow-by accumulated in the sump.

Wire wheels are a nightmare to keep clean, but a soap-and-water shooting brush speeds things up a bit. Wire wheels just plain need attention—let them rot and they'll fail with disastrous results. The Eastwood Company

The overdrive could be smartened up with a little black enamel paint. Smooth the paint into the lettering as accurately as possible, but anything that laps over the edge can be quickly wiped up with a rag moistened in thinner. Mike Lamm

Improper storage getting back at an owner. Quick temperature changes let water condense inside this rearview mirror. It quickly destroyed the silvering.

If you're going to get a cover for your car it had better be a good one. Cheap covers cause more harm than good. Moss Motors, Ltd.

If the car's off the road because of salt in the wintertime, you might as well mothball it completely and prepare for the long winter months ahead. Drain the coolant and replace it with a 50:50 mix (30:70 in very cold climates) of distilled water and high-quality antifreeze. Drive the car for about twenty minutes to circulate the new coolant, and turn the heater on briefly toward the end.

Fill the tank completely and add a fuel stabilizer. Let the engine run for another minute or two to get the stabilizer all the way through the lines. Drain and replace the oil and transmission fluid. (Old oil has acids in it that can harm the bearings.) Change the coolant and replace it with a 50:50 mix of distilled water and high-quality antifreeze.

Wash the car thoroughly and coat the paint and chrome with a heavy layer of wax. (Before you lay on the wax, it's a good idea to look the car over for chips and scratches, which must be touched up first.) Pay special attention to the underside and wheelwells—now's the time to get all the dirt and mud out, or else it will sit there all winter and soak up rust-causing moisture like a sponge. Some people also like to coat the underside of the car with a spray of clean motor oil. That's pretty gunky, but it does seem to keep rust off the floor pan.

Clean the interior well and coat any varnished wood with a silicone spray or straight wax. Wipe some silicone spray onto the weatherstripping and bump stops with a rag. Make sure that *all* the holes into the interior are plugged up. If a rat or a mouse takes a shine to your car it's likely to start a family inside, and the padding of your seats will be a lovely nest.

Right before you push the car into its resting place, remove the spark plugs and shoot a few drops of oil into each cylinder. Crank the engine once with the coil wire removed, and store the coil wire somewhere inside the house—that won't stop most thieves, but it might slow them down a bit. (You can also make a fake coil wire out of vacuum hose and spark plug caps and install it on the engine.) The last thing to do is to pull out the battery and hook it to a trickle charger in a warm (not cold), dry place for the winter. (Barring that, charge it up once a month with a regular charger.) Coat the terminals in petroleum jelly, check the water every month and rest the battery on a piece of wood instead of metal or concrete.

Where you store the car is as important as *how* you store it. Any covered area is better than none, but all storage sites are not created equal. Dirt and gravel floors will soak up moisture when it's cold and then steam it up when it's warm, effectively soaking the underside of the car each time—try to find a new concrete floor for the storage site. Large, fast changes in temperature are also harmful, though there's not always much you can do about it. Fiberglass insulation is probably your best insurance.

Many people jack up the car out of habit and leave it on blocks for the winter, which is fine if the suspension arms are compressed instead of left hanging. There's nothing wrong with leaving the car on the ground, though, as long as you push it backward or forward every month or so to prevent the tires from becoming square. Leave the emergency brake off while the car sits, and block up the rear wheels if needed.

If you can find large desiccant packs (try electronics, marine and appliance stores) by all means put one inside the interior, one in the trunk and one in the engine bay. Each should sit on a solid ceramic plate, not the metal or cloth or carpeting itself.

212

Maintenance

In your own service or owners manual, you'll find everything you need to know about maintaining your car in proper shape. All you have to do is follow the directions to the letter. Since you don't know when the last full service took place, attend to everything listed in the most comprehensive service interval as soon as you buy the car. This is going to be a major job—it means changing all the hydraulic fluid, checking the brake pads and shoes, repacking the wheel bearings, lubing the U-joints and water pump, filling the shock absorbers and on and on. From there, though, you'll know when 3,000 miles or three months has passed, and there will never be any doubt about what needs doing when.

One thing you should consider is cutting the oil change interval down from whatever is specified to once every 2,000 miles. That seems like an awful lot of oil changing, but engineers are beginning to find that changes as frequent as this aid engine life considerably, particularly in older cars. Replace the oil filter at least every other oil change (smear a film of oil on the gasket and tighten the filter by hand), and check the level of all the engine compartment fluids once a week. Transmission, rear end and shock levels should be checked at least once a month or at the interval specified in your manual.

A lot of English car owners get into the habit of running one grade heavier oil than specified in

Maintenance checks in unsuspecting places. Shown is access panel to Healey gearbox level and filler.

their engines and transmissions. This seems, surprisingly, to do little harm and definitely cuts down on noise while increasing pressure somewhat. It's certainly not *good* for the car, but doesn't seem to hurt it, either.

Finally, there's one other very important way to get a long and happy life out of your classic English sports car: Get out there and drive it!

English-American Translations

British car manuals are supposedly written in English, but I refuse to believe it. I adopt their words out of habit sometimes, though—this list should get you through their books and mine.

British term	American equivalent
actuator	switch
apron	valance
baulk ring	synchro ring
big-end bearing	rod bearing
bonnet	hood
boot	trunk
Bowden cable	sheathed cable
brake pipe	brake hose
bulkhead	firewall
bush	bushing
cam follower	lifter
choke tube	venturi
clutch housing	bell housing
control box	voltage regulator
crosshead	Phillips
crown wheel	ring gear
damper	shock absorber
distance piece	spacer
door casing	door panel
drop arm	Pitman arm
earth	ground
estate	wagon
extractor	bearing or wheel puller
fascia	dashboard
flat	sand
float chamber	float bowl
first motion shaft	input shaft (gearbox)
gearchange	shift linkage
grub screw	leadless Allen bolt
gudgeon pin	wristpin
hoist	engine crane or cherry picker
hood	convertible top
HT lead	main coil wire
bumper irons	brackets

British term	American equivalent
jointing compound	gasket sealant
LHS	*right*-hand side

(Americans usually use right and left meaning looking at the car from the front; the English usually mean sitting in the driver's seat looking forward. Stick to "driver's" and "passenger's" side to be safe.)

British term	American equivalent
linish	grind
methylated spirits	denatured alcohol
mudguard	fender
paraffin	kerosene
perished	rotten
petrol	gasoline
pinking	knocking
prise	pry
proud	raised above
quarterlight	vent window
rev counter	tachometer
saloon	sedan
scuttle	cowl
self-tapper	sheet-metal screw
set screw	bolt
sidelight	side marker
silencer	muffler
sill	rocker panel
slacken	loosen
spanner	wrench
split pin	cotter pin
spring washer	lock washer
strip	disassemble
suction advance	vacuum advance
sump	oil pan
swarf	metal filings and crud
third motion shaft	output shaft (gearbox)
thrust bearing	throwout bearing
valve locks	valve cotters
washing-up liquid	dishwashing soap
Welch plug	freeze plug
wheel nut	lug nut
windscreen	windshield
wing	fender

Safety Considerations

Restoring a car is a lot of fun. It's also a great way to do yourself in; there are enough opportunities to crush, burn, cut, and maim oneself to keep the Three Stooges busy for weeks. As you go through this book you'll see safety notes in the text, captions and sidebars. For every one thing I can tell you about safety procedures, you're going to discover three other ways to get hurt. Your safety begins and ends with your own common sense—you've got to think for a minute about how each job you do could go wrong and result in an injury.

I won't say I've never done a job without all the proper safety equipment and precautions. I think we've all done it a lot more than we want to admit. But every close call I've had has made me pay that much more attention to safety procedures; if you're given warnings instead of accidents, it's dumb to push your luck. Besides, a beautiful car is no good if you're not able—or around—to drive it.

Basic Safety Guidelines
Here's a preliminary list of do's, don'ts and "rookie moves":

Eyes
Do wear approved eye protection whenever grinding, drilling, welding, working under the car, shooting solvents and blasting.

Don't let chemicals splash or drip into your eyes.

Don't look at a welding flame without eyewear specifically approved for that kind of welding.

Rookie move: Trying to get grit out of your eye with greasy fingers—wash hands well before trying to remove foreign objects.

Hands and Body
Do wear gloves appropriate for the job—plastic or rubber when working with fiberglass; thick leather when working with broken glass or sharp-edged panels; flame-retardant and insulated when welding, brazing or working around other heat sources like the exhaust system.

Do keep your hands clean and grease-free to avoid accidents.

Don't cut toward yourself with scissors or a knife.

Don't place your hands where a slipping wrench or screwdriver can hit them.

Don't apply lots of torque where a breaking bolt will send your hands into a solid object.

Don't try to catch a heavy object once it has started to fall—let it drop.

Don't get under a car that is supported by less than two solid jack stands.

Don't use cinder blocks, wood, bricks or jacks to support a car you're working near.

Don't loosen or tighten heavily torqued bolts while the car is in the air.

Do use proper-fitting wrenches and screwdrivers at all times.

Don't remove heavy components like bumpers, transmissions and so on without properly supporting them first.

Don't get near a moving fan.

Don't wear loose clothes or long hair near rotating parts.

Do tie up hair and dangling clothing before working.

Don't wear rings or jewelry that can get caught in components or cause a short circuit.

Don't let kids and pets play around the tools and vehicle unsupervised.

Do use only an approved engine hoist or stand in good condition.

Do ask someone to come in and check on you occasionally. (Have them bring you a Coke while they're at it.)

Don't forget to chock the wheels of any car with one end in the air.

Don't turn over the engine of a raised car unless you're *positive* it's out of gear and chocked.

Don't jack from the oil pan, middle of the floorboards, thin suspension points or under fuel or brake lines.

Do jack from underneath springs, recommended jacking points along the sill, the rear differential or a cross-member.

Do use a stout piece of wood (at least 3 in. thick) to spread out the load of the jack.

Do keep a sharp cutting edge on all saws, bits and so forth.

Do keep parts and tools where they can't fall on your head or feet.

Do store paints and other chemicals in a locked cabinet so kids can't get at them.

Do read all the safety warnings on every chemical and tool. If the manufacturer says "May cause injury or death," they mean it.

Do keep a good first-aid kit on the wall of the garage.

Rookie move: Absent-mindedly picking up a metal part after welding it or removing it from a hot engine.

Lungs

Do wear a good-fitting filter mask when sanding or cutting fiberglass, spraying lacquers and cellulose enamels, and working with plastic fillers.

Do insist on a legitimate air-supply respirator when spraying isocyanate (two-pack) paints and working with other toxic or carcinogenic chemicals.

Do work with paints, solvents, gasoline, fillers and cleaners only in a well-ventilated area.

Do study the product label of all aerosol and liquid chemicals and learn the dangers and treatments for that chemical.

Don't combine solvents or cleaners in a haphazard way—poisonous gases could result.

Don't let exhaust gas accumulate in a closed space—it can be fatal.

Fire

Do keep at least two fire extinguishers, Type A–B–C, in your garage handy and charged at all times.

Do store oil, rags, paint, chemicals, raw fiberglass, wood, paper and gasoline away from heat and flame.

Do keep all liquids in tightly covered containers. Gasoline and solvents will quickly evaporate and fill your workshop with flammable fumes.

Do wear flame-retardant clothing and gloves when welding, brazing or soldering.

Do check behind any panel or bolt being heated for undercoating, oil stains, rubber bushes, wood or fuel lines in the area.

Don't ever weld near a fuel tank; empty tanks are as dangerous or more dangerous than full ones.

Do clean up all spills quickly and thoroughly.

Do keep a dishwashing liquid bottle filled with water nearby when working with heat, to extinguish small fires without resorting to your larger extinguisher.

Don't let your shop area get cluttered with rags or papers.

Don't heat your garage with an open-flame heater.

Don't oil or lube the fittings or hoses of an oxyacetylene welding kit.

Don't charge a battery in an enclosed space—the vapors are extremely flammable.

Don't give a water heater pilot light or similar source of ignition an even break; control evaporative fumes and gases, keep all flammable items away and shut off the flame when in doubt of a material's volatility and flammability.

Do ensure that all trouble lights and power tools are properly grounded, wired through a fuse-protected circuit and free of worn insulation.

Don't grind or cut near a fuel tank, battery or other flammable source.

Parts, Services, Tools and Literature Sources

Abingdon Spares Ltd.
Box 37, South Street
Walpole, NH 03608
   MG parts

Adirondack Restoration and Reconditioning Inc.
19 Queensway
Queensbury, NY 12804
   Full and partial restoration

Apple Hydraulics Inc.
715 Route 25A
Miller Place, NY 11764
   SU carburetor and lever shock rebuilding,
   machine work

Bernard F. Wade, Ltd.
Unit L3, Meltham Mill Ind. Est.
Meltham, Huddersfield HD7 3DS, England
   Rare fasteners

Bob Akin Motor Racing
61 Water Street
Ossining, NY 10562
   Full restoration

Borla East
600A Lincoln Boulevard
Middlesex, NJ 08846
   Stainless-steel exhaust systems

Brit-Tek 6
6 Londonderry Commons, Suite 111
Londonderry, NH 03053
   Oil injection rustproofing supplies

British Auto/USA
92 Londonderry Turnpike
Manchester, NH 03104
   Jaguar parts and accessories

British Wire Wheel
1600 Mansfield Street
Santa Cruz, CA 95062
   Wire and Minilite wheels service, supplies, tires

Buzzard Products Incorporated
2617 W. Glendale Avenue
Phoenix, AZ 85051
   Plastic rechroming

Cargo Forwarding UK Ltd.
34 Wickam Road
Beckenham, Kent BR3 2JT, England
   Overseas England-US vehicle transportation

Caterham Cars
Seven House, Town End
Caterham CR3 5UG, England
   Lotus Super 7 replicas and kits

The Classic MG Shop
Box 2083
Tallahassee, FL 32304
   MG parts, SU carburetor service

Classic Motorbooks (Motorbooks International)
Box 1
Osceola, WI 54020
   Automotive books, manuals, videotapes

Coker Tire
1317 Chestnut Street
Chattanooga, TN 37407
   Antique tires

Concours West
644 B Terminal Way
Costa Mesa, CA 92627
   New and used Jaguar parts

Cooper, Love & Jackson
Box 139
Nashville, TN 37202
   Vintage racing insurance

D&G Valve Manufacturing Co.
8 Mount Vernon Street
Stoneham, MA 02180
  Grose-jet float valves

David Brownell
Box 531
North Bennington, VT 05157
  Automotive appraisals

Dayton Wheel Products
1147 Broadway Street
Dayton, OH 45408
  Wire wheel restoration, machining, repair

Delta Motorsports
2724 E. Bell Road
Phoenix, AZ 85032
  Jensen and Jensen-Healey parts

Eastern Lines
31 Tooley Street
London SE1 2PF, England
  Overseas England-US vehicle transportation

The Eastwood Company
580 Lancaster Avenue
Malvern, PA 19355
  Tools

Eightparts
4060 E. Michigan
Tucson, AZ 85714
  Triumph TR-8 and Stag parts

EWA
369 Springfield Avenue, Box 188
Berkeley Heights, NJ 07922
  Imported automotive books, magazines, models

Exclusively Jensen
Cropredy Bridge Garage, Riverside Works
Cropredy, Banbury, Oxon OX17 1PQ, England
  Jensen and Jensen-Healey restoration and
  parts

Foreign Parts Unlimited
352 Washington Street
Somerville, MA 02143
  MGB performance parts

Gear & Machine Specialty Co.
5741 Nanjack Circle
Memphis, TN 38115
  Gear testing, repair, creation

Genuine Classic Brakes
341 Knickerbocker Avenue
Bohemia, NY 11716
  Brake system restoration, machining, repair,
  parts

Gran Turismo Jaguar
1351 E. 354 Street
Eastlake, OH 44095
  Jaguar performance and racing parts

Halibrand Engineering
9344 Wheatlands Road
Santee, CA 92071
  Halibrand wheels, Hewland gearsets, racing
  equipment

Hemmings Motor News
Box 100
Bennington, VT 05201
  Sales and service advertising

High-Speed Salvage
77-10 Allwood Avenue
Islip, NY 11722
  Cylinder head and block welding and repair

Horseless Carriage Carriers, Inc.
61 Iowa Avenue
Paterson, NJ 07503
  Vehicle transportation

Houston Metal Stripping
5017 Needham Road
Conroe, TX 77385
  Chemical stripping

Intercity Lines, Inc.
River Road
Warren, MA 01083
  Vehicle transportation

Jaguar Interiors, Inc.
Box 47
Muncie, IN 47308
  Jaguar interior parts and kits

Jaguar Motorsports Ltd.
1876 S.W. Second Street, Suite B
Del Ray Beach, FL 33445
  Jaguar restoration, race preparation

Jaguar Motor Works
3701 Longview Drive
Atlanta, GA 30341
  New and used Jaguar parts

Jahns/Quality Pistons
1465 W. El Segundo Boulevard
Compton, CA 90222
  Rare and specialty pistons

J.C. Taylor Antique Auto Insurance Agency, Inc.
320 S. 69th Street
Upper Darby, PA 19082
  Antique vehicle insurance

Joe Corto SU Carburetor
230-22 58th Avenue
Bayside, NY 11364
    SU carburetor parts, repair, tuning, restoration

John's Cars
888 Jaguar Lane
Dallas, TX 75226
    Jaguar parts, domestic engine conversion kits

Just Dashes Inc.
5949 Hazeltine Avenue
Van Nuys, CA 91401
    Hard vinyl repair

Kampena Motors
140-B S. Linden
S. San Francisco, CA 94080
    Lotus Europa and Elan parts, service,
    restoration

Mini City Ltd.
876 Turk Hill Road
Fairport, NY 14450
    Mini and Mini-based parts

Mini Mania
31 Winsor Street
Milpitas, CA 95035
    Mini parts, service, restoration

Morgan Spares, Ltd.
Box 1761
Lakeville, CT 06039
    Morgan stock and performance parts

Moss Motors, Ltd.
7200 Hollister Avenue
Goleta, CA 93117
    British parts, supplies, tools, accessories

Motorhead Ltd.
3221 Wilson Boulevard
Arlington, VA 22201
    British parts, supplies, tools, service

Mr. G's
5613 Elliot Reeder Road
Fort Worth, TX 76117
    Plastic rechroming, interior fasteners

The New Dash Group
4747 E. Elliot Street, Unit 29
Phoenix, AZ 85044
    Hard vinyl refinishing

Newport Imports
1200 W. Coast Highway
Newport Beach, CA 92663
    Aston Martin, Jaguar, Lotus parts

NOS Locators
587 Pawtucket Avenue
Pawtucket, RI 02860
    British glass

PAECO Import Parts
2400 Mountain Drive
Birmingham, AL 35226
    Service, machine work, performance parts

Pot Metal Restorations
4794C Woodlane Circle
Tallahassee, FL 32303
    Pot metal repair and replating

RD Enterprises
290 Raub Road
Quakertown, PA 18951
    Lotus parts

Redi-Strip
9910 Jordan Circle
Sante Fe Springs, CA 90670
    Chemical stripping

Road Atlanta Driver Training Center
Route 1
Braselton, GA 30517
    Driver training

Robert DeMars Ltd.
989 40th Street
North Oakland, CA 94608
    Automotive appraisals

SascoSports
110 Seymour Street
Stratford, CT 06497
    Full restoration

Scarborough Faire
1151 Main Street
Pawtucket, RI 02860
    British parts and accessories

Shirlstar Forwarding
259 Cranbrook Road
Ilford, Essex IG1 4TH, England
    Overseas England-US vehicle transportation

Skip Barber Racing School
Route 7
Canaan, CT 06018
    Driver training

Skip Barber Racing School West
Box 629
Carmel Valley, CA 93924
    Driver training

Special Interest Car Parts
1340 Hartford Avenue
Johnston, RI 02919
  British parts and accessories

Sports & Classics
512 Boston Post Road
Darien, CT 06820
  British parts, import and export

Steering Wheel Classics
13723 Balm-Picnic Road
Wimauma, FL 33598
  Steering wheel restoration

Steve Cram
1080 Eddy Street #607
San Francisco, CA 94109
  Automotive appraisals

SVRA
Box 261898
Tampa, FL 33615
  Vintage racing sanctioning body

Terry's Jaguar Parts
117 E. Smith Street
Benton, IL 62812
  Jaguar supplies

Tingle's Lotus Center
1615 Shawsheen Street #8
Tewksbury, MA 01876
  Lotus parts

TiP Sandblast Equipment
Box 649
Canfield, OH 44406
  Blasting supplies

Trans Ocean
390 Olive Tree Lane
Sierra Madre, CA 91024
  Lucas electrical components

TruePerformance, Inc.
3854 Fisher Road
Columbus, OH 43228
  Full restoration, racing parts, fabrication

Vanguard Engine Rebuilders
942 W. Liberty Street
Medina, OH 44256
  Performance and vintage racing engine work

Victoria British Limited
Box 14991
Lenexa, KS 66215
  British parts and supplies

Vintage Sports Car Drivers Association (VSCDA)
Box C
15 W. Burton Place
Chicago, IL 60610

Wefco
Sixth Floor, Beacon Tower
Fishponds Road
Fishponds, Bristol BS16 3HQ, England
  Leather spring gaiters

Welsh Jaguar Enterprises, Inc.
223 N. 5th Street
Stuebenville, OH 43952
  Jaguar parts

White Post Restorations
White Post, Virginia 22663
  Full restorations, hydraulic system sleeves and
  repair

XK's Unlimited
850 Fiero Lane
San Luis Obispo, CA 93401
  Jaguar parts and supplies

Disposal of Parts and Fluids

One of the real problems of doing your own automotive work is what to do with the junk and poisonous fluids you inevitably generate. Everybody knows these days that two of our largest environmental problems are the related ills of landfill overuse and groundwater contamination. Unfortunately, our interest in environmental problems far outstrips our ability to find answers to them right now.

Some areas have remarkably advanced programs for disposal of hazardous waste, but most locales don't. Your first step in being a responsible garbage maker will have to be doing some of your own research. The city or county listings in your telephone blue pages will have an entry for Waste Disposal, Hazardous Waste Management or something similar. Don't expect to get many answers the first time—it can be a real trick to finally find the right outfit, since there are still no uniform rules across the country for waste management. There are, however, hazardous waste disposal sites and procedures for every location—it just may be one heck of a long way off, and your local government may not have heard about it yet. If you come across a situation like this, it'll be your ironic duty to find the answers yourself and educate your leaders.

If you strike out with the government at first, call around to local garages, body shops, and restoration specialists; they're generally forced by law to dispose of toxics in an organized manner, so they should be helpful. You may ultimately be forced to offer one of these groups some money to add your own volatiles to theirs for disposal.

The best rule of thumb as you work with chemicals and fluids is to remember that if you can smell it, it's bad news. And the stronger the odor the more dangerous it is, both to your immediate health and to the atmosphere and water table. Cleaners, paints, and all oil-derived liquids are the big things to watch out for. Dumped carelessly by the wayside, these toxic chemicals will quickly enter the water cycle and come back to haunt everybody.

The easiest solution, of course, is not to make any more of these wastes than necessary in the first place. Except for motor oil, the greatest volume of volatiles is generated by cleaning, not the actual changing of a car's fluids. It's best to start off with the mildest cleaners possible at first—soap and water can, in fact, do a lot of work—not just for the environment's sake but because these are also the easiest on the car itself.

You'll inevitably generate some hazardous materials no matter what you do, however. Things like spray cleaners and naptha, for example—real health and environmental nightmares—are just too convenient to realistically swear off of completely. The trick is simply to catch as much of these fluids as possible after use, and to keep them tightly covered in glass or metal containers until you can safely get rid of them. Leaving pans of cleaners uncovered sends these toxins directly into the atmosphere through evaporation, so keep them covered, always.

Caked grease and ruined rags should also be kept tightly wrapped up in a cool place and disposed of along with actual fluids—they're simply volatiles that are currently trapped in solid form.

All toxics should be kept separated since cross contamination simply makes the disposal issue harder. Motor oil, for example, can actually be recycled and used as fuel for ships and other things. If it's contaminated with minute traces of brake fluid, though, the entire batch in the collection tank will be ruined.

Actual pieces of mechanical junk are generally more of a pain than a danger to dispose of. Assuming that the pieces aren't filled with fluid or particularly greasy, metal parts will sit happily inert in a landfill and actually decompose over time, albeit often a long time. If possible, you should bring big metal parts to a local junkyard; often yards will accept these pieces and use them for their scrap value. Smaller metal pieces, well, there's not much more you can do than to throw them away. The residual grease and oil won't make the local dump an ideal whooping crane nesting site, but at this point in time there aren't a lot of alternatives.

The same goes for plastic and small rubber parts, which actually do release a number of carcinogenic chemicals as they—if they—decompose. Again, though, until a coherent method of disposal is hit on, you don't have a lot of choice here but to throw them out.

Tires, on the other hand, are so well known as a dumping hazard that standards and methods for their disposal have been developed. Generally, the response has simply been to tell people that they can't dump their tires here—which ultimately is the wrong answer, since many people just get frustrated and toss them by the side of the road or in a vacant lot. A relatively recent and common development are mandatory tire buy-back laws; some areas have regulations that force tire dealers to accept used tires for disposal, usually with a small fee attached. Though there's no really good way for the dealer to get rid of the tires either, at least the problem is concentrated down to one source instead of many. Look into it.

Since regulatory agencies are currently far behind the scale of the waste problem, something else I encourage you to do is start making some noise about getting a comprehensive disposal plan developed for your city or county. Grass-roots organizations have formed in most places to look at the issue, and automotive enthusiasts need to be involved. We're the ones making a lot of the problems, so we'll need to be the ones helping to sort them out.

Index